ASSER International Sports Law Series

More information about this series at http://www.springer.com/series/8858

Johan Lindholm

The Court of Arbitration for Sport and Its Jurisprudence

An Empirical Inquiry into Lex Sportiva

ASSER PRESS

Springer

Johan Lindholm
Department of Law
Umeå University
Umeå, Sweden

ISSN 1874-6926 ISSN 2215-003X (electronic)
ASSER International Sports Law Series
ISBN 978-94-6265-284-2 ISBN 978-94-6265-285-9 (eBook)
https://doi.org/10.1007/978-94-6265-285-9

Library of Congress Control Number: 2018966862

Published by T.M.C. ASSER PRESS, The Hague, The Netherlands www.asserpress.nl
Produced and distributed for T.M.C. ASSER PRESS by Springer-Verlag Berlin Heidelberg

This T.M.C. ASSER PRESS imprint is published by the registered company Springer-Verlag GmbH, DE part of Springer Nature
The registered company address is: Heidelberger Platz 3, 14197 Berlin, Germany

Series Information

Books in this series comprehensibly chart and analyse legal and policy developments in the emerging field of European and international sports law.

The series uniquely features contributions from leading sports law scholars and is the most cited in its field. It is a valuable resource for practitioners, academics, sports officials, and anyone interested in or impacted by sports and the law.

Series Editors:

Prof. Dr. Ben Van Rompuy
Leiden University, The Netherlands
Vrije Universiteit Brussel, Belgium

Dr. Antoine Duval
T.M.C. Asser Instituut, The Netherlands

Editorial Office

ASSER International Sports Law Centre
T.M.C. Asser Instituut
P.O. Box 30461
2500 GL The Hague
The Netherlands
AISLC_books@asser.nl

international sports law centre

Preface

If I had to write one of those snappy back cover blurbs for this book, I might go with "a book written by a law geek for other law geeks". I first encountered and began conducting empirical studies of large sets of legal materials about six years ago. Ever since I began working on my doctoral thesis, I have had one foot in constitutional law and particularly the constitutional law of the European Union. Researching EU law inevitably involves sifting through a substantial number of decisions by the Court of Justice, searching for patterns and meaning that are sometimes rather obscure. It has therefore been very exciting to discover, together with my friend and colleague Mattias Derlén, that methods commonly used in other research fields provide great assistance when exploring the proverbial haystack. Through this process, I have become a great believer in the promise of exploring legal questions and legal assertions using real-world data, an approach to legal research that is frequently referred to as empirical legal studies.[1]

Since my other foot is firmly placed in the field of sports law, I naturally began to consider how this field might benefit from empirical legal studies and the Court of Arbitration for Sport (CAS) was an obvious candidate. CAS is a central actor in international sports and in the development of international sports law, and the institution has therefore attracted much attention by lawyers and non-lawyers alike.[2] Also, the data necessary to conduct such studies is available as it is relatively easy to get access to at least a significant portion of CAS's decisions. I therefore started collecting CAS decisions wherever I could find them in 2014 and, with the help of my research assistants Ellen Dalsryd and Johan Olsson (thank you guys!), began extracting information from the decisions and compiling a dataset. With indispensable economic backing by the Swedish Research Council for Sport and the School of Sport Science at Umeå University (thank you for believing in this project!), I began analysing this dataset seeking to empirically explore questions and

[1] This is a quite broad field of research that includes a rich variety of research interests and approaches.

[2] As evidenced by the fact that when I have told people at parties that I am writing a book about CAS, many have actually been interested!

claims about CAS posed by sports stakeholders and sports lawyers and to replicate previous empirical studies of arbitration institutions for CAS. I would estimate that somewhere between 10,000 and 15,000 lines of code went into conducting what you now have in front of you. I want to thank the people at T.M.C. Asser, particularly Antoine, Ben, and Frank, for giving me this great opportunity to study CAS and to experiment with methods that are not part of the legal researcher's standard toolbox.

I imagine that the main audience for this book are sports lawyers. In my experience, sports lawyers are very interested in CAS and its jurisprudence but generally neither familiar with nor particularly interested in such things as statistics, network analysis or machine-learning-assisted text analysis. I have therefore sought to strike a balance where I try as far as possible to concentrate the main text on legal questions and legal implications. That has, however, not always been possible, and I thank in advance for the reader's patience if I at times geek out. However, I am hoping that this book may also provide something to readers that are interested in empirical legal studies, arbitration law and transnational law.

Having conducted and presented empirical legal studies for some time, I have received different types of responses and I expect the same will be true for this study. This book is not intended to provide and does not provide answers to all questions relating to CAS, nor will it provide the final answers to the questions that it seeks to answer just because it is based on empirical evidence. I hope that this book can inspire and assist further research into CAS and its jurisprudence.

Paris, France
July 2018

Johan Lindholm

Contents

Abbreviations

ADD	Anti-Doping Division
AHD	Ad Hoc Division
AOC	Australian Olympic Committee
ATF	Arbitration Tribunal for Football
BAT	Basketball Arbitral Tribunal
BOA	British Olympic Committee
CAS	Court of Arbitration for Sport/Tribunal arbitral du sport
CAS Code	The Code of Sports-related Arbitration
CJEU	Court of Justice of the European Union
CONI	Comitato Olimpico Nazionale Italiano (Italian Olympic Committee)
CPC	The Swiss Civil Procedure Code
ECHR	European Convention for the Protection of Human Rights and Fundamental Freedoms
ECtHR	European Court of Human Rights
FEI	Fédération Equestre Internationale
FFTri	Fédération Française de Triathlon
FIFA DRC	FIFA Dispute Resolution Chamber
FIFA RSTP	FIFA Regulations for the Status and Transfer of Players
FINA	Fédération Internationale de Natation Amateur
FIS	Fédération Internationale de Ski
FISA	International Rowing Federation
IAAF	International Association of Athletics Federations
IBA	International Bar Association
ICAS	International Council of Arbitration for Sport
ICC	International Chamber of Commerce
ICCA	International Council for Commercial Arbitration
ICF	International Canoe Federation
ICSID	International Centre for Settlement of Investment Disputes

IF	International Sport Federation
IIHF	International Ice Hockey Federation
IOC	The International Olympic Committee
ITU	International Triathlon Union
LSHG	Ligue Suisse de Hockey sur Glace
New York Convention	The 1958 Convention on the Recognition and Enforcement of Foreign Arbitral Award
NOC	National Olympic Committee
PCA	Permanent Court of Arbitration
PILA	The Swiss Private International Law Act of 1987
SCOTUS	United States Supreme Court
SFT	Swiss Federal Tribunal (Bundesgericht/Tribunal federal)
SGB	Sports governing body, i.e. associations and corporations, that organize and govern sport through regulations, decisions and agreements
TFEU	Treaty on the Functioning of the European Union
UCI	Union Cycliste Internationale
USADA	United States Anti-Doping Agency
WADA	The World Anti-Doping Agency
WADC	The World Anti-Doping Code

Part I
Introduction

Chapter 1
Cour Suprême du Sport Mondial

Abstract More than thirty years have passed since CAS was created. During those three decades, CAS has evolved from a relatively marginal arbitration institution to the international "supreme court" for sports that decides many of the most important cases in sports and in doing so has a profound effect on sports more generally. CAS is also one of the key actors driving the establishment and continued development of arguably one of the best examples of a transnational legal order, the lex sportiva. This warrants an in-depth analysis of CAS as an institution, the actors involved in its activities, and its decisions. This chapter introduces CAS and the book. It describes the questions that the book seeks to answer and the theoretical framework from which it departs. It then goes on to describe the data and the methods used to study that data. This includes, in particular, a brief introduction to some of the key concepts of network analysis.

1.1 The First Thirty Years

The idea of establishing an international arbitration tribunal to handle sports-related disputes was introduced in 1981 at the XI Olympic Congress in Baden-Baden, Germany, by the then recently-appointed president of the International Olympic Committee (IOC), Juan Antonio Samaranch. The next year, during its 85th session in Rome, the IOC established a working group entrusted with the task of developing an arbitration court for sport. The year after that, on 6 April 1983 in New Delhi, the IOC ratified the statutes of the Court of Arbitration for Sport (CAS)[1] and on 30 June 1984 CAS commenced its activities in Lausanne, Switzerland.

These may not seem like extraordinary events. CAS was not an entirely new or unique type of institution. On the contrary, the practice of resolving disputes

[1] CAS also has an alternate but equally official French name, le Tribunal arbitral du sport or TAS. For consistency and clarity, I will only refer to the institution's English name, including when citing its decisions.

J. Lindholm, *The Court of Arbitration for Sport and Its Jurisprudence*,
ASSER International Sports Law Series,
https://doi.org/10.1007/978-94-6265-285-9_1

through arbitration rather than in ordinary national courts is so old that its origin is "lost in obscurity"[2] and the national and international legal framework governing arbitration courts, such as the 1958 Convention on the Recognition and Enforcement of Foreign Arbitral Award (the New York Convention), was in place long before CAS.[3] Indeed, in a way, CAS was and still is but one among several international arbitration institutions.[4]

Nor did sports stakeholders receive CAS with extraordinary enthusiasm.[5] CAS's initial workload must accurately be described as quite modest: during its first decade in existence, CAS issued on average about three decisions per year.[6] This initially quite humble level of operations was likely somewhat of a disappointment to those who were hoping and expecting great things of CAS. This included Samaranch who intended for CAS to become a true "cour suprême du sport mondial,"[7] a supreme court for world sports, or "a kind of Hague Court in the sports world."[8] This was a bold ambition and a challenge for CAS to live up to.

However, every court needs and deserves time to establish itself.[9] As expressed by the head of the working group developing CAS and its first president, Kéba Mbaye,[10] shortly after the establishment of the institution, only the future would be able to reveal whether CAS's creation was cause for celebration.[11] We now find ourselves some distance into that future as CAS has been operational for thirty-four years.[12] While CAS is still quite young compared to many dispute resolution institutions, sufficient time has passed to both warrant and enable a description and evaluation of how it has fared thus far.[13]

This book seeks to provide such a description and evaluation, focusing both on CAS as an institution, its jurisprudence, and the actors involved. This entails,

---

[2] Wolaver 1934, p. 132. Cf. Emerson 1970, pp. 155–156. By the time of the middle ages the practice was well-established and regulated in many jurisdictions. See e.g. Noussia 2010, p. 11.

[3] Blackaby et al. 2015, pp. 4–6. See further Sects. 2.1 and 10.1.

[4] Mbaye 2006, p. 19.

[5] Cf. Casini 2011, pp. 1321–1322.

[6] See further Sect. 3.3.

[7] Quoted in Mbaye 2002, p. xii. See also SFT's decision 27 May 2003 in case 4P.267–270/2002, 129 ATF 445 (*Lazutina & Danilova v. IOC*), para 3.3.3.3.

[8] IOC President Juan Antonio Samaranch's opening speech at the 85th session of the IOC.

[9] See Sect. 3.3. See also Hess 2015, pp. 59–60.

[10] In accordance with Juan Antonio Samaranch's vision, Kéba Mbaye was recruited from the International Court of Justice.

[11] Mbaye 2006, p. 19.

[12] However, this book focuses on the first 30 years, i.e. the period between 1984 and 2014. See further below Sect. 1.5.

[13] That being said, this book does not represent the first endeavor to evaluate CAS's progress. See e.g., in chronological order, Mbaye 2002, pp. xi–xii (concluding after eighteen years that the CAS had made remarkable, extraordinary, and rapid progress towards its goals); Yi 2006, p. 339 ("After twenty-two years, Juan Antonio Samaranch's dream is reaching fruition."); Reilly 2012, p. 80 ("Having celebrated its 25th birthday in 2009, the CAS is today firmly established as the Supreme Court for sport internationally.").

among other things, studying the litigants that bring disputes before CAS and the arbitrators that resolve those disputes, identifying and analyzing structures among these actors and in CAS's jurisprudence, and examining how CAS and its jurisprudence has developed over time to identify trends and shifting tendencies.[14] In this regard, this book can perhaps be described as a sort of biography of a legal institution, detailing its life thus far, identifying key characteristics and key moments. In doing so, we will go back and forth between, on one hand, describing CAS and its jurisprudence on a general or systematic level and, on the other, diving more deeply into specific episodes, decisions, actors, and issues.

One thing that characterizes this book and distinguishes it from most other studies of CAS, as well as from many studies of other judicial institutions,[15] is its relatively heavy reliance on empirical data and quantitative analysis. In this sense, this book can be described as an empirical inquiry into CAS and its jurisprudence. However, as explained in greater detail later in this chapter, the empirical approach is integrated with more traditional legal theory and methods for the purpose of achieving a richer and more complete understanding of CAS and its jurisprudence. Also, more fundamentally, the study relies on more traditional legal theory and scholarship, which also guides the choice of research questions.

1.2 Studying the Judge: CAS as an Arbitration Court

Why should we be interested in studying CAS and its jurisprudence? The first reason, which is perhaps the reason that is most obvious to lawyers, is that CAS constitutes a powerful dispute settlement institution that decides many important cases in the field of sports. CAS plays a particularly significant role when it comes to sports-related disputes involving high-level competition, such as the Olympic Games, or large amounts of money, such as football players transfers. Thus, the impact that CAS exerts on sports and its stakeholders through its decisions is direct, concrete, and significant.

One of the reasons for establishing CAS as a "supreme court for international sports"[16] was to unify all sports under a common dispute resolution body that would ensure fair, equal, and consistent enforcement of sports rules across all

[14] As explained in greater detail below, this book seeks to cover the development from CAS's inception to the end of 2014.

[15] There are, however, noteworthy exceptions, e.g. Drahozal and Naimark 2002; Hansford and Spriggs II 2008; Segal et al. 2005. My own previous research includes several studies where empirical data was used to describe and analyze the jurisprudence and method of the Court of Justice of the European Union (CJEU). See e.g. Derlén et al. 2013; Derlén and Lindholm 2014, 2015, 2016, 2017a. Where appropriate, this book draws on the experiences of previous empirical research of other judicial institutions, including for the purpose of comparison.

[16] See above Sect. 1.1.

nations and all sports.[17] In other words, one of the main purposes of CAS is to establish an international level playing field with regard to sports adjudication. In this sense, CAS has a clear place in the preexisting and well-established international structure where sports is organized on a sport-by-sport basis by federations and other sports governing bodies[18] (SGBs) on national, regional, and international levels. Within this structure, CAS has an internal, coordinating, and harmonizing role. CAS also plays an important role in legitimizing this structure and its claim for self-governance to external actors, such as political institutions and courts.

In this manner, how CAS functions and acts has far-reaching implications for its own legitimacy and the legitimacy of organized sports more generally. This is particularly clear when it comes to CAS's involvement in disputes between, on one hand, SGBs and, on the other, individual clubs and athletes. In such cases, CAS acts as an arbiter in a conflict between, on one hand, a rule- and decision maker and, on the other, those governed by those rules and decisions, not entirely dissimilar to the role played by national courts resolving disputes between public entities and individuals.[19] CAS's ability and willingness to resolve such disputes in a fair, competent, independent, and consistent manner can significantly impact not just the legitimacy of CAS but also of SGBs and organized sports more generally, both in the eyes of other sport stakeholders (thereby enhancing the internal legitimacy of the system) and in the eyes of the general public, politicians, ordinary courts, corporations, and other external actors (thereby enhancing its external legitimacy).[20] For these reasons, one of the aims of this book is to describe how CAS is organized and operates, and to evaluate this from the perspective of such fundamental values as fairness, competence, independence, and consistency.

In carrying out this examination, we will primarily study CAS and its jurisprudence on a general level, looking for trends and tendencies, in a manner that is likely more or less familiar to most lawyers.[21] However, like other courts and dispute resolution institutions, CAS is not at its core a building or an entity but ultimately a collection of individuals interacting with each other. Studying CAS and its jurisprudence should therefore include and will include studying social relations between different actors – most importantly between CAS arbitrators, between parties before CAS, and between arbitrators and parties – and the characteristics of different actors, particularly those that exert a particularly high degree of influence over CAS and its decisions.

[17] Cf. McLaren 2001, pp. 380–381 (specifically discussing the role of CAS when it comes to combating doping).

[18] Associations, corporations etc. that organize and govern sport through regulations, decisions, and agreements, e.g. national federations, international federations, the IOC, national Olympic Committees, and the World Anti-Doping Agency (WADA).

[19] See further Chap. 10.

[20] Cf. McArdle 2015, pp. 19–35.

[21] Even if the use of a combination of more traditional legal methods and empirical methods to carry out that examination may perhaps be less familiar to some.

These parts of the study are inspired by existing research on international arbitration courts, including research conducted by scholars in the fields of law, sociology, and international relations.[22] One might therefore say that this book in parts adopt not only an empirical approach but also a multidisciplinary approach to CAS and its jurisprudence. Understanding how actors involved in CAS's activities interact, what characterizes those who participate in and exercise influence over CAS and its jurisprudence, and these actors' tendencies adds depth to the description but also, and more importantly, has direct bearing on CAS's legitimacy, how sport-related disputes are resolved, and the development of international sports law more generally.[23]

This book focuses squarely on CAS. I nevertheless hope that it can also make a modest contribution to existing knowledge of how arbitration and arbitration institutions function generally. Even though arbitration is an old and well-established form for resolving disputes,[24] existing knowledge of how arbitration courts work is limited.[25] Although it is by no means universal and absolute, one major reason why parties traditionally have elected to resolve their disputes through arbitration is the confidentiality of the proceedings and the resulting awards.[26] As a consequence, studying how arbitrators operate and reach their decisions has been likened to studying a black box.[27] Although arbitration courts have generally become more transparent and therefore more accessible to researchers,[28] CAS is a comparatively transparent arbitration institution. The fact that a substantial portion of CAS's jurisprudence is publicly available and considered in this book gives extensive insight into how CAS and, perhaps, other arbitration institutions function.[29]

1.3 Studying a Legal Bumblebee: CAS and the Development of a Transnational Legal Order

A second major reason motivating this study is the role that CAS and its jurisprudence play in the development of a transnational legal order, often referred to as lex sportiva.[30] There is a steadily increasing wealth of legal literature

---

22 See Chap. 9.

23 Schill 2012.

24 See above Sect. 1.1.

25 Drahozal 2003.

26 Blackaby et al. 2015, p. 30.

27 See e.g. Berger 2013, p. 7; Rogers 2006, p. 1345; Tucker 2016.

28 See below Sect. 1.5.

29 While I will be drawing on existing research of other arbitration institutions for understanding and evaluating CAS, I generally leave to experts on other arbitration institutions to determine whether the findings made here regarding CAS are generalizable or valid for those other institutions.

30 However, as explained in more detail immediately below, the term lex sportiva is somewhat problematic as it is ambiguous and used in various ways.

discussing transnational legal orders[31] or, as they are alternatively referred to, private legal orders,[32] a national law,[33] or "private law beyond the state."[34] To claim that something constitutes a transnational legal order essentially means claiming that it is a legal order created by private institutions, not governed by national legal systems and that is in this regard autonomous, with norms applying across nations.[35] To use Teubner's words, the development of "global law without a state."[36]

There are innumerable candidates for transnational legal order's in the world. However, much of the existing literature has focused on three: the (new) lex mercatoria (the law merchant), the lex digitalis (the law of the internet), and the lex sportiva (the law of sports).[37] Despite appearances, the term lex sportiva is neither old nor proper Latin but relatively recently created from the term lex mercatoria.[38] By making this connection, lex sportiva positions itself in the context of transnational legal orders and by way of comparing itself to lex mercatoria, lex sportiva draws on the pedigree of its older and more well-established cousin.[39] While this book can hopefully make some small relevant contribution to our understanding of transnational legal orders more generally,[40] its study object is limited to lex sportiva.

CAS and its jurisprudence is not only a possible object of study when exploring transnational law but a particularly well-suited one. As one author puts it, "CAS represents one of the world's more successful attempts at bringing order to transnational issues."[41]

But what exactly is meant by lex sportiva? The concept of transnational legal orders is by itself quite complex and elusive. However, the term lex sportiva is additionally problematic as it is used to refer to different things and not always with great precision.[42] Although some internal differences can be detected, it is possible to discern two main uses of the term lex sportiva.

[31] See generally Jansen and Michaels 2008.

[32] See e.g. Teubner 2002.

[33] See e.g. Michaels 2007.

[34] See e.g. Jansen and Michaels 2008.

[35] See e.g. Foster 2003, p. 2.

[36] Teubner 1997.

[37] For an introduction and comparison of the three, see Vieweg and Staschik 2015, pp. 34–36. The proposition that a transnational legal order was developing in sports was supposedly first put forth by Giannini in 1949. See Wax 2015, p. 147.

[38] In CAS 98/200, *AEK Athens*, quoted immediately below, CAS also expressly invokes lex mercatoria.

[39] Beloff 2005, p. 49; Erbsen 2006, p. 441; Latty 2011, p. 37; Siekmann 2011, p. 4.

[40] As some of the findings made herein may be applicable to other private legal orders as well.

[41] Yi 2006, p. 290.

[42] See e.g. Erbsen 2006, p. 441 ("Commentators do not agree on what Lex Sportiva means, but many share a belief that it exists."); Vieweg and Staschik 2015.

The first main use focuses heavily on CAS and the normative impact of its jurisprudence. Somewhat simplified one could say that this use of the term, which is the narrower of the two, primarily views lex sportiva as "judge-made sports law."[43] Under this definition, lex sportiva refers to a number of (general) principles that CAS has identified, developed, or created and expressed in its jurisprudence.[44] An early example of this view can be found in CAS's decision in *AEK Athens*:[45]

> Sports law has developed and consolidated along the years, particularly through the arbitral settlement of disputes, a set of unwritten legal principles – a sort of lex mercatoria for sports or, so to speak, a lex ludica – to which national and international sports federations must conform, regardless of the presence of such principles within their own statutes and regulations or within any applicable national law, provided that they do not conflict with any national "public policy" ("ordre public") provision applicable to a given case.

CAS in this instance adds confusion by using the term lex ludica in *AEK Athens* but in subsequent decisions replaces it with the term lex sportiva while seemingly referring to essentially the same thing.[46] While it is not always clear what is meant by the term lex sportiva, when CAS uses the term in its decisions it frequently appears to refer to the body of rules and principles recognized in its previous decisions.[47] There are also many examples of legal researchers using the term in essentially the same way.[48]

In *AEK Athens* and many subsequent decisions, CAS emphasizes that these unwritten legal principles apply globally to all stakeholders in sports regardless of sports rules to the contrary. Thus, one of the key characteristics of lex sportiva, under this narrower definition, is the superior position of these principles in the hierarchy of sports norms. In this way, the term lex sportiva, as understood here, is closely connected to CAS's above-mentioned mission to provide fair, equal, and consistent enforcement in the world of sports.[49]

---

[43] Casini 2011, p. 1319.

[44] Which of these verbs most accurately captures reality depends on the particular situation and perhaps also on the perspective of the observer. See further Chap. 7.

[45] CAS 98/200, para 156.

[46] CAS 2002/O/373, *Scott*, para 14 ("CAS jurisprudence has notably refined and developed a number of principles of sports law, such as the concepts of strict liability (in doping cases) and fairness, which might be deemed part of an emerging 'lex sportiva'."). Whether any relevant distinction can be made between lex sportiva and lex ludica has been the subject of scholarly discussion, see e.g. Foster 2006; Parrish 2012; Siekmann 2011. Foster uses the term "lex ludica" to refer to sporting rules in a narrow sense, "the actual rules of the game", including formal rules and regulations and "equitable principles of sports". Foster 2006, para 8.

[47] See e.g. CAS 2002/O/410, *GFA v. UEFA*, p. 4; CAS 2002/A/417, *Witteveen*, para 84; CAS 2004/A/707, *Millar*, para 53; CAS 2004/A/776, *FCP v. FIRS*, para 16; CAS 2007/A/1424, *FEB v. FIQ*, para 17; CAS 2008/O/1455, *Boxing Australia v. AIBA*, para 42; CAS 2010/A/2268, *I v. FIA*, para 75; CAS 2011/A/2646, *Club Randewrs de Talca*, para C.1.ii.

[48] See e.g. Erbsen 2006; McLaren 2001; Mitten and Opie 2010; Nafziger 2004; Wax 2015, p. 148.

[49] Cf. Reeb 1998, p. xxxi ("Centralizing the resolution of sports disputes within the CAS should encourage the harmonization of certain major legal principles which are still applied haphazardly by the top sports bodies…").

There is some disagreement regarding which principles should properly be included in lex sportiva thus defined and differences in opinion reveal more deep-rooted differences in how lex sportiva is understood. Many of the principles that CAS has recognized and applied in its jurisprudence are not unique for the area of sports but rather general legal principles found in various national or international legal orders.[50] CAS, SGBs, and other sport stakeholders are in practice required to respect these general legal principles, at least if they want to be sure that their rules, decisions, and agreements will survive courts reviewing them. This most importantly includes certain basic fundamental rights. CAS has however also recognized and applied a number of other general legal principles, including for examples certain contractual principles and public law principles. These principles have become part of the norms governing sports through a process of borrowing and sometimes modifying norms developed in national and international legal orders.[51] These principles are frequently covered by the term lex sportiva, not least when CAS uses it.

However, some argue that including all these principles in the term lex sportiva overly extends it and advocate using a narrower definition that only covers principles that are uniquely applicable in the field of sports. These commentators frequently focus on the transnational nature of lex sportiva and, in particular, the autonomy of transnational legal orders vis-à-vis national legal orders. From this perspective, one of the key advantages of lex sportiva is its ability to enhance the autonomy of sports and its governing bodies[52] and the application and enforcement of general legal principles does not support the existence of a legitimate, independent, and unique transnational legal order in the field of sports.[53] Depending on what level of uniqueness one requires – or, differently phrased, what level of similarity with existing legal principles one allows – on may end up with a very narrow definition of lex sportiva that contains little substantive content.[54] However, one can in CAS's jurisprudence identify certain principles that are more unique to

---

[50] See e.g. CAS 98/200, *AEK Athens*, para 156 ("Certainly, general principles of law drawn from a comparative or common denominator reading of various domestic legal systems and, in particular, the prohibition of arbitrary or unreasonable rules and measures can be deemed to be part of such lex ludica."). See further Chap. 7.

[51] Beloff et al. 2012, pp. 308–309; Beloff 2005, p. 52 ("in locating these principles and rules, sports law borrows, magpie-like, from private law as well as public, appropriately mixing Latinisms with French phrases, civil and common law concepts."); Hess 2015, pp. 68–69; Latty 2007, pp. 305–323.

[52] See e.g. Beloff 2005, p. 53 ("one of [lex sportiva's] key objectives is to immunise sport from the reach of the law, to create in other words a field of autonomy within which even appellate sports tribunals should not trespass.").

[53] See e.g. Beloff 2005; Foster 2003; Foster 2006, paras 4–9; Vieweg and Staschik 2015, pp. 23–24.

[54] See e.g. Erbsen 2006 ("CAS's nominally unique Lex Sportiva is really an amalgam of general due process and equity norms tailored to sporting disputes…" Ibid. p. 454.).

sports,[55] and that can be referred to as sui generis principles[56] or *principia sportiva*[57], such as "the fundamental principle of sport that all competitors must have equal chances…"[58]

The theory and perspective that drives this narrowing of lex sportiva to only include sui generis sports principles are closely related to the theory and perspective that drives the second and broader use of lex sportiva: lex sportiva as a transnational legal order. This use of the term includes, besides the general principles discussed above,[59] also other transnational sports rules.[60] Thus, under this definition of lex sportiva, CAS is one among several important actors in the field of sports that contribute to the creation of an autonomous, global, and transnational legal order. Similarly, under this view, CAS's jurisprudence is but one of the sources of that legal order, albeit a rather important one. Other important actors include national, regional, and international SGBs and other sources include the sports rules they establish, that is written, formalized norms established by SGBs in the shape of for example statutes, charters, rules, codes, and regulations, which if they achieve global application constitute an important source of lex sportiva in this broader sense. The extensive inclusion of written rules established by institutions sets lex sportiva apart from more "spontaneous" legal orders, such as lex mercatoria.[61] From this perspective, CAS and other actors cooperate in responding to the need of a system of internationally applicable, non-state-based rules and principles governing sports.[62] Consequently, lex sportiva can be understood as a body of anational rules and principles that allows sport-related activities and disputes to be disconnected from the rules and principles of various national legal systems.[63]

CAS's role in relation to these regulations is not limited to interpretation and application. As explained by Foster, CAS's functions include identifying best practice standards from these regulations.[64] Some of these best practices are given

---

[55] Beloff et al. 2012, p. 309; Hess 2015, pp. 67–68; Latty 2007, pp. 323–332.

[56] See Foster 2003, p. 9. Cf. Panagiotopoulos 2013, p. 132 (describing lex sportiva as a "sui generis sporting legal order").

[57] Latty 2007, p. 323.

[58] CAS 2001/A/317, *Aanes*, para 24.

[59] Whether this only includes principles that are unique to sports or also a broader range of principles varies.

[60] See e.g. Buy et al. 2015, pp. 140–141; Casini 2011, p. 1319; Duval 2013, pp. 827–828; Latty 2011, p. 37.

[61] Buy et al. 2015, pp. 140–141.

[62] See e.g. CAS 2006/A/1082 & 1104, *Barreto Càceres*, para 36 ("…il convient de passer outre les règles étatiques internes qui seraient contraires aux principes et au cadre juridique des règles que la FIFA a pour but d'instaurer. Dans le domaine particulier du droit du sport, il est important de pouvoir recourir à des normes transcendant tel ou tel système étatique particulier. Cette possibilité de développer des règles dégagées, dans la mesure du possible, de toute référence à un système de normes étatiques particulières, répond en effet à un besoin spécifique découlant de l'organisation du sport.").

[63] Rigozzi 2005, p. 628.

[64] Foster 2006, para 6.

the status of general principles and are applied as part of lex sportiva,[65] for example in the area of doping based on the World Anti-Doping Code (WADC).[66] Best practices are also given broad force through SGBs implementing them in their own rules and regulation.[67]

Using the same term with different meanings does of course confuse things, but it does not appear possible to solve this issue by selecting one definition as inherently superior. Rather, it seems that the divergence stems from a difference in perspective.[68] If one is primarily concerned with the norms governing sports and their application in individual cases, as is for example primarily the situation for CAS panels, the first, narrower definition is quite sufficient and a broader definition complicates matters unnecessarily. However, if one's interest in lex sportiva is rooted in an interest in the autonomy of sports or the nature of law more generally, only the latter, broader definition will suffice.

I find it difficult not to be fascinated by these issues and this discussion considering the radical implications. The concept of transnational legal orders is problematic under traditional legal theory as it is difficult, if not outright impossible, to reconcile transnational legal orders with the well-established state-based theory of law that has dominated modern legal thinking.[69] The claim that there are self-regulatory private-based orders constitutes a strong and quite controversial challenge to the Westphalian connection between law and state,[70] and to the division between private and public entities.[71] If private actors engaged in a particular field are capable of establishing their own legal order, it can hardly be true that states have a monopoly on lawmaking.[72] National courts have consequently been unwilling to accept the existence of private legal orders, including lex sportiva. For example, in *Baumann* the German Oberlandesgericht Frankfurt unequivocally stated that there is no such thing as a lex sportiva independent of national law,[73] and similar stances

---

65 CAS 2002/A/373, *Scott*, para 14.

66 See e.g. CAS 2005/C/841, CONI, para 44 ("based on the WADC, which constitutes more and more a fundamental 'lex sportiva', a sanction is possible if there is an anti-doping rule violation…"); CAS 2008/A/1545, *Anderson*, paras 65–66.

67 Foster 2006, para 6.

68 Cf. Nafziger 2015, pp. 161–162.

69 See e.g. Teubner 2002.

70 Tuori 2011, pp. 296–304 ("The most serious challenges to links between law and state arise from legal relationships transcending nation-state boundaries. Phenomena questioning the state's internal sovereignty, such as self-regulation of the economy and sports, also tend to have a transnational background and transnational links." Ibid. p. 296).

71 Teubner 2008.

72 See e.g. Anter 2014, pp. 173–188 (regarding the connection between the state's legitimate monopoly on force and its legal monopoly).

73 OLG Frankfurt's decision 18 April 2001 in case 13 U 66/01 (*Baumann v. DLV*), para 56 ("eine von jedem staatlichen Recht unabhängige lex sportiva gibt es nicht.").

have been taken by Swiss[74] and English[75] courts. There are thus good arguments why lex sportiva, in the sense of a "true" transnational legal order that is actually and completely autonomous of national law, does not and cannot exist.

However, the fact that the notion of law as state-based has thoroughly dominated our understanding of law for a long time does not preclude that notion from shifting gradually. Researchers have previously pointed out that the idea of law as being exclusively state-based is strongly challenged by many real-world phenomena,[76] and as explored in this book there are some tangible indications of the existence of such a private legal order in the area of sports.

Thus, researchers studying lex sportiva are confronted with a seemingly paradoxical situation. On one hand, national courts and traditional legal theory dictate that private legal orders do not and cannot exist, but the researchers' observations do not always clearly fit that theory. Much like bumblebees, according to a popular myth,[77] lex sportiva can be observed doing things that it should not be able to do.[78]

This book departs from and engages with the theory of lex sportiva presented above. However, it does not aim to definitively answer whether lex sportiva constitutes a transnational legal order.[79] Rather, we will explore how CAS and its jurisprudence contribute to the establishment of lex sportiva because how CAS functions and acts support the creation and legitimacy of a transnational legal order in the sports area.[80]

In doing so, a number of questions will be considered. Is CAS independent and impartial in relation to SGBs and other sport stakeholders? The answer to this question is crucial for both the internal and external legitimacy of lex sportiva. They are also closely related to respecting the principle of legality, which is indispensable in an order claiming to be a legal order.[81] Does CAS otherwise support the effective adjudication of disputes and enforcement of rules, regulations, and principles in the area of sports? In order to make a credible claim for the existence of an autonomous

---

74 SFT's decision 20 December 2005 in case 4C.1/2005, BGE 132 III 285 (*X. AG v. Y*), pp. 288–289 ("Von privaten Verbänden aufgestellte Bestimmungen stehen vielmehr grundsätzlich zu den staatlichen Gesetzen in einem Subordinationsverhältnis und können nur Beachtung finden, so weit das staatliche Recht für eine autonome Regelung Raum lässt… Sie bilden kein 'Recht' im Sinne von Article 116 Abs. 1 IPRG und können auch nicht als 'lex sportiva transnationalis' anerkannt werden, wie dies von einer Lehrmeinung befürwortet wird").

75 See Foster 2003, p. 14.

76 See e.g. Barents 2004, pp. 17–19; Duval 2013, p. 823; MacCormick 1999; Schultz 2014, pp. 4–6.

77 The often repeated "fact" that bumblebees should not be able to fly according to the laws of physics, is in fact a myth. See e.g. Zetie 2003.

78 See also Paulsson 2011, pp. 315–317.

79 See e.g. Hess 2015, p. 61 ("Lex sportiva is assumed to be an autonomous legal order…"). I am doubtful about my ability to provide a valuable contribution to a field where much impressive research has already been done, see e.g. Casini 2011; Erbsen 2006; Foster 2003; Latty 2007.

80 In the second, broader sense of the term. For a similar reasoning, see e.g. Panagiotopoulos 2011.

81 See also Sect. 7.2.

legal order there must be institutions with powers necessary to transform it into reality. To what extent does CAS define and contribute to the substantive content of lex sportiva? Rules are the basic building block of a legal order and no legal order can exist without rules.[82] Does CAS act in a consistent, transparent, and foreseeable manner? Does CAS and its jurisprudence contribute to structure and unity? Rules do not by themselves a system make; it is when rules are organized in a consistent and coherent manner that a system starts to take shape.[83] Consistency and predictability is of central importance for the legitimacy of the order as a whole.[84]

1.4 Descriptive and Critical, Doctrinal and Empirical

As already touched upon, a range of methods and perspectives will be applied and combined to achieving the aims of this book. This book is in many regards quite descriptive, and intentionally so. For example, it aims to describe how requests turn to decisions and how this process has developed over time,[85] what types of issues CAS resolves,[86] and what characterizes CAS arbitrators[87] and parties that come before CAS.[88] These types of empirical questions are somewhat different than the normative questions that legal researchers traditionally and primarily engage with. That is not to say that normative questions cannot be empirical questions. On the contrary, to ask what is the law governing a particular issue (*de lege lata*) is to ask an empirical question.[89] However, while those types of question can be and predominantly are resolved using a doctrinal approach, at least some of the empirical questions posed in this book requires using different methods. For example, to what extent female arbitrators are represented in CAS is an empirical question with a quantifiable answer that is attainable given sufficient and accurate data.[90]

In order to answer that question and many of the other questions posed in this book, a combination of methods commonly used in social science will be

---

[82] It is, however, equally obvious that unlike national legal orders, lex sportiva, as a "specialized legal order" neither needs nor aims to be "complete" in the sense that it contains a rule for every situation.

[83] In formulating these questions, I have drawn generally on the thoughts of Duval 2013; Kerchove & Ost 1994; Schultz 2014.

[84] Franck et al. 2017, p. 1128. Cf. Brower and Schill 2009, p. 473 (discussing investment-treaty arbitration).

[85] See Sects. 3.3–3.6.

[86] See Chap. 6.

[87] See Chap. 9.

[88] See Chap. 10.

[89] To state that the law *is* one thing or the other is to make a factual or empirical statement or, one could argue, a prediction.

[90] See Sect. 9.2.2.

employed, including in particular statistical analysis, network analysis, and text mining. In doing so, I hope to demonstrate to the reader that such methods are valuable, if not indispensable, for answering not only questions of a more socio-legal nature such as the one in the example above, but also many core legal questions. For example, as demonstrated below it is possible to empirically observe and quantify a particular decision's role as precedent and how this shifts over time.[91] To answer this and similar questions, this book spends quite extensive attention on how CAS (or perhaps more accurately how actors involved with CAS) have actually acted as evidenced by the cases that were brought before it and how those cases were decided.[92]

I choose to describe this as empirical legal research in that it seeks to answer legal questions by capturing a legal reality. This is not particularly novel. Empirical questions and statements are relatively common in legal studies,[93] and can for example concern how law works, how changes in law affects the application of law, how courts interpret and apply the law, and how legal services are performed.[94] Nor is it necessarily uncontroversial. For example, it is an empirical fact that CAS delivered 309 decisions in 2014 and that that is exactly 103 times more decisions than it delivered in 1987.[95] Some of the empirical claims provided in this book are perhaps more controversial, for example that *Quigley* is CAS's premiere landmark decision.[96] However, they are not different in kind and should not be treated in a fundamentally different manner.

Nor are the research questions asked in this book particularly novel. Most of the questions have previously been asked by other researchers or are based on claims previously made by other researchers. In this regard, this study follows in the methodological footsteps of several, previous studies examining CAS and its jurisprudence.[97] What may however distinguish this study from some studies seeking to answer same or similar questions is the size of the material considered and, as a consequence, some of the methods used to study that material. Empirical legal research has become significantly more common in the last decade.[98] It allows us to empirically test theoretical statements about the law and to draw normative conclusions from empirically supported findings.[99]

---

[91] See Chap. 5. See also Derlén and Lindholm 2017b.

[92] Although it takes a slightly different approach and asks some quite different questions, this book is in part inspired by Segal et al. 2005 who empirically examine the role of the Supreme Court of the United States (SCOTUS) in the American legal system.

[93] Epstein and King 2002, p. 3.

[94] See generally Cane and Kritzer 2010.

[95] See Sect. 3.3.

[96] See Sect. 5.3.

[97] See e.g. Bersagel 2012; Erbsen 2006; Foster 2006.

[98] See e.g. Cane and Kritzer 2010.

[99] Cahoy 2010, p. vi; George 2006, p. 146.

There are many arguments for conducting empirical legal research. One of them is to enhance the legitimacy of legal reasoning that may otherwise be viewed as a smokescreen, particularly by external actors (i.e. non-lawyers).[100] Empirical research supports the development of legal theory by allowing for testing and developing theories in and about law and helps to separate the normative from the descriptive.[101] To base our understanding of law and legal institutions on anecdotes is dangerous. While anecdotes can be accurate, reliable, and representative, they may also instead be atypical and misleading. In this sense, empirical data "contextualizes anecdotes."[102]

1.5 Data Collection, Confidentiality, and Public Access

In conducting empirically-based research, the quality of the research is dependent on the quality of the underlying data. In the case of this study, the primary underlying data is CAS's decisions.[103] One traditional characteristic of arbitration is that the proceedings and the awards are confidential, and from the litigants' perspective this was one of the advantages of arbitration over adjudicating disputes in ordinary courts.[104] However, the confidentiality of the proceedings and the awards is a major methodological challenge when studying arbitration tribunals, particularly when conducting quantitative research that requires a representative data sample. The level of transparency differs between arbitration institutions and in recent years there has been a trend towards increased transparency.[105] Collecting large, representative sets of arbitration awards can however still be problematic.

CAS proceedings and awards are to some extent guarded by confidentiality. The arbitrators participating in CAS panels are generally bound by confidentiality.[106] Moreover, according to the CAS Code, cases brought under Ordinary Arbitration Procedure[107] are as a general rule confidential but the proceedings and the awards can be made public "if all parties agree or the Division President so decides."[108] This binds all parties and includes any information relating to the dispute.[109] It is

---

100 Posner 1995, p. 3.

101 Heise 1999, pp. 813–814.

102 Drahozal 2003, pp. 23–24; Franck 2007, pp. 13–14 (p. 14 quoted).

103 However, we will also explore data on decisions by other sports dispute resolution institutions and the backgrounds of CAS arbitrators. See Sect. 4.3 and Chap. 9.

104 See above Sect. 1.2.

105 See e.g. Malatesta and Sali 2013; Rogers 2006; Smeureanu 2011.

106 Article S19 CAS Code ("CAS arbitrators and mediators are bound by the duty of confidentiality, which is provided for in the Code and in particular shall not disclose to any third party any facts or other information relating to proceedings conducted before CAS.").

107 See further Sect. 2.2.

108 Article R43 CAS Code.

109 Mavromati and Reeb 2015, p. 312.

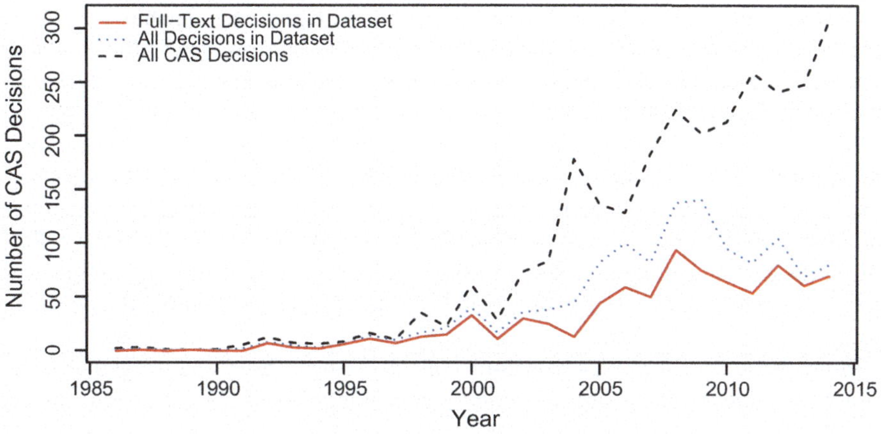

Fig. 1.1 Dataset Representativeness. [*Source* The author]

generally quite rare that the parties agree to make such awards public. At the time of writing, the CAS jurisprudence database contains 33 CAS decision in if we assume that cases brought under the Ordinary Arbitration Procedure. This is a rather low number considering that CAS received 602 such cases during the studied period. Overall, CAS ends up issuing an award in roughly two out of three requests.[110] Thus, if we assume that cases brought under the Ordinary Arbitration Procedure follow the overall trend we can estimate that less than one in ten decisions issued under the Ordinary Arbitration Procedures has been made public. This is a quite modest publication rate. However, it does provide at least some public access to these CAS decisions.

The rules governing the confidentiality of cases brought to CAS under the Appeals Arbitration Procedure[111] are essentially reversed compared to the rules governing the Ordinary Arbitration Procedure: they are as a general rule made public subject to an opt-out system. According to the CAS Code, in these cases "[t]he award, a summary and/or a press release setting forth the results of the proceedings shall be made public by CAS, unless both parties agree that they shall remain confidential."[112] While CAS does not publish all its decisions rendered under the Appeals Arbitration Procedures, it does publish a significant portion. This allows for and encourages the systematic creation of and adherence to jurisprudence.[113]

The term "published CAS decision" is in this book used broadly to refer to all CAS decisions that I through my best effort was able to access in full text. This primarily includes decisions that CAS has actively made public, early on in the

110 CAS, Statistics 2016.

111 See further Sect. 2.2.

112 Article R59 CAS Code.

113 See Blackshaw 2012, p. 7.

CAS Digest and more recently through its online jurisprudence database.[114] These decisions can be considered published in a more narrow and official sense. However, the dataset also includes a number of decisions that are publicly accessible through other channels.

All in all, I have been able to collect and study 830 CAS awards and opinions, which for the sake of simplicity hereinafter will be referred to as "CAS decisions", issued between CAS's inception and the end of 2014. Because CAS sometimes combines several proceedings in a single decision the collected decisions reflect 946 requests for a decision. The decisions collected and considered in full text represent approximately 31 percent of all CAS decisions issued during the period in question.[115]

From the text of the CAS decisions collected I have been able to gather some information about a quite significant number of unpublished CAS decisions, that is CAS decisions rendered during the studied period that I were not able to access in full text. CAS frequently refer to its previous decisions in its decisions.[116] Such references frequently contain information about a rule or principle relied upon, but may also contain information about the parties, the procedure, the nature of the dispute, when the decision was rendered, and so on. Most of these references are to published CAS decisions, that is decisions included in the dataset. However, analyzing these references have also resulted in partial but reliable information about 295 additional, unpublished CAS decisions.[117] As discussed below, this quite extensive practice of referencing to unpublished decisions is problematic from a legal standpoint.[118]

Altogether, the combined body of published and unpublished CAS decisions considered here, altogether 1,125 decisions, represents almost 42 percent of all decisions issued by CAS during the studied period. The data thus includes a substantive share of all CAS decisions. It would obviously be preferable to consider every decision issued by CAS. However, as discussed above, the confidentiality of CAS proceedings and decisions does not allow this.

The data considered is on the whole likely to be quite representative for CAS's body of jurisprudence. For the purpose of evaluating data representability it is initially relevant to note that data considered is well distributed over time relative to the number of decisions issues by CAS.[119] Thus, it is unlikely that the data selection will cause the study to miss developments over time. It is also encouraging that the

---

[114] http://jurisprudence.tas-cas.org. Accessed 7 September 2018.

[115] According to statistics released by CAS it issued 2,695 decisions between 1986 and 2014. CAS, Statistics 2016.

[116] See further Chap. 4.

[117] When such references are discussed in the context of network analysis, they are referred to as "out-of-network references". This is the reason why certain reference to CAS decisions are below named "*Unknown*".

[118] See Sect. 4.5.

[119] See above Fig. 1.1 *Dataset Representativeness*.

languages of the collected decisions follow the same distribution as CAS decisions generally.[120]

There are however some issues relating to the data and its representativeness that should be addressed. First, the portion of CAS decisions considered is lower for cases brought under Ordinary Arbitration Procedure than for cases brought under Appeals Arbitration Procedure and Ad Hoc Procedure.[121] This is unfortunate but unavoidable since the former to a greater extent than the latter are confidential. The fact that CAS decisions in Ordinary Arbitration Procedure are underrepresented in the data should have a limited impact on the accuracy of findings regarding CAS's overall jurisprudence. Cases brought under the Ordinary Arbitration Procedure constitute a relatively small part of CAS's total case load: only 15 percent of all cases submitted to CAS during the studied period came under the Ordinary Arbitration Procedure.[122] The limited data may however provide a non-representative picture of Ordinary Arbitration Procedures as such.

However, the data does include more than a marginal number of cases and there are good reasons to believe that the data includes most of the more structurally important CAS decisions brought under the Ordinary Arbitration Procedure. Because CAS's decisions in ordinary arbitration procedure are more difficult to access they are naturally less likely to be of high precedential value. This is also supported by the data. As discussed above, the data includes a large portion of CAS's jurisprudence and those decisions only include references to a small number of decisions in cases brought under Ordinary Arbitration Procedure. Considering that they are both unpublished and have never been referred to in the relatively large portion of CAS decisions that was accessed and considered in full text, it seems highly likely that the non-included decisions are of more limited precedential value.

Moreover, as discussed above, decisions in Ordinary Arbitration Procedures that are publicly available have been particularly selected for publication. It is therefore reasonable to expect that the awards in Ordinary Arbitration Procedures that are included in the dataset are – or at least were perceived to be – particularly important as precedents compared to those that were not published and therefore are not included in the dataset. This reasoning is at least in part empirically supported by the fact that, when it comes to the decisions considered herein, CAS decisions in Ordinary Arbitration Procedures are, on average, cited more frequently than decisions in Appeals Arbitration Procedures.[123] This effect is further exasperated by the

[120] The dataset consists to 81% of decisions written in English and to 18% of decisions written in French. This compares well with the composition of CAS decisions overall where 72% are in English and 21% are in French. Mavromati 2012, p. 48.

[121] In its official statistics, CAS does not break down issued decisions by procedure. However, assuming that the ratio of issued decisions to incoming requests is the same for all procedure types (64%), CAS should have issued approximately 294 decisions in cases brought under ordinary arbitration procedure during the time studied. In total, the data includes information about 53 of those decisions. This portion, 18%, is significantly lower than the overall inclusion rate of 42%.

[122] CAS, Statistics 2016.

[123] An average of 3.3 citations per award compared to 2.8.

fact that decisions in Ordinary Arbitration Procedures considered tend on average to be older than decisions in Appeals Arbitration Procedures[124] and have therefore had more time to be cited.

Consequently, there is a risk that the data may somewhat exaggerate the precedential power of awards in Ordinary Arbitration Procedures. Because the decisions in Ordinary Arbitration Procedures are on average older than decisions under the Appeals Arbitration Procedures and the average number of references to previous decisions made in CAS decisions has increased over time,[125] the Ordinary Arbitration Procedures studied also tend to contain fewer citations.[126] While these factors will be taken into consideration in the analysis below, their effects on the findings should be negligible considering that Ordinary Arbitration Procedure cases make up a relatively small part of all CAS decisions.

It should finally be pointed out that the relatively limited number of decisions brought under Ordinary Arbitration Procedure has some relevance for the study of sole arbitrators. Sole arbitrators are relatively common in cases brought under Ordinary Arbitration Procedure[127] and not having access to many of those decisions impacts the examination.[128]

Second, the fact that parties can decide by mutual agreement to make a decision in a case brought under Appeals Arbitration Procedures confidential may affect the dataset's representativeness. It is for example possible that decisions in cases of a particularly sensitive nature will not be made public. However, the fact that there are plenty of examples of decisions containing information about personal and sensitive matters suggests that this is not a very strong tendency. Bersagel has suggested that it is also possible that parties may prefer to keep decisions where CAS deviated from previous jurisprudence confidential.[129] I am skeptical of the existence of such a tendency as I fail to see why the party that was disadvantaged by the deviation from previous case law would have an interest in keeping it a secret. I am also uncertain why the party that benefitted from the deviation would particularly care to keep it secret considering how difficult it is to have a rendered decision overturned.

Third, we would expect CAS Divisional Presidents, repeat litigants, like the major SGBs,[130] and to some extent CAS administrators to prioritize publishing and disseminating decisions of particular precedential importance. Consequently, it is possible that the CAS decisions collected and considered in full text is of a higher precedential value than those not included in the dataset. At the same time, the fact that a decision is published greatly increases its chances of being read, considered,

124 The mean decision year of these awards are 2004 and 2008 respectively.

125 See Sect. 3.5.

126 An average of 1.2 references per award compared to 3.1.

127 Mavromati and Reeb 2015, p. 274.

128 See further Sect. 8.10.

129 Bersagel 2012, p. 199.

130 See Sect. 10.4.

and cited. This reasoning is supported by the fact that, among all decisions considered in this study, the published CAS decisions are on average 50 percent more frequently cited than the unpublished CAS decisions.[131] This may at first glance appear expected and obvious. However, one should keep in mind that the unpublished CAS decisions that are included in the dataset are included only because they have been cited by CAS. This is a quite strong selection bias in favor of unpublished decisions of particularly high precedential value. At the same time, that unpublished decisions are more rarely cited is and ought to be true: parties' and panels' ability to cite unpublished decisions is severely limited by the fact that they are not publicly available.[132] Moreover, we assume and below confirm that the importance of decisions as a source of law to some extent differ depending on the nature of the dispute. Thus, any selection bias in this regard should not affect the overall validity of conclusions and had it been possible to consider a larger sample, most tendencies would likely be even stronger.

1.6 Law as Network

In order to answer some of the questions posed, this study uses a combination of statistical methods and network analysis. As some readers may not be quite so familiar with these methods, a short introduction is in order.

Network analysis has developed from graph theory, which in turn came about as a mathematical tool for solving geometrical and topological problems.[133] Broadly speaking, network analysis involves mapping relationships between individual components, which for example can be individuals or websites, for the purpose of understanding how a system, such as the movie industry or the Internet, is structured and functions. Networks may be so large that they are difficult to survey but are fundamentally uncomplicated, in their basic form consisting only of connections, or *edges* in network analysis terminology, between their components, or *vertices* in network analysis terminology.[134] A network may for example be constructed based on actors that have appeared together in films[135] or on websites that link to each other.[136]

[131] On average 3.0 times per published decision compared to on average 2.0 times per unpublished decision.

[132] In this regard, it is surprising and somewhat worrisome that CAS panels do quite frequently cite unpublished decisions. See further Sect. 4.5.

[133] Euler 1741 is generally claimed to constitute the origin of graph theory.

[134] Edges are sometimes also referred to as links or arcs and vertices as nodes.

[135] A popular example is the game Six degrees of Kevin Bacon where players try to connect any actor to Kevin Bacon through chains of association based on movies in which actors have appeared together.

[136] This is for example the basis for the Google search engine.

This book relies on two networks. The first network, which we can refer to as the CAS case law network, is based on references between CAS decisions, that is instances where CAS panels in their decisions referred to other CAS decisions.[137] In making such a reference the CAS panel is communicating the reasons for why it reached a particular decision with the parties as well as a broader audience that includes other stakeholders in sports and subsequent CAS panels. The data contains 2,985 such references between the 1,125 studied CAS decisions. Because such references can obviously only be made from newer decisions to older decisions this is a (time-)directed network. This is a type of citation network that reflects how CAS decisions relate to each other, the strength of those connections, and the general structure of CAS's jurisprudence.

The second network is based on connections between actors involved in CAS proceedings, that is arbitrators and parties. The nature of those connections varies. Arbitrators are connected to each other by appearing together on the same CAS panel and connected to parties by being nominated by them. Parties are connected to each other by appearing as litigants, either on the same side or on opposite sides. This is a type of social network that reflects which actors are connected to which and their positions in CAS.

Although networks are simple to construct and understand, they are powerful analytical tools. In this book, the networks are analyzed to determine the centrality of decisions/actors relative to other decisions/actors and to identify community structures. What this means requires further explanation.

A network that is created by randomly adding edges between vertices will have no vertices that hold particularly important positions in the network. But in real-world networks, such as networks representing CAS's jurisprudence or actors in the CAS, edges are not distributed randomly. It is intuitive that decisions that deal with the same legal issue will be more strongly connected to each other, that certain arbitrators appear more frequently together with certain arbitrators,[138] that some CAS decisions are cited more frequently than others, that some CAS arbitrators are appointed more frequently than others, and so on.

Thus, vertices have different positions and this reflects a difference in the roles they play in the network. There are different ways to think about the different roles that vertices may play in a network and while a vertex may not be structurally important in one sense, it may be in another. For example, in the CAS jurisprudence network, a particular decision can be considered important because it is used as a source of law in many subsequent decisions or because it has made some crucial contribution on a particular legal issue, but both are not necessarily true at the same time.[139]

[137] Any situation where the parties referred to a previous decision as part of their arguments is excluded, as are references contained in quotes. That a decision contains multiple references to the same previous decision is not given any consideration.

[138] For example, the data includes eight CAS decisions where both UCI and WADA appears as parties, most often on the same side of the dispute.

[139] For more discussions on different meanings of importance in precedent and the possibility of using network analysis to capture these, see Derlén and Lindholm 2014.

Centrality measurements are used for identifying and quantifying the important vertices in a network. Simply explained, centrality is a quantitative measurement of the relative importance of a vertex, in this context a decision or an actor, in the network. Network analysis contains a number of different centrality measurements.

An obvious and straightforward centrality measurement is degree centrality. A vertex's *degree* is simply the number of edges connected to it. For example, when studying the composition of CAS panels, each arbitrator's degree is equal to the number of other arbitrators that he or she has appeared on panels with.[140] In a directed network, such as the CAS case law network, it is possible to distinguish between a vertex's *outdegree*, the number of edges starting from the vertex and ending at another vertex, and its *indegree*, the number of edges pointing to the vertex. In the CAS case law network, a CAS decision's outdegree is equal to the number of decisions it cites and its indegree is equal to the number of decisions that cites it. The main advantages of degree centrality are that it is easy to understand and simple to calculate. Comparing different decisions' indegree can be used to measure how frequently they are relied upon in subsequent decisions, a measurement of their relative *precedential power*.[141] Outdegree can similarly be treated as a type of measurement of how extensively the decisions are based in previous case law, a measurement of their relative *persuasive power*.[142]

Degree centrality does however have significant limitations. First, degree centrality is egalitarian in the sense that it treats every reference equally. While egalitarianism is often positive, it does not always reflect reality. For example, indegree centrality does not accurately capture that a decision may have a structural impact on the development of the law that is not reflected in how many times it has been cited. To use an illustrative example, imagine two decisions, A and B, that each have been cited in two different subsequent decisions, X and Y respectively, and therefore both have an indegree of 1. Thus, indegree suggests that A and B are equal important as precedents. However, what if X has never been cited while Y has been cited a hundred times? Assuming that Y is being cited on the point of law for which Y cites and builds upon B, most lawyers would agree that B's contribution to the law is greater than A's and that indegree centrality fails to reflect this.

Second and somewhat similarly, outdegree centrality does not accurately represent whether a particular decision is well-grounded in existing case law. A decision that cites a few, important decisions can on good grounds be considered better grounded in existing jurisprudence than a decision that cites a large number of relatively insignificant decisions.[143]

---

[140] When two arbitrators appear on more than one panel together, these edges can be simplified as a single edge with higher weight with the same result.

[141] See further Chap. 5 and Sect. 6.3.1.

[142] See further Sect. 6.3.2.

[143] To use a similar example from the university context, a student paper that cites three well-argued and novel research articles is arguably better supported than one that cites a hundred Wikipedia articles.

Third, because degree centrality is an absolute rather than relative measurement, it poorly reflects change over time. For example, a CAS decision's outdegree will always be the same[144] even though how well-grounded or persuasive it is in a legal sense may change, for example if it in a crucial way relies upon previous case law that is subsequently overturned.[145] While a decision's indegree can and often does go up as subsequent decisions cite it, it can only increase, not decrease, even if it is overturned.

To address these issues, degree centrality will here below be supplemented by other network centrality measures. First, this study uses the *PageRank* algorithm that was introduced in 1998 and that serves as the basis for how Google ranks webpages. Very simplified, PageRank uses a "random walker" to explore a network's structure by extensively and randomly following edges, occasionally teleporting to a random vertex.[146] A vertex's PageRank, which is expressed as a percentage value, represents the relative probability that the random walker at a particular point in time finds herself in a particular vertex.[147] When applied to a directed network, PageRank constitutes a powerful alternative to indegree centrality.[148] In the CAS's case law network, this constitutes a measurement of different CAS decisions' precedential value as it provides a relative measurement of importance that changes over time and that does not inappropriately premier neither the oldest nor the newest decisions.

The second algorithm used is the HITS algorithm.[149] HITS has many similarities with PageRank: it was developed in the late 1990s for the purpose of ranking websites, produces relative centrality scores that changes over time, distinguishes between edges based on the characteristics of the connected vertices, and individual vertices' centrality scores can therefore (unlike for degree centrality) only be calculated on the basis of the larger network. However, instead of using a random walker to explore the network, HITS does it by assigning two scores to all vertices: an *authority score* and a *hub score*. A vertex's authority score is equal to the sum of the hub score of all vertices with an originating edge to the vertex. Thus, in the CAS case law network a decision with high authority score is a decision that has been

144 Equal to the number of decisions it cites.

145 See further Derlén and Lindholm 2017b.

146 The chance of a teleport at each vertex explored, in the algorithm expressed as the damping factor (d), affects how many edges backwards the random walker will explore. Because of the comparatively limited size of the network, in this study I use a factor of 0.5 (50% chance of a teleport), compare to the original of 0.85 (15% chance of a teleport).

147 Brin and Page 1998; Page et al. 1998. As a law teacher, I like to think about PageRank as the chance that a law student doing research by reading court decisions and following reference backwards in time (like a random walker) at any given point in time is reading a particular court decision.

148 In a directed network, the random walker follows edges from originating vertices to target vertices. In an undirected network, by comparison, the random walker can follow the edge in either direction.

149 This is frequently used as a measurement of persuasive power in studies of case law. See e.g. Fowler et al. 2007; Lupu and Voeten 2012.

cited by many and/or good hubs. Similarly, a vertex's hub score is equal to the sum of the authority score of all vertices targeted by the vertex and a decision with high hub score is a decision that cites many and/or good authorities. Hub score is in this book used as a measurement of persuasive power.[150] A decision's hub score reflects not only the number of decisions it cites but also the relative importance of the cited decisions.[151] Instead of treating all cited decisions equally, the HITS algorithm assigns greater importance when an important decision is cited.[152] Thus, a decision with a high hub score is a judgment that cites many and/or important judgments.[153]

Like most citation networks, including other case law networks, and many other real-world networks, such as the Internet,[154] centrality in the CAS case law network follows a power law distribution rather than a normal distribution.[155] In a normal or "bell curve distribution" most values cluster around the middle of the range, the mean, and gradually decrease towards the lower and upper end of the spectrum. By comparison, in a power law distribution, also known as a "long tail distribution", most of the values are on the lower end of the spectrum with an increasingly small group of values on the higher end.[156] When values are distributed in this manner it can be difficult to determine whether mean values for groups are statistically significant.[157] In order to determine whether differences in mean centrality are statistically significant the scores will, as described in greater detail below, be compared with the mean score of a large number of randomly created sets of identical size.

Another characteristic of real-world networks is the existence of communities of vertices within networks that are more densely connected to each other than to other vertices in the network.[158] These vertices constitute a community because they share some characteristic and/or play a similar role in the network.[159] When studying a real-world network, network communities represent real-world communities. In this manner, community detection or clustering, as it is also known, can for example be used to identify groups of individuals that are socially connected or

[150] PageRank is here used instead of authority score.

[151] Kleinberg 1999.

[152] In the HITS algorithm, "importance" is measured as authority score and calculated on the basis of the judgments citing it. A good authority is a vertex pointed to by many good hubs and a good hub is a vertex that points to many good authorities.

[153] In a network of case law, authorities and hubs can be translated as influential judgments and judgments that are well founded in law. See Fowler et al. 2007, p. 331. For a discussion of important hubs in the case law of the CJEU, see Derlén and Lindholm 2014, p. 685.

[154] Barabási and Réka 1999.

[155] See e.g. Sect. 5.2.

[156] The mechanisms behind this distribution can frequently be described as a "rich-get-richer" phenomenon. See e.g. Barabási and Réka 1999.

[157] As the inclusion or exclusion of a single member may have a massive impact on the group's mean score.

[158] Girvan and Newman 2002, p. 7821; Radicchi et al. 2004, p. 2658.

[159] Fortunato 2010, pp. 76–77.

research publications that deal with the same topic.[160] As explained in greater detail below, community detection is in this book used to identify CAS decisions that deal with the same issues.[161]

1.7 Organization of the Book

This book consists of ten chapters divided into three parts. This chapter has introduced the topic and the study. This work continues in Chap. 2 that provides an introduction of the organizational aspects of CAS and the normative framework in which it operates. That chapter concludes this first introductory part of the book.

The second part of the book focuses on CAS's jurisprudence. In Chap. 3 we will explore some of the general characteristics of its jurisprudence. This provides a basic understanding of the process within CAS that turns requests for decisions into decisions, the connections between CAS decisions through references, and how these matters have developed over time. Chapter 4 maps to what extent CAS and other sports bodies rely on and adhere to previous decisions by CAS when making their decisions, that is, to what extent CAS decisions function as precedent. Chapter 5 ends the discussion about structure and precedent in CAS's jurisprudence by focusing on individual CAS decisions and exploring what may be considered CAS's most important decisions, its "landmark cases", under alternative meanings of the term. The subsequent two chapters then turn to the substance of CAS's jurisprudence. Chapter 6 employs a combination of methods in seeking to identify and describe the main issues dealt with by CAS and how they relate to each other. The last chapter of the second part, Chap. 7, maps the rules and principles developed in CAS's decisions, the normative contribution of its jurisprudence, as well as how CAS goes about establishing and developing such rules and principles.

The third and final part of the book turns the attention to CAS's main actors. Chapter 8 mainly focus on arbitrators from a structural perspective in the sense of identifying structures among arbitrators, structures in the relationships between arbitrators and parties, and the position of arbitrators in relation to the structure of CAS's jurisprudence. Chapter 9 continues to study arbitrators but does so with the aim of describing what characterizes CAS arbitrators and to what extent those characteristics affect how they function as arbitrators. Finally, Chap. 10 focuses on the parties that come before CAS and the roles that CAS plays in relation to different parties and in disputes between different types of parties.

[160] Girvan and Newman 2002, p. 7821.

[161] See Chap. 6.2.

References

Anter A (2014) Max Weber's Theory of the Modern State: Origins, Structure and Significance. Palgrave Macmillan, Basingstoke

Barabási A-L, Réka A (1999) Emergence of Scaling in Random Networks. Science 286:509–512

Barents R (2004) The Autonomy of Community Law. Kluwer Law International, The Hague

Beloff M (2005) Is there a lex sportiva? International Sports Law Review 3:49–60

Beloff M, Kerr T, Demetriou M, Beloff R (2012) Sports Law, 2nd edn. Hart Publishing, Oxford

Berger B (2013) The Legal Framework: Rights and Obligations of Arbitrators in the Deliberations. In: Berger B, Schneider M (eds) Inside the Black Box: How Arbitral Tribunals Operate and Reach Their Decisions. Juris Publishing, New York, pp. 7–12

Bersagel A (2012) Is There a Stare Decisis Doctrine in the Court of Arbitration for Sport? An Analysis of Published Awards for Anti-Doping Disputes in Track and Field. Pepperdine Dispute Resolution Law Journal 12:189–207

Blackaby N, Partasides C, Redfern A, Hunter M (2015) Redfern and Hunter on International Arbitration, 6th edn. Oxford University Press, Oxford

Blackshaw I (2012) Introductory Remarks. In: Wild A (ed) CAS and Football: Landmark Cases, T. M.C. Asser Press, The Hague, pp. 5–10

Brin S, Page L (1998) The anatomy of a large-scale hypertextual Web search engine. Computer Networks and ISDN Systems 30:107–117

Brower CN, Schill SW (2009) Is Arbitration a Threat or a Boon to the Legitimacy of International Investment Law? Chicago Journal of International Law 9(2):471–498

Buy F, Maramyou J-M, Poracchi D, Rizzo F (2015) Droit du Sport, 4nd edn. LGDJ, Paris

Cahoy D (2010) Considerations in the Rise of Empirical Legal Scholarship. American Business Law Review 47:v–ix

Cane P, Kritzer H (2010) The Oxford Handbook of Empirical Legal Research. Oxford University Press, Oxford

CAS (2016) Statistics 2016. http://www.tas-cas.org/fileadmin/user_upload/CAS_statistics_2016_pdf. Accessed 7 September 2018

Casini L (2011) The Making of Lex Sportiva by the Court of Arbitration for Sport. German Law Journal 12(5):1317–1340

Derlén M, Lindholm J (2014) Goodbye van Gend en Loos, Hello Bosman? Using Network Analysis to Measure the Importance of Individual CJEU Judgments. European Law Journal 20 (5):667–687

Derlén M, Lindholm J (2015) Characteristics of Precedent: The Case Law of the European Court of Justice in Three Dimensions. German Law Journal 16(5):1073–1098

Derlén M, Lindholm J (2016) Bosman: A Legacy Beyond Sports. In: Duval A, Van Rompuy B (eds) The Legacy of Bosman. T.M.C. Asser Press, The Hague, pp. 31–49

Derlén M, Lindholm J (2017a) Peek-a-boo, It's a Case Law System. German Law Journal 18 (3):647–686

Derlén M, Lindholm J (2017b) Is It Good Law? Network Analysis and the CJEU's Internal Market Jurisprudence. Journal of International Economic Law 20(2):257–277

Derlén M, Lindholm J, Mirshahvalad A, Rosvall M (2013) Coherence Out of Chaos: Mapping European Union Law by Running Randomly Through the Maze of CJEU Case Law. Europarättslig Tidskrift 16(3):517–535

Drahozal C (2003) Of Rabbits and Rhinoceri: A Survey of Empirical Research on International Commercial Arbitration. Journal of International Arbitration 20(1):23–34

Drahozal C, Naimark R (2002) Towards a Science of International Arbitration: Collected Empirical Research. Kluwer Law International, The Hague

Duval A (2013) Lex Sportiva: A Playground for Transnational Law. European Law Journal 19 (6):822–842

Emerson F (1970) History of Arbitration Practice and Law. Cleveland State Law Review 19 (1):155–164

Epstein L, King G (2002) The Rules of Inference. University of Chicago Law Review 69:1–133
Erbsen A (2006) The Substance and Illusion of Lex Sportiva. In: Blackshaw I, Siekman R, Soek J (eds) The Court of Arbitration for Sport 1984–2004. T.M.C. Asser Press, The Hague, pp. 441–454
Euler L (1741) Solutio problematis ad geometriam situs pertinentis. Commentarii academiae scientiarum Petropolitanae 8:128–140
Fortunato S (2010) Community Detection in Graphs. Physics Reports 486:75–174
Foster K (2003) Is There a Global Sports Law. Entertainment Law 2(1):1–18
Foster K (2006) Lex Sportiva and Lex Ludica: The Court of Arbitration for Sport's Jurisprudence. Entertainment and Sports Law Journal 3(2)
Fowler J, Johnson T, Spriggs II J, Jeon S, Wahlbeck P (2007) Network Analysis and the Law: Measuring the Legal Importance of Precedents at the U.S. Supreme Court. Political Analysis 15:324–346
Franck S (2007) Empirically Evaluating Claims About Investment Treaty Arbitration. North Carolina Law Review 86:1–88
Franck S, van Aaken A, Freda J, Guthrie C, Rachlinski J (2017) Inside the Arbitrator's Mind. Emory Law Journal 66(5):1115–1173
George T (2006) An Empirical Study of Empirical Legal Scholarship: The Top Law Schools. Indiana Law Journal 81:141–160
Girvan M, Newman M (2002) Community Structure in Social and Biological Networks. PNAS 99 (12):7821–7826
Hansford T, Spriggs II J (2008) The Politics of Precedent on the U.S. Supreme Court. Princeton University Press, Princeton
Heise M (1999) The Importance of Being Empirical. Pepperdine Law Review 26:807–834
Hess B (2015) The Development of Lex Sportiva by the Court of Arbitration for Sport. In: Vieweg K (ed) Lex Sportiva, Duncker and Humblot, Berlin, pp. 59–76
Jansen N, Michaels R (2008) Beyond the State? Rethinking Private Law: Introduction to the Issue. American Journal of Comparative Law 56(3):527–539
Kleinberg J M (1999) Authoritative Sources in a Hyperlinked Environment. Journal of the ACM 46:604–632
Latty F (2007) La lex sportiva: Recherche sur le droit transnational. Martinus Nijhoff, Leiden
Latty F (2011) Transnational Sports Law. The International Sports Law Journal 2011(1–2):34–38
Lupu Y, Voeten E (2011) Precedent in International Courts: A Network Analysis of Case Citations by the European Court of Human Rights. British Journal of Political Science 42:413–439
MacCormick N (1999) Questioning Sovereignty. Oxford University Press, Oxford
Malatesta A, Sali R (eds) (2013) The Rise of Transparency in International Arbitration. JurisNet, Huntington
Mavromati D (2012) Language of procedure before CAS: Practice, criteria and impact of the language on the outcome of the case. CAS Bulletin 2012(1):39–48
Mavromati D, Reeb M (2015) The Code of the Court of Arbitration for Sport: Commentary, Cases and Materials. Wolters Kluwer, Alphen aan den Rijn
Mbaye K (2002) Foreword. In: Reeb M (ed) Digest of CAS Awards 1998–2000. Kluwer Law International, The Hague, pp. xi–xii
Mbaye K (2006) Une nouvelle institution d'arbitrage: le tribunal arbitral du sport (TAS). Annuaire français de droit International XXX:409 (1984). Reprinted in: Blackshaw I, Siekman R, Soek J (eds) The Court of Arbitration for Sport 1984–2004. T.M.C. Asser Press, The Hague, pp. 6–20
McArdle D (2015) Dispute Resolution in Sport: Athletes, Law and Arbitration. Routledge, Oxon
McLaren R (2001) The Court of Arbitration for Sport: An Independent Arena for the World's Sports Disputes. Valparaiso University Law Review 35:379–405
Michaels R (2007) The True Lex Mercatoria: Law Beyond the State. Indiana Journal of Global Legal Studies 14(2):447–468
Mitten M J, Opie H (2010) 'Sports Law': Implications for the Development of International, Comparative, and National Law and Global Dispute Resolution. Tulane Law Review 85:269–322

Nafziger J (2004) Lex Sportiva. The International Sports Law Journal 2004(1–2):3–8
Nafziger J (2015) Defining the Scope and Structure of International Sports Law: Four Conceptual Issues. In: Vieweg K (ed) Lex Sportiva. Duncker and Humblot, Berlin, pp. 161–178
Noussia K (2010) Confidentiality in International Commercial Arbitration: A Comparative Analysis of the Position under English, US, German and French Law. Springer Verlag, Berlin
Page L, Brin S, Motwani R, Winograd T (1998) The PageRank Citation Ranking: Bringing Order to the Web, 29 January 1998. http://ilpubs.stanford.edu:8090/422/1/1999-66.pdf. Accessed 6 July 2018
Paulsson J (2011) Arbitration in Three Dimensions. International and Comparative Law Quarterly 60(2):291–323
Panagiotopoulos D (2011) Lex Sportiva and International Legitimacy Governing: Protection of Professional Players. US-China Law Review 8:121–136
Panagiotopoulos D (2013) Sporting Jurisdictional Order and Arbitration. US-China Law Review 10:130–140
Parrish R (2012) Lex sportiva and EU sports law. European Law Review 37(6):716–733
Posner R (1995) Overcoming Law. Harvard University Press, Cambridge
Radicchi F, Castellano C, Cecconi F, Loreto V, Parisi D (2004) Defining and identifying communities in networks. PNAS 101(9):2658–2663
Reeb M (1998) The Court of Arbitration for Sport (CAS). In: Reeb M (ed) Digest of CAS Awards I. Kluwer Law International, The Hague, pp. xxiii–xxxi
Reilly L (2012) An Introduction to the Court of Arbitration for Sport (CAS) and the Role of National Courts in International Sports Disputes. Journal of Dispute Resolution 2012(1):63–81
Rigozzi A (2005) L'arbitrage international en matière de sport. Helbing & Lichtenhahn, Basel
Rogers C (2006) Transparency in International Commercial Arbitration. Kansas University Law Review 54:1301–1345
Schill S (2012) International Arbitrators as System-Builders. American Society of International Law 106:295–297
Schultz T (2014) Transnational Legality: Stateless Law and International Arbitration. Oxford University Press, Oxford
Segal J, Spaeth H, Benesh S (2005) The Supreme Court in the American Legal System. Cambridge University Press, Cambridge
Siekmann R (2011) What is Sports Law? Lex Sportiva and Lex Ludica: A Reassessment of Content and Terminology. The International Sports Law Journal 2011(3-4):3–13
Smeureanu I (2011) Confidentiality in International Commercial Arbitration. Wolters Kluwer, Alphen aan den Rijn
Teubner G (ed) (1997) Global Law Without a State. Dartmouth, Andover
Teubner G (2002) Breaking Frames: Economic Globalization and the Emergence of Lex Mercatoria. European Journal of Social Theory 5(2):199–217
Teubner G (2008) State Policies in Private Law. American Journal of Comparative Law 56:835–843
Tucker T (2016) Inside the Black Box: Collegial Patterns on Investment Tribunals. Journal of International Dispute Settlement 7:183–204
Tuori K (2011) Ratio and Voluntas: The Tension Between Reason and Will in Law. Ashgate, Farnham
van de Kerchove M, Ost F (1994) Legal Systems Between Order and Disorder. Stewart I trans., Oxford University Press, Oxford
Vieweg K, Staschik P (2015) The Lex Sportiva: The Phenomenon and its Meaning in the International Sporting Arena. In: Vieweg K (ed) Lex Sportiva. Duncker & Humblot, Berlin, pp. 17–58
Wax A (2015) Public International Sports Law and the Lex Sportiva. In: Vieweg K (ed) Lex Sportiva, Duncker & Humblot, Berlin, pp. 145–160
Wolaver E (1934) The Historical Background of Commercial Arbitration. University of Pennsylvania Law Review 83(2):132–146

Yi D (2006) Turning Medals into Metal: Evaluating the Court of Arbitration for Sport as an International Tribunal. Asper Review of International Business and Trade Law 6:289–341
Zetie K (2003) Getting a buzz from flight. Physics Education November 2003:476 Education November 2003:476

Chapter 2
CAS: An Overview

Abstract Each time a case is referred to CAS a new arbitration panel is formed to resolve the specific dispute at hand. While each panel is independent of each other they operate within a shared organizational and regulatory framework. This framework provides panels with the power to issue binding and enforceable awards, but also governs how they may exercise this power. This chapter introduces the organizational and regulatory framework governing CAS. This includes the CAS Code which, among other things, governs CAS's organization, jurisdiction, and the formation of panels. The chapter also provides a general description of what characterizes the cases that come before CAS.

2.1 Organizational and Regulatory Framework

Since its creation, the Court of Arbitration for Sport (CAS) has had its seat and main headquarters in Lausanne, Switzerland,[1] where the International Olympic Committee (IOC) and many other sports governing bodies (SGBs) are also situated.[2] This means that CAS and its proceedings are governed by Swiss law, even though oral hearings may be and in fact are held in other places.[3] Since 1996 CAS has two decentralised offices for Oceania and North America, currently situated in Sydney and New York respectively. Since 2012 it has also set up a number of alternative hearing centres. Finally, beginning with the Atlanta Olympic Games in 1996, a number of special CAS Ad Hoc Divisions (AHDs) have been set up to resolve disputes in connection with certain major sporting events, including Olympic Summer and Winter Games, Asian Games, Commonwealth Games, European Football Championships, and FIFA World Cups, at the place of such events.[4]

---

[1] CAS is since 2005 housed in Château de Béthusy.
[2] Article S1 CAS Code.
[3] Article R28 CAS Code; Kaufmann-Kohler and Bärtsch 2006, p. 79.
[4] See Article S6, point 8, CAS Code.

J. Lindholm, *The Court of Arbitration for Sport and Its Jurisprudence*,
ASSER International Sports Law Series,
https://doi.org/10.1007/978-94-6265-285-9_2

Originally, under the CAS Statute of 1984, CAS's members were appointed directly by the IOC, international sport federations (IFs), National Olympic Committees (NOCs), and the IOC President. However, this was reformed in 1994 following concerns regarding CAS's independence voiced by the Swiss Federal Tribunal (SFT) in its decision in *Gundel*.[5] Through the so-called Paris Agreement, a new foundation, the International Council of Arbitration for Sport (ICAS), was formed and entrusted with the task of regulating, administrating, supervising, and financing CAS.[6] The purpose of this reorganization was to increase CAS's independence from the IOC.[7]

ICAS has twenty members of which twelve are appointed by the IOC, IFs, and NOCs who then, in turn, participate in the appointment of the remaining eight.[8] Among other things, ICAS "appoints the arbitrators who constitute the list of CAS arbitrators."[9] According to the CAS Code, "[e]very arbitrator shall appear on the list drawn up by ICAS."[10] This list shall contain at least 150 arbitrators,[11] but has in recent years been at least twice as long.[12] ICAS also appoints the CAS Secretary General who heads CAS's Court Office. The role of the Court Office is to organize and administer CAS's work.

Another result of the 1994 reform process is that CAS is organized into two permanent divisions: the Ordinary Arbitration Division and the Appeals Arbitration Division. These divisions correspond to the two main types of CAS jurisdiction to which in some regards diverging procedural rules apply.[13] Each division is headed by a Division President, appointed by ICAS,[14] who, among other things, plays an important part in panel formation.[15] This structural division only applies to the organizational level and does not extend to individual arbitrators; all arbitrators that appear on the list of CAS arbitrator are eligible to appear on a panel organized by either the Ordinary or Appeals Arbitration Division. However, following FIFA's adoption of CAS as its appellate institution, CAS maintains an additional list of arbitrators that are exclusively qualified to hear football-related disputes.[16]

---

[5] SFT's decision 15 March 1993 in case 4P.217/1992, ATF 119 II 271 (*Gundel v. FEI*). See also further Sect. 3.3.

[6] Article S2 CAS Code.

[7] See also Sect. 3.3.

[8] Article S4 CAS Code.

[9] Article S6 CAS Code.

[10] Article R33 CAS Code.

[11] Article S13 CAS Code.

[12] See Sect. 8.2.

[13] See below Sect. 2.2.

[14] Article S6 CAS Code.

[15] See below Sect. 2.3.

[16] See Sect. 8.5.

Because the seat of CAS and its arbitration panels is in Switzerland[17] it is ultimately governed, as the law of arbitration or *lex arbitri*, by the Swiss Law on International Arbitration set out in the Private International Law Act of 1987 (PILA).[18] The PILA addresses such issues as the arbitrability of disputes, the constitution of the tribunal, grounds and procedures for challenging arbitrators and awards, as well as certain procedural issues.

The organization of CAS and ICAS is governed by the Statutes of the Bodies Working for the Settlement of Sports-Related Disputes which are incorporated in the Code of Sports-related Arbitration (CAS Code). The statutes regulate such matters as the appointment of ICAS members and CAS arbitrators, the purpose and main responsibilities of these two organizations, and the organization of CAS.

The CAS Code also contains the procedural rules governing disputes before CAS.[19] These procedural rules, which are set by ICAS,[20] in part overlap with rules found in the PILA and must comply with the latter. However, the CAS Code regulates these matters in greater detail and also addresses several issues not addressed by the PILA.

The "foundation stone" of arbitration is that the parties have an arbitration agreement,[21] a written "agreement by the parties to submit to arbitration all or certain disputes which have arisen or which may arise between them in respect of a defined legal relationship,"[22] and an arbitration award that does not rest on a valid arbitration agreement can be set aside.[23] CAS jurisdiction therefore requires the existence of a valid arbitration agreement.[24]

In theory, the parties can through such arbitration agreements or subsequent agreement affect certain aspects of the framework governing the resolution of the dispute. The perhaps most important example of this is the power of the parties to decide the (substantive) law governing the merits of the disputes (the *lex causae*).[25] However, in practice, the substantive rules interpreted and applied by CAS will in a

---

[17] Article R28 CAS Code.

[18] Article 176(1) PILA. However, domestic disputes, i.e. disputes between parties that are domiciled or reside habitually in Switzerland, are governed by the Swiss Civil Procedure Code (CPC).

[19] Article R27 CAS Code. For an excellent commentary of these rules, see Mavromati and Reeb 2015.

[20] Article S6 CAS Code.

[21] Blackaby et al. 2015, p. 12.

[22] Article 7(1) UNCITRAL Model Law.

[23] Article V New York Convention; Article 190(2)(b) PILA.

[24] Article R27, R38, and R48 CAS Code. However, as highlighted by e.g. the *Pechstein*-case, athletes in practise have limited power over or alternative to agreeing to arbitration if they wish to compete. See BGH's decision 7 June 2016 in case KZR 6/15 (*Pechstein v. ISU*), para 56. This casts doubt over the consensual basis of CAS's jurisdiction in many cases. See Duval 2017. See also below Sect. 2.2.

[25] Articles R45 and R58 CAS Code.

majority of the disputes it resolves be found in various sporting rules and regulations, such as for example the World Anti-Doping Code (WADC).[26]

A consequence of CAS and proceedings before CAS being governed by Swiss arbitration law is that CAS awards can be annulled by the Federal Supreme Court of Switzerland (*Bundesgericht, Tribunal federal*, or SFT).[27] An award can be annulled on procedural grounds, including improper tribunal constitution, lack of jurisdiction, *ultra* or *infra petita* decisions, and violation of fundamental procedural rights, and on substantive grounds for breach of *ordre public*.[28] It is in practise rare for SFT to set aside CAS awards: less than one out of ten applications for the annulment of CAS decisions are wholly or partial successful,[29] and annulments on substantive grounds are particularly rare. However, the existence of and potential for review by SFT has some very tangible effects on CAS, its jurisprudence and, by extension, sports law generally.[30]

By merit of being an arbitration tribunal,[31] CAS and its awards are covered by the New York Convention of June 10, 1958 on the Recognition and Enforcement of Foreign Arbitral Awards (the New York Convention). This means that national courts of signatory states shall refuse to hear disputes that fall under the scope of an arbitration agreement.[32] It also means that CAS awards will be recognized and enforced in all signatory states,[33] which includes an obstacle to re-litigation of the dispute (negative *res judicata*).

This does not, however, completely isolate CAS and its awards from the requirements of national law or review by national courts. According to the New York Convention, the courts of a signatory state may decline to recognize an arbitral award on certain grounds,[34] one ground being that the award violates "national public policy."[35] The New York Convention's public policy exception is in most jurisdictions given a narrow interpretation that only includes more qualified

---

[26] See Article R58 CAS Code.

[27] Article 191(2) PILA. See also Kaufmann-Kohler and Bärtsch 2006, p. 80; Rigozzi 2010.

[28] Article 190(2) PILA.

[29] Dasser and Wójtowicz 2016, pp. 283–284 (noting that the success-rate for challenges of awards in the SFT is higher for sports-related than non-sport-related arbitration).

[30] See e.g. immediately above regarding *Gundel* and Chap. 7. An illustrative example is SFT's decision 27 March 2012 in case 4A_558/2011 (*Matuzalem v. FIFA*), para 4.5.3.

[31] Cf. SFT's decision 15 March 1993 in case 4P.217/1992, ATF 119 II 271 (*Gundel v. FEI*); SFT's decision 27 May 2003 in case 4P.267/2002, ATF 129 III 445 (*Lazutina & Danilova v. IOC*), at p. 463, para 3.3.4 ("le TAS est suffisamment indépendant du CIO, comme de toutes les autres parties qui font appel à ses services, pour que les décisions qu'il rend dans les causes intéressant cet organisme puissent être considérées comme de véritables sentences, assimilables aux jugements d'un tribunal étatique.").

[32] Article II(3) of the New York Convention. See also Mitten and Opie 2010, pp. 302–303; Blackshaw 2013, p. 16 (discussing examples from national courts).

[33] Article III of the New York Convention.

[34] Article V of the New York Convention.

[35] Article V(2)(b) of the New York Convention.

violations. Most national jurisdictions also largely agree on what constitutes such a severe breach of procedural requirements that recognition of an award may be declined on grounds of lack of procedural due process. What in this regard constitutes substantive public policy varies more significantly between jurisdictions.[36] For example, EU Member State courts shall decline to recognize CAS awards on public policy grounds if doing so would violate EU competition law.[37] This creates a possibility, albeit quite limited, for re-litigating disputes decided by CAS in national courts.[38]

2.2 Jurisdiction

As discussed above, CAS's jurisdiction over a dispute requires that the dispute falls within the scope of a valid arbitration agreement. Arbitration agreements conferring jurisdiction upon CAS may be found in various types of documents including statutes, rules, and agreements. For example, one specific but important ground for jurisdictions is the Olympic Charter which provides CAS with exclusive jurisdiction over "any dispute arising on the occasion of, or in connection with, the Olympic Games" and over challenges of many IOC decisions.[39] Additionally, participation agreements with individual athletes may include arbitration agreements conferring exclusive jurisdiction upon CAS to resolve all disputes arising in connection with a competition.[40] In principle it is up to the parties to an arbitration agreement to formulate it and agree what is covered by the agreement.[41] However, a large portion of the cases that come before CAS, particularly under the Appeals Arbitration Procedure, are based on CAS's model arbitration clauses.[42]

Both the CAS Code and the organization of CAS reflect that CAS jurisdiction rests on two distinguishable types of arbitration agreements and results in two distinguishable types of arbitration procedure. The first type is referred to as Ordinary Arbitration Procedure and includes all cases where CAS decides the dispute as a first (and typically final) instance. Cases heard under the Ordinary

[36] IBA 2015, pp. 15–18.

[37] See e.g. Case C-126/97, *Eco Swiss China Time Ltd v. Benetton International NV*, EU:C:1999:269, paras 36, 39; Joined Cases C-295-298/04, *Manfredi et al. v. Assitalia SpA.*, EU:C:2006:461, paras 31, 39; Case C-8/08, *T-Mobile Netherlands BV et al. v. Raad van bestuur van de Nederlandse Mededingingsautoriteit*, EU:C:2009:343, para 49.

[38] A current example of this is the case of *Pechstein v. ISU*, e.g. BGH's decision 7 June 2016 in case KZR 6/15; OLG München's decision 15 January 2015 in case 1110/14 Kart.

[39] Article 61 IOC Charter.

[40] See Yi 2006, p. 293 (reproducing the agreement for the 2004 Olympic Summer Games).

[41] Simma 2006, p. 26.

[42] Cf. Reeb 2004, xxiv. However, as illustrated by e.g. Cour d'appel Bruxelles's decision 29 August 2018 in case 2016/AR/2048 (*Doyen Sports et al. v. URBSFA et al.*), paras 14–17, national courts may decline to recognize and enforce overly broad general arbitration clauses.

Arbitration Procedure are similar to those heard by commercial arbitration tribunals, commonly involving contractual disputes.[43] The nature of these disputes and the basis for CAS's jurisdiction to resolve them is in many regards similar to those of commercial arbitration.[44]

The second type is Appeals Arbitration Procedure where CAS decides "disputes concerning the decisions of federations, associations or other sports-related bodies."[45] Cases brought under Appeals Arbitration Procedure are considerably more common than cases brought under Ordinary Arbitration Procedure. In recent years, 10–15 percent of all requests for decisions to CAS were brought under Ordinary Arbitration Procedure. By comparison, 75–90 percent of the requests were brought under Appeals Arbitration Procedure.[46] A majority of all cases brought under the Appeals Arbitration Procedure concern doping-related matters and other disciplinary matters, but it is not uncommon for appeals cases to also concern other matters.[47] While CAS's jurisdiction to hear cases under the Appeals Arbitration Procedure has a consensual basis, that jurisdiction is typically grounded in sport rules, participation agreements, or licensing agreements,[48] and an individual athlete or club has in practice very little or no room for negotiating the terms.[49]

A party that wishes to appeal a decision to CAS must first exhaust all remedies available within the body that made the decision.[50] This is similar to the requirement of exhaustion of domestic remedies that is common in international courts[51] and reflects that CAS's adjudication of disputes is intended to be subsidiary to their resolution by the appropriate bodies within each sport respectively. Consequently,

---

[43] Of the CAS decisions studied in full text, 17% of the decisions issued under Ordinary Arbitration Procedure concern doping and other disciplinary matters. This compares to almost 60% for CAS decisions issued under Appellate Arbitration Procedure. See also Mitten and Opie 2010, p. 286; Reilly 2012, p. 64.

[44] Paulsson 1993, p. 368; Pinna 2006, p. 388. See also Chap. 10.

[45] Rule S12 CAS Code.

[46] CAS, Statistics 2016. Depending on the year, another 2–4% of all requests fall under the Ad Hoc Procedure.

[47] For example, following the CAS's own subject matter classification, nearly 12% of all appellate cases studied concern contractual matters and a nearly equal portion concern transfer-related matters.

[48] Paulsson 1993, p. 368.

[49] See SFT's decision 22 March 2007 in case 4P.172/2006, ATF 133 III 235 (*Cañas v. ATP Tour*), at p. 243 ("Ainsi l'athlète qui souhaite participer à une compétition organisée sous le contrôle d'une fédération sportive dont la réglementation prévoit le recours à l'arbitrage n'aura-t-il d'autre choix que d'accepter la clause arbitrale, notamment en adhérant aux statuts de la fédération sportive en question dans lesquels ladite clause a été insérée, à plus forte raison s'il s'agit d'un sportif professionnel. Il sera confronté au dilemme suivant: consentir à l'arbitrage ou pratiquer son sport en dilettante."); CAS 2009/A/1782, *Volandri*, para 70; ECtHR's decision of 2 October 2018 in *Mutu & Pechstein v. Switzerland*, app. no. 40575/10 & 67474/10, paras 113–115. See also Rigozzi 2010, pp. 226–228.

[50] Article R47 CAS Code.

[51] See e.g. Article 35(1) ECHR.

which bodies have been involved in the making and review of a decision prior to it reaching CAS depends on how the particular sport in question is organized.

An additional requirement for CAS to have jurisdiction over a dispute is that it is "a sports-related dispute."[52] It follows from the CAS Code that "[s]uch disputes may involve matters of principle relating to sport or matters of pecuniary or other interests relating to the practice or the development of sport and may include, more generally, any activity or matter related or connected to sport."[53] The requirement has also been interpreted broadly and in practice constitutes no serious limitation to CAS's jurisdiction.[54]

Until 2011 CAS also had a Consultation Procedure. Unlike Ordinary and Appeals Arbitration Procedure, the Consultation Procedure would not entail CAS resolving a particular dispute or issuing a legally binding decision. Instead it would provide an "advisory opinion" on "any legal issue with respect to the practice or development of sport or any activity related to sport."[55] Similar procedures exist in national[56] and international legal orders.[57] Under this procedure, select SGBs would be allowed to request an advisory opinion. This request was received by the CAS President who would determine if it was appropriate to provide an opinion and, if that was the case, form a panel and formulate the questions that the panel should answer.[58] The power to reformulate the questions gave the CAS President significant power over the procedure and could affect the usefulness of the answer to the requesters.[59] CAS responded to 82 such requests before it was abolished 1 January 2011, the majority of which were received before 1995.[60]

Besides the aforementioned permanent divisions ICAS has, as discussed above, created Ad Hoc Divisions (AHDs) in connection with certain major sports events, such as the Olympic Games and the Commonwealth Games. The purpose of the AHDs is to provide accessible and rapid settlement of disputes that arise in connection with these events. Recently, in connection with the 2016 Rio Olympic Summer Games and the 2018 PyeongChang Winter Olympic Games, additional CAS Anti-Doping Division (ADDs) specialized in resolving doping-related disputes have also been established.[61] ICAS creates special lists of arbitrators to serve on these AHDs consisting of twelve arbitrators and among these appoints a

52 Article R27 CAS Code.

53 Ibid.

54 Kane 2003a; Reeb 2004, p. xxxiii; Yi 2006, p. 294.

55 Article R60 CAS Code (2004).

56 McLaren 2006, pp. 180–181. See also Blackshaw 2013, p. 14 (comparing it to commercial "expert determinations").

57 See e.g. Article 267 TFEU (giving the CJEU jurisdiction to issue preliminary rulings); Protocol 16 to the ECHR (providing the ECtHR jurisdiction to issue advisory opinions) (not yet in force).

58 Articles R60 and R61 CAS Code (2004).

59 McLaren 2006, pp. 183–186.

60 CAS, Statistics 2016.

61 See also Mavromati 2016.

Division President and Co-President.[62] When an AHD receives an application the Division President forms a panel by appointing three arbitrators from the list.[63]

This book will focus on these arbitration procedures. It is however worth mentioning that CAS also offer mediation.[64]

2.3 Formation

As discussed above, only those who have been appointed to the list of CAS arbitrators are eligible to serve on a CAS panel and only those who have "appropriate legal training, recognized competence with regard to sports law and/or international arbitration, a good knowledge of sport in general and a good command of at least one CAS working language" are eligible to be added to the list. The appointment of arbitrators to the list is done by ICAS who updates the list every four years.[65] Appointees must sign a declaration of objectivity, independence, impartiality, and conformity with the CAS Code.[66] Since 2010 those who serve as CAS arbitrators may not also appear as counsel before CAS.[67]

As discussed, all arbitrators on the list may handle both Ordinary and Appellate Arbitration Procedure. However, there are some differences between Ordinary and Appellate Arbitration Procedure with regard to panel formation.

Under the Ordinary Arbitration Procedure a CAS panel consists of either one arbitrator (sole arbitrator) or three arbitrators. If the arbitration agreement does not specify the panel size it is decided by the President of the Ordinary Arbitration Division.[68] Of the CAS decisions heard under Ordinary Arbitration Procedure studied here, 13 percent were decided by a sole arbitrator. The sole arbitrator is appointed by agreement among the parties or, if agreement cannot be reached, the Division President. When the panel is to consist of three arbitrators, each party nominates one arbitrator from the list who then together and by mutual agreement appoints a third arbitrator who serves as the panel president.[69]

---

[62] Articles 3–4 Arbitration Rules applicable to the CAS ad hoc division for the Olympic Games.

[63] Article 11 Arbitration Rules applicable to the CAS ad hoc division for the Olympic Games. While the Division President has the discretion to appoint a sole arbitrator this rarely occurred during the studied period, the notable exceptions being OG 06/003, *Azzimani*; OG 12/011, *ROC v. ISAF*. However, it can be noted that it was more common during the 2016 Rio Olympic Summer Games, possibly due to an extraordinary high number of disputes.

[64] According to Blackshaw, 85% of referred disputes are resolved through mediation. Blackshaw 2006, p. 2. See also Kane 2003b.

[65] Articles S13 and S14 CAS Code.

[66] See also Article R33 CAS Code.

[67] Article S18 CAS Code.

[68] Article R40.1 CAS Code.

[69] Article R40.2 CAS Code.

According to the CAS Code there is a presumption that a CAS panel sitting under the Appellate Arbitration Procedure will be composed of three arbitrators.[70] However, if the parties agree or the President of the Appellate Arbitration Division so decides, a panel composed of a sole arbitrator can be formed.[71] In practice, there appears to be no significant difference in panel size between the two procedures as 13 percent of the studied decisions issued under Appellate Arbitration Procedure were decided by a sole arbitrator. Sole arbitrators are appointed by the Division President.

Like under the Ordinary Arbitration Procedure, parties to a three-arbitrator appellate panel each nominate one arbitrator. However, the nominees must be confirmed by the Division President. This is intended to enhance the impartiality and independence of the nominees. The arbitrator nominated by the respondent nominates a panel president but the president is appointed by the Division President after consulting with both party-nominated arbitrators.[72] In these ways, the Division President exerts stronger influence over the panel formation under the Appellate Arbitration Procedure compared to under the Ordinary Arbitration Procedure.

2.4 Sports and Subject Matters

In order to understand CAS jurisprudence, it is important to understand some of its basic characteristics. One aspect of this is the types of disputes and subject matters that come before CAS. As laid out above, CAS has very broad jurisdiction, at least potentially, and what types of cases CAS hears is in principle primarily limited by the disputes that parties choose to bring before it.[73] As will be discussed in a number of different contexts below, CAS jurisprudence is quite diverse, containing cases on different subject matters.[74] Cases that come before CAS are also connected to a diverse range of sports. All subject matters and sports do not however appear in equal amount. On the contrary, CAS jurisprudence is dominated by a few subject matters, a few sports, and a few combinations of subject matters and sports.[75]

We begin by studying what sports appear in CAS jurisprudence. The dataset includes CAS decisions involving 73 different sports. However, of those 73 sports, 26 only appear in a single decision[76] and 52 sports appear in five or fewer

[70] Cf. Krähe 2006, p. 102.

[71] Article R50 CAS Code.

[72] Article R54 CAS Code.

[73] See above Sect. 2.2. Cf. Anderson 2010, p. 88.

[74] There are a number of different, alternative methods for identifying and classifying the issues that appear in CAS jurisprudence. See further Chap. 6. In this section, however, I will exclusively use the subject matter classification provided by CAS in its jurisprudence database.

[75] See below Fig. 2.1 *Subject Matters and Sports*.

[76] This includes for example wakeboard, netball, modern pentathlon, and billiards.

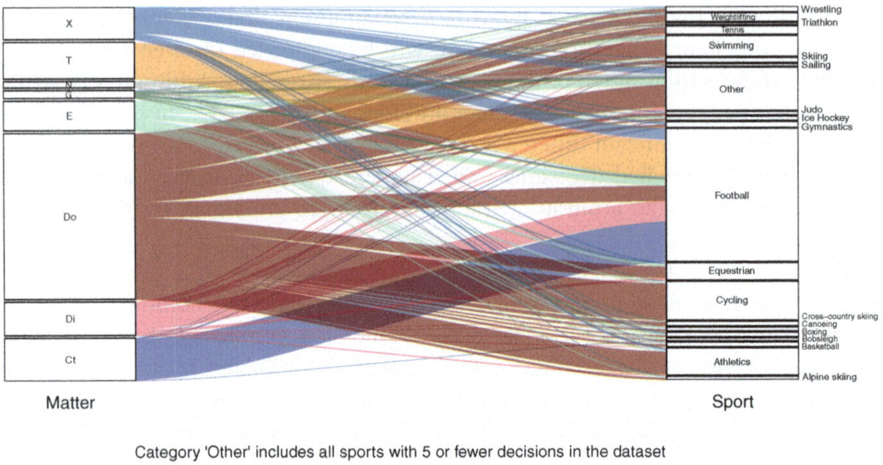

Fig. 2.1 Subject Matters and Sports. [*Source* The author]

decisions.[77] On the other end of the spectrum, there are a few sports that dominate CAS's jurisprudence.[78] Football, cycling, athletics, swimming, and equestrian sports constitute, in that order, a distinct top five. Two out of three CAS decisions in the dataset concern one of these five sports.[79] Football is the sport that by far gives rise to the largest number of CAS disputes: 38 percent of all decisions in the dataset concern a football-related dispute.[80]

The subject matters concerned follow a similar distribution with doping being dominant: 45 percent of all CAS decisions in the dataset concern doping-related matters. Another 40 percent of the decisions are fairly evenly split between cases concerning contract disputes, player transfers , other (non-doping) disciplinary matters, and eligibility.[81] Thus, it is clear that CAS jurisprudence is dominated by doping-related and football-related disputes.

---

[77] In Fig. 2.1 *Subject Matters and Sports* above, these 52 sports have been grouped together under the heading "Other" to improve readability.

[78] Like many other things in CAS jurisprudence, the distribution of decisions among sports follow a power law distribution. See further Sect. 5.2.

[79] See above Fig. 2.1 *Subject Matters and Sports* (football 315 decisions, cycling 91 decisions, athletics 64 decisions, swimming 47 decisions, and equestrian sports 43 decisions).

[80] Cf. Reilly 2012, p. 69 ("Of the cases heard at CAS, approximately 45% relate to appeals rendered by an organ of [FIFA]."). This was not always the case. In 2005, the number of football-related disputes in CAS jumped drastically. The impact of football's dominance is analyzed in greater detail in Sect. 3.3.

[81] See above Fig. 2.1 *Subject Matters and Sports* (contracts 11.3%, disciplinary 10.3%, transfers 10.3%, and eligibility 9.0%). The remaining approximately 15% are split among a variety of subjects that include nationality-related disputes and governance.

Patterns in the connections between sports and subject matters are slightly more complicated. Commensurate with its dominance on the subject matter side, doping-related CAS decisions can be found in nearly every sport, including football. Similarly, football-related CAS decisions concern virtually all subject matters. This is hardly surprising considering how many football-related disputes CAS hears. However, CAS decisions that concern *both* doping *and* football are relatively uncommon.[82] This is not a surprising finding as it is in line with previous research observing a relatively low prevalence of doping in football compared to many other sports.[83] It is however important for understanding CAS jurisprudence. Viewed from the perspective of most sports, CAS jurisprudence primarily, and for some sports exclusively, concerns doping. From the perspective of football, however, CAS jurisprudence primarily concerns three other subject matters: contracts, player transfers, and non-doping-related disciplinary actions (in that order). Conversely, CAS jurisprudence on these three subject matters are overwhelmingly dominated by decisions concerning football.[84] Thus, when actors engaged in other sports than football are involved in disputes concerning these subject matters they will encounter that almost all of the existing case law concerns football. A possible and natural consequence of this might be that the general principles developed by CAS in the areas of contracts, transfers, and non-doping-related disciplinary matters are influenced by the particular rules, practices, and other conditions found in football.[85]

References

Anderson J (2010) Modern Sports Law. Hart, Oxford

Blackaby N, Partasides C, Redfern A, Hunter M (2015) Redfern and Hunter on International Arbitration, 6th edn. Oxford University Press, Oxford

Blackshaw I (2006) Introductory Remarks. In: Blackshaw I, Siekman R, Soek J (eds) The Court of Arbitration for Sport 1984–2004. T.M.C. Asser Press, The Hague, pp. 1–5

Blackshaw I (2013) ADR and Sport: Settling Disputes Through the Court of Arbitration for Sport, the FIFA Dispute Resolution Chamber, and the WIPO Arbitration & Mediation Center. Marquette Sports Law Review 24(1):1–57

CAS (2016) Statistics 2016. http://www.tas-cas.org/fileadmin/user_upload/CAS_statistics_2016_pdf. Accessed 7 September 2018

Dasser F, Wójtowicz P (2016) Challenges of Swiss Arbitral Awards: Updated and Extended Statistical Data as of 2015. ASA Bulletin 34(2):280–300

[82] See above Fig. 2.1 *Subject Matters and Sports*. The dataset only includes 33 CAS decisions concerning doping in football. If the number was proportional to the number of doping cases in the entire dataset, there would be 142 or more than four times as many decisions concerning doping in football.

[83] See Davies et al. 2014.

[84] See above Fig. 2.1 *Subject Matters and Sports*.

[85] Whether this is actually the case and conditions in other sports are significantly different requires further research.

Davies T, Vernon M, Schofield J (2014) Is sport doing enough to catch drug cheats? In: Palmer C (ed) The Sports Monograph: Critical Perspectives on Socio-Cultural Sport, Coaching and Physical Education. SSTO Publications, Preston, pp. 65–78

Duval A (2017) Not in My Name! Claudia Pechstein and the Post-Consensual Foundations of the Court of Arbitration for Sport. Max Planck Institute for Comparative Public Law & International Law (MPIL) Research Paper No. 2017-01. https://papers.ssrn.com/sol3/papers.cfm?abstract_id=2920555. 7 September 2018.

IBA (2015) Report on the Public Policy Exception in the New York Convention. Report by the Subcommittee on Recognition and Enforcement of Foreign Arbitral Awards, October 2015. https://www.ibanet.org/LPD/Dispute_Resolution_Section/Arbitration/Recogntn_Enfrcemnt_Arbitl_Awrd/publicpolicy15.aspx. Accessed 7 September 2018

Kane D (2003a) Twenty Years On: An Evaluation of the Court of Arbitration for Sport. Melbourne Journal of International Law 4:611–635

Kane O (2003b) The CAS Mediation Rules. The International Sports Law Journal 2003(1):33–35

Kaufmann-Kohler G, Bärtsch P (2006) The Ordinary Arbitration Procedure of the CAS. In: Blackshaw I, Siekman R, Soek J (eds) The Court of Arbitration for Sport 1984–2004. T.M.C. Asser Press, The Hague, pp. 69–98

Krähe C (2006) The Appeals Procedure before the CAS. In: Blackshaw I, Siekman R, Soek J (eds) The Court of Arbitration for Sport 1984–2004. T.M.C. Asser Press, The Hague, pp. 99–104

Mavromati D (2016) The Rules governing the CAS Anti-Doping and Ad Hoc Divisions at the Olympic Games, 29 August 2016. https://ssrn.com/abstract=2816482. Accessed 6 July 2018

Mavromati D, Reeb M (2015) The Code of the Court of Arbitration for Sport: Commentary, Cases and Materials. Wolters Kluwer, Alphen aan den Rijn

McLaren R (2006) CAS Advisory Opinions. In: Blackshaw I, Siekman R, Soek J (eds) The Court of Arbitration for Sport 1984–2004. T.M.C. Asser Press, The Hague, pp. 180–193

Mitten M J, Opie H (2010) 'Sports Law': Implications for the Development of International, Comparative, and National Law and Global Dispute Resolution. Tulane Law Review 85:269–322

Paulsson J (1993) Arbitration of International Sports Disputes. Arbitration International 9(4): 359–369

Pinna A (2006) The Trials and Tribulations of the Court of Arbitration for Sport: Contribution to the Study of the Arbitration of Disputes Concerning Disciplinary Sanctions. In: Blackshaw I, Siekman R, Soek J (eds) The Court of Arbitration for Sport 1984–2004. T.M.C. Asser Press, The Hague, pp. 386–408

Reeb M (2004) The Court of Arbitration for Sport: History and Operation. In: Reeb M (ed) Digest of CAS Awards III, Kluwer Law International, The Hague, pp. xxvii–xxxv

Reilly L (2012) An Introduction to the Court of Arbitration for Sport (CAS) and the Role of National Courts in International Sports Disputes. Journal of Dispute Resolution 2012(1):63–81

Rigozzi A (2010) Challenging Awards of the Court of Arbitration for Sport. Journal of International Dispute Settlement 1(1):217–265

Simma B (2006) The Court of Arbitration for Sport. In: Blackshaw I, Siekman R, Soek J (eds) The Court of Arbitration for Sport 1984–2004. T.M.C. Asser Press, The Hague, pp. 21–30

Yi D (2006) Turning Medals into Metal: Evaluating the Court of Arbitration for Sport as an International Tribunal. Asper Review of International Business and Trade Law 6:289–341

Part II
The Jurisprudence

Chapter 3
The Lay of the Land: The Topography of CAS Jurisprudence

Abstract It can be difficult to approach and effectively describe a large body of individual decisions involving a range of unique circumstances and issues, such as CAS jurisprudence. A balance between overwhelming complexity and oversimplification must be struck carefully. One approach for doing so is to treat CAS's body of decisions as a network connected through references. Studying such a network allows for the detection of the basic structure of CAS jurisprudence, of how CAS relates to its own previous decisions, and how this has developed over time. In this chapter we will explore the basic structure of CAS jurisprudence but also more generally how CAS operates and interacts with the cases that come before it and with its previous decisions.

3.1 Treasure Islands(?)

This second part of the book, which consists of this and the following three chapters, studies Court of Arbitration for Sport (CAS) jurisprudence with the overarching aim of identifying substance and structure. Substance, in this context, refers to the normative content, that is rules and principles, found in and developed through CAS's decisions. By the merit of their nature and CAS's role in their development, these rules and principles constitute the normative bulk that is essential to the formation of a transnational legal order: legal orders are normative orders and an order without norms is hardly a normative order. As we shall see below, many of these norms are based on or borrow from norms found in sport regulations, national law, and international law, but have been developed, adapted, and adopted by CAS for use in sports.[1]

The work of identifying structures begins in this chapter. To accomplish this we will be studying the CAS case law network.[2] The CAS decisions that are connected

[1] See further Chap. 7.
[2] See Sect. 1.6.

J. Lindholm, *The Court of Arbitration for Sport and Its Jurisprudence*,
ASSER International Sports Law Series,
https://doi.org/10.1007/978-94-6265-285-9_3

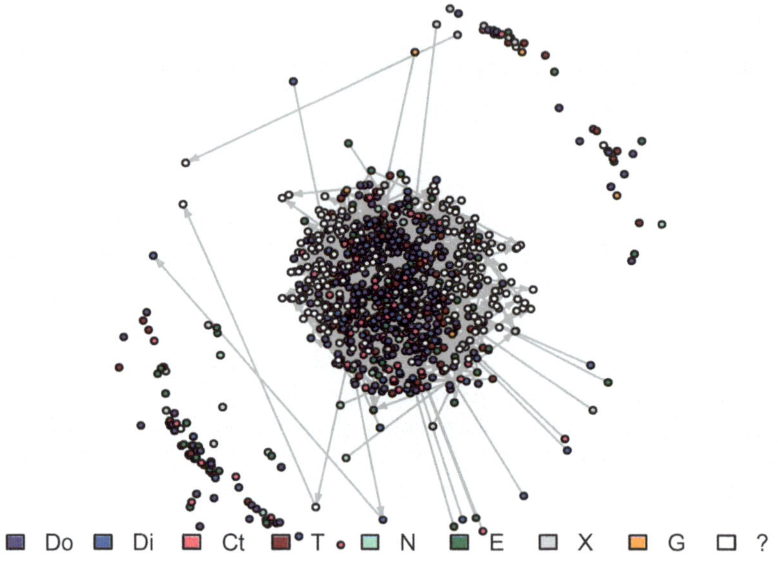

Fig. 3.1 CAS's Case Law Network. [*Source* The author]

to each other by references between them make up a ball-of-yarn-like mess in the middle.[3] This illustrates, in my opinion quite accurately, the methodological challenge with studying connected cases. How can we analyze and simplify this information, which at first sight appears too extensive and complex to be presented in an intelligible way, into something that reveals something relevant while at the same time not engaging in oversimplification? We will return to these decisions and those questions below.

Before we turn our attention to the connected cases we will, in this section, focus on the 148 CAS decisions that in the map of the CAS case law network look like unanchored dots dispersed around a dense and messy center.[4] These decisions will be referred to as islands. An island is a decision that is disconnected from the rest of the network since it does not refer to any other decision nor does any other decision refer to it. In this section, we will study what characterizes islands, particularly by comparing islands and non-islands, that is decisions that have at least one connection, inwards or outwards, to the rest of the jurisprudence, in the CAS case law network.

Before we do so, it should for methodological purposes be noted that islands are generally a little younger than non-islands. Consequently, the islands have had less opportunity to be cited than the non-islands.[5] It is therefore possible that some of the

[3] See above Fig. 3.1 *CAS's Case Law Network*.

[4] See above Fig. 3.1 *CAS's Case Law Network*.

[5] See below Fig. 3.2 *Islands and Non-Islands by Decision Year*. Overall, islands are about six months newer than non-islands in both median and mean age.

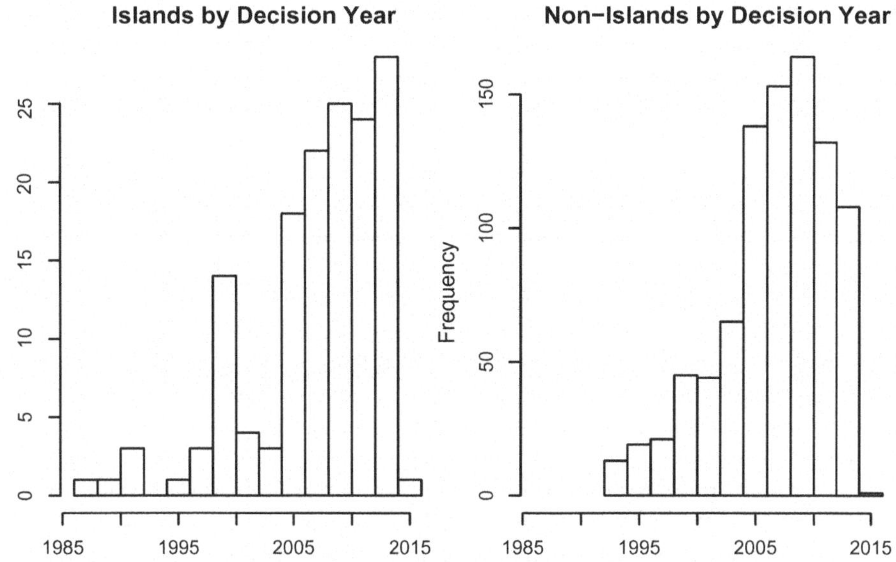

Fig. 3.2 Islands and Non-Islands by Decision Year. [*Source* The author]

CAS decisions that are islands in the dataset will eventually be cited (and thereby become non-islands) if given more time. But the age difference is limited and it is impossible to say with any reasonable degree of accuracy which of the decisions that are islands might in the future be cited. Also, the fact that the islands are overall slightly more recent than the non-islands do not explain why they do not refer to any prior decisions. In fact, quite the opposite: the more recent a decision is, the greater the number of existing decisions available to be referred to and recent decisions do in fact refer to existing decisions more frequently and to a greater extent. This suggests that there might be something that characterizes islands and sets them apart from the parts of CAS jurisprudence that are connected to each other in some way.

As we explore the CAS jurisprudence further, in this and subsequent chapters, it will become increasingly clear that to find patterns in what may at times be despairingly complex information and, after we find such patterns, make sense of them constitutes a major methodological challenge. This is not a problem when it comes to islands. Islands provide no information about the rest of the CAS jurisprudence and cannot, consequently, tell us anything relevant about other CAS decisions. Since we rely on that kind of information to detect the structure of the network, islands also have little value from a structural perspective. Since the islands have never been cited we can say little about the information contained in the case and where or when they might be relevant. The absence of connections does however reveal something relevant and interesting about CAS jurisprudence in two regards.

First, islands are relevant and interesting because they can reveal something about when decisions are *not* an important source of law. The fact that decisions that are islands have never been referred to in other decisions suggest that they have limited relevance as a source of law. We cannot definitively determine why subsequent decisions have not referred to the islands. For example, we cannot absolutely rule out that there are some islands that establish novel points of law that very well could have been relevant to cite in subsequent decisions but were overlooked by the parties and the arbitrators. However, oversight is unlikely to be a major explanatory factor on an aggregate level. The most reasonable explanation why the islands have not been referred to is that they do not contain information that is relevant to consider and refer to when CAS decides subsequent decisions, such as interpreting or developing a general rule or principle that is subsequently applied.

That a decision has never or rarely been cited does not make it special. As we shall discuss in more detail below, in CAS's case law network, much like in other legal citation networks, inward citations, i.e. references to a decision, follow a power law distribution where most decisions are never or rarely referred to and a few decisions receive most such references.[6] In other words, not being referred to is the norm for decisions.

Thus, it is not the lack of inward citations as such that distinguishes islands from other CAS decisions. What is special about the islands is that they *both* are not cited by other citation *and* that they do not cite other decisions. This raises the question of what the reasons for this might be. Do islands exhibit some common characteristics that distinguish them from non-islands and that can explain the limited use of previous decisions as a source in these cases? This is interesting and relevant when answering the questions explored in this book. Identifying when jurisprudence is irrelevant also reveals something about when jurisprudence is relevant. This involves exploring whether there is correlation between a case having particular characteristics and it being an island.[7]

In my mind, there are primarily three characteristics worth examining in this context. First, because the number of citations in the CAS case law network has changed over time with regard to both inward and outward citations,[8] one possible such distinguishing characteristic might be age. As discussed and illustrated in the figure above,[9] there are some difference between islands and non-islands regarding when they were decided by CAS. However, the differences are quite small and overall islands and non-islands have roughly the same age profile. Thus, it seems highly unlikely that age is more than a marginally contributing factor.

A second characteristic that is worth considering is the sport involved. Are there distinct differences in the sports concerned in decisions that are islands and non-islands respectively? To test this, we can break down islands and non-islands by the relative prevalence of the sports concerned in these decisions. When we do

---

[6] See further Sects. 1.6 and 5.2. This is true for CAS as well as most national and international courts.

[7] Below we will be returning to this question and exploring more generally whether there is correlation between the characteristics of individual CAS decisions and their precedential and persuasive power, which is essentially the same type of inquiry applied to the entire data.

[8] See below Sects. 3.5–3.6.

[9] See above Fig. 3.2 *Islands and Non-Islands by Decision Year.*

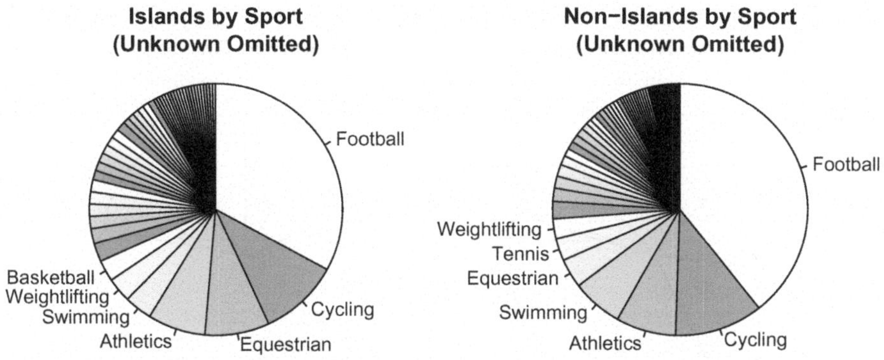

Fig. 3.3 Islands and Non-Islands by Sport (Color figure online). [*Source* The author]

this, we see that the differences in distribution by sport between islands and non-islands are fairly small. For both groups of decisions, the largest sport by far is football. About one-third of all studied decisions, islands and non-islands alike, concerned a football-related matter. Both groups also include many and roughly equal proportions of decisions where the underlying dispute has its origin in cycling or athletics. For both islands and non-islands, 55–60 percent of all decisions concern either football, cycling, or athletics.[10]

There is only one sport that clearly distinguishes itself in prevalence when comparing islands and non-islands to each other: equestrian sports. The relative portion of decisions concerning equestrian sports is about twice as large for island decisions compared to non-island decisions.[11] Although equestrian sports are distinctly overrepresented among islands, the extent of the overrepresentation is not extremely disproportionate and equestrian sports do not have any obvious characteristics that distinguish them from other sports in such a way that it could explain why case law would be less important in equestrian sports than in other sports. The reason why cases concerning particular sports tend to more commonly be islands is not necessarily because of some characteristic of the sport *per se* but could also be because the characteristics of the disputes that typically arise in those sports and therefore end up being adjudicated by the CAS. However, as we shall discuss in more detail below, it is not immediately obvious why this would be true for equestrian sports.

This brings us to the third and final characteristic worth considering in this context: the subject matter concerned. As we shall examine in closer detail below, there are some clear differences between CAS decisions depending on the subject matter involved when it comes to both the frequency of references to prior decisions (outward citations) and the likelihood of a decision being cited (inward citations).[12]

[10] See above Fig. 3.3 *Islands and Non-Islands by Sport*.

[11] 8.2% compared to 4.3%.

[12] See Sect. 6.3.1.

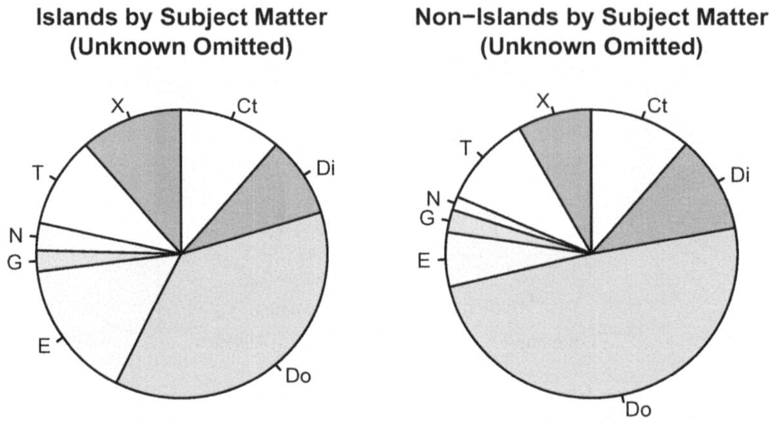

Fig. 3.4 Islands and Non-Islands by Subject Matter (Color figure online). [*Source* The author]

Thus, it is worth exploring whether disputes concerning certain subject matters are more frequent among islands than non-islands.

When we map and compare the relative prevalence of different subject matters among islands and non-islands we find that the two groups of cases have roughly the same portions when it comes to most subject matters. There are, however, some clear differences between the two: islands more rarely than non-islands concern doping and, instead, more frequently concern issues regarding eligibility on other grounds than nationality.[13]

This difference between islands and non-islands in subject matter distribution is clearer than the difference in distribution by sport. Cases concerning issues of eligibility unconnected to issues of nationality are almost three times more common among islands than non-islands.[14] This makes sense. While the outcome of an eligibility case may affect the concerned athlete as deeply as a disciplinary action,[15] the written rules governing eligibility are frequently more extensive and detailed than those governing disciplinary actions and differ distinctly between different sports. Eligibility cases tend to turn on the interpretation of the written rules governing particular sports. Consequently, both the need for and the potential role of previous CAS decisions as a source of law when deciding subsequent cases concerning eligibility is generally diminished compared to cases concerning many other subject matters. There are some CAS decisions concerning eligibility that go against the overall trend and that both cite and have been cited by other decisions, but many of those cases are disputes between clubs and federations concerning the

---

[13] See above Fig. 3.4 *Islands and Non-Islands by Subject Matter*.

[14] Among non-islands with a known subject matter, 6.8% concern eligibility on other grounds than nationality. Among islands, 19.3% of all decisions with a known subject matter concern non-nationality eligibility.

[15] Arroyo 2013, p. 1075.

clubs' eligibility to compete in national, regional, and international competitions.[16] There are of course exceptions,[17] but generally speaking, case law has comparatively low relevance in cases concerning individual athlete's eligibility on non-nationality related grounds.[18]

As an illustrative example, take CAS's decision in *Pistorius* in 2008. The case concerned whether Oscar Pistorius, a South African sprint runner and double-leg amputee, was allowed to compete against "able-bodied athletes" in the 2008 Beijing Olympic Games using prosthetic legs. The International Association of Athletics Federations (IAAF) concluded that the prosthetic legs gave Pistorius a competitive advantage and denied him the right to compete. In its ruling, CAS concluded that the IAAF had not met its burden of proof to show a competitive advantage and overturned the IAAF's decision.[19]

Pistorius has been commented on extensively in the literature,[20] which may give the impression that the decision is an important element of CAS jurisprudence. However, CAS's decision in *Pistorius* does not build on prior CAS decisions, nor has it ever, even once, been referred to in the studied CAS decisions. Thus, *Pistorius* is an island with no connection to the rest of CAS jurisprudence. This does not rule out the possibility that *Pistorius* may have had some meaningful impact, for example on the development of selection requirements and procedures. However, the decision has no measurable impact on how CAS resolves subsequent disputes. This should perhaps not come as a surprise given that CAS was careful to explicitly limit the scope of its ruling in *Pistorius*;[21] the *Pistorius* panel pointed out that "[e]ach [eligibility] case must be considered… on its own merits".[22] This can perhaps help explain why cases concerning eligibility are over-represented among islands.

This can possibly also help explain the observation that equestrian sports are over-represented in the island population. Although islands that involve equestrian sports concern quite different matters,[23] many CAS decisions that are islands and concern equestrian sports also concerned the issue of eligibility. Take, for example,

---

16 See e.g. CAS 2004/A/676, *Ismailia*; CAS 2008/A/1583 & 1584, *Benfica & Vitória*.

17 See e.g. CAS 2008/A/1574, *D'Arcy*; CAS 2008/A/1594, *Sheykhov*.

18 See Sect. 6.3.1 and Table 6.2 *Precedential Power of Communities: Subject Matters*.

19 CAS 2008/A/1480.

20 See e.g. Casini 2011, p. 1328; Cornelius 2013; Mitten and Davies 2008, pp. 89–90; Ravjani 2009, pp. 283–284; Wolbring 2008.

21 CAS 2008/A/1480, *Pistorius*, paras 53–56.

22 Ibid. para 56.

23 See e.g. CAS 92/71, *SJ v. FEI* (upholding a decision in a doping matter regarding a horse testing positive for multiple banned substances); CAS 2004/A/544, *CBH v. FEI* (overturning a decision regarding eligibility to participate in the Olympic Games); CAS 2008/A/1636, *Hoy* (overturning a decision in a disciplinary action regarding animal cruelty); CAS 2013/A/3151, *Millar* (overturning in part, through a particularly brief reasoning referring only to evidence and the panel's discretion, ibid. paras 78–83, a decision in a doping matter regarding an equestrian testing positive for a banned doping substance).

the case of *Beresford* where CAS in a short and straightforward decision relying only on interpretation of by-laws and written rules concluded that the NOC's exclusion of one rider from the 2012 London Olympic Games did not give rise to a right for the applicant to be included.[24] However, it should be noted that we are now talking about a rather small sample size from which we should be careful not to draw too far-reaching conclusions.

Whereas general eligibility cases are overrepresented in the island population, cases concerning doping and other disciplinary actions are underrepresented. This is consistent with the observation that CAS decisions in cases concerning doping and other disciplinary actions generally tend to be more central in the CAS case law network compared to other decisions, both in terms of relying on prior decisions as sources of law and being relied upon by other decisions.[25]

3.2 Let's Stay Connected

As we saw in the preceding section, studying the islands in the CAS case law network can reveal some information about when decisions are not an important source of law. The characteristic that defines islands, the absence of connections to other decisions, is also relevant when it comes to determining the strength of the CAS case law network. The elements of a network can be more or less strongly connected. For example, a social network can be described as weak if each member of the network is only connected to one other member and as vulnerable if many members are only connected to the same member.[26]

How strong the connections between CAS's decisions are is relevant from a legal perspective as a weak structure is susceptible to swift change. That, in turn, may cast doubt over whether CAS jurisprudence constitutes the backbone of a transnational legal order. Conversely, a finding that CAS decisions are strongly connected to each other suggests that CAS jurisprudence has a strong structure and, by extension, indicates the existence of a case law-based system.

One measurement used in network analysis to measure and describe the relative level of connectedness of a network is *density*. A network's density is calculated by comparing the network's actual number of edges to its potential number of edges, i.e. the number of edges that do exist compared to the edges that would exist in the network if every vertex was connected to every other vertex. The latter can also be referred to as a complete network. By dividing the former number with the latter

---

[24] CAS 2012/A/2837.

[25] See Sect. 6.3.

[26] Another element of the strength of the network is the strength of the connections between its components. For example, a pair of arbitrators that have appeared on the same CAS panel many times together can be said to be more strongly connected than a pair that only appeared once on the same panel. See further Sect. 8.4. In the network this can be represented in the weight of the edge connecting two vertices.

one derives at a number somewhere between 0 and 1 where 0 is the density of a network only consisting of islands and 1 is the density of a complete network.

The density of the CAS case law network is 0.00239. The large number of decimals may make it seem like a rather sparse network and in a sense it is. In order to put this value in proper perspective one must however be aware that legal citation networks generally tend to have rather low density. The number of relevant references to prior decisions that a court can reasonably make in a single decision is for practical purposes limited. For example, the density of the citation network of the Supreme Court of the United States (SCOTUS) is 0.00048[27] and that of the Court of Justice of the European Union (CJEU) is 0.00096.[28] Thus, the CAS case law network is many times denser than those two courts, both of which can be described as courts that rely extensively on prior decisions and through their jurisprudence play a major role in the development of the law.

From this comparison, it may now appear as if the CAS case law network is particularly dense; it is after all almost five times denser than the SCOTUS case law network. However, the density of a network is naturally connected to the size of the network as density tends to decrease with size.[29] For example, a court that has only issued two previous decisions can cite both those decisions in its third decision, and as lawyers we could reasonably expect it to do so if both previous decisions are relevant to the case at hand. However, this obviously becomes untenable very quickly, both because the number of previous decisions that the court is comfortable citing in a single decision is limited and because there is an awareness cost for lawyers to be familiar with and remember previous decisions. The CAS decision that contains the single most references to unique previous CAS decision is the 2009 decision in *Costa* that cites to 23 previous CAS decisions.[30] Even if every CAS decision contained as many references as *Costa*, the CAS case law network's density would fall below that of a complete network by the time the CAS issued its twenty-fifth decision.[31] For these reasons, real-world complete networks are very rare, even when it comes to relatively small networks.

Thus, although CAS has steadily increased the average number of citations in its decisions over time,[32] it is natural and all but inevitable that the density of its case law network declines over time. We can confirm that this is indeed the case by tracking the density of the CAS case law network over time. From this we can see that although the case law network of CAS is currently much denser than those of SCOTUS and the CJEU, the CAS case law network's density is declining steadily. Unless there is a break in the current trend, which for the reasons laid out above is

---

[27] Calculated on the basis of the numbers reported by Fowler and Jeon 2008.

[28] Derlén and Lindholm 2017.

[29] Scott 2017, pp. 81–84.

[30] CAS 2009/A/1919.

[31] Based on CAS's statistics, this occurred sometime during 1992.

[32] See below Sect. 3.5.

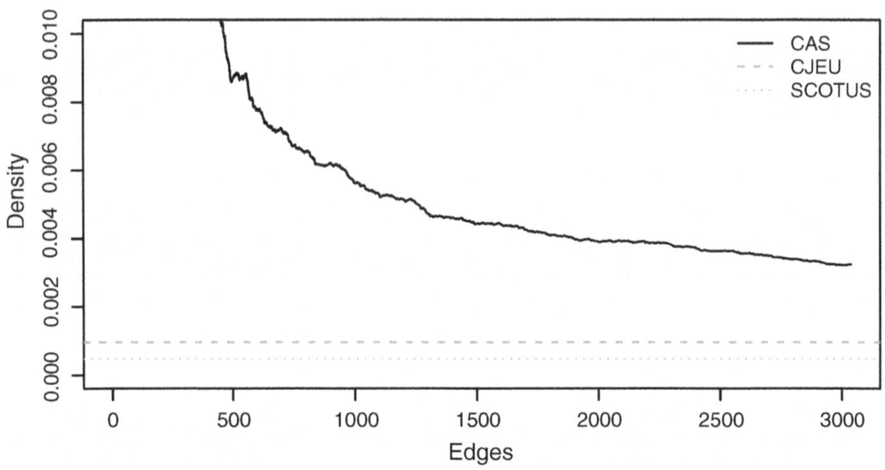

Fig. 3.5 Network Density Over Time. [*Source* The author]

highly unlikely, the CAS case law network's density will eventually reach a level that is similar to those of the SCOTUS and CJEU case law networks.[33]

It is in this regard interesting to compare the CAS case law network with the case law network of the European Court of Human Right (ECtHR). The ECtHR case law network is closer in size to the CAS case law network than those of SCOTUS and the CJEU. According to Lupu and Voeten, the ECtHR had, during the period studied by them, issued 3,369 decisions that contained a total of 35,962 references to previous decisions.[34] This means that the ECtHR case law network had a density of 0.00634.[35] This is two-and-a-half times as dense as the CAS case law network. This is quite impressive given that the ECtHR's case law network is also fifty percent larger than the CAS case law network and thus ought, for the reasons explained above, have lower density than CAS case law network, all else being equal.

It is however not entirely fair, in my mind, to expect the CAS case law network to have similar density as the ECtHR case law network. The ECtHR only hears

[33] See above Fig. 3.5 *Network Density Over Time*. Note that time is here measured in edges, i.e. references between CAS decisions in chronological order, rather than some more conventional time measurement. The main reason for and advantage of using edges as a time measurement is that it is independent of changes in the average number of decisions or references, which in CAS have been quite significant. It should be noted that the figure does not take into consideration islands for the purpose of calculating the density of the CAS case law network.

[34] Lupu and Voeten 2011. Excluded from this is 3,950 cases that were disposed by through so-called pilot procedures. It should be noted that Lupu and Voeten only consider decisions issued by the ECtHR until 2006 and the numbers are thus somewhat outdated. However, for the purpose of comparing how connected two legal citation networks are at a given point in time and at a particular size, these numbers provide adequate information.

[35] Calculated on the basis of the numbers reported in Lupu and Voeten 2011.

cases concerning violations of the European Convention for the Protection of Human Rights and Fundamental Freedoms (ECHR). This affects ECtHR jurisprudence and the ECtHR's use of previous decisions as a source of law in two important ways.

First, every case that comes before the ECtHR concerns one of the articles in the ECHR or, if the concerned convention state has elected to sign on, one of the protocols. This means that the ECtHR and its decisions concern a relatively limited number of issues compared to most other national and international courts. This naturally contributes to the density of the ECtHR's citation network. The more decisions concern the same legal issues, the more relevant decisions there are that can be cited, and the more relevant decisions that a court can cite, the more decisions it will tend to cite. We will below more closely explore what issues come before CAS,[36] but for the purposes of this context it suffices to say that while the cases that come before CAS are not as diverse as those of many national courts, they are arguably more diverse than those of the ECtHR.

Second, case law plays a particularly important role as a source of law in the ECHR system. The ECHR and its protocols are written in a broad and general manner that requires extensive interpretation and there are very few sources that can be used when interpreting the text of the ECHR. For example, there are hundreds of ECtHR decisions interpreting the phrase "a fair and public hearing within a reasonable time by an independent and impartial tribunal established by law."[37] Rights under the ECHR are also dynamic and develop with society. Because of these factors, ECtHR jurisprudence is exceptionally important for determining the scope and application of the Convention rights and this can be expected to be reflected in the density of the ECtHR case law network.

Thus far we have focused on density. Another measurement that can be used to measure the level of connectedness of a network is *inclusiveness*. A network's inclusiveness is expressed as the number of connected vertices, i.e. non-islands, in the network as a percentage of the total number of vertices in the network.[38] A legal citation network where every decision at least cites one prior decision or is cited by a subsequent decision has an inclusiveness of 100 percent and a legal citation network (if one could call it that) where no decisions contain any citations has an inclusiveness of 0 percent. Real-world citation networks tend to lie somewhere between these two extremes.

One advantage of inclusiveness over density as a measurement of connectedness when it comes to analyzing legal citation networks is that it is less dependent on the size of the network. While it is more difficult for a court with an extensive body of

---

36 See Chap. 6.

37 Article 6 ECHR.

38 Scott 2017, p. 81. In other words, what percentage of all vertices in the network that are non-islands.

jurisprudence than one with a limited one to cite *all* of its previous decisions, it is not more difficult for the former to cite *any* of its previous decisions.[39]

This greatly helps explaining why the CAS case law network is quite similar to other courts' case law networks using inclusiveness, and much more so than when using density. The CAS case law network has an inclusiveness of 87 percent. This is very close to and right between, on one side, SCOTUS and ECtHR case law networks (84 and 85 percent respectively) and, on the other, the CJEU case law network (89 percent).[40] Judging by those three courts, it seems that one should not expect a legal citation network to have total inclusiveness. Differently phrased, the existence of a certain number of islands is a natural element that is to be expected in a legal citation network. Even well-established national and international courts that have an extensive body of jurisprudence and that are active in legal systems and areas of law where jurisprudence plays a crucial role as a source of law, issue a noteworthy number of decisions, about one in six or seven, that neither refers to previous decisions nor are referred to by subsequent decisions. Based on these findings, the inclusiveness of the CAS case law network appears to be par for the course.

As discussed above, inclusiveness and density are two network analysis measurements that are frequently used to measure how well-connected the vertices in a network are. A related but slightly different approach is to examine the distance between the vertices. This is a measurement of the size of the network but instead of measuring size by how many vertices the network contains it measures network size in terms of the distance between the vertices. A network with a short distance between the vertices is a dense network, but in a different sense than what is captured by the density measurement discussed above. The difference between these concepts is more easily explained if we instead of a case law network consider a social network consisting of individuals, such as CAS arbitrators. The network can be large in terms of it including a large number of individual arbitrators but that does not necessarily say anything about to what extent those individuals are personally in contact with each other (density) or how many of them are in contact with at least one other individual (inclusiveness).

The size of a network is most commonly measured in two ways: diameter and average path length. Both of these measures are based on the network concept of *shortest paths*.[41] A shortest path is the shortest path that connects two vertices in a network, directly or through other vertices.

The concept of shortest paths has gained significant popular renown when applied to social network as the foundation of the small-world phenomenon. Broadly summarized, the small-world phenomenon refers to the idea that

---

[39] In fact, there is somewhat of a bias in the opposite direction: the fewer previous decisions the court has, the less likely it is that there is one decision that is relevant to cite. However, the impact of this connection to network size is much smaller than the one for density since it only takes citing a single decision to be included in the network.

[40] Derlén and Lindholm 2017, p. 661; Lupu and Voeten 2011, p. 424 n 54.

[41] Also referred to as geodesic paths.

individuals are more closely connected than they might think if they include the acquaintances of their acquaintances, and so on. For each step in the network or, to use network analysis terminology, degree, an individual's network expands quickly and will eventually include a significant portion of the world's population.[42] Based on Stanley Milgram's study that first brought major attention to the small-world phenomenon, there is a popular notion that all individuals in the world are connected to each other within an average of six degrees.[43] Using network analysis terminology, this notion can be rephrased as that the global social network's average shortest path length is 6 or, differently phrased, that the average distance between the global social network's vertices (i.e. all individuals on Earth) is six degrees.[44]

Legal citation networks function differently than social networks and its edges represent one-way flow of information, ideas, and argument that are different in nature to more dynamic, interpersonal relationships and shortest paths consequently have a slightly different meaning in a legal citation network than in a social network. Shortest paths are nevertheless a valuable tool for measuring distances between individual decisions and across a case law network. Short distances across a case law network are generally preferable from a legal perspective. If distances in the legal citation network are short it means that there are relatively few intermediary steps that information, ideas, and arguments flow through, i.e. there is a more direct connection between all decisions, and this in turns suggests greater coherency. However, at the same time, the distances within a case law network will and should depend on the diversity of the issues addressed in the decisions included in the network.

Shortest paths can be used to measure network distances in two different ways. The first is *diameter* which can be defined as the distance between the outer-most positions in the network. A network's diameter is the longest of all shortest paths between any two vertices in the network. The diameter of the CAS case law network is 11. This means that one never needs to follow more than 11 references (degrees) to link two CAS decisions directly or indirectly connected through references.[45] Another, arguably more relevant measurement of distance is the average length of the shortest path connecting two decisions. The average path length in the CAS case law network is much shorter than its diameter: the average distance between any two CAS decisions in the CAS case law network is 3.4.

The average distance between CAS decisions in the CAS case law network has increased significantly over time, both in terms of diameter and average path

---

[42] See e.g. Watts and Strogatz 1998; Kleinberg 2000.

[43] Milgram 1967. Milgram's study does not actually make or support a claim regarding the distance of the global population. However, subsequent empirical studies suggest that it may not be entirely erroneous. See e.g. Leskovec and Horvitz 2008 (the average user distance on MSN Messenger is 6.6 degrees); Kwak et al. 2010 (the average user distance on Twitter is 4.1 degrees); Viswanath et al. 2009 (the average user distance on Facebook is 3.7 degrees).

[44] Which explains why the notion is often referred to simply as six degrees of separation.

[45] This obviously does not include islands.

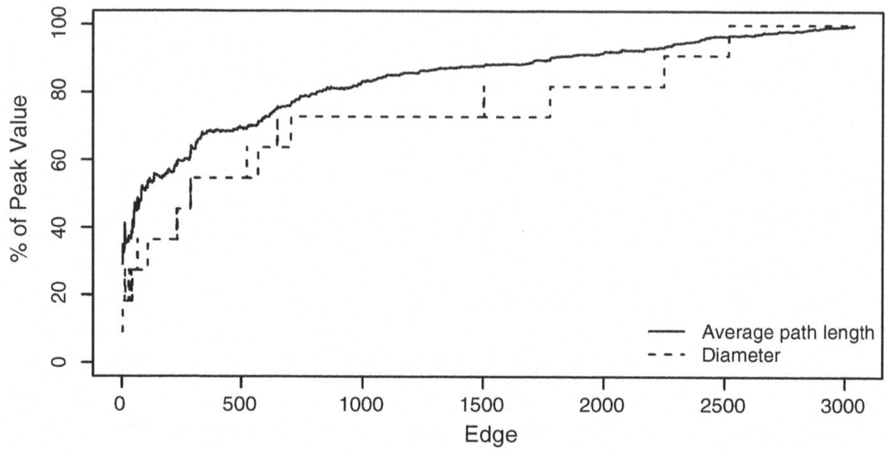

Fig. 3.6 Network Distance Over Time. [*Source* The author]

length.[46] This finding is consistent with CAS citing cases in a chain, that is that it cites the most recent CAS decision on a particular point of law rather than going all the way back to the decisions where the point was first made. While there are individual examples of this, it is uncertain to what extent this is typical. Increased distance over time can also indicate that the disputes that have been brought before CAS and the issues that it has been asked to decide have become increasingly diverse over time. If so, the CAS case law network would essentially have to stretch out to encompass this increased diversity.

The diameter and average shortest path decrease if one focuses on a smaller part of the network. For example, a sub-network consisting of all doping-related CAS decisions has a diameter of 8 and an average path length of 3.0.[47] This makes sense. A group of decisions are more likely to refer to the same decisions and to each other if they concern similar issues and this results in decreasing distances. Conversely, a group of decisions concerning a more diverse set of issues may be directly or indirectly connected but that connection will be more tenuous and this is reflected in an increased distance.

It may initially seem like CAS decisions concerning doping violations largely deal with the same issues and that they would be rather naturally connected to each other. However, as discussed immediately above, the distances between the doping cases are quite long, albeit unavoidably shorter than for the entire network. This suggests that CAS decisions dealing with doping-related matters does not perhaps

[46] See above Fig. 3.6 *Network Distance Over Time*. Regarding the measurement of time in terms of edges, see above Fig. 3.5 *Network Density Over Time*.

[47] See below Fig. 3.7 *Doping Sub-Network*. This sub-network consists of 1,269 edges (citations) connecting 383 vertices (CAS decisions). 46 unconnected vertices (islands) are not represented in order to increase the figure's legibility.

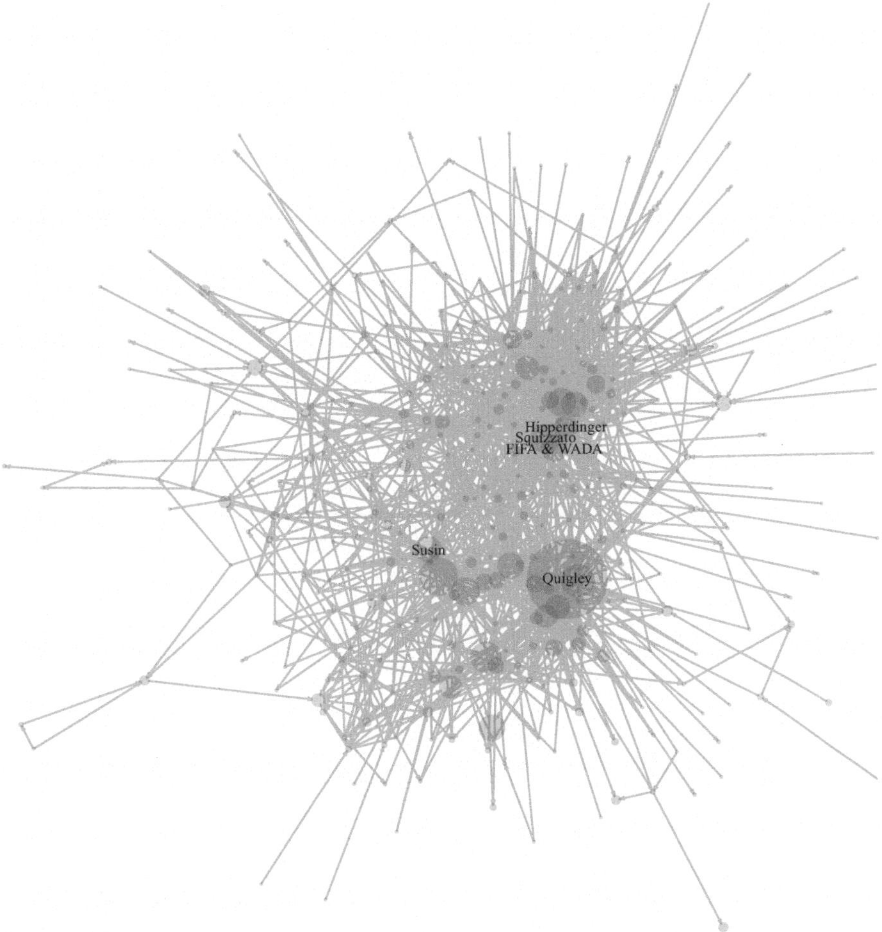

Fig. 3.7 Doping Sub-Network (Color figure online). [*Source* The author]

form a natural, heterogeneous cluster. In fact, doping-related cases that come before CAS frequently concern a number of rather diverse issues. Take for example, the case of *Schumacher*. In 2010, CAS decided two cases concerning Stephan Schumacher, a German cyclist who leading up to the 2008 Olympic Games in Beijing had been deemed to have committed an anti-doping rule violation. The more recent of the two *Schumacher* decisions[48] can be connected to CAS's decision in *Quigley*,[49] the most prominent decision in the sub-network and arguably one of

[48] CAS 2009/A/2011.

[49] CAS 94/129.

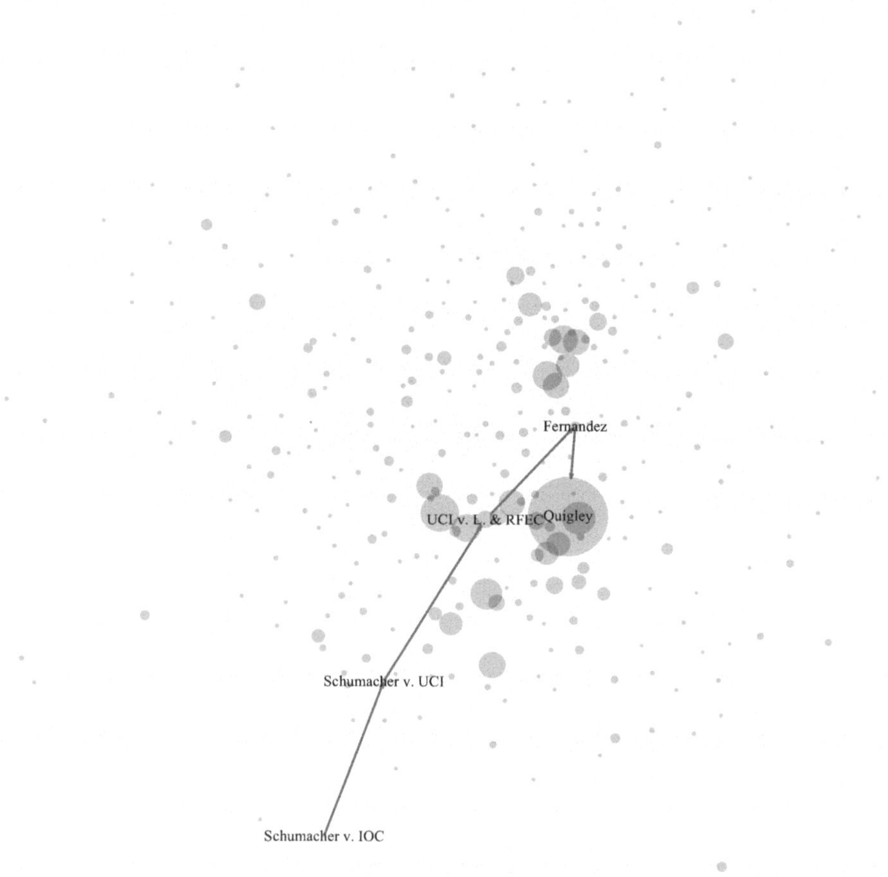

Fig. 3.8 Doping Sub-Network—*Schumacher* to *Quigley* (Color figure online). [*Source* The author]

CAS's foremost landmark decisions.[50] However, if one manually examines the four steps involved in linking the two cases, one will discover that the connection in legal reasoning becomes increasingly weak.[51] Two decisions that are directly linked (have a distance of 1) can safely be presumed to concern at least one shared issues, but the likelihood that two cases deals with the same issue decreases with distance. This illustrates why it is necessary to use more advanced methods for identifying well-fitting clusters within a case law network.[52]

---

[50] See Sect. 5.3.

[51] See above Fig. 3.8 *Doping Sub-Network:* Schumacher *to* Quigley.

[52] See Sect. 6.2.

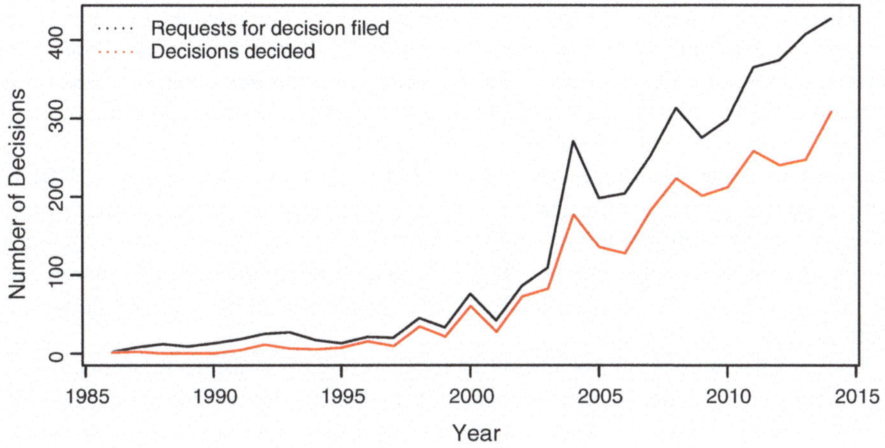

Fig. 3.9 Requests and CAS Decisions Over Time. [*Source* The author]

3.3 Requests In, Decisions Out

An exciting aspect of studying the CAS case law network is its dynamic character. As discussed on numerous occasions in this book, these shifts create certain methodological challenges. In drawing conclusions about CAS and its jurisprudence we must consider that CAS of today is not CAS of yesterday, and the same goes for its jurisprudence. Thus, a "dynamic perspective" will be employed in many parts of this book. However, in order to support that discussion, it is necessary to first identify some of the overarching trends in CAS jurisprudence. That is the purpose of this section.

A first factor that is important to consider is the development of the number of cases coming before CAS and the number of decisions coming out of CAS. Overall, it is clear that CAS's case load has increased dramatically over time. The number of awards issued by CAS in a given year is on average 40 percent higher than the number of awards issued in the preceding year.[53] This is a quite consistent and radical increase.[54]

CAS's history can from this perspective be divided into two major periods: the period before and after 2001. Until and including 2001, the number of requests for a CAS decision was quite modest, on average just under 2 requests per month. For obvious reasons, the number of CAS decisions delivered during this period was even lower and follows the number of requests for a decision. In 2002, the number

---

[53] Calculated on the basis of CAS, Statistics 2016. See also above Fig. 3.9 *Requests and CAS Decisions Over Time*.

[54] This is significantly higher than the yearly increase of 5% predicted by Cavalieros and Kim 2015, p. 238.

of requests for a decision filed with CAS increased dramatically and has since followed a steep and fairly constant increase. In 2013, CAS received almost five times as many requests as in 2001 and more requests than in the entire period from 1986 to 2001.[55] There is no indication that this trend is about to slow down.

The importance of the development after 2001 for CAS, its jurisprudence, and international sports law can hardly be overstated. The influx of cases after 2001 is both evidence of and a contribution to CAS's relevance, both on the micro level when it comes to settling individual disputes and on the macro level when it comes to shaping international sports law. If CAS's annual jurisprudence had remained at its pre-2001 levels there would likely be little reason for writing a book about the institution or its jurisprudence.

Because the increase in the number of requests and the consequential increase in the number of CAS decisions is important, it becomes relevant to investigate what may explain this dramatic development. It seems that there are two major events that fit with the timeline and that may have significantly contributed to the observed development. First, in 2002, FIFA and ICAS entered into an agreement whereby CAS assumed the jurisdiction of the Arbitration Tribunal for Football (ATF) and has since functioned as the appellate body for decisions by the FIFA Dispute Resolution Chamber (FIFA DRC). With this agreement, the number of football-related disputes that could reach CAS increased significantly.[56]

In this context, it is worth noting that previous research points to 1991 as being an important year for similar reasons. In 1991, following the so-called Paris Agreement,[57] CAS published a "Guide to Arbitration" in order "to facilitating understanding of the Code of sports-related arbitration and, in a more general way, encouraging access to the Court of Arbitration for Sport (CAS)."[58] The guide contained model arbitration clauses that international federations were invited to incorporate in their statutes, regulations, and agreements. Since four out of five cases that come before CAS fall under the Appeals Arbitration Procedure,[59] the introduction of arbitration clauses in federation statutes and regulations has shown to be greatly important to the development of CAS's role. Thus, when FEI as the first international federation in March 1991 decided to include such an arbitration clause and appoint CAS as its appellate instance, this was a principally important moment in CAS's history.[60] However, the event had a marginal impact on the number of cases arriving before CAS.[61] CAS did see a temporary surge in equestrian-related cases: deciding six such cases in 1992 contributed to a small

[55] 407 requests in 2013 compared to 381 requests 1986–2001. See above Fig. 3.9 *Requests and CAS Decisions Over Time*. The figure is based on CAS, Statistics 2016.

[56] Blackshaw 2006, p. 4; Blackshaw 2012, p. 9; Weger 2016, pp. 106–107.

[57] See further immediately below.

[58] CAS 1991, foreword.

[59] CAS, Statistics 2016.

[60] See e.g. Blackshaw 2013a, p. 3; Coccia 2013, p. 24.

[61] See above Fig. 3.9 *Requests and CAS Decisions Over Time*.

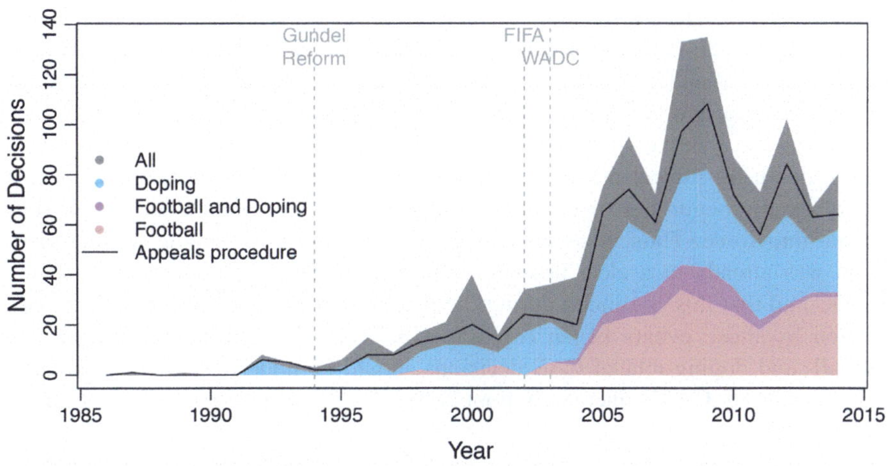

Fig. 3.10 CAS Decisions Over Time: Football, Doping, and the Rest. [*Source* The author]

bump in its total number of decisions. The impact was however overall and over time small. Nor did FEI's example cause other SGBs to follow suit, most of them refrained for some time from adopting similar arbitration clauses in their statutes and regulations.[62]

The second major event that took place in the early 2000s was that the first version of the World Anti-Doping Agency's (WADA) World Anti-Doping Code (WADC) entered into effect in 2003. The WADC designates CAS as the final body of appeal in international disputes. Its adoption meant a significant increase in the potential number of doping-related decisions that could be brought before CAS.[63]

The data supports the proposal that the 2002 FIFA-ICAS agreement and the WADC entering into force in 2003 significantly contributed to CAS's case load and its jurisprudence. In 2005, the number of decisions that CAS issued each year increased suddenly and significantly to a much higher level where it has since remained.[64] The time period that passed between the identified events and CAS issuing more decisions seems quite reasonable and it conversely seems unlikely that the two are unrelated.[65] Indeed, if we study the subject matter of the collected CAS decisions, we can see that a large portion of the bump between 2004 and 2005 consist of decisions that relate to either football, doping, or both. Football- and doping-related cases have also made up more than a majority of CAS's yearly decisions since 2005, and for some years significantly more than a majority.

---

[62] Kane 2003, p. 614.

[63] Kaufmann-Kohler and Rigozzi 2015, p. 42.

[64] See above Fig. 3.9 *Requests and CAS Decisions Over Time* and above Fig. 3.10 *CAS Decisions Over Time: Football, Doping, and the Rest.*

[65] For football-related cases from 2002 to 2005 and for doping-related cases from 2003 to 2005.

However, the data also suggests that these two events are not exclusively responsible for the increase in CAS decisions over time: CAS decisions that concern neither football nor doping constitute a significant portion of all CAS decisions issued each year and this holds true for both before and after 2005. In some years, these decisions make up more than 40 percent of CAS's decisions. When the data is broken down by subject matter it also seems quite clear that the trends identified above actually begun before the agreement with FIFA was struck and the WADC entered into force. Thus, it seems that CAS's position as a dispute settling institution was already in a clear upswing before the FIFA-ICAS agreement and the WADC and that this continued during the period after those event but before cases affected by those events began reaching CAS. For this reason, the increase in football- and doping-related CAS decisions should be understood both as a cause and a result of CAS's increased popularity[66] or "one positive indicator of its success."[67]

If this is correct, the explanation for CAS's increased popularity should be sought further back in time. Commentators have suggested that a key factor behind the increased number of cases coming before CAS are the organizational and jurisdictional changes made in 1994.[68] That development can, in turn, be traced back to 10 September 1992, when CAS issued a decision that can be described as a defining moment in CAS's history and what may very well be CAS's single most commented case: *Gundel*.[69]

In June 1991, Elmar Gundel, a professional German equestrian, competed in a jumping event in Aachen with the horse Life is Life. Life is Life performed well in the competition but subsequently tested positive for a banned substance, isoxsuprine. This lead to a series of proceedings. The FEI Judicial Committee found that Gundel was guilty of a doping violation, having acted with the intent of improving the horse's performance, disqualified Gundel and Life is Life from the competition in question, and imposed a fine and a three-month suspension on Gundel.[70] Gundel appealed FEI's decision to CAS where his challenge of the testing procedure was unsuccessful. CAS did however overturn FEI's finding that Gundel had acted intentionally and as a consequence thereof decreased the fine and the length of the suspension.[71]

CAS's decision in *Gundel* has had a major impact on later CAS decisions. The approach established and applied in *Gundel* for determining whether a doping violation was intentional was subsequently adopted and applied by several CAS

---

66 "Popularity" is here meant purely in terms of the number of cases brought before it, not e.g. in terms of the perception of CAS among the general public or athletes.

67 McLaren 2011, p. 52.

68 Mangan 2009, p. 593.

69 CAS 92/63. See e.g. Anderson 2010, pp. 80–81; Blackshaw 2013b; Gardiner et al. 2012, p. 141; James 2013, pp. 51–52; Wise and Meyer 1997, p. 1450.

70 As described in CAS 92/63, *Gundel*.

71 CAS 92/63, *Gundel*, paras 15–16.

panels deciding doping-related cases, many of which, in turn, have also had a significant impact on CAS's jurisprudence.[72]

Gundel's most significant and long-lasting impact was however brought about by events that toke place after CAS issued the decision. Unhappy with CAS's decision, Elmar Gundel appealed the decision to the Swiss Federal Tribunal (SFT), arguing that CAS was not a fair and impartial arbitral body. SFT upheld the CAS decision, concluding that it was a "true court of arbitration." However, SFT also expressed concerns about the close ties between CAS and the International Olympic Committee (IOC) and what this meant for CAS's independence.[73]

The Swiss Federal Tribunal's dicta caused a number of important institutional, procedural, and jurisdictional changes. Through the so-called Paris Agreement of 1994 the IOC created some distance between itself and CAS by placing CAS under a new foundation, the International Council of Arbitration for Sport (ICAS).[74] Also, CAS's funding sources were diversified. These changes were effectuated through the Code of Sports-related Arbitration (CAS Code) that entered into force in November 1994. The CAS Code also included other provisions ensuring the independence of CAS and its arbitrators and provided for the establishment of two divisions within CAS: the Ordinary Arbitration Division and the Appeals Arbitration Division.[75]

The creation of the Appeals Arbitration Division can be seen as "formalizing CAS's operation in its appeals capacity"[76] in relation to decisions taken by sports governing bodies (SGBs) in individual sports and allows CAS to act as a "court of 'last instance'" for sport-related disputes.[77] This was also ensured as several international federations after 1994 undertook the necessary regulatory changes to make CAS a compulsory last instance for reviewing internal decisions. In these ways, the 1994 reforms had a deep impact on CAS and on international sports law.[78]

The appeals process and the appeals body have been described as important factors when it comes to explaining CAS's growth.[79] This causal connection is not obvious when examining the collected data. It is true that most CAS decisions are appellate awards and that the number of appellate procedures in CAS rose after 1994. However, so did the number of other procedures and the ratio of appellate to

---

[72] See e.g. CAS 95/141, *Chagnaud*, paras 17–18; CAS 96/156, *Foschi*, para 12.2; CAS 98/214, *Bouras*, para 16; CAS 2001/A/317, *Aanes*, paras 37–39.

[73] SFT's decision 15 March 1993 in case 4P.217/1992, ATF 119 II 271 (*Gundel v. FEI*). See also Vaitiekunas 2014, pp. 132–135. Cf. ECtHR's decision 2 October 2018 in *Mutu & Pechstein v. Switzerland*, appl. no. 40575/10 & 67474/10, paras 154–157.

[74] Reprinted in Digest of CAS Awards vol. III, pp. 767–769. See also Sect. 2.1.

[75] See also Paulsson 1993, pp. 367–368; Vaitiekunas 2014, esp. pp. 37–39, 139–142, 149; Yi 2006, pp. 13–15. See also Sect. 2.2.

[76] Vaitiekunas 2014, p. 38.

[77] Anderson 2010, p. 81.

[78] Cf. Kane 2003, p. 618 ("The year 1994 can be seen as a turning point for international sports jurisprudence.").

[79] Duval 2015, pp. 382–383; Mangan 2009, p. 593.

non-appellate decisions have been roughly the same over CAS's lifetime, both before and after the 1994 reforms.[80] Also, the data suggests that there was indeed an increase in the number of appellate decisions after 1994, but that it was quite modest compared to the development after 2005, more than a decade after the reform.[81]

This does not prove that the 1994 reforms were meaningless for the consistent and powerful increase in the number of cases referred to CAS. The data does however suggest that there is no clear and direct correlation between the two. It is possible that there is a correlation but that it is less direct and therefore not immediately obvious in the data. Perhaps the post-*Gundel* reforms of CAS's appellate system contributed to the independence and quality of CAS – or at least the perception of such independence and quality – that in turn increased CAS's attractiveness as a dispute resolution institution.[82] This would be consistent with the observations above.

3.4 Requests In, and Then What?

A few words ought to be said about CAS's case turnover and how this has changed over time. First, it is worth pointing out that not all requests for a decision that is delivered to CAS result in decisions. A request may for example be retracted as a consequence of the underlying dispute having been reconciled. According to the statistical information provided by CAS, roughly two in three requests result in a CAS decision.[83] Until the mid- to late-1990s, the portion of requests leading to a decision varied significantly from year to year.[84] However, since around the year 2000, the decision-to-request ratio has been quite stable around 70 percent.[85]

Another, arguably more important factor is the length of time that it takes for CAS to resolve a dispute. Expediency is often presented as one of the major benefits of and reasons for resorting to arbitration.[86] Expediency is of great importance in

[80] See above Fig. 3.10 *CAS Decisions Over Time: Football, Doping, and the Rest.* See also Kaufmann-Kohler and Rigozzi 2015, p. 42.

[81] See above Fig. 3.10 *CAS Decisions Over Time: Football, Doping, and the Rest.*

[82] Kane 2003, p. 618.

[83] CAS, Statistics 2016.

[84] These fluctuations are in part a result of the small sample size during those early years, but a contributing factor may also be a shift in how CAS deals with cases that are successfully conciliated. Until 1999, those cases were terminated by issuing a termination order, but since then they result in a consent award. Mavromati and Reeb 2015, p. 308.

[85] See below Fig. 3.11 *Requests Leading to a Decision Over Time* (based on CAS, Statistics 2016).

[86] Kaufmann-Kohler and Rigozzi 2015, p. 14 (noting that the expediency of arbitration often has more to do with the fact that the award is not subject to appeal than the length of the proceeding itself).

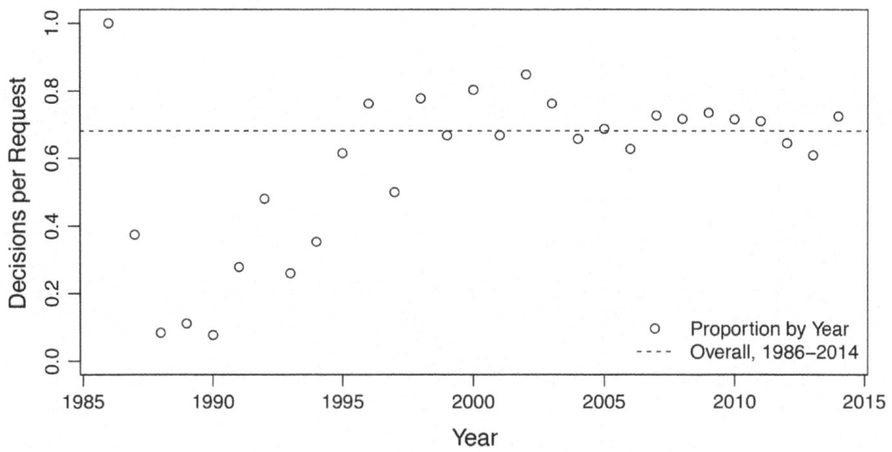

Fig. 3.11 Requests Leading to a Decision Over Time. [*Source* The author]

the area of sports where justice delayed frequently means justice denied.[87] For example, an athlete that finds out that he or she was eligible to participate in the Olympic Games will benefit little from this if it is established after the Games are over.[88] One of the key goals behind the establishment of CAS was therefore to create a forum that would be able to resolve sports-related disputes swiftly.[89] The expediency of the procedure is also a key factor when it comes to justifying why arbitration before CAS constitutes a reasonable and proportional balance between opposing interests.[90] For example, in finding that CAS decisions constitute "true awards" in *Lazutina & Danilova v. IOC*, the SFT attached relevance to the fact that there seemed to exist no other solution that could resolve international sports-related disputes as rapidly as CAS.[91] Similarly, CAS's ability to rapidly resolve sports-related disputes was one of the factors that led the German Bundesgerichtshof to conclude in *Pechstein* that SGBs requiring athletes to agree to CAS arbitration does not constitute abuse of a dominant position.[92] Also, CAS

[87] See e.g. Mavromati and Reeb 2015, p. 587; Mitten and Opie 2010, p. 288.

[88] Reilly 2012, p. 71.

[89] Ibid. p. 63.

[90] See e.g. SFT's decision 22 March 2007 in case 4P.172/2006, ATF 133 III 235 (*Cañas*), para 4.3.2.3; ECtHR's decision 2 October 2018 in *Mutu & Pechstein v. Switzerland*, app. no. 40575/10 & 67474/10, para 98.

[91] SFT's decision 27 May 2003 in case 4P.267–270/2002, 129 ATF 445 (*Lazutina & Danilova v. IOC*), para 3.3.3 ("Il n'est pas certain que d'autres solutions existent, qui soient susceptibles de remplacer une institution à même de résoudre rapidement et de manière peu coûteuse des litiges internationaux dans le domaine du sport.").

[92] BGH's decision 7 June 2016 in case KZR 6/15 (*Pechstein v. ISU*), para 59.

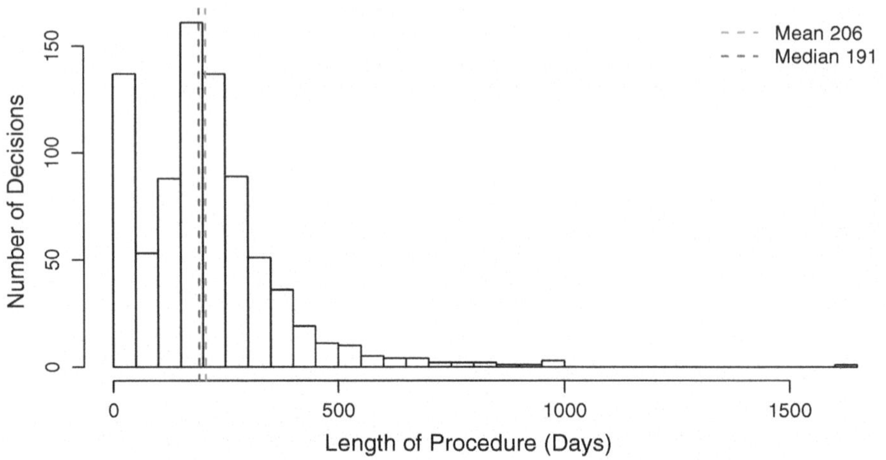

Fig. 3.12 CAS Procedure Length Distribution (Color figure online). [*Source* The author]

chooses to emphasize its swift procedure as one of its characteristic traits when it describes itself.[93]

Thus, the time taken by CAS to decide a case is an important issue in several regards and we can gain valuable insight into the matter by examining how long it took CAS to decide the cases included in the dataset. The length of the procedure before CAS is here calculated as the number of days that transpired between, on one hand, the date of submission of the statement of appeal or request for arbitration[94] and, on the other hand, the date of the decision.

In measuring this, we can see that the length of the CAS procedure follows what resembles a normal distribution around a median and a mean of roughly 200 days or approximately six-and-a-half months.[95] The vast majority of all CAS cases cluster around the mean and nine out of ten cases that are filed with CAS are decided within one year of the initial request. One notable deviation from a normal distribution is the large number of cases before CAS that are decided within 50 days. These are for the most part cases decided by Ad Hoc Divisions, where the procedure length for obvious reasons is very short, and cases concerning eligibility,[96] where, as discussed above, time is often of the essence.

---

[93] See e.g. CAS 92/71, *L v. Y. SA*, para 7 ("Le TAS est une institution arbitrale qui met à disposition des parties une procedure arbitrale rapide et peu coûteuse.").

[94] In most CAS decisions, this date is explicitly stated as part of CAS's presentation of the procedural history of the case. Where the filing date was unclear, the decision was disregarded for the purpose of calculating the length of the procedure. The dataset contained a total of 817 CAS decisions where the procedure length could be determined with certainty.

[95] See above Fig. 3.12 *CAS Procedure Length Distribution*.

[96] See below Table 3.1 *Procedure Length*.

Table 3.1 Procedure Length. [*Source* The author]

Variable	n	Mean procedure length (Days)
All cases	817	206.3
Case type		
A	699	223.7***
AUS	7	95.3
C	10	123.2
H	63	3.7***
O	38	265.0***
Matter		
Ct	94	263.6***
Di	86	191.9**
Do	368	230.0***
E	71	56.1*
G	20	159.5*
N	16	100.3
T	86	246.5***
X	76	166.5***
Outcome		
Admissible	15	237.4***
Allowed	12	77.5
Dismissed	309	185.0***
Inadmissible	10	174.8
Jurisdiction denied	38	154.0*
Partially upheld	175	258.4***
Set aside	23	233.5***
Upheld	145	225.0***

Particularly worthy of highlighting in this context is the fact that it takes CAS on average 224 days, or almost seven-and-a-half months, to decide a case brought under the Appeals Arbitration Procedure.[97] This can be compared with the CAS Code which states that "[t]he operative part of the award [in an Appeals Arbitration Procedure] shall be communicated to the parties within three months after the transfer of the file to the Panel."[98] However, according to the same provision, that time limit can be extended by the Division President and such extensions are frequently given.[99]

The equivalent provision governing awards in cases brought under the Ordinary Arbitration Procedure contains no time limit and a CAS panel deciding such a case

[97] See above Table 3.1 *Procedure Length*. See however Benz and Sternheimer 2015, p. 7 (noting a significantly shorter procedure length).

[98] Article R59 CAS Code.

[99] Rigozzi 2010, p. 5.

could in theory take a long time to render its decision.[100] However, based on the studied cases it takes in practice on average 265 days or a little less than nine months between a request for arbitration and CAS issuing its decisions in an Ordinary Arbitration Procedure.[101] It is both difficult and hazardous to make sweeping assumptions about the similarities and differences between cases brought under Ordinary and Appeals Arbitration Procedure respectively. However, it is not immediately obvious that it should be easier or quicker for CAS to resolve cases brought under the Ordinary Arbitration Procedure, many of which involve rather complicated contractual disputes and transfer disputes, than cases brought under the Appeals Arbitration Procedure. If this impression is correct, the relatively small difference in the length of Ordinary and Appeals Arbitration Procedures raises some doubt concerning the efficacy of the time limit on issuing awards under the Appeals Arbitration Procedure.

Without denying the importance of expedient resolution to the parties, for example an athlete facing a suspension, we should acknowledge that the expediency of dispute resolution can and should be subject to certain limitations. First, before the process can begin in earnest a panel must be constituted and this will in most cases take some time.[102] It is uncertain how much time can realistically be shaved off compared to the current situation.[103] It has been noted that the time limits for parties to file their submissions and to react to the opposing side's submissions are already quite stringent.[104] Relatedly, it is questionable how much quicker the process can or should be made given the need to ensure the parties' due process right of having an effective opportunity to present their cases and to, as far as possible, achieve just substantive outcomes in individual cases. Increased expediency is not cost-free. McAuliffe and Rigozzi have pointed out that parties would be wise to appoint experienced counsel that is familiar with CAS's procedure and jurisprudence and who are therefore able to act within the already demanding time limits.[105]

Before leaving the topic of procedure length, there is one last observation to be made: the development of procedure length over time or, more correctly stated, the lack of development in this regard. While the average length of the procedure before CAS has varied somewhat between individual years, the variations have been rather minor, there is no clear trend towards decreased or increased procedure

---

[100] See Article R46 CAS Code.

[101] See above Table 3.1 *Procedure Length*. See also Benz and Sternheimer 2015, p. 7 ("the total average duration of such a procedure is less than one year…").

[102] Blackaby et al. 2015, p. 37 (noting that this is common complaint in arbitration).

[103] It can here be noted that the system used in Ad Hoc Divisions with a set of arbitrators on standby, see Sect. 2.3, does allow for a very rapid procedure, see above Table 3.1 *Procedure Length*. To use a similar system to handle the vast bulk of CAS's cases is however hardly realistic.

[104] McAuliffe and Rigozzi 2013, p. 16; Rigozzi 2010, p. 5.

[105] McAuliffe and Rigozzi 2013, p. 16.

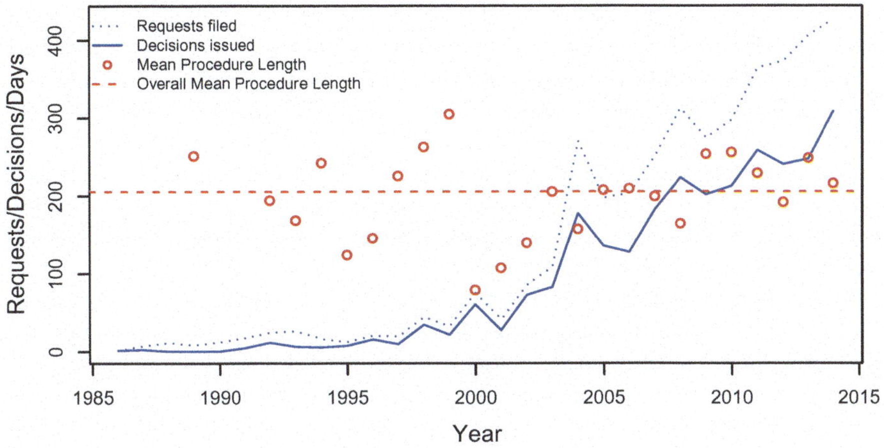

Fig. 3.13 CAS Procedure Length Over Time. [*Source* The author]

length over time, and the yearly mean procedure time has been very stable around the overall mean during the last twelve years of the studied period.[106]

This is far from given as adjudication institutions run a strong risk of being victims of their own success. As more litigants seek its services and the institution's case load increases, this tends to lead to an increased backlog and procedure length.[107] The fact that CAS has been able to maintain the same average procedure length while the number of requests filed and decisions issued has increased eight-fold speaks strongly to CAS's ability to effectively scale to handle large amounts of cases.

3.5 References Out

Much of the discussion in this book concerns and is based on CAS's references to its own, previous decisions. It is therefore relevant to consider whether CAS's practice of self-reference has shifted over time when studying CAS and its jurisprudence. Just like the number of CAS decisions issued has shifted over time, so has CAS's tendency to refer to its own decisions and this may both affect and explain various findings.

[106] See above Fig. 3.13 *CAS Procedure Length Over Time*. The figure shows that the average length varied significantly year-by-year from 1985 to 2002. However, it should be noted that the number of decisions during those years were quite low and that the length of the procedure in individual cases may thus have a disproportionally large impact on the yearly mean.

[107] This is for example a well-known issue with the European Union's court system. See e.g. Kinsella and Duke 2014; Kye 2015; Prechal 2016, pp. 1287–1288.

There are two ways to think about citation practice and these are closely associated with the distinction between inward and outward references. Each reference is at once both an inward and an outward reference: the referring decision is the object of the outward reference and the decision being referred to is the object of the inward reference. If we think about a reference as an arrow, the originating decision is at its tail and the target decision is at its head.[108] The distinction between inward and outward references may perhaps appear technical and theoretical but it illustrates a rather important and practical distinction that is perhaps particularly important when considering change over time.

We begin by focusing on outward references over time, that is, how frequently CAS refers to its previous decisions and whether its practice in this regard has shifted over time. Mean outdegree, that is the average number of references made, per year is a good measurement in this regard. It is a straightforward and simple measurement but should do a good job of capturing the general trend in a reliable and representative manner.[109]

The development can be divided into three rather distinct phases: lack, growth, and establishment of the use of case law as a source of law. From the outset, we know that CAS's average number of outward references must by necessity have begun at a very low level since no one can cite that which does not exist. Consequently, every adjudication institution will initially have a period where it does not refer to its own previous decisions. This initial phase is for similar reasons followed by a period where the average number of outwards references remains at a relatively low level and then rises slowly. In theory, it is possible for an institution to in its eleventh decision cite all its ten prior decisions. However, this is not how it works in practice. It takes time to build a body of case law and for its average number of references to previous decisions to rise.

That citation practice follows these general trends appear to be a general, if not universal, trait that has been observed in multiple legal orders. How long each stage lasts does however differ, sometimes quite strongly. For example, Fowler and Jeon have shown that the reference practice of the Supreme Court of the United States (SCOTUS) over time follows this pattern. It took roughly 25 years after its formal creation before SCOTUS's mean number of outward references to its own decisions rose noticeably above zero and about 135 years before the average number of references per decision was firmly established above one.[110] This can be compared to the Court of Justice of the European Union (CJEU). During the CJEU's first 23 years of existence, its average decision contained close to zero references to previous decisions. After this period, however, the numbers began rising fairly steadily and rose to above one reference per decision roughly 30 years after the CJEU was established.[111]

---

[108] See Sect. 1.6.

[109] See Sect. 1.6.

[110] Fowler and Jeon 2008, p. 19.

[111] Derlén and Lindholm 2017, p. 667.

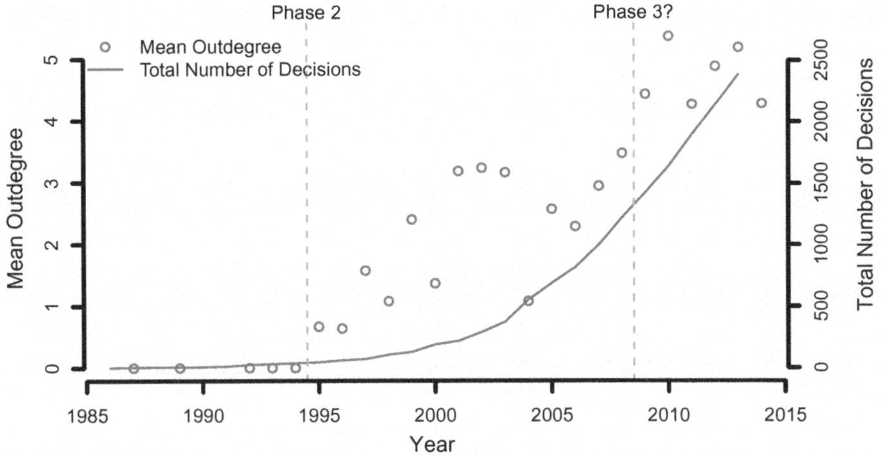

Fig. 3.14 Outdegree Centrality Over Time (Color figure online). [*Source* The author]

If we track how many references to previous decisions CAS has made and how this has developed over time, we find that its early citation practice follows the same general trends as those institutions. However, CAS's development was much faster than both SCOTUS's and the CJEU's and the initial phases was significantly shorter for CAS than both those institutions.[112] The phase during which CAS made no references to its previous decisions lasted less than a decade, from 1986 to 1994.[113]

As far as I have been able to ascertain from the collected decisions, the first time that a CAS panel referred to a previous CAS decision was on 31 August 1994 in the advisory opinion in *FFTri & ITU*. The background to the case was that two French triathlon athletes had tested positive for doping and were subsequently suspended from competing for one year by the disciplinary commission of the French triathlon federation, Fédération Française de Triathlon (FFTri), a sanction that was subsequently confirmed by the French sports minister. This provoked a reaction from the international triathlon federation, International Triathlon Union (ITU), whose rules mandated a two-year suspension for the violation in question. FFTri argued that certain principles of natural justice, including the proportionality of the sanction, must be guaranteed, regardless of ITU's rules. Referring to and directly quoting its earlier advisory opinion in *IOC*,[114] the CAS panel declared that an athlete that is accused of doping is entitled to a fair procedure in conformity with national and international legal principles, including the establishment of to what extent the doping violation was intentional, that it is in this spirit that the anti-doping rules

[112] See above Fig. 3.14 *Outdegree Centrality Over Time.*

[113] One could argue that the period started two years earlier, in 1984 when CAS was created. However, no cases were submitted to CAS during the first two years.

[114] CAS 86/02.

must be understood, and that minimum sanctions established by an international federation are not binding on national federations in so far as they are incompatible with these requirements.[115]

Interestingly, when a CAS panel four months later made the second reference ever to previous CAS decisions,[116] it was to this part of the decision in *FFTri & ITU* and it was made in yet another advisory opinion: *UCI & CONI*.[117] Thus, it appears that, at least early on, advisory opinions were driving CAS's use of prior decisions as a source of law: both many early decisions referring to previous decisions and many of the decisions referred to early were advisory opinions.[118] It is difficult to empirically determine whether this is a general trait of advisory opinions since there are relatively few advisory opinions,[119] they were more common, relatively speaking, in the early years, and the procedure has since been abolished.[120]

It does however seem reasonable that the distinct role of advisory opinions in CAS's early jurisprudence is not accidental. First, unlike an award in a particular dispute, an advisory opinion is not binding on the parties[121] and for CAS panels to openly rely on previous decisions in support of its conclusions may therefore be less controversial, both to the parties and to outside observers, if it is done in an advisory opinion.[122] However, the more times a dispute resolution institution uses its previous decisions as a source of law, the more used to the practice its audience becomes and the less controversial it seems. In this manner, non-binding advisory opinions can serve as a vehicle for introducing the use of previous decisions as a source of law, a Trojan horse of sorts for introducing a precedent-like system.[123]

Second, and somewhat relatedly, a procedure like the consultation procedure where the questions to be answered are broader and more open to reformulation[124] is a great opportunity for those answering those questions to introduce or develop general principles and doctrines. For example, legal scholars active in the field of European Union law are of the opinion that the CJEU's development of European Union law has primarily been achieved through its decisions in cases brought as

115 CAS 93/109. See also McLaren 2006, p. 192.

116 At least as far as I was able to ascertain based on the decisions included in the dataset.

117 CAS 94/128, *UCI & CONI*, para 28.

118 See also, e.g., CAS 95/144, *COE* (extensively discussing CAS 94/128, *UCI & CONI*).

119 According to CAS's statistics, only about 1% of all CAS decisions between 1986 and 2013 were advisory opinions.

120 Mavromati and Reeb 2015, p. 603. According to CAS's statistics, 3 of the 7 decisions rendered in the first four years (1986–1989) were advisory opinions. By comparison, during its last four years of existence, 7 out of 891 CAS decisions were advisory opinions.

121 Article R62 CAS Code (now abolished).

122 Cf. Pinna 2006, p. 407 (noting that CAS's statements about the principle of legality were in non-binding legal opinions).

123 See also further Chap. 4.

124 CAS had significant discretionary power to reformulate the questions posed by the parties. McLaren 2006, pp. 183–184.

preliminary references.[125] The consultation procedure in CAS has many things in common with the CJEU's preliminary reference procedure.

After the initial, near-zero level there tends to come a point in the development of a case law-based legal order when the order has sufficiently "matured" and its average number of references begin to increase steadily. In order for this to occur, the institution must have established an adequate body of jurisprudence to which it can refer. Adequacy in this sense is not merely a quantitative question of the institution having issued a certain number of decisions. As discussed below, empirical comparisons of different judicial institutions suggest that there is no strong correlation between, on one hand, the size of its body of jurisprudence and, on the other hand, how frequently it refers to that jurisprudence.[126] Rather, the institution's collective jurisprudence must exhibit a certain qualitative character where it deals with a sufficient number of the key issues that comes before it. An increase in reference to prior decisions may reasonably also require a certain level of respect and/or acceptance, both within the institution and among those with which the institution communicates.

While we know from studying other legal orders that a phase of steady growth tends to follow the first phase, this phase can follow different patterns. For example, after the initial phase described above, SCOTUS experienced more than a century during which its average number of references to previous case law increased clearly, strongly, and overall consistently. There were, however, some breaks in this trend. Most obviously, during the so-called Warren Court (1953–1969) the average outdegree dipped considerably, but afterwards the average increased and in line with the previous trend.[127] We have in a previous study shown that the CJEU follows largely the same pattern as SCOTUS but thus far without any significant dip. The CJEU's development was also significantly faster than SCOTUS's.[128] For example, whereas it took SCOTUS about ninety years before its decisions contained on average five references to previous decisions, the same development took the CJEU only half the time, about forty-five years.[129] If CAS is building a body of jurisprudence, we expect it to follow the same general pattern of behavior as SCOTUS and the CJEU when it comes to citing to its own decisions.

Indeed, CAS's aforementioned decision in *FFTri & ITU* in 1995 signaled the beginning of a new, second phase in CAS's use of its prior decisions as a source of law. During this period, CAS panels began citing previous CAS decisions to a steadily increased extent. The average number of references to previous decisions

---

[125] See e.g. Alter 1998, pp. 126–129, 122; Craig 2001, pp. 182–183; Jacob 2014, p. 19; Schepel and Blankenburg 2001, pp. 41–42; Stone Sweet and Brunnell 1998, pp. 65–66.

[126] See immediately below.

[127] Fowler and Jeon 2008, p. 19.

[128] Derlén and Lindholm 2017, pp. 667–669.

[129] Compare Fowler and Jeon 2008, p. 19, and Derlén and Lindholm 2017, pp. 667–669.

found in CAS decisions increased by eight times between 1995 and 2010,[130] from 0.67 to 5.36.[131] This means that it took CAS half the time of the CJEU to reach an average of five references, which, in turn, took half the time of SCOTUS to reach the same point. When viewed in this comparison, CAS's rapid pace of developing its practice of referring to previous decisions can be described as astonishing, perhaps even aggressive. As discussed in greater detail below, the question of precedent in arbitration is both complicated and, in some regards, controversial.[132] With this in mind, it is interesting that CAS has relied on previous decisions significantly more frequently and sooner than two premier examples of case law-driven courts.

One way of measuring and understanding just how fast CAS's use of references to previous decisions developed is to compare the average number of references and the size of the body of accumulated decisions. At the beginning of a judicial institution's lifetime there is, as discussed above, a natural correlation between the number of references in a decision and the number of previous decisions in existence when the decision is written. When an institution's body of decisions reaches "critical mass", a number large enough to allow for references, and then how many references does however seem to vary between judicial institutions. For both SCOTUS and the CJEU the body of decisions has been leading the average number of references, meaning that the total number of decisions increased faster than the average number of references.

When it comes to CAS, the average number of decisions that CAS panels refer to have deviated in several regards from the accumulated size of CAS's body of jurisprudence. CAS's increased reference to prior decisions was significantly steeper than the increase in its accumulated body of decisions between 1993 and 2003.[133] CAS's trend in this regard was starkly different from SCOTUS's and the CJEU's. For example, when the CJEU in 1994 first reached the level where it on average referred to three prior decisions it had issued almost 4,000 previous decisions.[134] When CAS reached the same level in 2001 it did so on the basis of an accumulated jurisprudence of less than 200 decisions. One possible interpretation of the data is that CAS after a few initial years of building a body of decisions was quite comfortable to follow and develop what was decided in those decisions.

The quite dramatic differences between CAS on the one hand and SCOTUS and the CJEU on the other may tempt some readers to view CAS's extensive and rapidly increasing reference of prior decisions with suspicion. However, it is important to remember that there are some rather important differences between the cases that come before CAS and those that come before SCOTUS and the CJEU. In

130 How one should interpret the development in CAS after 2009 is, as discussed in greater detail below, a little complicated.

131 See above Fig. 3.14 *Outdegree Centrality Over Time.*

132 See Chap. 4.

133 See above Fig. 3.14 *Outdegree Centrality Over Time.*

134 Derlén and Lindholm 2017, pp. 667–668.

particular and arguably most importantly, the cases that come before CAS involve a less diverse group of issues than those that reach the other two institutions. As touched upon above and further explored below, CAS jurisprudence deals with a fairly limited number of distinct subject matters and is particularly dominated by doping-related disputes.[135] The lower the diversity of the issues adjudicated, the higher the average number of references to previous decisions one can expect. All else being equal, an institution whose activities are concentrated on a relatively limited number of issues is more likely to find relevant decisions to consider and cite when adjudicating a new case compared to an institution that deals with a broad range of issues. Such differences should reasonably even out over time as both institutions will eventually reach a point where it has more relevant decisions on all issues than it in practice can consider and refer to. However, it could help explain why the average number of cited decisions in CAS has increased comparatively fast.

Relatedly, the area of doping is dominated by a few regulatory acts, importantly the WADC. The WADC and the regulatory acts that preceded it are applied in a large number of cases with far-reaching consequences for those involved but are fairly general in terms of language. It is therefore natural that previous decisions have played an important role when CAS interprets and applies the text.

After CAS's average first climbed to this level it shifted again. Two "plateaus" dominate the subsequent development, one between 2001 and 2006 and a second between 2009 and the end of the studied period.[136] A development where a judicial body increases the number of references it makes to its previous decisions is in practice not infinitely sustainable. Considering that the time that CAS panels can spend formulating each decision and that the decisions' length is in practice, albeit not formally, limited, CAS, much like other adjudicatory bodies, will eventually need to prioritize which prior decisions it refers to and as it begins to do so the average number of cited decisions will stabilize. We have in a previous study seen signs of the CJEU reaching such a point in recent years,[137] and it is possible to interpret the collected data as CAS reaching this third stage of development around 2009. Between 2009 and 2014 the average number of references found in CAS decisions have hovered around five with some variations up and down between individual years.[138] The fact that CAS's total body of decisions during these years has increased by more than two hundred new decisions yearly suggests that we might in fact witness a more sustained plateau in the development.[139] However, it is important to point out that we are dealing with a relatively short time period of six years and it is too early to say with certainty whether this constitutes a stable break with the previous trend.

---

[135] See Sect. 6.2.

[136] See above Fig. 3.14 *Outdegree Centrality Over Time.*

[137] Derlén and Lindholm 2017, p. 669.

[138] As explored in Sect. 6.3, there are some significant differences in this regard between different issues and areas.

[139] See above Fig. 3.14 *Outdegree Centrality Over Time.*

3.6 References In

As we saw in the previous section, outward references and their development over time can reveal several things about CAS. As discussed, one can and, in my opinion, should also consider the other side of CAS's references, that is to focus on the decisions that are the targets as opposed to the sources of such references. One approach that can provide potentially interesting findings regarding how CAS treats and uses its previous decisions is to track mean indegree centrality by year. This approach mirrors the one used in the previous section, but instead of tracking outward references (outdegree) we focus on inward references (indegree). To explain the difference, whereas a year with high mean outdegree is a year when CAS decisions contained many reference, a year with high mean indegree is a year when CAS issued decisions that it subsequently referred to frequently.[140]

Another difference between outdegree and indegree is to what extent they are affected by time. A decision only contains the references to previous decisions that it contained when it was published and it will never contain any other references. Thus, the mean outdegree of a group of CAS decisions, such as those issued in a particular year, will be the same regardless of when it is studied. By contrast, CAS decisions' indegree centrality changes with every new reference. Every time CAS publishes a decision that contains at least one outwards reference the indegree of the decisions referred to changes. This means that indegree centrality of individual decisions and the mean indegree centrality of decisions issued in a particular year changes constantly. We will study this by taking inward references in the CAS case law network,[141] breaking them down by the decision year of the target decisions.[142]

A rather obvious observation that one can make is that the history of CAS's inward references can be divided into three distinct periods. The first period (circa 1986–1996) is characterized by the mean indegree fluctuating strongly from year to year, varying from zero to above twelve. These shifts should be interpreted with great caution as we are dealing with a small sample size during this first period. In the beginning CAS decided few decisions each year,[143] and the indegree of an individual decision consequently greatly impacts the mean indegree for all decisions issued that year. The most obvious example of this is 1995. CAS decisions rendered in 1995 have a mean indegree that is more than twice as high as decisions from most other years. CAS issued only eight decisions that year, but two of those decisions are among those that CAS refers to most frequently: the aforementioned *UCI & CONI* and *Quigley*, which is the single most frequently cited decision.[144] The presence of these landmark cases distinguishes 1995 from many other years. However, had these decisions been handed down in later years together with more

---

[140] See Sect. 1.6.

[141] See Sect. 1.6.

[142] See below Fig. 3.15 *Indegree Centrality Over Time*.

[143] See above Fig. 3.9 *Requests and CAS Decisions Over Time*.

[144] CAS 94/128 and CAS 94/129 respectively. See further Sect. 5.3.

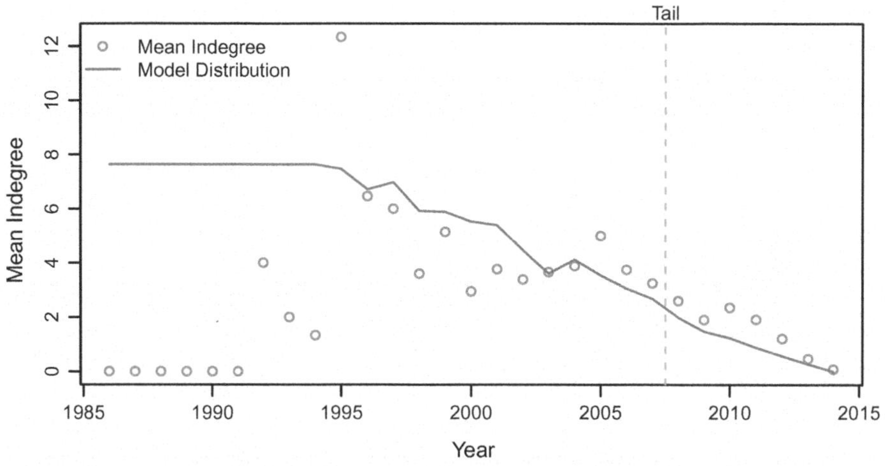

Fig. 3.15 Indegree Centrality Over Time (Color figure online). [*Source* The author]

average decisions, 1995 would not stick out in the same way. Also, in CAS's and most other court's jurisprudence most references are made to a small group of decisions[145] and whether those top-cited decisions show up in a particular year can have a disproportionally large impact on that year's mean indegree centrality. For these reasons, mean indegree centrality is a tricky and sometimes deceptive measurement of precedential power.

However, despite these problems, there is some value to tracking mean indegree centrality. This becomes clearer when we turn our attention to the second period (1997–2007) during which the mean indegree centrality is quite stabile around four with only relatively small variations between individual years.

It seems that the level established during this second phase can be described as CAS's "indegree baseline", at least thus far. First, we generally do not expect indegree centrality to develop in as smooth fashion as outdegree centrality and this trend is comparatively stable.[146] Second, it is not a given that indegree centrality in the CAS case law network and other legal citation networks stabilizes in this manner. On the contrary, in legal citation networks[147] there is a natural correlation between a decision's age and its indegree centrality; the older a decision is, the more opportunities it has had to be cited. If CAS panels treat all decisions equally regardless of age all decisions would accumulate references over time but older decisions would always have accumulated more references than newer decisions. This would result in a situation where the mean indegree of the oldest CAS

[145] See Sect. 5.2.

[146] See, for comparison, Fowler and Jeon 2008; Derlén and Lindholm 2017.

[147] And most other time-directed networks for that matter.

decisions is the highest and where newer decisions have progressively lower indegree.[148]

As is evident from the figures below and discussed in greater detail immediately below, it is true that the yearly mean indegree for CAS decisions decline during the most recent years, but the development of mean indegree does not follow this model if we go further back in time. The mean indegree between 1997 and 2002 are overall lower than this model predicts and the mean indegree from 2005 and onwards is slightly higher. This finding suggests that the assumption that CAS panels treat all decisions equally regardless of age is wrong.

CAS's inwards citation tendencies are to some extent exposed by studying the third period (2008–2014) during which the mean indegree of CAS decisions steadily decrease from the aforementioned baseline towards zero. Much like the fact that mean outdegree will begin at zero,[149] this is an inevitable phenomenon. Just like the first decision cannot contain any references to previous decisions,[150] the most recent decision cannot yet have been cited by any more recent decisions.[151]

What is more interesting to observe is the length of the "tail", that is the amount of time it takes before decisions reach their more mature indegree. For example, CAS decisions rendered in 2013 and 2014 have the lowest mean indegree centrality of all CAS decisions rendered in any year since 1988 (which has zero),[152] but there is nothing to suggest that CAS decisions rendered during those years were of particularly poor precedential value. It is very likely that those decisions' indegree centrality will rise over time and reveal their precedential value. It is very difficult to determine what will constitute these decisions' "proper" indegree level or when they will reach it.[153] However, based on the trend established by older, more established decisions, it is possible to make an educated guess. Based on the trend set by CAS decisions issued between 1997 and 2007, the mean indegree centrality for CAS decisions decided in an average year is roughly four. It is not impossible that CAS's decisions issued in 2013 and 2014 are of exceptionally low or exceptionally high precedential value; we cannot with certainty say anything about their precedential value in this sense other than how CAS has treated them up to this point in time. At the same time, knowing nothing else,[154] it is most reasonable to

[148] See the model distribution above in Fig. 3.15 *Indegree Centrality Over Time*. The model was constructed by taking all outwards references actually made in CAS decisions and assuming (contrary to what actually happened) that inwards references were distributed equally among all prior decisions in existence when the references were made.

[149] See above Sect. 3.5.

[150] I.e. the oldest decision's outdegree centrality must be zero.

[151] I.e. the most recent decision's indegree centrality must be zero.

[152] See above Fig. 3.15 *Indegree Centrality Over Time*.

[153] Also, remember that indegree unlike outdegree can and in fact does change continuously over time.

[154] This assumption is of course not necessarily reasonable if there is other evidence to the contrary. However, at least with regard to the particular case of CAS's 2013–2014 jurisprudence I am not aware of any such evidence.

expect that those decisions – as a group of decisions with individual variations – are of comparable precedential value as the decisions that came before them and has had more time to be cited. Along this line of reasoning it seems from the data that the "proper" average level of indegree for CAS decisions is four. One can then infer from the data that it seems to take between six and eight years for CAS decisions to reach this level, this being the length of the "tail" during which CAS decisions' mean indegree drop from four to zero.

This would then seem to suggest that CAS generally tends[155] to cite new CAS decisions for about six to eight years, during which their indegree centrality rises until they have on average accumulated roughly four references. The data suggests that after these six to eight years, CAS moves its attention from those decisions, which it now cites to more or less the same extent as older decisions, to newer decisions.

It is uncertain why CAS seems to take this approach when it comes to referring to its previous decisions, but there are several, possibly co-contributing explanations for the observed tendencies. While it is difficult to rule out, it seems unlikely that it is the result of a formalized practice or some other conscious effort. If I were to interview individual arbitrators, I believe they would truthfully claim that they were not aware of these citation tendencies. Another possible but unlikely explanation is that the (collective) memory of CAS arbitrators is limited and that they have a hard time remembering decisions that are more than six or eight years old. However, if this was a relevant explanation, we would expect to find a clear inverse correlation between the number of decisions CAS delivers each year (which increases steadily) and average mean indegree centrality (which appears to be fairly stable). One final explanation is that the normative and institutional framework governing sports operates on six-to-eight-year cycles that become a more general pace of development.

References

Alter K J (1998) Who are the 'Masters of the Treaty'? European Governments and the European Court of Justice. International Organizations 52:121–147

Anderson J (2010) Modern Sports Law. Hart, Oxford

Arroyo M (2013) Arbitration in Switzerland: The Practitioner's Guide. Kluwer Law International, Alphen aan den Rijn

Benz J, Sternheimer W (2015) Expedited Procedures before the Court of Arbitration for Sport. CAS Bulletin 2015(1):6–11

Blackaby N, Partasides C, Redfern A, Hunter M (2015) Redfern and Hunter on International Arbitration, 6th edn. Oxford University Press, Oxford

---

[155] It is worth emphasizing that what we are measuring here is the CAS's general approach throughout its entire history to all of its decisions and which seems to follow rather specific patterns. However, if one were to study individual CAS decisions one should expect to find deviations from these patterns, sometimes quite extensive ones.

Blackshaw I (2006) Introductory Remarks. In: Blackshaw I, Siekman R, Soek J (eds) The Court of Arbitration for Sport 1984–2004. T.M.C. Asser Press, The Hague, pp. 1–5
Blackshaw I (2012) Introductory Remarks. In: Wild A (ed) CAS and Football: Landmark Cases. T. M.C. Asser Press, The Hague, pp. 5–10
Blackshaw I (2013a) ADR and Sport: Settling Disputes Through the Court of Arbitration for Sport, the FIFA Dispute Resolution Chamber, and the WIPO Arbitration & Mediation Center. Marquette Sports Law Review 24(1):1–57
Blackshaw I (2013b) CAS 92/A/63, Gundel v. FEI. In Anderson J (ed) Leading Cases in Sports Law. T.M.C. Asser Press, The Hague pp. 65–74
CAS (1991) Guide to Arbitration. http://sportrecht.org/cms/upload/10verbands/CASguideArbitration.pdf. Accessed 7 September 2018
CAS (2016) Statistics 2016. http://www.tas-cas.org/fileadmin/user_upload/CAS_statistics_2016_.pdf. Accessed 7 September 2018
Casini L (2011) The Making of Lex Sportiva by the Court of Arbitration for Sport. German Law Journal 12(5):1317–1340
Cavalieros P, Kim J (2015) Can the Arbitral Community Learn from Sports Arbitration? Journal of International Arbitration 32(2):237–260
Coccia M (2013) International Sports Justice: The Court of Arbitration for Sport. European Sports Law Bulletin 2013(1):23–76
Cornelius S (2013) CAS 2008/A/1480 Pistorius v. IAAF. In: Anderson J (ed) Leading Cases in Sports Law. T.M.C. Asser Press, The Hague, pp. 229–238
Craig P (2001) The Jurisdiction of the Community Courts Reconsidered. In: de Búrca G, Weiler J (eds) The European Court of Justice. Oxford University Press, Oxford, pp. 177–214
de Weger F (2016) The Jurisprudence of the FIFA Dispute Resolution Chamber. T.M.C. Asser Press, The Hague
Derlén M, Lindholm J (2017) Peek-a-boo, It's a Case Law System. German Law Journal 18 (3):647–686
Duval A (2015) La Lex Sportiva Face au Droit de l'Union Européenne: Guerre et Paix dans l'Espace Juridique Transnational. Academic thesis, European University Institute, Florence
Fowler J, Jeon S (2008) Authority of Precedent. Social Network 30:16–30
Gardiner S, O'Leary J, Welch R, Boyes S, Naidoo U (2012) Sports Law. 4th edn. Routledge, Oxon
Jacob M (2014) Precedent and Case-Based Reasoning in the European Court of Justice. Cambridge University Press, Cambridge
James M (2013) Sports Law. 2nd edn. Palgrave Macmillan, Basingstoke
Kane D (2003) Twenty Years On: An Evaluation of the Court of Arbitration for Sport. Melbourne Journal of International Law 4:611–635
Kaufmann-Kohler G, Rigozzi A (2015) International Arbitration: Law and Practice in Switzerland. Oxford University Press, Oxford
Kinsella S, Duke A (2014) Who are the Real Winners and Losers in the General Court? Competition Policy International Europe Column. http://www.competitionpolicyinternational.com/who-are-the-real-winners-and-losers-in-the-general-court. Accessed 6 June 2018
Kleinberg J M (2000) The Small-World Phenomenon: An Algorithmic Perspective. Proceedings of the Thirty-Second Annual ACM, pp. 163–170
Kwak H, Lee C, Park H, Moon S (2010) What is Twitter, a social network or a news media? Proceedings of the 19th International Conference on the World Wide Web, ACM, pp. 591–600
Kye C (2015) A Quagmire of Delays at the European General Court: Any Escape? Maastricht Journal of European and Comparative Law 22(3):453–471
Leskovec J, Horvitz E (2008) Planetary-scale views on a large instant-messaging network. Proceedings of the 17th International Conference on the World Wide Web, ACM, pp. 915–924
Lupu Y, Voeten E (2011) Precedent in International Courts: A Network Analysis of Case Citations by the European Court of Human Rights. British Journal of Political Science 42:413–439
Mangan M (2009) The Court of Arbitration for Sport: Current Practice, Emerging Trends and Future Hurdles. Arbitration International 25(4):591–602

Mavromati D, Reeb M (2015) The Code of the Court of Arbitration for Sport: Commentary, Cases and Materials. Wolters Kluwer, Alphen aan den Rijn

McAuliffe W, Rigozzi A (2013) Sports Arbitration. The European, Middle Eastern and African Arbitration Review 2013:15–22

McLaren R (2006) CAS Advisory Opinions. In: Blackshaw I, Siekman R, Soek J (eds) The Court of Arbitration for Sport 1984–2004. T.M.C. Asser Press, The Hague, pp. 180–193

McLaren R (2011) The Court of Arbitration for Sport. In: Nafziger J, Ross S (eds) Handbook on International Sports Law. Edward Elgar Publishing, Cheltenham, pp. 32–64

Milgram S (1967) The Small World Problem. Psychology Today 1:61–67

Mitten M J, Davis T (2008) Athlete Eligibility Requirements and Legal Protection of Sports Participation Opportunities. Virginia Sports and Entertainment Law Journal 8:71–146

Mitten M J, Opie H (2010) 'Sports Law': Implications for the Development of International, Comparative, and National Law and Global Dispute Resolution. Tulane Law Review 85:269–322

Paulsson J (1993) Arbitration of International Sports Disputes. Arbitration International 9(4):359–369

Pinna A (2006) The Trials and Tribulations of the Court of Arbitration for Sport: Contribution to the Study of the Arbitration of Disputes Concerning Disciplinary Sanctions. In: Blackshaw I, Siekman R, Soek J (eds) The Court of Arbitration for Sport 1984–2004. T.M.C. Asser Press, The Hague, pp. 386–408

Prechal S (2016) The Many Formations of the Court of Justice: 15 Years After Nice. Fordham International Law Journal 39(5):1273–1288

Ravjani A (2009) The Court of Arbitration for Sport: A Subtle Form of International Delegation. Journal of International Media and Entertainment 2:241–284

Reilly L (2012) An Introduction to the Court of Arbitration for Sport (CAS) and the Role of National Courts in International Sports Disputes. Journal of Dispute Resolution 2012(1):63–81

Rigozzi A (2010) The recent revision of the Code of sports-related arbitration (CAS Code). Jusletter 13 September 2010

Schepel H, Blankenburg E (2001) Mobilizing the European Court of Justice. In: de Búrca G, Weiler J (eds) The European Court of Justice, Oxford University Press, Oxford, pp. 9–42

Scott J (2017) Social Network Analysis, 4th edn. Sage, London

Stone Sweet A, Brunell T (1998) Constructing a Supranational Constitution: Dispute Resolution and Governance in the European Community. American Political Science Review 92:63–81

Vaitiekunas A (2014) The Court of Arbitration for Sport: Law-making and the question of independence. Stämpfli Verlag, Bern

Viswanath B, Mislove A, Cha M, Krishna G (2009) On the evolution of user interaction in Facebook. Proceedings of the 2nd ACM Workshop on Online Social Networks, ACM, pp. 37-42

Watts D, Strogatz S (1998) Collective Dynamics of 'Small-World' Networks. Nature 393:440–442

Wise A, Meyer B (1997) International Sports Law and Business. Kluwer Law International, Boston

Wolbring G (2008) Oscar Pistorius and the future nature of Olympic, Paralympic and other sports. Scripted 5(1):139–160

Yi D (2006) Turning Medals into Metal: Evaluating the Court of Arbitration for Sport as an International Tribunal. Asper Review of International Business and Trade Law 6:289–341

Chapter 4
CAS Decisions as Precedent

Abstract To follow previous decisions or, differently stated, to adhere to precedent is a central element of the application and development of law in many legal orders where adherence to precedent upholds fundamental legal values. The role and use of previous awards as precedent in arbitration is more complex and arbitral precedent is a contested concept. At the same time, the question of whether and to what extent CAS jurisprudence functions as precedent is a central issue for understanding CAS and the development of lex sportiva. This chapter explores to what extent CAS decisions function as precedent in subsequent cases, both those that come before CAS and other sports dispute resolution bodies. The chapter also explores CAS's reliance on unpublished decisions as precedent.

4.1 Precedent and Non-arbitrary Arbitration

Mitten and Opie have identified a number of research questions concerning the Court of Arbitration for Sport (CAS) and its case law that they suggest ought to be answered. One of these questions concerns precedent: "Is CAS jurisprudence functioning as a de facto body of common law legal precedent?"[1] This question is directly relevant for the establishment of lex sportiva: a legal order based on the rule of law requires for its legitimacy the consistent and foreseeable application of general norms and that cases are decided alike, at least as far as possible.[2] This chapter hopes to provide a contribution towards answering this question.

Relying on precedent can be understood as the act of being guided by an earlier decision when making a subsequent decision in a situation that is sufficiently similar and therefore relevantly comparable to the previous situation.[3] Thus, in a

---

[1] Mitten and Opie 2010, p. 291. As discussed below, the term "de facto" is highly important in this context.

[2] See Dworkin 2016, e.g. pp. 217–225.

[3] Of course, no two real-world situations are identical. The problem of distinguishing between relevant and irrelevant factual differences is a key issue with using precedent. See e.g. Alexy 2011, p. 275; Gascón 2012, p. 35.

J. Lindholm, *The Court of Arbitration for Sport and Its Jurisprudence*,
ASSER International Sports Law Series,
https://doi.org/10.1007/978-94-6265-285-9_4

general sense, "[t]o follow a precedent is to draw an analogy between one instance and another."[4] This also describes the practice of appealing to precedent outside the legal realm,[5] and reliance on precedent can be described as "a fundamental feature of any orderly decision process."[6]

But the discussion here is limited to courts and other judicial bodies following previous decisions. When used in this context, the term precedent can refer either to an entire previous decision or more narrowly to a *ratio decidendi*.[7] Like precedent, *ratio decidendi* can be understood in different ways,[8] and is a contested concept.[9] However, a simple yet appropriate definition of the concept is "the minimum rule… necessary to explain the outcome of the case."[10]

While this chapter focuses on CAS decisions as precedent, it will be drawing on scholarship studying and making comparisons with how precedent is used in national courts, international courts, and arbitration. Such an examination reveals that precedent is a more complex concept than the simple description presented above suggests. Many questions relating to precedent lack clear and undisputed answers. This is true even within single legal orders with considerable experience with precedent.[11] Such problems seem to some extent inherent and unavoidable when one seeks to make a decision by drawing conclusions from previous decisions.[12]

Such an examination also reveals significant differences between legal orders in terms of the normative doctrines and theories regarding whether and to what extent judicial bodies ought to follow precedent, that which we can call *de jure* precedent. One aspect where one can find differences between different systems concerns to what extent judges are expected to follow prior decisions, that is the relative (normative) level of bindingness of precedent and the theoretical basis for such doctrines. For example, in legal systems belonging to the common law family, the concept of precedent is intrinsically connected with the doctrine of *stare decisis*.[13]

---

[4] Duxbury 2008, p. 2.

[5] Schauer uses the illustrative example of "the child who insists that he should not have to wear short pants to school because his older brother was allowed to wear long pants when he was seven." Schauer 1987, p. 572. Cf. Alexander 1989, pp. 5–6 (describing this as an example of "the natural model of precedent").

[6] Schreuer and Weiniger 2008, p. 1189. See e.g. OG 96/001, *US Swimming v. FINA*, paras 13–16 (holding the IOC to a flexible practise to allow formally deficient entries).

[7] Chiassoni 2012, p. 14 (referring to these as precedent-judgment and precedent-holding respectively).

[8] See Ibid., pp. 17–22.

[9] Douglas 2010, p. 107.

[10] Landes and Posner 1976, p. 250.

[11] See e.g. Hart 2012, pp. 134–135 (discussing the theory of precedent under English law).

[12] As Hart explains, the legal use of precedent is communication by example and as such "may leave open ranges of possibilities, and hence of doubt." Ibid., pp. 124–125 (p. 125 quoted).

[13] Common law's influence on the theory of precedent is so extensive that examples of adherence to precedent that deviates from the common law model risk being overlooked.

Selecting a particular doctrine or theory of precedent as a point of departure and focusing too narrowly on that doctrine or theory risks leading to missing or excluding relevant models of adherence to precedent. For example, previous decisions frequently guide subsequent decision making even in legal orders that do not adhere to a principle of *stare decisis*. In practice, precedent is used in all systems, albeit to varying degrees.[14] There are different types of precedent.[15] Thus, rather than thinking of bindingness of precedent as a binary state (binding/non-binding) it is better to imagine a scale that ranges from, on one side, systems prohibiting precedent from having any relevance to, on the other side, systems where precedent is strictly binding without exception.[16] However, at the same time, the ways that judicial bodies in fact relate to precedent, which can be referred to as *de facto* precedent, can also differ significantly.

On the basis of these considerations, the examination of CAS decisions as precedent in this chapter takes a broad and practical approach to the concept of precedent. This is in line with Legum who defines precedent in two ways: from counsels' perspective as "any decisional authority that is likely to affect the decision in the case at hand" and from arbitrators' perspective as "any decisional authority that is likely to justify the award to the principal audience for that award."[17]

There is no single correct answer to why precedent ought to be followed and, if so, in what way and to what extent. Much intellectual effort and ink have been spent pondering the validity and strength of various arguments for and against adhering to precedent,[18] and it is not possible to do full justice to this discussion within the limits of this chapter. For the purpose of understanding and analyzing how CAS uses its prior decisions as precedent it is however motivated to briefly recap some of the main values that adherence to precedent seeks to promote.

A first reason for following previous decisions is that doing so contributes to the foreseeability of the law and its consistent application. The value of this in a legal order is so obvious that it hardly requires further explanation. It is a fundamental element of the rule of law that those who are governed by the law can determine their legal rights and obligations, thereby allowing them to adjust their behavior accordingly. In order for its subjects to be able to be ruled by the law, the law must be prospective, open, clear, and relatively stable.[19] It can be questioned whether law

---

[14] See e.g. Douglas 2010, p. 104; Guillaume 2011, p. 6.

[15] Cross and Harris 1991, p. 4.

[16] See Chiassoni 2012, pp. 27–33. Such a scale can be imagined even though one would be hard-pressed to find real-world examples at the extreme ends of that spectrum.

[17] Legum 2008, pp. 7–8. Other scholars have used similar functional definitions with only minor differences. For example, Stone Sweet et al. defines precedent as "accreted legal materials, issuing from prior awards, that counsel and arbitrators use as building blocks to construct frameworks for argumentation and justification." Stone Sweet et al. 2017, p. 582. Weidemaier considers that "arbitration generates precedent if awards have some observable relevance of the future conduct of system participants." Weidemaier 2010, p. 1901.

[18] See e.g. Duxbury 2008, pp. 150–182.

[19] Raz 2009, pp. 213–215. See also Schreuer and Weiniger 2008, p. 1189.

that severely fails in terms of predictability and consistency should even be considered law.[20] Adherence to precedent promotes the predictability and consistency of law. Also, viewed from a more practical perspective, the reason why we legally prescribe how individuals ought to behave is to influence their behavior, and this is only possible if the rules are clear and foreseeable. That courts interpret and apply the law in a consistent, foreseeable, and uniform manner allow others to direct their actions accordingly.[21]

Second, adherence to precedent can relatedly be viewed as protecting legitimate expectations. By establishing a precedent on a particular issue, a court gives rise to a public expectation of how that issue will be decided in the future and allows individuals to act accordingly. If the same issue arises in a future case, an individual that acted in reliance of that precedent will reasonably expect the deciding court to decide the issue in the same way as the preceding court.[22] This can be described as the backwards-looking flip-side of foreseeability. As one scholar opines, "reliance has always counted as an important consideration in the overruling calculus; indeed, the protection of reliance interests from judicial flip-flops is the doctrine's animating force."[23]

The more courts communicate that they will follow their previous decisions, the greater the public expectation that they will do so and the greater the interest in protecting such expectations. For example, when a CAS panel cites or otherwise indicates that it is following a previous decision in making its decision it signals that it considers that it ought to follow that previous decision. Doing this increases public expectations that future panels will decide similar cases in the same way. In this way, the citing panel makes it more difficult for future panels to deviate.[24] This reliance-expectation effect is not limited to individual decisions but also has system-wide consequences. When judicial bodies signal that they follow – and ought to follow – precedent when making decisions, most obviously by referring to individual previous decisions, they contribute to the perception that previous decisions constitute an important source of law that judicial bodies should follow and a general expectation that they will in fact do so.

Third, adherence to precedent is closely connected to general and equal application of law. That two situations where the relevant facts are the same ought to be decided in the same way is one of the most basic elements of fairness.[25] This applies

[20] See Fuller 1969, pp. 38–39.

[21] Gascón 2012, pp. 37–38. Cf. Hart 2012, p. 138.

[22] Cf. Weidemaier 2010, pp. 1926–1927. See also Legum 2008, p. 10 (defining a precedent from the public's perspective as "any decisional authority in which the factual and legal issues are sufficiently similar to the case at hand that the public reasonably expects the issues to be handled similarly.").

[23] Barrett 2003, p. 1061.

[24] Nafziger 2004, p. 3 ("An obvious purpose for developing a lex sportiva is to guide later awards and thereby stabilize expectations about arbitration of particular issues."). Cf. Ramberg 2017, pp. 80–81.

[25] Alexy 2011, p. 275 (discussing this in the context of the principle of universalizability).

in a clear and direct way to the use of precedent as adhering to precedent contributes to the equality and fairness of the legal system.[26] As Dworkin explains, "[t]he gravitational force of a precedent may be explained by appeal... to the fairness of treating like cases alike."[27]

A fourth and final major reason for following precedent is efficiency. It would require considerable time and resources for courts to consider every legal issue relevant in every single case "from scratch".[28] Thus, an argument can be made that adherence to precedent allows decision makers to benefit from the work performed by those who came before.[29] As formulated by a famous American jurist, "the labor of judges would be increased almost to the breaking point if every past decision could be reopened in every case, and one could not lay one's own course of bricks on the secure foundation of the courses laid by others who had gone before him."[30]

In the same way as national, regional, and international courts developing their jurisprudence promotes these values, so does CAS when it develops its jurisprudence. As explained by Nafziger, a "fully developed lex sportiva would help apply three values that the principle of *stare decisis* serves: efficiency of the legal process, predictability or stability of expectations, and equal treatment of similarly situated parties."[31]

It should finally be noted that it is not a given that arbitration awards are capable of constituting precedent in the same or a similar way as court decisions. An argument can be made that there are important differences between, on one hand, previous arbitration awards as precedent in arbitration systems (arbitration precedent) and, on the other, previous judgments as precedent in national and international courts (judicial precedent).

Historically, it was commonly held that arbitrators neither follow nor create precedent.[32] There are several reasons for this position, including the view that each arbitration is a unitary, ad hoc phenomenon without the capacity to create precedent. It has also been suggested that arbitrators may not enjoy the same legitimacy as judges to engage in norm making through precedent and that arbitrators may be reluctant to establish or rely upon precedent, at least explicitly, for fear of losing business.[33]

These expectations of how arbitration tribunals relate to precedent has come to be challenged on an empirical basis. It is undeniable that at least some arbitration

---

[26] See e.g. Alexander 1989, pp. 9–13.

[27] Dworkin 2013, p. 139.

[28] I.e. on the basis of statutes, general principles, preparatory works etc. and without consulting previous decisions.

[29] See e.g. Gascón 2012, p. 38; Schauer 1987, p. 599.

[30] Cardozo 1921, p. 149.

[31] Nafziger 2004, p. 3.

[32] See e.g. Bjorklund 2009, p. 1273; Weidemaier 2010, p. 1899. See also Kaufmann-Kohler 2007, p. 357 ("it is common knowledge that international arbitration lacks a doctrine of precedent, at least as it is formulated in the common-law system.").

[33] See Commission 2007, p. 135; Weidemaier 2010, pp. 1934–1938; Weidemaier 2012, p. 1092.

tribunals in recent years do in practice adhere to previous decisions, even if it should be noted that there are significant variations among different arbitration systems in this regard.[34] This supports this study taking a broad and practical approach to the concept of precedent when studying how CAS engages with its own previous decisions.

The remainder of this chapter is divided into five sections. The following two sections address the role of CAS decisions as horizontal and vertical precedent respectively. This distinction is inspired by legal orders that follow the doctrine of *stare decisis* and where the term horizontal precedent refers to courts following its own previous decisions or decisions by courts on the same hierarchical level,[35] and vertical precedent refers to courts following decisions by courts that are hierarchically superior to themselves. The main purpose of this distinction lies in that the level of constraint and the duty to follow previous decisions is generally greater, all else being equal, when they were rendered by superior courts.[36]

These concepts cannot be directly transferred to the context of CAS and its jurisprudence: CAS is not subject to the principle of *stare decisis*[37] and the hierarchical organization of sports dispute resolution bodies is different than for example courts belonging to the same national legal order.[38] For the purpose of analysis, it is nevertheless reasonable to distinguish between the role of CAS decisions as precedent in CAS itself (horizontal precedent) and in other sports dispute resolution bodies (vertical precedent). Whereas the horizontal dimension covers both establishment and use of precedent, as a continuous and circular process, the vertical dimension covers to what extent the precedent-making process within CAS affects other bodies in a discernable way.

Both the horizontal dimension and the vertical dimension approach CAS decisions as precedent from a backward-looking perspective, that is by focusing on how previous CAS decisions are relied upon in making more recent decisions. The subsequent section of this chapter reverses the perspective and examines how CAS from a forward-looking perspective in issuing a decision relates to the fact that it may be relied upon as precedent when future cases are settled. The second to last section addresses the practice of and problem with relying on unpublished

---

[34] See e.g. Bjorklund 2009, p. 1294 ("While it is axiomatic that decisions of international courts and tribunals do not have formal precedential value, it is nearly as axiomatic that such decisions often have a practical precedential value."); Commission 2007, pp. 150–151; Kaufmann-Kohler 2007, pp. 361–378; Stone Sweet et al. 2017, p. 573 (regarding investment disputes); Weidemaier 2010, pp. 1100. See also Ten Cate 2013, pp. 420–421. Authors disagree to what extent it is possible and desirable that arbitration tribunals establish systems of precedent. See e.g. Bjorklund 2009; Guillaume 2011; Kaufmann-Kohler 2007; Ten Cate 2013.

[35] These two are sometimes distinguished as self-precedent and horizontal precedent respectively. Gascón 2012, p. 36.

[36] See e.g. Barrett 2003, p. 1015; Schauer 2007, p. 385.

[37] See below Sect. 4.2.1.

[38] See below Sect. 4.3.

decisions. Based on the findings in the previous sections, the final section seeks to summarize and draw some general conclusions regarding CAS decisions as precedent.

4.2 Horizontal Precedent

4.2.1 What CAS Says: CAS on CAS Decisions as Precedent

The CAS Code is silent on the topic of whether CAS may, should, or must adhere to previous decisions, but most scholars agree that there is no formal principle of binding precedent that require CAS panels to adhere to precedent.[39] CAS has explicitly confirmed this in several decisions.[40] CAS also acts as if it is free to deviate from its jurisprudence. For example, in *Webster* the CAS panel declared that when calculating a club's damages when a player unilaterally terminates his or her employment contract without just cause, the employer "is not entitled to claim any part of the Player's alleged market value."[41] Later, in *Matuzalem*, while explicitly pointing out its cognizance of *Webster*, the panel held that "the loss of a possible transfer fee can be considered a compensable damage."[42] Finally, the right of arbitration panels to deviate from previous decisions has also been supported by the SFT.[43] Hence, it is undisputed that CAS is not formally bound to follow precedent.

But does CAS nevertheless consider itself to have a duty to follow its own previous decisions and, if so, to what extent? CAS has explicitly addressed the issue in five decisions. In these five decisions, CAS has consistently spoken out in favor

---

[39] See e.g. Casini 2011, p. 1331; Mavromati and Reeb 2015, p. 375; Nafziger 2004, p. 3 (making the conclusion based on the fact that "[a]rbitral awards are normally binding only in the cases and on the parties to which they are addressed."); Reilly 2012, p. 75; Rigozzi 2005, pp. 227–228. See however Kaufmann-Kohler 2007, p. 366, who argues for "the existence of a true *stare decisis* doctrine within the field of sports arbitration." However, by this the author appears to mean that CAS through its decisions are in practice creating rules and frequently, systematically, and increasingly cite its previous decisions. Kaufmann-Kohler 2007, pp. 365–366. Thus, "true *stare decisis*" does not seem to entail a doctrine of formal bindingness.

[40] See e.g. CAS 97/176, *UCI v. Jogert & NCF*, para 40, quoted in CAS 2008/A/1545, *Anderson*, para 53 (the decision is not publicly available); CAS 2004/A/628, *Young*, para 19; CAS 2008/A/1545, *Anderson*, para 55; CAS 2008/A/1574, *D'Arcy*, para 33.

[41] CAS 2007/A/1298, *Webster*, para 82.

[42] CAS 2008/A/1519-1520, *Matuzalem*, para 117. The *Matuzalem* panel did also note that there was pre-*Webster* case law supporting its decision. Ibid. para 117 and n. 16.

[43] SFT's decision 9 October 2012 in 4A_110/2012 (*Paulissen*), para 3.2.2 ("les arbitres, dont le pouvoir résulte essentiellement de la volonté des parties, ne rendent pas des sentences dont les solutions s'imposeraient nécessairement à un autre tribunal arbitral appelé à trancher la même question, de sorte qu'il paraît difficile, en théorie du moins, de considérer la jurisprudence arbitrale comme étant une source du droit de l'arbitrage.").

of following its own previous decisions, but if one considers them in order, one can notice that its position on this issue has developed somewhat over time.

The first time that CAS explicitly addressed the issue, as far as I have been able to determine, was in its decision in *Cullwick* in 1997. The case concerned an asthmatic water polo player, Cullwick, who tested positive for Salbutamol in connection with the 1995 Junior Men's Water Polo World Championship. Salbutamol was the active ingredient in the inhaler that he had been prescribed by his doctor. According to FINA's rules, the use would not have constituted a doping violation had Cullwick declared it in advance since it served "bona fide, medically sanctioned, therapeutic purposes."[44] The central issue was whether the absence of a declaration as such caused the use to constitute a doping violation. One year earlier, CAS had addressed that issue in a factually similar case, *Lehtinen*.[45] The *Cullwick* panel noted that while it was not bound to follow *Lehtinen*, it was "disposed to do so, both out of a sense of comity and because of the desirability of consistent decisions of the CAS, unless there were a compelling reason, in the interest of justice, not to do so."[46] CAS did not stress many of the values traditionally associated with a system of precedent,[47] and to use comity as an argument to support adherence to precedent is unusual.

CAS addressed the issue again one year later, in 1998, in the case of *Jogert*:[48]

> [t]he Panel feels that CAS rulings form a valuable body of case law and can contribute to strengthen legal predictability in international sports law. Therefore, although not binding, previous CAS decisions *can, and should, be taken into attentive consideration* by subsequent CAS panels, in order to help developing legitimate expectations among sports bodies and athletes.

The decision in *Jogert* adds to *Cullwick* and clarifies that CAS is not only able to consider its previous decisions when deciding cases, but that it is desirable that it does so. The quoted section of *Jogert* makes it clear that this normative position rests on the twin interests of predictability and legitimate expectations that are frequently relied upon in promoting adherence to precedent.[49] However, it is not clear what more specifically a duty of "attentive consideration" entails. It does not follow from the quoted section that CAS has a duty to follow precedent or to explain itself if it decides to deviate from its previous decisions, merely that it has a duty to consider previous decisions.

CAS returned to the issue six years later in *Young* where it concluded that it "will obviously *try*, if the evidence permits, to come to the same conclusion on matters of

---

[44] CAS 96/149, *Cullwick*, para 18.

[45] CAS 95/142, *Lehtinen*, para 20.

[46] CAS 96/149, *Cullwick*, para 22. CAS went on to conclude that no such compelling reason existed in the case at hand.

[47] See above Sect. 4.1.

[48] CAS 97/176, *Jogert*, para 40, quoted in CAS 2008/A/1545, *Anderson*, para 53 (the decision is not publicly available, emphasis added).

[49] See above Sect. 4.1. *Jogert* differs somewhat from *Cullwick* in this regard.

law as a previous CAS Panel."[50] It is not clearly stated in *Young* why CAS will try to follow precedent.[51] It seems to be either "a matter of comity, or an attempt to build a coherent corpus of law," but the *Young* panel explicitly declined to examine this issue in greater detail.[52] The ambition to follow previous decisions articulated in *Young* can arguably be viewed as a more stringent standard of adherence to precedent compared to the attentive-consideration-standard expressed in *Jogert*. However, *Young* still does not suggest that CAS is under any normative duty to follow precedent, not even a weak one. *Cullwick*, *Jogert*, and *Young* can in this regard be distinguished from CAS's subsequent decisions on the matter.

In *D'Arcy*, decided in 2008, CAS stated "that subsequent panels *should not* take a different approach to that adopted by earlier panels unless satisfied that the approach or view of the earlier panel is an erroneous one or is inapplicable because of different circumstances or different contractual language."[53] Unlike the decisions already discussed, *D'Arcy* contains a normative statement on the issue of adherence to precedent: while CAS is not bound to follow precedent, it ought to do so.[54] *D'Arcy* goes further and defines the two situations when it would be acceptable for CAS not to follow a previous decision, these being when the previous decision was erroneously decided and when it is distinguishable from the case at hand. The rationale for this view is also slightly different from those previously expressed, at least those expressed in *Young*. The values supporting the position laid out in *D'Arcy* are certainty and consistency. Both the standard and the reasons laid out in *D'Arcy* resemble those found in many legal orders.[55] *D'Arcy* is however not quite as clarifying as it may first seem. *D'Arcy* specifically concerned precedent relating to provisions of the CAS Code and there is nothing in the decision indicating one way or the other whether the same standard applies to CAS decisions as precedent generally.

CAS most recently addressed the issue of adherence to precedent in *Anderson*, which is also its most illuminating decision on the matter. *Anderson* concerned whether the United States' women's relay teams should forfeit medals won at the 2000 Sydney Olympic Games as a consequence of one of its members, Marion Jones, being disqualified for a doping violation.[56] CAS had examined this issue in a previous case with very similar facts[57] and concluded that an individual team

---

[50] CAS 2004/A/628, *Young*, para 19 (emphasis added).

[51] Nor is it, at least to me, obvious.

[52] Ibid., para 19. *Young* here appears to speak to the above-quoted section in CAS 96/149, *Cullwick*, para 22.

[53] CAS 2008/A/1574, *D'Arcy*, para 33 (emphasis added). It is worth noting that the panel subsequently emphasized that while its conclusion was the same as previous decisions, it arrived at it though independent reasoning. Ibid., para 34.

[54] Ibid., para 33.

[55] See above Sect. 4.1.

[56] The case is presented in greater detail in Sect. 7.2.

[57] Both cases concerned U.S. relay teams' forfeiture of medals in Olympic Games following the suspension of an individual team member for a doping violation after the competition.

member's disqualification does not result in a team forfeiture.[58] A key question in *Anderson* was to what extent the *Anderson* panel was bound by that previous decision.

CAS in *Anderson* quoted with approval the reasoning in *Jogert* and *Young*[59] and formulated for itself the most stringent duty to follow precedent thus far:[60]

> Therefore, although a CAS panel in principle might end up deciding differently from a previous panel, it *must accord to previous CAS awards a substantial precedential value* and it is up to the party advocating a jurisprudential change to submit persuasive arguments and evidence to that effect. Accordingly, the CAS 2004/A/725 award is a very important precedent and the Panel will draw some significant guidance from it.

It follows from *Anderson*, like *D'Arcy* before it, that CAS can deviate from precedent that it finds erroneously decided.[61] However, *Anderson* establishes a presumption that previous decisions are correctly decided, places the burden of showing an error and need for change on the party claiming so, and, in the absence of such showing,[62] expects CAS to be "significantly guided" by previous decisions.

This is supported by the fact that CAS will generally "take care to distinguish earlier cases if their decision is going in a different direction."[63] There are examples of CAS explaining why it is not appropriate to follow certain previous decisions, either because the *ratio decidendi* of the previous decision does not apply to the present case or because the underlying facts are materially different.[64] It would be unnecessary for CAS to justify why it is not following previous decisions unless it has some obligation to consider them in the first place. Thus, the fact that CAS takes care to distinguish previous decisions indicates that it perceives that it has a duty to consider previous decisions and to explain why it is not following them.

4.2.2 What CAS Does: Habit of Adherence

In their study of the Supreme Court of the United States (SCOTUS), Fowler and Jeon use the portion of all decisions that cite at least one previous decision as an

---

[58] CAS 2004/A/725, *USOC v. IOC & IAAF*. It is a curious coincidence that the disqualified athlete concerned in *USOC v. IOC & IAAF* is Jerome Young, the defendant in CAS 2004/A/628, *Young* discussed above.

[59] It appears circular that CAS followed previous decisions in deciding to what extent it should follow previous decisions. The circularity is lessened somewhat, but only somewhat, by the statement "the Panel shares the view of other CAS panels," indicating that the *Anderson* panel's conclusion is not exclusively based on previous decisions.

[60] CAS 2008/A/1545, *Anderson*, para 55.

[61] While not explicitly stated in *Anderson*, unlike in *D'Arcy*, it follows from the very nature of precedent that CAS is not required to follow a decision in a distinguishable situation.

[62] As was the case in *Anderson*. CAS 2008/A/1545, *Anderson*, para 61.

[63] Reilly 2012, p. 75.

[64] See e.g. CAS 98/218, *Hall*, para 8; CAS 2004/A/690, *Hipperdinger*, para 42.

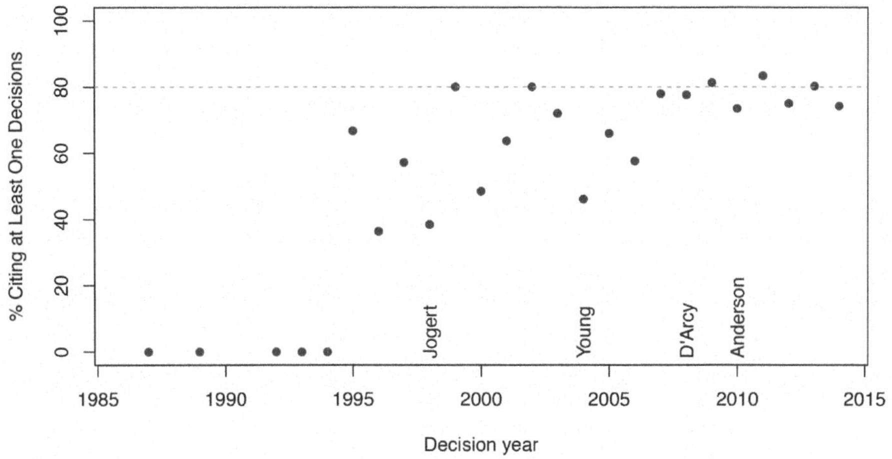

Fig. 4.1 Percentage of Decisions Citing at Least One Decision (Color figure online). [*Source* The author]

indication of the growing strength of *stare decisis*. They argue that if the principle of *stare decisis* is strengthened over time, the portion of decisions that cite previous decisions should increase.[65] It is questionable whether this measurement is capable of capturing whether judges are bound to follow prior decisions in the normative sense (*de jure*) as associated with the principle of *stare decisis*. It does however reflect to what extent judges actually (*de facto*) follow previous decisions. This is the reason why a number of scholars studying arbitral precedent have used this measurement.[66] The measurement reveals whether arbitrators are in the habit of referring to previous decisions. Furthermore, if arbitrators exhibit a clear and consistent habit of citing a particular type of source, this reasonably reflects their understanding of what constitutes an appropriate and persuasive methodology. In this manner, measuring the portion of decisions citing previous decisions is capable of empirically capturing many key aspects of adherence to precedent.

In studying the collected decisions, we find that the portion of CAS decisions that cite previous decision has increased over time.[67] However, even more striking is CAS's increased consistency in citing decisions.

The development can be divided into three rather distinct periods. The first period lasts until 1995 before which CAS did not cite its previous decisions. The second period begins in 1995 and ends in 2006. During this period, the portion of decisions that cited previous decisions varies greatly from 40 to 80 percent on a year-to-year basis and there is no discernable trend. For example, when *Jogert* and *Young* were

---

[65] Fowler and Jeon 2008, p. 19 (studying the United States Supreme Court).

[66] See e.g. Commission 2007, pp. 149–150; Kaufmann-Kohler 2007, pp. 365–366; Weidemaier 2012, p. 1125.

[67] See above Fig. 4.1 *Percentage of Decisions Citing at Least One Decision.*

decided in 1998 and 2004, 38 and 46 percent respectively of all CAS decisions cited previous decisions. However, during the surrounding years those numbers were in the 70–80 percent range. The third, more stable period, during which *D'Arcy* and *Anderson* were decided, begins in 2007 and stretches until the end of the studied period. Since 2007, CAS has cited previous decisions in roughly 80 percent of its decisions and it has done so with an almost remarkable consistency.

These findings confirm Kaufmann-Kohler's observation in 2006 of "a strong evolution towards reliance" on previous decisions within CAS.[68] However, the data shows no continuation of that trend after 2007. Rather, the data shows that CAS then hit what, at least for now, appears to constitute a ceiling citation rate of 80 percent. CAS has not deviated from that mark by more than a few percentage points over the last seven years of the studied time period. There is no obvious explanation why such a ceiling should exist.[69] For example, there are hardly any discernable differences based on subject matter that may help explain the findings.[70]

On the contrary, one would expect this number to increase as CAS's body of jurisprudence increases in size. We can reasonably assume that the number of cases of first impression, where no relevant and citable previous decisions exist, appearing before CAS would decrease as its body of jurisprudence grows.[71] While the average number of decisions cited by CAS has risen with the number of decisions rendered and has increased to do so after 2007,[72] the same is not true for the portion of decisions citing at least one previous decision. The correlation between the mean number of previous decisions cited[73] and the portion of decisions citing previous decisions in a given year is generally low. However, in years when CAS has on average cited four previous decisions or more it has consistently cited previous decision in around 80 percent of its decisions.[74]

It is not immediately obvious whether 80 percent is a low or high number. It is clearly higher than in most other arbitration systems. For example, it has been found that of arbitration awards applying the Vienna Sales Convention and arbitration awards published by the International Chamber of Commerce (ICC), only 6 and 15 percent respectively contained references to prior awards.[75] Similarly, a study of labor-related arbitration found that roughly 25 percent of all awards cited at least one previous award.[76] Thus, the rate of references to previous decisions in CAS is

---

68 Kaufmann-Kohler 2007, p. 365.

69 However, as discussed immediately below, it does appear to be a pattern that many institutions share.

70 The sole exception are decisions concerning Eligibility which cite previous decisions 48% since 1985 and 54% since 2007.

71 See Sect. 3.3.

72 After 2007, the mean outdegree has varied between 2.9 and 5.4.

73 Also known as mean outdegree.

74 See below Fig. 4.2 *Mean Outdegree and Percent Citing Previous Decisions.*

75 Kaufmann-Kohler 2007, p. 362.

76 Weidemaier 2012, p. 1125. This varied significantly depending on the type of dispute.

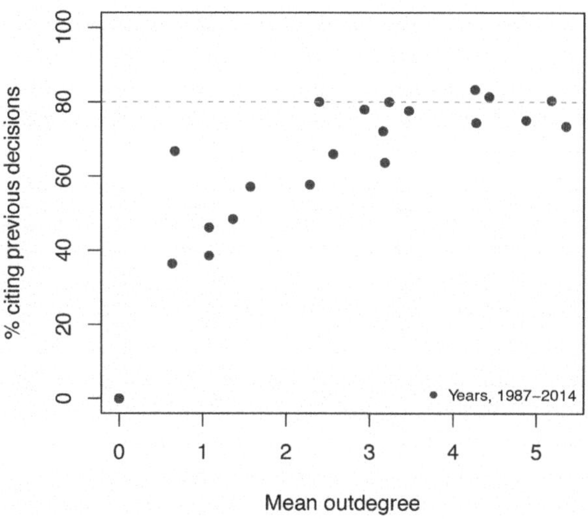

Fig. 4.2 Mean Outdegree and Percent Citing Previous Decisions (Color figure online). [*Source* The author]

significantly higher than in those bodies. CAS's citation rate is however quite comparable to that of the private bodies that are associated with ICANN and that resolve domain name disputes. These have been found to refer to its previous decisions in 78 percent of its cases.[77] It is also comparable to the citation rate in arbitration awards and decisions by the International Centre for Settlement of Investment Disputes (ICSID).[78] However, CAS's 80 percent citation rate falls short of that of some courts that rely heavily on precedent. For example, SCOTUS cites previous judgments in more than 90 percent of its judgments and in some years that number is closer to 100 percent.[79] The same is true for the Court of Justice of the European Union (CJEU) in recent decades.[80]

One conclusion that can be drawn from this comparison is that previous decisions constitute an important source in CAS. Based on its consistent reliance on previous decisions in four out of five decisions and the fact that this generally holds true across subject matters,[81] one can conclude that CAS arbitrators in practice treat previous CAS decisions as a nearly indispensable source. This is evidence of a system of *de facto* arbitration precedent that challenges traditional thinking and distinguishes CAS from many arbitration bodies.

However, it must also be acknowledged that CAS is not unique or incomparable in this regard. There are other arbitration systems where previous decisions are cited to a comparable extent and there is room for further development before CAS

---

[77] Kaufmann-Kohler 2007, p. 367.

[78] Commission 2007, pp. 149–150.

[79] Fowler and Jeon 2008, p. 19. SCOTUS consistently exceeded 90% around 1900 and has remained at those levels with the exception of during the Warren Court (1953–1969). Ibid.

[80] Derlén and Lindholm 2017, pp. 669–670.

[81] Eligibility is however, as previously discussed, somewhat of an exception in this regard.

decisions attain the same level of indispensability as a source of law that case law enjoy under American and EU law. It also remains to be seen if CAS's use of previous decisions – as measured here – has peaked. Judging by the examples of SCOTUS and the CJEU, it seems common that the increase in citation rate slows down after reaching 80 percent and it may take CAS several decades to reach levels of 90 or 100 percent if it follows those courts' examples.[82]

The common law doctrine of *stare decisis* is frequently juxtaposed with the civil law doctrine of *jurisprudence constante* as an alternative model of precedent.[83] The essential element of the doctrine of *jurisprudence constante* is that while a court is not expected to adhere to a single, previous decision, it ought not to deviate from an established line of case law.[84] Scholars have used *jurisprudence constante* as a model for understanding how arbitration precedent works and how it should work.[85] In her study of doping-related CAS decisions in track and field, Bersagel concludes that CAS's adherences to its own prior decisions bares more resemblance to the civil law doctrine of *jurisprudence constante* than to the common law doctrine of *stare decisis*.[86] There are indeed examples of CAS decisions that can be understood as supporting this view,[87] and CAS will sometimes explicitly point to the existence of a *jurisprudence constante*.[88]

However, the existence of a consistent line of case law does not appear to be a condition for CAS to follow precedent. CAS appears perfectly willing to cite and follow a single decision, and even if it was recently decided.[89] This is for example evidenced by the average age of cited CAS decisions. The likelihood of a decision being cited peaks after only six months and then declines quite linearly. References

[82] Derlén and Lindholm 2017, p. 670.

[83] See e.g. Bersagel 2012 (regarding CAS); Bjorklund 2009, pp. 1294–1295 (regarding investment arbitration); Commission 2007, p. 132 (regarding investment arbitration).

[84] Cross and Harris 1991, pp. 10–11; Kaufmann-Kohler 2007, p. 360 (both noting that in most legal orders there are exceptions to this rule).

[85] See e.g. Bjorklund 2009, pp. 1294–1297 (regarding investment arbitration); Guillaume 2011, p. 23.

[86] Bersagel 2012, p. 206.

[87] See e.g. CAS 2007/A/1352, *Petacchi*, para 7.24.

[88] See e.g. CAS 2000/A/289, *UCI v. C. & FFC*, para 7.

[89] As discussed, there are findings consistent with CAS "chain-citing", i.e. that it cites only the most recent decision or decisions on a point where there are other, older decisions. See Sect. 3.2. If this is correct, it is possible that CAS adheres to a doctrine of *jurisprudence constante*, i.e. that it follows precedent when there is an established line of case law, but also to a practice of referring not to those of lines of case law but only the most recent decision. It is extremely difficult, if not impossible, to accurately capture CAS's use of precedent if it obscures it in this manner. It is however highly unlikely that this is the case. The main reason for referring to previous decisions is to legitimize the outcome in the present case and for CAS to more or less intentionally hide the existence of an established line of case law would be counterproductive for the purpose of legitimizing its decisions.

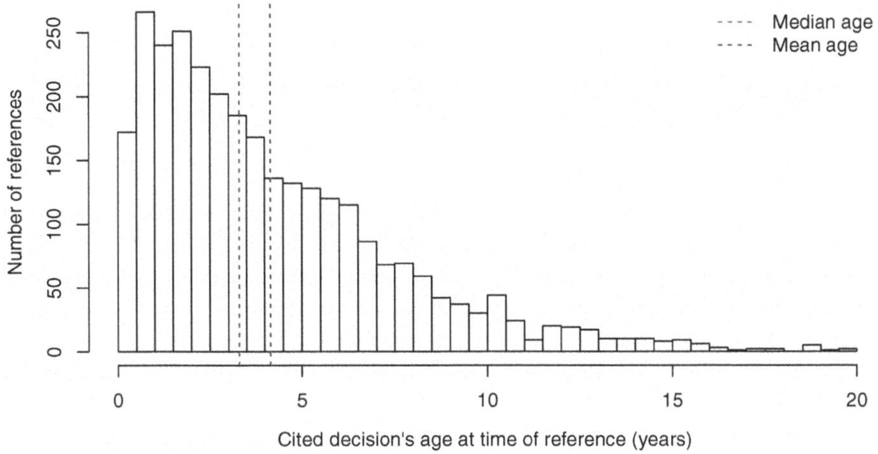

Fig. 4.3 Age Distribution of Cited Decisions. [*Source* The author]

to decisions that are older than ten years are quite rare.[90] This is not the pattern we would expect to see in a system where judicial bodies follow a doctrine of *jurisprudence constante*, at least in a strict sense. If courts only cited and adhered to decisions that belong to an established line of case law, we would expect to find that the age of cited decisions was more evenly distributed.

Consequently, when CAS points to the existence of a consistent line of case law it seems to constitute an additional argument for adhering to precedent rather than a condition for doing so.[91] This should not be misconstrued as that the existence of an established line of case law is irrelevant when it comes to adherence to precedent in CAS: the burden placed on a party that seeks to convince CAS from deviating from previous decisions increases with the length and consistency of previous decisions on the matter.

Such an approach also makes sense considering the values that adherence to precedent seeks to promote. On one hand, the efficiency gains that follow from relying on previous courts' work is the same regardless of whether and how many times it has been upheld. However, the longer the line of case law, the greater the public reliance and the need to protect those who have adjusted their behavior accordingly.[92]

[90] See above Fig. 4.3 *Age Distribution of Cited Decisions*.

[91] See e.g. CAS 2013/A/3411, *Bresciano*, para 103. It should however be noted that this concerned the calculation of damages following a player breach of contract without cause, an issue on which there had been conflicting case law. See above Sect. 4.2.1.

[92] See above Sect. 4.1.

4.2.3 De Facto *Stare Decisis*

As shown above, CAS's use of its own previous decisions has not been static but has developed significantly over time. Consequently, we should take care to clarify that the discussion here focuses on the role of previous decisions as horizontal precedent in recent years, particularly after 2007.

First, in line with CAS's consistent position it is clear that previous decisions do not constitute binding precedent,[93] at least if we by this mean that CAS is normatively constrained in the sense that it must either follow or distinguish previous decisions and that a decision that fails to do so is unlawful.[94] There is no legal principle of formal bindingness that mandates that CAS panels respect the bindingness of previous decisions and that failure to follow precedent constitutes grounds for challenge.[95]

However, at the same time, it is also clear that previous decisions are not non-binding or merely persuasive in a sense that may for example be said of scholarly work.[96] If adherence to a previous decision was exclusively a function of the persuasive quality of its reasoning,[97] it would be irrelevant whether that reasoning appeared in a previous CAS decision or in a scholarly work. It follows clearly from both what CAS expresses regarding to what extent it ought to adhere to precedent[98] and empirical observations of how CAS actually relates to precedent[99] that this is not the case and that it finds itself more strongly compelled to be guided by previous CAS decision. CAS is in this regard not entirely dissimilar from the CJEU who, although normatively free to disregard them, in practice generally and frequently both cites and adheres to its previous decisions.[100]

This can be understood against the backdrop of the American discussion regarding the constraining force of precedent on precedent as a duty for courts to follow previous decisions even if they were incorrectly decided.[101] Such an

---

[93] See above Sect. 4.2.1.

[94] MacCormick and Summers 1997, pp. 554–555; Schauer 1987, pp. 592–593.

[95] Chiassoni 2012, p. 27.

[96] I intentionally avoid using the term "persuasive authority". Compare Bersagel 2012, p. 195; Reilly 2012, p. 75 (characterizes CAS's previous decisions as persuasive authority). The reason for this is that the term is used as the opposite of "binding authority" and both can be and frequently is understood as a content-dependent, non-binding authority. See Schauer 2008a, p. 1940. The term and the associated dichotomy is inappropriate as it obscures many relevant nuances. Cf. Bhala 1999, pp. 918–919.

[97] This could be characterized as a content-dependent reason for adherence. Cf. Schauer 2008a, p. 1935.

[98] See above Sect. 4.2.1.

[99] See above Sect. 4.2.2.

[100] Cross and Harris 1991, p. 17. The same can be said about investment tribunals. Schreuer and Weiniger 2008.

[101] See e.g. Alexander 1989; Nelson 2001; Schauer 2008b. This can be described as the content-independent authority of precedent. Cf. Schauer 2008a, pp. 1935–1936.

approach highlights the relevant question of what distinguishes (at least certain) previous decisions from other sources in terms of authority.[102] It follows from the discussion above that CAS considers that it ought to adhere to previous decisions, not exclusively because they agree with their substance but also because of the nature of the source. Thus, previous decisions enjoy content-independent authority in CAS, something that legislation and sport rules have but that scholarly work generally lacks.[103]

As discussed above, the duty to adhere to precedent is not the result of a formal normative doctrine. Casini has noted that CAS panels "demonstrate a consistent deference to [and] tend to follow their own prior 'jurisprudence'" in a way that is similar to international courts and tribunals and fittingly refers to this as an "informal but consistent rule of precedent."[104] Guillaume explains that adherence to precedent is necessary "in new branches of law where the norm is yet uncertain."[105] This may help explain the finding that precedent is a seemingly indispensable source of law in CAS. While it has developed greatly over the last decades, (international) sports law must still be characterized as a new legal order containing many uncertain norms.

To better understand the role of previous decisions as precedent we can use the distinction between *de jure stare decisis* and *de facto stare decisis* proposed by Bhala. Under both of these concepts there is an obligation to adhere to precedent and neither is non-binding in the sense that precedent has a merely persuasive force. However, whereas under *de jure stare decisis* the obligation to adhere is based in law, *de facto stare decisis* means that "the adjudicator has an institutional memory and *puts it to work at every, or almost every, opportunity*."[106] This description fits quite well the findings made in this chapter and by previous scholars studying how CAS relates to its previous decisions as precedent.[107]

The difference between CAS and the role that previous decisions play as precedent in other systems does not seem fundamental. There are few examples of judicial bodies that are absolutely bound to follow previous decisions, in law and in practice.[108] A general account that can be used to describe the *de facto* situation in most systems is that while it is possible to depart from precedent they are respected "as a matter of principle" and anyone proposing a departure has a "burden of

---

[102] Cf. Hart 2012, p. 136.

[103] Of course, the room for deviating from a rule found in a statute is significantly smaller than for a rule established in precedent.

[104] Casini 2011, p. 1331.

[105] Guillaume 2011, p. 23.

[106] Bhala 1999, pp. 936–941 (studying precedent in international trade law), p. 941 quoted (emphasis added).

[107] Cf. Schreuer and Weiniger 2008, p. 1196 (concluding that "a *de facto* practice of precedent certainly exists" in investment tribunals).

[108] The law of England between 1898, the decision in *London Street Tramways Co Ltd v. London County Council* [1898] AC 375, and 1966, the Practice Statement, is arguably the most stringent doctrine of binding precedent.

argument" and must present "sufficiently good reasons" for doing so.[109] This description seems to capture quite well the standard articulated by CAS in *Anderson*.[110] While what constitutes sufficiently good reasons may differ, this description fundamentally captures the situation in most legal orders and can also be applied to the role of CAS's jurisprudence as precedent.

4.3 Vertical Precedent

CAS's adherence to its own prior decisions was discussed above and in that context characterized as horizontal precedent. This section examines whether and in what way other sports dispute resolution bodies[111] follow CAS's decisions. This will be referred to as *vertical precedent*, a term that implies that those other sports dispute resolution bodies are inferior in relation to CAS.[112] This is however not intended to indicate that those other bodies are under an obligation to obey the commands of CAS by merit of its authority in the way that the term vertical precedent may indicate in legal orders that adhere to the doctrine of *stare decisis*.[113] In the context of sports, the vertical ordering of sports adjudication bodies does not derive from a normative position that other bodies ought to obey CAS as a matter of principle but from the empirical observation that other bodies' decisions *de facto* are subject to review by CAS. Because of this, CAS decisions has a form of vertical precedential effect that arbitration awards normally lack.[114]

An obvious object of examination in this regard is the FIFA Dispute Resolution Chamber (FIFA DRC). There are several reasons for this. First, football-related disputes are by far the most common among all sports in CAS's jurisprudence and there is consequently a relatively large body of football-related CAS decisions.[115] In other words, the FIFA DRC has ample opportunities to consider and follow CAS's jurisprudence. Second, CAS is the appellate body of the FIFA DRC and has been so since 2002.[116] The risk of its decisions being overturned on appeal creates a clear and substantial incentive for the FIFA DRC to ensure that its decisions conform with CAS jurisprudence. Third and finally, as discussed in greater detail below, ICAS maintains a list of arbitrators that are specialized in and approved for resolving football-related disputes.[117] The use of specially qualified and selected

[109] Alexy 2011, p. 275.

[110] See above Sect. 4.2.1.

[111] For simplicity's sake henceforth referred to simply as "other bodies".

[112] See above Sect. 4.2.

[113] See e.g. Schauer 2008a, pp. 1935–1936.

[114] Cf. Weidemaier 2010, fn. 5.

[115] See Sect. 2.4.

[116] See Sect. 3.3.

[117] See Sect. 8.5.

arbitrators can reasonably be expected to result in decisions of high substantive quality and a judicial body's interest in considering and citing a previous decision will reasonably increase with its quality.[118]

In order to test the impact of CAS jurisprudence on the FIFA DRC, 2,332 English-language FIFA DRC decisions rendered between 2002 and 2017 were analyzed.[119] This examination reveals that roughly 30 percent of the FIFA DRC's decisions contain some form of reference to CAS's jurisprudence.[120] The portion of FIFA DRC decisions referring to CAS jurisprudence varies between individual years but has hovered around this level since 2005. It should however be noted that the term "reference" is in this context used broadly to include not only explicit references to specific CAS decisions but also, and more commonly to CAS jurisprudence in general.[121] This is less than half as frequently as CAS itself refers to its jurisprudence.[122] However, the fact that the FIFA DRC refers to CAS jurisprudence in about three out of ten decisions indicates that the former has an appreciable impact on the latter.

The process of analyzing what characterizes CAS decisions that are relied upon by the FIFA DRC is severely complicated by the fact that the FIFA DRC frequently makes sweeping references to CAS jurisprudence in general rather than to specific CAS decisions. References to specific CAS decisions are also sometimes concealed in the published versions of the FIFA DRC's decisions.[123]

---

[118] This is true even though, as discussed above, the binding nature of a precedent is not based on content-dependent factors.

[119] All decisions publicly available on the FIFA DRC's website (http://www.fifa.com/about-fifa/official-documents/governance/dispute-resolution-chamber.html) on 18 February 2018 were downloaded. However, due to the problem of ensuring accurate data extraction in a multi-language set, 343 non-English decision (predominantly decisions written in Spanish and French) were excluded from consideration. There were also some additional files that could not be processed. The texts of these decisions were extracted and processed, searching for (i) references to specific CAS decisions, (ii) more general references to CAS jurisprudence, and (iii) general references to the FIFA DRC's own jurisprudence. While the FIFA DRC, as discussed below, frequently refers to its own jurisprudence, it more rarely refers to its own individual decisions.

[120] As seen below in Fig. 4.4 *Percentage of FIFA DRC Decisions Referring to Jurisprudence* the portion of FIFA DRC decisions containing a reference to CAS jurisprudence in a given year varies between about 25 and 40%.

[121] See e.g. FIFA DRC decision of 10 December 2009, *Club C v. Player M & Club S*, para 37; FIFA DRC no. 4919, para 17; FIFA DRC decision of 6 May 2010, *Player M v. Club K.*, para 31; FIFA DRC decision 5 February 2010, *Player X v. Club FC-S*, para 35 (all regarding the concept of the specificity of sports and containing the same expression); FIFA DRC decisions of 23 January 2013, *Club F v. Club B*, para 22 ("the Chamber pointed out that, so far, both the Dispute Resolution Chamber as well as the CAS have adopted a strict approach").

[122] As discussed above in Sect. 4.2.2, CAS in recent years refers to its jurisprudence in 80% of its decisions.

[123] The published versions of FIFA DRC decisions sometimes refer to specific CAS decisions in an anonymized form that makes it difficult or impossible to determine which CAS decision the FIFA DRC refers to. See e.g. FIFA DRC decision of 10 December 2009, *Club C v. Player M & Club S*, para 16 ("As clearly stated in the award CAS 2008/X/XXXX FC S v/ Mr M & RZS &

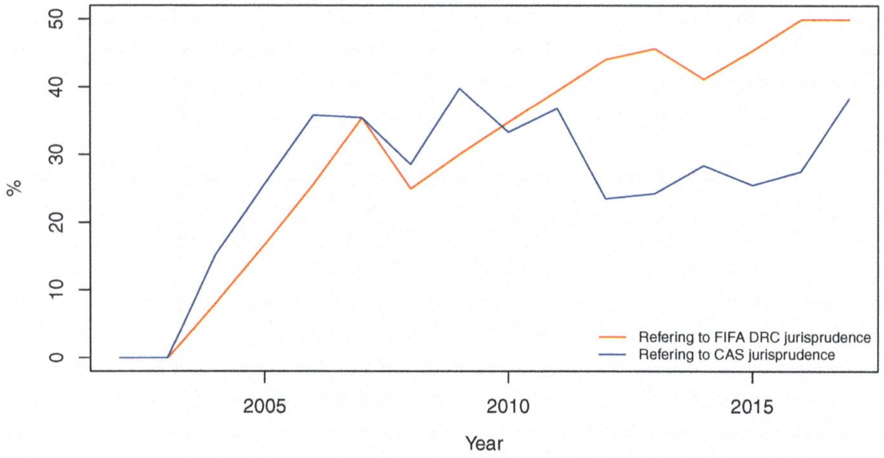

Fig. 4.4 Percentage of FIFA DRC Decisions Referring to Jurisprudence. [*Source* The author]

That being said, the available data provides a clear and unambiguous picture: all publicly available CAS decisions that the FIFA DRC explicitly cites in a legible form concern football-related disputes. With the caveat that the data is limited in these regards, it thus appears as if the FIFA DRC tends to exclusively consider football-related CAS decisions. It is conceivable that other sports adjudicatory bodies in the same way as the FIFA DRC primarily or exclusively consider CAS decisions that specifically relate to their sports. However, to determine if this is actually the case requires further examination of the jurisprudence of dispute resolution bodies in other sports.[124]

The CAS decision that is most commonly cited by the FIFA DRC is *Aston Villa v. B.93*.[125] In 2003, the English football club Aston Villa signed a three-year "Scholarship Agreement" with the Danish football player Magnus Troest. Under this agreement, Troest would train and play exclusively with Aston Villa, attend educational training provided by the club, and receive a weekly "Scholarship Allowance" and certain travel expenses. Troest had previously played for the Danish football club B.93 that requested that Aston Villa pay training compensation. The issue in the dispute that followed was whether Troest was an amateur, for which no training compensation would be given, or a non-amateur. CAS found that according to the FIFA Regulations for the Status and Transfer of Players (FIFA RSTP), the only criterion when classifying a player was whether he or she had received remuneration exceeding expenses actually incurred, which was the case

FIFA 2008/X/XXXX Mr M & RZS v/ FC S & FIFA…"); FIFA DRC decisions of 23 January 2013, *Club N v. Club R*, para 28 ("e.g. CAS 2006/X/XXXX").

[124] For at least one example where this was not the case, see Sect. 5.1.

[125] CAS 2006/A/1177, *Aston Villa FC v. B.93 Copenhagen*.

with Troest.[126] This is the point for which the decision is most commonly invoked by the FIFA DRC,[127] but the decision also addresses other issues pertaining to training compensation.[128]

Finally, it is interesting to note to what extent the FIFA DRC will adhere to its own previous decisions and whether it differs from how it treats CAS jurisprudence. While the FIFA DRC's tendency to refer to CAS jurisprudence has remained relatively stable over time, its tendency to refer to its own jurisprudence has increased steadily over time and in recent years such references appear in nearly half of the FIFA DRC's decisions.[129] Much like CAS, the FIFA DRC's increased adherence to precedent helps achieving FIFA's aim of enhancing uniformity, equality, and certainty within the field of football.[130] It does however detract from this development that the FIFA DRC relatively rarely refers to specific, named previous decisions and in most cases instead opts to refer to its body of jurisprudence in general.

The FIFA DRC will refer to its previous decisions using different expressions to signal to what extent it does or finds itself bound to follow those previous decisions. However, it is difficult to draw any clear conclusions from these statements regarding how it views the role of its previous decisions as precedent.[131] Like CAS,[132] the FIFA DRC will emphasize when its own jurisprudence is "well-established"[133] or "long-standing",[134] although it seems that the FIFA DRC more commonly than CAS points to the existence of an established line of case law. However, a single and/or recent decision do not appear irrelevant when the FIFA DRC decides a dispute.[135]

---

[126] Ibid., paras 30–31.

[127] See e.g. FIFA DRC decisions of 16 July 2009, *Club H v. Club M*, para 13; FIFA DRC decisions of 17 January 2014, *Club R v. Club G*, para 12; FIFA DRC decisions of 17 June 2016, *Club A v. Player C*, para 13.

[128] See e.g. FIFA DRC decision of 27 February 2014, *Club J v. Club P*, para 8.

[129] See above Fig. 4.4 *Percentage of FIFA DRC Decisions Referring to Jurisprudence*.

[130] See de Weger 2016, pp. 4–5.

[131] See e.g. FIFA DRC decision of 3 October 2008, *Club A v. Club O*, para 8 ("the Chamber recalled its jurisprudence applied in similar cases"); FIFA DRC decision of 28 March 2008, *Club AAA v. Club BBB*, para 11 ("the Chamber referred to its jurisprudence relating to the Solidarity Mechanism"); FIFA DRC decision of 30 August 2013, *Player L v. Club Y*, para 18 ("Such conduct constitutes, in line with the jurisprudence of the Chamber, a clear breach of contract.").

[132] See above Sect. 4.2.2.

[133] See e.g. FIFA DRC decision of 3 July 2008, *Club J v. Club A*, para 10; FIFA DRC decision of 3 September 2015, *Player A v. Club C*, para 19; FIFA DRC decision of 18 August 2016, *Club A v. Club C*, para 10.

[134] See e.g. FIFA DRC decision of 25 September 2015, *Player A v. Club C*, paras 15, 27; FIFA DRC decision of 3 September 2015, *Player A v. Club C*, para 11; FIFA DRC decisions of 8 September 2016, *Player A v. Club C*, para 23.

[135] See e.g. FIFA DRC decision of 19 February 2009, *Club B FF v. Club S*, para 26.

4.4 Looking Forward and Setting the Right Precedent

It is easy to think of precedent as mainly backwards-looking as much of the discussion regarding precedent tends to focus "on the use of yesterday's precedents in today's decision."[136] In line with this, the discussion in this chapter has thus far focused on the most overt manifestation of a system of precedent: references to previous decisions as support for a present decision.

However, decisions in the present can also be understood and approached from a forward-looking perspective as potential precedent for future cases.[137] What in the present constitutes a decision in a specific situation risks being interpreted as a general rule in the future.[138] To a body that is about to render a decision, the forward-looking aspect of precedent means having to consider what consequences a contemplated decision in the case at hand will have on future cases.[139] In choosing between different possible rulings, the decision maker must not only consider the outcome of the case in question, but also the outcome of hypothetical future cases where those deciding those cases will tend to adhere to the contemplated decision.[140] As elegantly expressed by Schauer, decision makers cannot shirk this responsibility by only focusing on the case at hand:[141]

> Today is not only yesterday's tomorrow; it is also tomorrow's yesterday. A system of precedent therefore involves the special responsibility accompanying the power to commit the future before we get there.

Obviously, the body that issues a decision does not fully control whether and how it will impact future decisions; the impact of a decision as a precedent is ultimately determined by subsequent decision makers when they decide whether to adhere to the decision. However, at the same time, the decision-making body is not completely powerless over its decision's function as precedent going forward. There are a number of strategies that the decision-making body can employ. For example, a decision-making body can enhance its decision's persuasive force and thereby increase the likelihood of it subsequently being adhered to by subsequent decision-makers by more extensively embedding the decision in existing jurisprudence.[142]

It can be argued that the responsibility of arbitrators to be forward-looking and consider the precedent they set when issuing an award is substantially different than that of a judge issuing a judgment. The foremost duty of an arbitrator is to perform

---

[136] Schauer 1987, p. 572.

[137] Llewellyn 1960, p. 26 (discussing the role of precedent in American law).

[138] Schauer 1987, pp. 572–575. Schauer uses the familiar example of a child extrapolating a general rule from his or her parents' previous decisions regarding bedtimes. Ibid., pp. 573–574.

[139] Llewellyn 1960, p. 26.

[140] See MacCormick 2003, pp. 105–116 (aptly describing this as rule-utilitarianism).

[141] Schauer 1987, pp. 572–573.

[142] Ten Cate 2013, p. 476.

the service that he or she was hired to perform: to resolve the dispute for which the arbitration tribunal was formed. As such, it is both natural and expected that arbitrators generally prioritize dispute resolution over precedent setting.[143]

CAS does however at least occasionally reveal that it is aware of the precedent-setting effect of its decisions and acts accordingly. One example of a strategy employed by CAS to limit a decision's unwanted precedential effect is to emphasize the exceptional nature of the facts. This sends a message that the panel does not intend to establish a general rule and enhances subsequent panels' ability to distinguishing their cases from the one decided.

An example of this can be found in *Puerta*. In connection with the 2005 French Open, Argentinian tennis player Mariano Puerta tested positive for small traces of etilefrine. CAS accepted Puerta's explanation that he had unknowingly consumed a small amount of the banned substance by drinking from a glass that his wife had used for her medicine but concluded that he had failed to exercise "utmost caution". This conclusion can be seen as the *Puerta* panel both respecting and taking responsibility for CAS decisions as precedent. The arbitrators could have modified or departed from CAS precedent defining what constitutes "utmost caution" in order to excuse Puerta, but doing so would have weakened existing precedent.

By adhering to its previous decisions, CAS put itself in a difficult position as it found that the applicable rules did not allow for a just and proportionate sanction.[144] According to the rules, Puerta was to receive a suspension not shorter than eight years, which in the panel's opinion in practice was tantamount to a lifetime ban. Even though the applicable anti-doping rules were clear, CAS found that it could depart from them as they contained a "gap" since they did not allow for a proportional sanction.[145] The *Puerta* panel also stated that it believed its conclusion to be consistent with the interests of the World Anti-Doping Agency (WADA) who, "as a responsible lawmaker," would not want "the WADC [World Anti-Doping Code] to be seen as an instrument of oppression and injustice…"[146] On those grounds, CAS reduced Puerta's suspension to two years.

CAS sought to limit the precedential impact of its decision by stating multiple times that the case at hand was exceptional; that it was unlike any previous case; that a similar case would likely never again arise; that it was fully in support of the standardized sanctions that the WADC provides; that "in all but the very rarest of cases" those sanctions are just and proportional; and that the ruling did not suggest that CAS panels enjoy discretion to set an appropriate penalty beyond what follows

---

[143] See Landes and Posner 1979, pp. 238–239; Ten Cate 2013, p. 474. One might possibly also argue that confidential arbitral awards, which are still common, are incapable of guiding future decisions and consequently have no forward-looking effect that arbitrators need to consider. However, as discussed immediately below, arbitrators do in fact rely on confidential prior awards.

[144] CAS 2006/A/1025, *Puerta*, paras 11.3–11.4, 11.7.

[145] In order to reach this conclusion, the *Puerta* panel used the threat of national courts overturning the decision and the resulting weakening of the rules as an argument. *Id.* paras 11.7.23–11.7.24.

[146] Ibid., para 11.7.32.

from the WADC.[147] The *Puerta* panel's strategy appears to have been successful. Subsequent panels have declined to apply the holding in *Puerta* in subsequent cases, distinguishing the circumstances of those cases as not being of the same exceptional nature as those in *Puerta*.[148]

4.5 Unpublished Decisions as Precedent

CAS frequently cites previous CAS decisions that are not publicly available. CAS decisions collected and analyzed in full text in this study contained a total of 3,039 individual references to previous CAS decisions. 577 of those references were to decisions not included in the dataset (out-of-network citations).[149] Thus, roughly one in five references made by CAS to previous decisions is to a decision that is not publicly available in a broad sense of the word.[150] All-in-all, the dataset contains references to 295 unique, non-publicly-accessible CAS decisions. This is made possible because parties have access to unpublished decisions, most obviously decisions in cases where they were a party, and CAS arbitrators have access to such decisions through CAS.[151]

An illustrative example of this practice is *Korneev & Gouliev*.[152] The case was decided by the CAS Ad Hoc Division created for the 1996 Olympic Games in Atlanta to settle a doping-related dispute. Two Russian athletes, Andrei Korneev and Zakhar Gouliev, had each won an Olympic bronze in their respective sports, swimming and wrestling, but subsequently tested positive for bromantan, a performance-enhancing substance that has properties of both steroids and stimulants, and works as a masking agent, and the International Olympic Committee (IOC) decided to remove the two athletes' medals. The principal question put before CAS was whether bromantan was a prohibited substance. The substance was not specifically listed and the key issue was therefore whether it could be considered to fall under the ban of "related substances". CAS found that the IOC had not proved to a sufficient degree of certainty that bromantan was comparable to explicitly banned substances. CAS therefore overturned the IOC's decisions against

---

147 Ibid., para 11.7, para 11.7.27 quoted. Most interestingly, the *Puerta* panel explicitly stated that "its decision does not weaken either the WADC or WADA" or "the war against doping." Ibid., paras 11.7.32–11.7.33. Of course, declaring this to be the case does not necessarily make it true.

148 See e.g. CAS 2006/A/1165, *Ohuruogu*, para 17; CAS 2008/A/1489 & 2008/A/1510, *Despres*, paras 7.19–7.20; CAS 2011/A/2364, *Butt*, paras 56–57, 73–75. See also Sect. 3.1 regarding CAS 2008/A/1480, *Pistorius*.

149 See also Sect. 1.6.

150 Regarding what in this context is considered publicly available, see Sect. 1.5.

151 Latty 2007, pp. 262–263 (discussing this as a factor that contributes to the coherence of CAS jurisprudence).

152 CAS OG/96/003 & 004, *Korneev & Gouliev v. IOC*. Sometimes also referred to as the bromantan decision.

Korneev and Gouliev.[153] However, in deciding the case, CAS declared, for the first time, that the standard of proof in doping cases, which it subsequently extended to other disciplinary offences,[154] is "comfortable satisfaction."[155]

CAS panels frequently refer directly to *Korneev & Gouliev* on this point,[156] and the decision's extended impact on CAS jurisprudence is extensive.[157] Some of the Atlanta Ad Hoc Division's decisions have been made publicly available in the CAS jurisprudence database, but not *Korneev & Gouliev*.[158] As far as I have been able to determine, CAS's decision in *Korneev & Gouliev* has only ever been published in a private publication that is expensive to access.[159]

Another example is *Associação Portuguesa de Desportos v. Club Valencia*.[160] CAS cites this decision frequently and in important cases: the decision is the twenty-seventh most frequently cited CAS decision in terms of direct citations (in-degree), but when considering the relative importance of the decisions that cite it (PageRank) the decision is CAS's twentieth most important decision, right below *Korneev & Gouliev*.[161] From CAS's references we can learn that the decision in *Associação Portuguesa de Desportos v. Club Valencia* settles some important issues regarding arbitration clauses and when an appeal is filled in a timely manner.[162] Despite dealing with such important issues and its actual use as a point of authority on such issues, the decision in *Associação Portuguesa de Desportos v. Club Valencia* is unpublished and, despite my best efforts, impossible to access. The case is, most likely relatedly, almost entirely ignored in academic literature[163] and we therefore do not even have access to basic information about the dispute and the underlying facts.

Finally, consider the award in CAS 2003/A/506. The decision is the principal precedent on the allocation of the burden of proof, frequently cited for the following principle:[164]

---

[153] Beloff 2001, pp. 50–51; Bowers 2010, p. 521; McLaren 1998, pp. 9–10.

[154] See e.g. CAS 2014/A/3628, *Eskişehirspor v. UEFA*, para 123 and cited sources.

[155] Beloff et al. 2012, pp. 249, 309. Regarding the substantive meaning of this standard, see further Sect. 7.4.

[156] See e.g. CAS 2001/A/337, *Bray*, para 26; CAS 2001/A/343, *UCI v. H.*, para 20; CAS 2001/A/345, *Meier*, para 22; CAS 2002/A/383, *Dos Santos*, para 85; CAS 2011/A/2625, *Bin Hammad*, para 154; CAS 2012/A/2699, *Al-Birair*, para 89.

[157] Ranked by PageRank, *Korneev & Gouliev* is CAS's nineteenth most important decision. See further Sect. 5.3.

[158] According to CAS's official statistic, six cases were submitted to the Ad Hoc Division and its decision in three of these cases are publicly available.

[159] Mealey's International Arbitration Report.

[160] CAS 2004/A/574, *Associação Portuguesa de Desportos v. Club Valencia*.

[161] See Sect. 5.3.

[162] See e.g. CAS 2006/A/1153, *Lopes de Almeida*; CAS 2011/A/2425, *Fusimalohi*. See also Rigozzi and Hasler 2013.

[163] See however Rigozzi and Hasler 2013.

[164] See e.g. CAS 2009/A/1810 & 1811, *SV Wilhelmshaven v. Club A. Excursionistas & Club A. River Plate*, para 18; CAS 2009/A/1908, *Parma FC SpA. v. Manchester United FC*, para 42; CAS

> [I]n CAS arbitration, any party wishing to prevail on a disputed issue must discharge its burden of proof, i.e. it must meet the onus to substantiate its allegations and to affirmatively prove the facts on which it relies with respect to that issue. In other words, the party which asserts facts to support its rights has the burden of establishing them.... The Code sets forth an adversarial system of arbitral justice, rather than an inquisitorial one. Hence, if a party wishes to establish some facts and persuade the deciding body, it must actively substantiate its allegations with convincing evidence.

CAS has also referred to CAS 2003/A/506 on the hierarchical order of sport rules.[165] Despite its significant impact on CAS jurisprudence and its practical importance to those who are parties to disputes before CAS (and possibly also other sports dispute resolution bodies), even basic information about the circumstances of the case, including any information about who the parties were, or the reasoning that led CAS to the conclusion quoted above is inaccessible.[166] *Korneev & Gouliev*, *Associação Portuguesa de Desportos v. Club Valencia*, and CAS 2003/A/506 are only three examples of CAS's quite extensive practice of relying on unpublished decisions.

Is this practice problematic and, if so, how problematic is it? From a more traditional understanding of arbitration, the practice of relying on unpublished decisions may not be shocking. Generally speaking, parties to arbitration have extensive control over the law applicable to the dispute and arbitration tribunals enjoy greater discretion than ordinary courts in deciding what to consider in making their decisions. This is reflected in CAS where parties have influence over the applicable rules.[167] As explained by CAS in *Beckie Scott*, when parties that in their pleadings refer to previous CAS decisions this can constitute a choice of applicable law that includes CAS jurisprudence and the principles of lex sportiva.[168] Other times, the terms governing the arbitration gives CAS broad discretion that can be used to consider previous decisions. This is for example the case with Article 17 of the Court of Arbitration for Sport Arbitration Rules for the Olympic Games:

> The Panel shall rule on the dispute pursuant to the Olympic Charter, the applicable regulations, general principles of law and the rules of law, the application of which it deems appropriate.

When CAS is endowed with such broad discretion there is nothing to suggest that it is precluded, as a matter of law, from considering unpublished decisions.

2009/A/1919, *Costa*, para 31; CAS 2013/A/3297, *FC Metalist v. UEFA & PAOK FC*, para 8.33 (quoted); CAS 2014/A/3546, *Dixon*, para 7.3; CAS 2014/A/3536, *Racing Club Asociación Civil v. FIFA*, para 9.2. See also Coccia 2013a, p. 59.

165 See e.g. CAS 2005/A/889, *Mathare United FC v. Al-Arabi SC*, para 8; CAS 2006/A/1125, *Hertha BSC Berlin v. Stade Lavallois Mayenne FC*, para 27.

166 We can however deduce from some of the references that the decision appears to have concerned a football-related dispute.

167 See Sect. 2.1. One example of this can be found in the FIFA Statutes: "CAS shall primarily apply the various regulations of FIFA and, additionally, Swiss law." Article 57.2 FIFA Statutes.

168 CAS 2002/O/373, *Scott*, para 14.

This finds some support in the decision of the Swiss Federal Tribunal (SFT) in *Paulissen*. Roel Paulissen was a Belgian mountain biker who had tested positive for the banned substance clomifene and was subsequently suspended. The subsequent proceedings came to concern whether Paulissen in addition to the suspension should also be fined and, if so, the proper amount such a fine. The international cycling federation (UCI) appealed the decision of the disciplinary body of the national cycling federation (Royale Ligue Vélocipédique Belge, RLVB) to impose a fine of € 7,500 and asked CAS to raise the amount to € 104,432.[169] The key issue before CAS was what the principle of proportionality requires. In making its decision on this issue, CAS considered and cited a number of previous CAS decisions,[170] including two unpublished decisions with which Paulissen and his counsel were unfamiliar and that had not been raised or discussed during the procedure before CAS.[171] Paulissen challenged CAS's award before the SFT claiming that his right to be heard had been violated and that CAS's award should therefore be annulled.[172] The SFT found three reasons why Paulissen's procedural rights had not been violated, one of which was that CAS decisions are not "necessarily" binding on subsequent panels,[173] and do not establish "legal principles"[174] that a party must be allowed to address as a matter of his or her procedural rights.

The SFT's conclusions do not, however, mean that there is no cause to be critical of CAS's reliance on unpublished precedent. A first, rather straight-forward argument against relying on unpublished decisions as precedent is basic fairness. To allow litigants to present arguments based on unpublished decisions to which they happen to have access provides those litigants with an unfair advantage over other litigants.[175] There are two elements to this unfair advantage. The first is that the party opposing the litigant relying on an unpublished decision is unprepared to discuss its relevance to the case at hand. This type of surprise effect can be mitigated by granting the other party access to the decision and sufficient time to present arguments. A second, more fundamental problem that is more difficult to resolve is that one party has an inherent advantage in terms of knowledge going into the process. Repeat parties, actors that frequently appear as parties before CAS, such as major sports governing bodies,[176] will have access to a number of unpublished

[169] CAS 2011/A/2325, *Paulissen*, paras 1–31.

[170] Ibid., paras 159–203 (concluding that a fine of € 20,800, corresponding to 20% of Paulissen's annual earnings, constituted a proportional fine).

[171] CAS 2010/A/2203 & 2214, *Larpe*; CAS 2010/A/2288, *Giunti*.

[172] SFT's decision 9 October 2012 in case 4A_110/2012 (*Paulissen*), para 3.

[173] Ibid., para 3.2.1 ("à l'inverse du Tribunal fédéral qui, en sa qualité d'autorité judiciaire suprême de la Confédération, prononce des arrêts ayant valeur de précédents pour les juridictions inférieures, les arbitres, dont le pouvoir résulte essentiellement de la volonté des parties, ne rendent pas des sentences dont les solutions s'imposeraient nécessairement à un autre tribunal arbitral appelé à trancher la même question.").

[174] "Principes juridiques".

[175] Cf. Reynolds and Richards 1978, p. 1185.

[176] See Sect. 10.4.

decisions and will therefore particularly benefit from the use of unpublished decisions as precedent.

Second, as discussed above, one of the main reasons for establishing a system of adherence to precedent is that doing so promotes the consistent and equal application of the law and one can argue that this reason is undermined by using unpublished precedent. In order to know whether a previous decision should guide a latter, one must know whether the situations are comparable or distinguishable and if we are unaware of the circumstances in the previous case we are unable to determine if adherence to previous decisions strengthens or weakens the consistent and equal application of law.[177] Moreover, the interest of adhering to precedent for the purpose of honoring reasonable expectations and actions taken in reliance on those expectations does not apply to unpublished decisions. If actors were unaware of a previous decision they can hardly have relied upon it and have no established positions that would be harmed by a failure to adhere to that previous decision.[178] Thus, adherence to unpublished decisions is unsupported by at least some of the core values motivating a system of precedent and may even run counter to those values.

The third and final criticism of adherence to unpublished precedent is that it undermines the rule of law. According to Raz, the rule of law does not only entail "that people should be ruled by the law and obey it," but also "that the law should be such that people will be able to be guided by it."[179] A system where people are incapable of determining what the law is and to adjust their actions accordingly fails to comply with the rule of law and undermines the authority of the law. Similarly, according to Fuller, the principle of legality requires that rules are understandable and accessible in advance and "there can be no rational ground for asserting that a man can have a moral obligation to obey a legal rule that… is kept secret from him."[180]

How severe the problems of adherence to unpublished precedent in this regard are depends on the relative degree of bindingness of precedent. In a system where precedent establishes rules that are comparable to rules in statutory law in terms of content, effect, and degree of bindingness, reliance on unpublished precedent is problematic in the same way and to the same extent as reliance on unpublished statutes. However, if previous decisions on the other side of the scale have no binding authority, that is that they are merely content-dependent persuasive, comparable to scholarly works in most orders, it is significantly less problematic to

177 Cf. Alexander 1989, p. 12; Reynolds and Richards 1978, pp. 1185–1186.

178 It is of course possible and likely that the parties to a case relies on the decision regardless of it being confidential. Whereas their reliance in the particular relationship is protected by the principle of res judicata, reliance against actors that are not and could not be aware of the confidential decision is less worthy of protection.

179 Raz 2009, p. 213.

180 Fuller 1969, p. 39.

consider the reasoning and conclusions in unpublished decisions.[181] Such a situation can perhaps be compared to a court considering an *amicus curiae* brief.

It is in this context no defense that CAS lacks a normative doctrine of formal bindingness *de jure* and that previous CAS decisions are not absolutely binding on subsequent CAS panels. What is relevant is how CAS *de facto* treats its previous decisions. On the basis of the observation that CAS in practice is "extremely reluctant to depart from precedent" and "[i]n the interest of fairness to the parties," Bersagel concludes that it is "critical that the CAS publish all nonconfidential awards, and refrain from allowing parties to rely on confidential awards."[182]

I agree. Not all CAS decisions have great or any precedential value,[183] and it is reasonable that certain decisions are kept confidential in a situation where the parties' interest in privacy clearly outweighs the decision's precedential value,[184] although even then it can be questioned whether total and absolute confidentiality is necessary.[185] However, as concluded above, CAS adheres to previous decisions to an extent that can be described as *de facto stare decisis*.[186] It is deeply unsatisfactory that decisions that in practice establish rules of direct and substantial importance in disputes, that directly affect clubs and individuals, and that may lead to severe consequences, including both extensive disciplinary sanctions and monetary damages, cannot in practice be read, reviewed, considered, evaluated, or criticized. These are exactly the kind of decisions that the CAS Division Presidents should as far as possible exercise their discretion to make publicly available.[187]

4.6 System-Arbitrator-Precedent

Many arbitration systems are not set up in a way that is conducive for the creation of or adherence to precedent. Arbitration awards may not be well-reasoned and are relatively rarely made available to the public.[188] Also, if one views arbitration as a free market for dispute resolution services there are no strong economic incentives for parties or arbitrators to participate in the formation of a system of precedent.[189] Landes and Posner argue that arbitral precedent is "an uncompensated benefit, not

181 See Barrett 2003, p. 1024.
182 Bersagel 2012, p. 205.
183 See Sect. 5.2.
184 Cf. Blackshaw 2011, p. 143.
185 See Mavromati and Reeb 2015, p. 320.
186 See above Sect. 4.2.
187 See Article R43 CAS Code.
188 Weidemaier 2010, p. 1914.
189 Landes and Posner 1979, pp. 238–239.

only on future parties but also on competing judges" that might hurt arbitrators' businesses by "reduc[ing] the incidence of disputes."[190]

The role of previous decisions as precedent is different in CAS compared to in many other arbitration tribunals,[191] largely because CAS is different.[192] One important factor is that CAS issues reasoned and regularly publicly available awards.[193] Also, arbitration tribunals are frequently constituted for each dispute without them being part of a robust and more permanent institutional framework. They therefore neither realistically can establish a body of jurisprudence nor do they have clear incentives for doing so.[194] The institutional stability of CAS enhances the conditions conducive for a system of arbitral precedent compared to less strongly institutionalized arbitration systems.[195] To a greater extent than arbitrators in many other arbitration systems, and more akin to judges in national and international courts, CAS arbitrators and CAS decisions form part of a system.

The fact that arbitral precedent is a *de facto* phenomenon in CAS suggests that CAS should not be described and understood merely as "a free market in judicial services."[196] The existence of arbitration precedent indicates that there exists a community, something greater than the individual arbitrators, that has an interest in the development of and adherence to precedent, and that the arbitrators' interest in belonging to this community creates an incentive to contribute to this system of precedent.[197] Well-reasoned decisions, that engage with and add to previous jurisprudence, enhance the legitimacy of the individual arbitrator and of the arbitration system as a whole.[198]

However, as a final note, it should be pointed out that although CAS exhibit a quite extensive adherence to precedent, its jurisprudence is not devoid of conflicting strands of case law.[199] The adjudicatory system in sports could also contain additional institutional safeguards to ensure that CAS panels interpret and apply lex sportiva in a consistent manner, such as an internal review system.[200]

---

190 Ibid., p. 238.

191 Kaufmann-Kohler 2007, p. 365.

192 Cf. Ioannidis 2016, pp. 31–32.

193 Cf. Weidemaier 2010, pp. 1914–1916 (regarding what distinguishes ICSID and labor arbitration from other arbitration systems and that contributes to the formation of arbitral precedent).

194 See e.g. Guillaume 2011, p. 14.

195 Cf. Stone Sweet 2006, p. 641.

196 Landes and Posner 1979, p. 248 ("a free market in judicial services would not lead to the production of precedents as a by-product of the competing judges to demonstrate their competence and impartiality through the issuance of judicial opinions.").

197 Cf. Ibid., pp. 248–249.

198 Weidemaier 2010, pp. 1919, 1942–1947.

199 Rigozzi 2005, pp. 638–640; Segan 2013.

200 Weston 2009, p. 128.

References

Alexander L (1989) Constrained by Precedent. Southern California Law Review 63:1–64
Alexy R (2011) A Theory of Legal Argumentation: The Theory of Rational Discourse as Theory of Legal Justification. Oxford University Press, Oxford
Barrett A C (2003) Stare Decisis and Due Process. University of Colorado Law Review 74:1011–1075
Beloff M (2001) Drugs, Laws and Versapaks. In: O'Leary J (ed) Drugs and Doping in Sport: Socio-Legal Perspectives. Cavendish, London, pp. 39–56
Beloff M, Kerr T, Demetriou M, Beloff R (2012) Sports Law, 2nd edn. Hart Publishing, Oxford
Bersagel A (2012) Is There a Stare Decisis Doctrine in the Court of Arbitration for Sport? An Analysis of Published Awards for Anti-Doping Disputes in Track and Field. Pepperdine Dispute Resolution Law Journal 12:189–207
Bhala R (1999) The Myth About Stare Decisis and International Trade Law. American University International Law Review 14:845–956
Bjorklund A (2009) The Emerging Civilization of Investment Arbitration. Penn State Law Review 113:1269–1300
Blackshaw I (2011) Towards a "Lex Sportiva". The International Sports Law Journal 2011(3/4):140–144
Bowers L (2010) Science and the Rules Governing Anti-Doping Violations. In: Thieme D, Hemmersbach P (eds) Doping in Sports. Springer, Berlin, pp. 513–531
Cardozo B (1921) The Nature of the Judicial Process. Yale University Press, New Haven
Casini L (2011) The Making of Lex Sportiva by the Court of Arbitration for Sport. German Law Journal 12(5):1317–1340
Chiassoni P (2012) The Philosophy of Preced: Conceptual Analysis and Rational Reconstruction. In: Bustamante T, Bernal Pulido C (eds) On the Philosophy of Precedent. Proceedings of the 24th World Congress of the International Association for Philosophy of Law and Social Philosophy III. Franz Steiner Verlag, Stuttgart, pp. 13–33
Coccia M (2013a) International Sports Justice: The Court of Arbitration for Sport. European Sports Law Bulletin 2013(1):23–76
Commission J (2007) Precedent in Investment Treaty Arbitration: A Citation Analysis of a Developing Jurisprudence. Journal of International Arbitration 24(2):129–158
Cross R, Harris J W (1991) Precedent in English Law, 4th edn. Clarendon Press, Oxford
de Weger F (2016) The Jurisprudence of the FIFA Dispute Resolution Chamber. T.M.C. Asser Press, The Hague
Derlén M, Lindholm J (2017) Peek-a-boo, It's a Case Law System. German Law Journal 18(3):647–686
Douglas Z (2010) Can a Doctrine of Precedent Be Justified in Investment Treaty Arbitration? ICSID Review 25(1):104–110
Duxbury N (2008) The Nature and Authority of Precedent. Cambridge University Press, Cambridge
Dworkin R (2013) Taking Rights Seriously. Bloomsbury, London
Dworkin R (2016) Law's Empire. Bloomsbury, London
Fowler J, Jeon S (2008) Authority of Precedent. Social Network 30:16–30
Fuller L (1969) The Morality of Law, 2nd edn. Yale University Press, New Haven
Gascón M (2012) Rationality and (Self) Precedent: Brief Considerations Concerning the Grounding and Implications of the Rule of Self Precedent. In: Bustamante T, Bernal Pulido C (eds) On the Philosophy of Precedent. Proceedings of the 24th World Congress of the International Association for Philosophy of Law and Social Philosophy III. Franz Steiner Verlag, Stuttgart, pp. 35–50
Guillaume G (2011) The Use of Precedent by International Judges and Arbitrators. Journal of International Dispute Settlement 2(1):5–23
Hart H L A (2012) The Concept of Law, 3rd edn. Oxford University Press, Oxford

Ioannidis G (2016) The Influence of Common Law Traditions on the Practice and Procedure Before the Court of Arbitration for Sport (CAS). In: Duval A, Rigozzi A (eds) Yearbook of International Sports Arbitration 2015. T.M.C. Asser Press, The Hague, pp. 17–38
Kaufmann-Kohler G (2007) Arbitral Precedent: Dream, Necessity or Excuse? Arbitration International 23(3):357–378
Landes W M, Posner R A (1976) Legal Precedent: A Theoretical and Empirical Analysis. The Journal of Law and Economics 19:249–307
Landes W M, Posner R A (1979) Adjudication as a Private Good. The Journal of Legal Studies 8 (2):235–284
Latty F (2007) La lex sportiva: Recherche sur le droit transnational. Martinus Nijhoff, Leiden
Legum B (2008) The Definitions of 'Precedent' in International Arbitration. In: Gaillard E, Banifatemi Y (eds) Precedent in International Arbitration. Juris Publishing, New York, pp. 5–14
Llewellyn K N (1960) The Common Law Tradition: Deciding Appeals. Little, Brown and Co., Boston
MacCormick N (2003) Legal Reasoning and Legal Theory. Oxford University Press, Oxford
MacCormick N, Summers R (1997) Appendix: Final Version of the Common Questions, Comparative Legal Precedent Study, September 1994. In: MacCormick N, Summers R, Goodhart A (eds) Interpreting Precedent. Ashgate, Farnham, pp. 551–562
Mavromati D, Reeb M (2015) The Code of the Court of Arbitration for Sport: Commentary, Cases and Materials. Wolters Kluwer, Alphen aan den Rijn
McLaren R (1998) A New Order: Athletes' Rights and the Court of Arbitration at the Olympic Games. Olympika: The International Journal of Olympic Studies 7:1–24
Mitten M J, Opie H (2010) 'Sports Law': Implications for the Development of International, Comparative, and National Law and Global Dispute Resolution. Tulane Law Review 85:269–322
Nafziger J (2004) Lex Sportiva. The International Sports Law Journal 2004(1–2):3–8
Nelson C (2001) Stare Decisis and Demonstrably Erroneous Precedents. Virginia Law Review 87 (1):1–84
Ramberg C (2017) Prejudikat som rättskälla i förmögenhetsrätten. Wolters Kluwer, Stockholm
Raz J (2009) The Authority of Law, 2nd edn. Oxford University Press, Oxford
Reilly L (2012) An Introduction to the Court of Arbitration for Sport (CAS) and the Role of National Courts in International Sports Disputes. Journal of Dispute Resolution 2012(1):63–81
Reynolds W, Richards W (1978) The Non-Precedential Precedent: Limited Publications and No-Citation Rules in the United States Courts of Appeal. Columbia Law Review 78:1167–1206
Rigozzi A (2005) L'arbitrage international en matière de sport. Helbing & Lichtenhahn, Basel
Rigozzi A, Hasler E (2013) Sports Arbitration under the CAS Rules. In: Arroyo M (ed) Arbitration in Switzerland: The Practitioner's Guide. Wolters Kluwer, Alphen aan den Rijn, pp. 936–1206
Schauer F (1987) Precedent. Stanford Law Review 39(3):571–605
Schauer F (2007) Has Precedent Ever Really Mattered in the Supreme Court? Georgia State University Law Review 24:381–401
Schauer F (2008a) Authority and Authorities. Virginia Law Review 94(8):1931–1961
Schauer F (2008b) Why Precedent in Law (and Elsewhere) is Not Totally (or Even Substantially) About Analogy. Perspectives on Psychological Science 3(6):454–460
Schreuer C, Weiniger M (2008) A Doctrine of Precedent? In: Muchlinksi P, Ortino F, Shreuer C (eds) The Oxford Handbook of International Investment Law. Oxford University Press, Oxford, pp. 1188–1206
Segan J (2013) Does the Court of Arbitration for Sport need a 'Grand Chamber'? Sports Law Bulletin, 19 April 2013. https://www.sportslawbulletin.org/does-the-court-of-arbitration-for-sport-need-a-grand-chamber/. Accessed 9 January 2018
Stone Sweet A (2006) The New Lex Mercatoria and Transnational Governance. Journal of European Public Policy 13(5):627–646

Stone Sweet A, Chung M Y, Saltzman A (2017) Arbitral Lawmaking and State Power: An Empirical Analysis of Investor–State Arbitration. Journal of International Dispute Settlement 8 (4):579–609

Ten Cate I (2013) The Costs of Consistency: Precedent in Investment Treaty Arbitration. Columbia Journal of Transnational Law 51:418–478

Weidemaier W C M (2010) Toward a Theory of Precedent in Arbitration. William and Mary Law Review 51:1895–1958

Weidemaier W C M (2012) Judging-Lite: How Arbitrators Use and Create Precedent. North Carolina Law Review 90:1091–1146

Weston M (2009) Simply a Dress Rehearsal? U.S. Olympic Sports Arbitration and De Novo Review at the Court of Arbitration for Sport. Georgia Journal of International and Comparative Law 38:97–129

Chapter 5
CAS's Landmark Decisions

Abstract In most legal orders there are a few key decisions that all lawyers are well-familiar with and that are frequently described as landmark decisions. Such decisions occupy a central position in the story of the legal order but one can also seek to quantify the landmark qualities of a decision by how centrally placed it is in a case law network. This chapter explores the existence of landmark CAS decisions, that is decisions that have a particularly significant impact on CAS jurisprudence. It will do so using different measurements that represent different ways of thinking about the systemic impact of decisions. Doing this identifies and highlights particularly important individual decisions but also provides a richer understanding of the structure of CAS jurisprudence.

5.1 Importance of Important Decisions

The main stories of many legal orders center around a number of judicial decisions that are supposedly particularly important. Depending on the legal order and the context, such decisions may varyingly be referred to as classic cases, *grands arrêts*, or landmark decisions, which is the term that will be used here. While there are significant differences in meaning between such terms, they are all based on roughly the same idea: some decisions are, for lack of a more precise word, more important than others. Landmark decisions are not merely aids in legal teaching and storytelling. In orders where legal development occurs through judicial decisions, certain decisions are particularly important because they constitute a starting, turning, or ending point of a branch of "judge-made law". Thus, in most legal orders, and particularly in case law-based legal orders, it makes sense to identify and focus on landmark decisions. By extension, the existence of landmark decisions is a typical and important element of a case law-based legal order.

The jurisprudence of the Court of Arbitration for Sport (CAS) contains landmark decisions, at least if we believe CAS itself. For example, in *Al-Wehda v. SAFF*, CAS referred to its previous decision in *Cole*[1] as a landmark decision when it

[1] CAS 2005/A/952.

J. Lindholm, *The Court of Arbitration for Sport and Its Jurisprudence*,
ASSER International Sports Law Series,
https://doi.org/10.1007/978-94-6265-285-9_5

comes to basing CAS's jurisdiction on the statutes of a national federation referring to the international federation statutes.[2] Similarly, the panel in *Benjamin* referred to CAS's decision in *Mellouli*[3] as "a recent landmark decision" that establishes that CAS has considerable discretion to determine what constitutes an appropriate sanction.[4]

Other sports dispute resolution institutions also sometimes refer to certain CAS decisions as landmark decisions. For example, in its decision in *Hawkins* the Basketball Arbitral Tribunal (BAT) referred to CAS's decision in *Matuzalem*[5] as a landmark decision when it comes to calculating damages in cases of contract termination without proper cause.[6] Finally, legal scholars frequently refer to certain decisions as landmark decisions, including in the area of sports law and, more specifically, CAS decisions.[7]

What distinguishes landmark decisions like (if we believe CAS and BAT) *Cole*, *Mellouli*, and *Matuzalem* from other, ordinary, less important CAS decisions? Despite the ubiquitous use of the term, there is no established definition of what constitutes a landmark decision and it is difficult to firmly distinguish landmark decisions from other decisions.

In order to approach the concept of landmark decisions, we must first accept two propositions: (i) that the process of adjudication involves declaring what the law is and that this a creative process that on some level involves developing the law,[8] and (ii) that decisions serve as models for subsequent cases. Judicial decisions may thus carry some authoritative force or, differently phrased, have "normative implications beyond the context of the particular case in which it was delivered"[9] or, again differently phrased, serve as precedents.

The role of CAS decisions as precedent was studied extensively above.[10] Departing from the conclusion above that CAS decisions do in fact have substantial precedential force, what is it that characterizes and distinguishes landmark decisions from other CAS decisions? First of all, as we shall explore further below, a binary distinction into important decisions and unimportant decisions is much too simplified. Rather, precedential power follows a more fluid distribution. Maduro and Azoulai, commenting on the jurisprudence of the Court of Justice of the European Union (CJEU), highlight "judgments of systematic impact", that is judgments "that survive the passing of time but also those which, even when their concrete legal

---

[2] CAS 2011/A/2472, para 17.

[3] CAS 2007/A/1252.

[4] CAS 2007/A/1415, para 39.

[5] CAS 2008/A/1519–1520.

[6] BAT 436/11, para 71.

[7] See e.g. Anderson 2013; Martens 2006; Wild 2012.

[8] Cf. *Anastasoff v. United States*, 223 F.3d 898, 899 (8th Cir. 2000) ("Inherent in every judicial decision is a declaration and interpretation of a general principle or rule of law.").

[9] Komárek 2011, p. 4.

[10] See Chap. 4.

answer has become obsolete or has even been overturned, have lived on through their multiple effects in other areas of law."[11] In my opinion, this definition captures the most important characteristic of judicial decisions that lawyers recognize as being landmark decisions: decisions that have a broad or deep effect on the legal order on a systemic level.

The focus on systemic effect means that what constitutes a landmark decision under this definition is not necessarily the same as what some would consider a "classic". For example, when teaching law students, many law professors, including myself, frequently ask students to read classic cases and refer to those cases in textbooks. Sometimes we do this because those decisions have a broad or deep effect on the legal system, but this is not always the case. Other possible reasons for focusing on such classic cases include that they are historically important, involve captivating facts, provide illustrative examples, are particularly well-reasoned, are objects of considerable public attention or controversy, or simply because reading them is a law school tradition.[12]

Maduro and Azoulai's definition also brings attention to the fact that it is not always immediately obvious when a decision is rendered whether it is a landmark decision, and that its systemic effect may only become apparent through its use and development in subsequent decisions.[13] However, as the above-used example of CAS's decision in *Benjamin* illustrates, a decision does not necessarily need to mature over time in order for lawyers to identify it as a landmark decision. Sometimes well-trained lawyers are able to identify a decision's greatness immediately when it is issued. For the purpose of this study it is however a problem that it is extremely difficult, if not impossible, to empirically capture a decision's systemic importance until some time has passed.[14]

5.2 Degree Distribution: A Few Good Cases

One approach for studying the structure of CAS's jurisprudence, how CAS relates to its own jurisprudence, and whether this conforms to our expectations of a case law-based legal order is to consider how CAS's references to previous decisions is distributed across its body of jurisprudence. We do not expect citations to be distributed evenly across a legal citation network. Previous research has shown that

---

[11] Maduro and Azoulai 2010, p. xiii.

[12] See Derlén and Lindholm 2015; Derlén and Lindholm 2016a; Lupu and Voeten 2011.

[13] See also Vauchez 2016.

[14] We can however identify some common characteristics of important decisions and make an educated guess about whether a particular decision is likely to become important based on whether it has such characteristics. See Derlén and Lindholm 2015.

courts' references to previous decisions strongly tend to center around a few, really important decisions and that the vast majority of all decisions are rarely cited.[15] Differently phrased, references to previous decisions generally tend to follow a power law distribution.[16]

For example, Fowler and Jeon have shown that the reference of the United States Supreme Court (SCOTUS) to its own case law follows a power law distribution,[17] and Neale has shown that the same is true in Canada.[18] Perhaps some would argue that this is to be expected from legal orders that belong to the common law tradition, particularly when it comes to complex issues of constitutional law where there are few statutory rules, law to a greater extent develop through case law, and adherence to case law enhances consistency and foreseeability.[19] However, this "rich-get-richer" phenomenon can also be observed in international courts, such as the International Criminal Court,[20] and Lupu and Voeten have shown that the inward references of the European Court of Human Rights (ECtHR) follow a power law distribution similar to that of SCOTUS.[21] Also, we have found that the CJEU's inward citations follow a power law distribution.[22] One might argue that both European Union law and European Convention law are two non-national legal orders where case law is of particular importance. Considering that the same is supposedly true for lex sportiva, we should expect CAS's references to its own previous jurisprudence to follow a pattern that is similar those of the ECtHR and the CJEU.

Moreover, this pattern does not appear to be dependent on the legal order placing particular emphasis on case law as a source of law. For example, researchers have found that inward references in the citation networks of the Austrian Supreme Court,[23] the Italian Constitutional Court,[24] and the Netherland's Supreme Court[25] all follow this distribution. For a previous research project, we studied the published jurisprudence of the Swedish Supreme Court between 1981 and 2014.[26] The Swedish legal order is traditionally not considered to be particularly case

[15] Case law networks can in this regard be viewed as an example of a "small–world network" where edges are organized in neither an orderly or random way and which also includes social networks and many other real-world networks. See Watts and Strogatz 1998.

[16] Also sometimes referred to as a "long tail distribution". A scale-free network is a network with a power law degree distribution. Barabási and Albert 1999.

[17] Fowler and Jeon 2008, p. 19.

[18] Neale 2013, pp. 21–22.

[19] Cf. David and Brierley 1985, pp. 376–377; Siems 2014, pp. 46–47.

[20] See Tarissan and Nollez-Goldbach 2014.

[21] Lupu and Voeten 2011, p. 426.

[22] See below Fig. 5.1 *CJEU Indegree Distribution*. For more information about the dataset and its distribution, see Derlén and Lindholm 2017.

[23] Geist 2010, p. 144.

[24] Agnoloni 2014, p. 26.

[25] van Opijnen 2012.

[26] The data is described in greater detail in Derlén and Lindholm 2016b, p. 148.

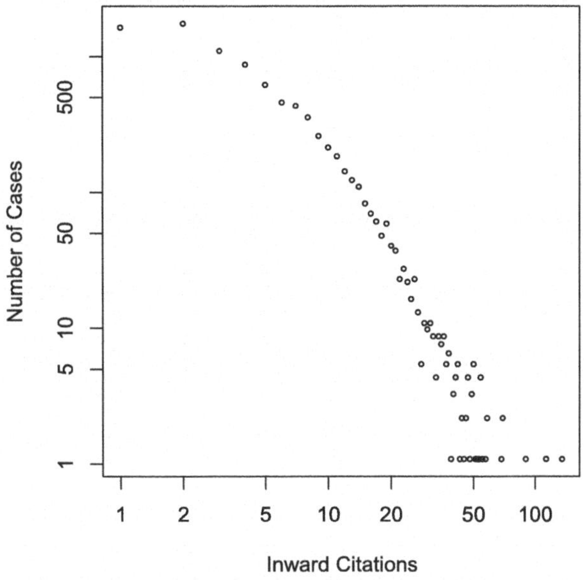

Fig. 5.1 CJEU Indegree Distribution. [*Source* The author]

law-based,[27] which is also reflected in that the court makes relatively few references to its previous case law in term of absolute numbers. However, the distribution of those references still clearly follow a power law distribution.[28]

Thus, in practice, references to decisions tend to follow a power law distribution and this is true in most legal orders, whether it is a national or international one, whether it is more influenced by the common law tradition or the civil law tradition.

That references to decisions follow a power law distribution is not only empirically supported, it also makes theoretical sense. First, it is consistent with the very nature of precedents that most references will point to a small group of decisions. In legal orders where the law governing legal issues to some extent develop through judicial decisions, certain decisions will be the primary sources for particular points of law and, in the absence of a convention against citing case law, courts will cite these decisions as authorities when faced with these points of law. Such decisions have great precedential value beyond their function of deciding the particular case and will therefore be used as a source of law relatively frequently. Conversely, in all systems where this has been studied, most decisions are never or very infrequently cited, and this is true even of the decisions of the highest courts. Even in SCOTUS, the ECtHR, and the CJEU, most decisions have in practice fairly limited precedential value simply because most decisions' novel contributions to the law are rather marginal and they are consequently rarely cited.

Second, there is also a much more practical reason why a very small number of decisions receive the overwhelming majority of references: references are made by humans who have imperfect knowledge and memory. If a decision is cited it is more

27 See e.g. Strömholm 2000, pp. 40–41.

28 See below Fig. 5.2 *Swedish Supreme Court Indegree Distribution*.

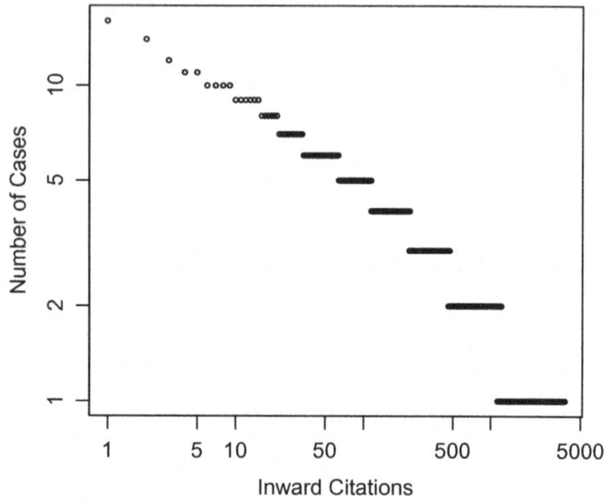

Fig. 5.2 Swedish Supreme Court Indegree Distribution. [*Source* Derlén and Lindholm 2016b]

likely to attract attention and if it attracts more attention it is more likely to be cited.[29] For this reason, power law distributions are not unique for networks of jurisprudence. On the contrary, power law distributions are a common and natural occurrence in many real-world networks, including business networks, social networks, transportation networks, and the Internet.[30] For example, citations of academic papers generally follow a power law distribution; almost half of all research papers are never cited whereas the top 0.01 percent are cited more than 1,000 times.[31]

For the reasons stated above, we expect to find that CAS's references to its own decisions follow a power law distribution. Of course, a power law distribution does not constitute definitive, end-of-all-discussion evidence of a case law-based legal order. However, it would certainly be one factor leaning in that direction if it was clear that CAS – like most national, regional, and international courts – has developed some "centers of gravity" in its jurisprudence that it refers back to on a consistent basis. Conversely, if we find that CAS distributes its references equally among all of its previous decisions, this would cast some doubt over the proposition that CAS jurisprudence is an integral part of the development of a case law-based legal order.[32]

When we examine how CAS's references to its own case law are distributed, we see that it resembles a power law distribution. 60 percent of all CAS decisions have

---

[29] See Redner 1998, p. 4.

[30] See e.g. Barabási and Albert 1999.

[31] Redner 1998. See also Watts and Strogatz 1998.

[32] For example, we have argued that the fact that Swedish courts of precedent cite so many different CJEU decisions (796 references to 533 different CJEU decisions) suggests a rather inexperienced, instrumental, and casuistic approach to CJEU case law. Derlén and Lindholm 2015, pp. 173–174.

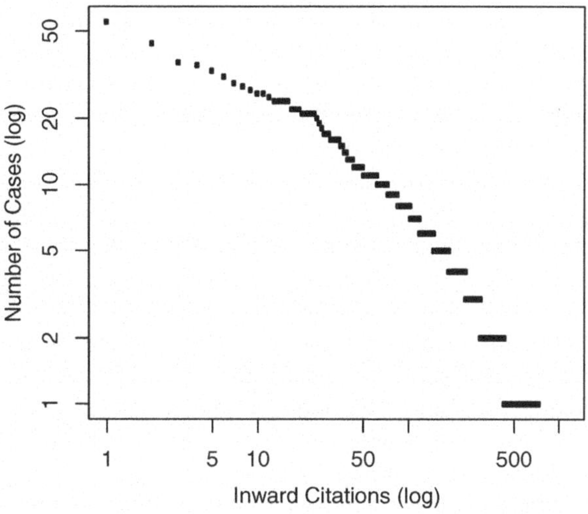

Fig. 5.3 CAS Indegree Distribution. [*Source* The author]

never been cited or have only been cited once.[33] On the other side of the scale the top 1 percent of all CAS decisions has received more than 13 percent of all of CAS's references. It is however not quite as clear a power law distribution as the courts previously discussed. This supports the picture of CAS's jurisprudence exhibiting some of the signs of a case law-based court, but it also suggests that it might not distribute its references quite in the same way as some of the more established courts.[34]

As we will explore in greater detail below, there is a correlation between indegree distribution and what issues the decisions concern. For example, decisions that concern doping sanctions and doping procedure tend to belong to the higher end of the indegree distribution whereas decisions concerning eligibility on grounds of nationality or contractual obligations generally tend to reside on the lower end of the spectrum.[35]

5.3 CAS's High Impact Decisions

Having concluded above that in reasoning with its previous decisions CAS does, at least to some relevant extent, distinguish between ordinary and extraordinary decisions, we are now ready to tackle the task of identifying CAS's landmark

---

[33] Of all 978 decisions included in the complete dataset, 322 decisions had never been cited and 265 had only been cited once.

[34] See above Fig. 5.3 *CAS Indegree Distribution*.

[35] See Sect. 6.3.1.

decisions, that is, decisions that have had a broad or deep impact on a systemic level.[36]

However, before doing so, we should acknowledge that there is no one right approach for answering this question and, consequently, no single answer. First, as explored in this and the subsequent sections, there are multiple ways by which a decision can have systemic impact. Second, as explored further below,[37] the answer changes as the legal order develops and to consider the dynamic forces in play provides a different perspective on the matter.

Having addressed these important caveats, a natural starting point for exploring these issues is to consider and compare the top decisions ranked by indegree and PageRank. Both of these centrality measurements seek to capture decisions' precedential value by considering to what extent they are being relied upon as a source for future development but, as developed above, PageRank takes into consideration not only direct references but also the indirect impact of the decision on jurisprudence in the long term.[38]

Many decisions are represented on both of these lists, the most obvious one being *Quigley* which holds the top spot on both lists. George Quigley was an American shooter who in connection with a skeet event in Cairo in 1994 contracted bronchitis resulting in a high fever and hallucinations. After he had been handed a list of banned substances, the doctor at the hotel where Quigley was staying provided him with antibiotics and an unmarked bottle of cough syrup. In response to a direct question, the doctor stated that neither of these contained a banned doping substance. After winning the shooting event, Quigley tested positive for the banned substance ephedrine, which was an active ingredient in the cough syrup. Neither the international federation in question, UIT, nor CAS questioned Quigley's explanation of how the substance ended up in his body. In its decision, CAS explained the underlying reasons for the principle of strict liability for doping offenses and why it is justified.[39] However, the panel ultimately found that Quigley should not be disqualified, despite having tested positive, because the rules in question were not sufficiently clear.[40]

CAS's decision in *Quigley* is of significant structural importance in several regards and this helps explain its central position in the CAS case law network. First, *Quigley* provides the first, clear jurisprudential support for the validity of the principle of strict liability, a principle that is of immense practical importance in many disputes concerning doping violations,[41] an area of sports law that in turn makes up roughly half of all CAS decisions.[42] Moreover, *Quigley* was not only first

[36] See above Sect. 5.1.

[37] See below Sect. 5.4.

[38] See Sect. 1.6.

[39] CAS 94/129, *Quigley*, paras 14–15.

[40] Ibid., paras 33–34.

[41] See further below Sect. 5.4.

[42] See Sect. 2.4.

in upholding this principle, it was also particularly balanced and well-reasoned in a way that makes it convincing.[43] For these reasons, *Quigley* is often quoted in support for the principle of strict liability.[44]

Quigley is however also an important precedent concerning the principle of respect for fundamental rights, particularly procedural rights.[45] *Quigley* is one of the first CAS decisions[46] to recognize a right to be heard,[47] and is sometimes cited on this point.[48] Relatedly, *Quigley* deals with the consequences of a party's right to a fair hearing being violated and, more specifically, the ability to "cure" a previous, deficient hearing by a sports dispute resolution institution by having CAS hear the case *de novo* on appeal.[49]

Finally, *Quigley* establishes, again in a particularly well-reasoned and convincing manner, that sports governing bodies (SGBs) are subject to what can broadly be referred to as legal principles upholding or relating to the rule of law,[50] and that CAS will enforce these immensely important principles,[51] even when doing so conflicts with important sport values:[52]

> [T]he rule-makers and the rule-appliers must begin by being strict with themselves. Regulations that may affect the careers of dedicated athletes must be predictable. They must emanate from duly authorised bodies. They must be adopted in constitutionally proper ways. They should not be the product of an obscure process of accretion. Athletes and officials should not be confronted with a thicket of mutually qualifying or even contradictory rules that can be understood only on the basis of the de facto practice over the course of many years of a small group of insiders.[53]

As important as the principle of strict liability and the right to a fair hearing are, this is perhaps the most important element of *Quigley*. The paragraph quoted above is, in my humble opinion, arguably one of the most important that CAS has ever formulated. The basic principles that relate to the rule of law applies to every case

---

[43] There are several similarities between *Quigley* and the CJEU's landmark decision in Case C-415/93, *Bosman*, EU:C:1995:463. Cf. Derlén and Lindholm 2016a.

[44] See e.g. CAS 95/142, *Lehtinen*, para 12; CAS 2000/A/310, *Leipold I*, para 25; CAS 2004/A/651, *French*, para 47 n 3.

[45] See also Sect. 7.3.

[46] It was not, however, the first decision to do so. See e.g. CAS 91/53, *G. v. FEI*, para 11.

[47] CAS 94/129, *Quigley*, paras 58–59.

[48] See e.g. CAS 98/200, *AEK Athens*, para 58.

[49] CAS 94/129, *Quigley*, para 59, cited in support in e.g. CAS 2001/A/317, *Aanes*, para 7; CAS 2001/A/354-355, *IHA v. LHF & FIH & LHF v. FIH*, para 6; CAS 2004/A/714, *Fazekas*, para 11; CAS 2005/A/835 & 942, *Bomfim*, para 26.

[50] Cf. Foster 2006, para 25 (presenting this element of *Quigley* as establishing a requirement of good governance).

[51] See also CAS OG 04/009, *Kaklamanakis*, para 24 ("CAS will always have jurisdiction to overrule the Rules of any sport federation if its decision making bodies conduct themselves with a lack of good faith or not in accordance with due process.").

[52] Louw 2012, p. 685. See also further Sect. 7.2.

[53] CAS 94/129, *Quigley*, para 34.

that comes before CAS and by extension the creation, application, and enforcement of sports rules outside of CAS. While *Quigley* is frequently cited on other issues, its holding on the principles related to the rule of law has had a clear impact on subsequent decisions.[54]

Looking beyond *Quigley* at the top, there are some significant differences between the two lists, and these differences signify that there may be a difference between how frequently a particular decisions is referred to and its overall impact on CAS's jurisprudence and sports law more generally.

Take for example CAS's decision in *Ekimov v. Hamilton*. The American cyclist Tyler Hamilton won a gold medal in the 2004 Olympic Games in Athens. In a subsequent anti-doping test, Hamilton left blood samples that initially were considered "suspicious for blood transfusion", but the International Olympic Committee (IOC) later concluded that the test was inconclusive and therefore wrote a letter to Hamilton declaring its intention to refrain from pursuing the matter further.[55] The Russian Olympic Committee and the Russian cyclist Viatcheslav Ekimov, who had finished second in the race, sought to appeal the IOC's decision to CAS. One of the main issues to be decided by CAS was whether the letter constituted a "true" and final decision that could be appealed. CAS concluded that the letter, regardless of its form, was to be considered a true decision since it materially affected the legal situation of the addressee, the appellants, and other concerned athletes.[56]

The dataset contains twenty-two references to *Ekimov v. Hamilton*, which places it a respectable tie for the seventeenth most-cited decision,[57] ahead of many cases and not far below CAS's decisions in *Aris I*[58] that dealt with many of the same issues as *Ekimov v. Hamilton*, including the definition of what constitutes an appealable decision.[59]

Aris I concerned Aris FC, a Greek football team from Thessaloniki that was facing relegation from the highest division of the Greek football system (*Alpha Ethniki*) to the second highest division (*Beta Ethniki*). Another team in the same division, Panionis, had been the subject of a FIFA DRC decision according to which the team would be deducted points unless it paid an outstanding amount to two football players. Panionis failed to do so within the prescribed time limit and should therefore, according to Aris, be deducted points and consequently relegated

---

[54] See e.g. CAS 96/149, *Cullwick*, para 21; CAS 2000/A/281, *Haga*, para 12; CAS 2001/A/330, *Reinhold*, para 17; CAS 2004/A/725, *USOC v. IOC & IAAF*, paras 17–21; CAS 2011/A/2612, *Hui*, paras 100–104. See further Sect. 7.2.

[55] The test was inconclusive due to a lack of red blood cells. After that decision, but before CAS's decision in *Ekimov v. Hamilton*, CAS had in a separate case, CAS 2005/A/884, *Hamilton*, found that Tyler Hamilton had indeed engaged in blood doping.

[56] CAS 2004/A/748, *Ekimov v. Hamilton*, paras 14–18.

[57] See below Table 5.1 *Top Decisions by Indegree*. *Ekimov v. Hamilton* shares this spot with the older and in many senses important decision in CAS 95/141, *Chagnaud*.

[58] CAS 2005/A/899.

[59] Ibid., para 61.

Table 5.1 Top Decisions by Indegree. [*Source* The author]

Case	Indegree
CAS 94/129, *Quigley*	55
CAS 2005/A/830, *Squizzato*	44
CAS 2000/A/274, *Susin*	36
CAS 2005/C/976 & 986, *FIFA & WADA*	35
CAS 2004/A/690, *Hipperdinger*	33
CAS 2005/A/847, *Knauss*	31
CAS 98/211, *Smith de Bruin*	29
CAS 98/200, *AEK Athens*	28
CAS 2006/A/1025, *Puerta*	27
CAS 2001/A/317, *Aanes*	26
CAS 2005/A/899, *Aris I*	26
CAS 2005/A/983, *Club Atletico Penarol et al.*	25
CAS 96/156, *Foschi*	24
CAS 98/208, *Wang et al.*	24
CAS 2007/A/1370 & 1376, *Lucas Dodo*	24
CAS 2009/A/1920, *FK Pobeda et al.*	24
CAS 95/141, *Chagnaud*	22
CAS 2004/A/748, *Ekimov v. Hamilton*	22
CAS 2006/A/1153, *Almeida*	22
CAS 96/149, *Cullwick*	21
CAS 98/214, *Bouras*	21
CAS 2003/O/486, *Fulham FC v. Olympique Lyonnais*	21
CAS 2006/A/1180, *Ribery*	21
CAS 2009/A/1870, *Hardy*	21
CAS 2004/A/659, *Galatasaray v. FIFA et al.*	20
OG 04/003, *Edwards*	19
CAS 2004/A/574, *Associacao Portuguesa de desportos v. Club Valencia*	18
CAS 94/128, *UCI & CONI*	17
CAS 2003/A/484, *Vencill*	17
CAS 2010/A/2172, *O. v. UEFA*	17

instead of Aris. Aris made this request to FIFA, who in a letter addressed to Aris replied that the matter fell under the jurisdiction of the Hellenic Football Federation. Aris sought to appeal what it considered constituted a decision on the part of FIFA to CAS. CAS concluded that it lacked jurisdiction because FIFA's letter did not constitute an appealable decision and Aris had access to other remedies through its national federation.[60]

[60] CAS 2005/A/899, *Aris I*, para 20.

Even though *Aris I* is older than *Ekimov v. Hamilton* and served as a foundation for the latter[61] the two decisions are separated by only two references, suggesting that the two are nearly comparably important. However, when ranked by PageRank, *Ekimov v. Hamilton* drops down to the thirty-fourth position, far below *Aris I*.[62] This reveals that despite the small difference in references between the two decisions, *Aris I* has had a deeper impact on CAS's overall jurisprudence than *Ekimov v. Hamilton*.

Aris I is also a good example of a CAS decision whose relevance as a source of law might easily be overlooked.[63] As we can see below, the decision in *Aris I* was cited in several other CAS decisions that, as evident from their high PageRank, in turn were cited in many and/or important decisions. One of these is *Ekimov v. Hamilton*. Thus, part of *Aris I*'s importance is based on it establishing the principles applied and expanded on in *Ekimov v. Hamilton*, and rightfully so. This is a good illustration of why PageRank in many ways is a better measurement of precedential power than indegree centrality.

Moreover, CAS decisions citing *Aris I* concern a wide range of subject matters, including governance, doping, other (non-doping) disciplinary actions, contract disputes, and eligibility.[64] The fact that the decision has broad application supports it being considered a landmark CAS decision. *Aris I* appears to have the type of broad and deep impact on a systemic level that we look for in a landmark decision.[65]

There are other decisions that appear to have had a deep systemic impact on CAS's jurisprudence without being cited by CAS particularly frequently. One example of this is CAS's advisory opinion in *UCI & CONI* which has the second highest PageRank of any CAS decision, right after *Quigley*, but is tied for twenty-eight when it comes to indegree.

The background to *UCI & CONI* was that an Italian cyclist, Gianni Bugno, had tested positive for caffeine and was subsequently suspended by the Italian cycling federation for three months following the directives of the Italian Olympic Committee (Comitato Olimpico Nazionale Italiano, CONI) that, in turn, were based on the rules of the IOC. The suspension did however conflict with the anti-doping rules of the international cycling federation (UCI).[66] The situation thus involved a conflict between the rules and regulations of different SGBs and to settle the matter CAS was asked to clarify several important issues, including the division of regulatory competence between the IOC, national Olympic Committees (NOCs), and

---

[61] CAS 2004/A/748, *Ekimov v. Hamilton*, paras 13–14. See also below Fig. 5.4 *Decisions Referring to Aris I*.

[62] *Aris I*'s PageRank is 50% higher than that of *Ekimov v. Hamilton*.

[63] Legal commentators appear to have paid little attention to the decision.

[64] See below Fig. 5.4 *Decisions Referring to Aris I*.

[65] See above Sect. 5.1.

[66] CAS 94/128, *UCI v. CONI*, para 1.

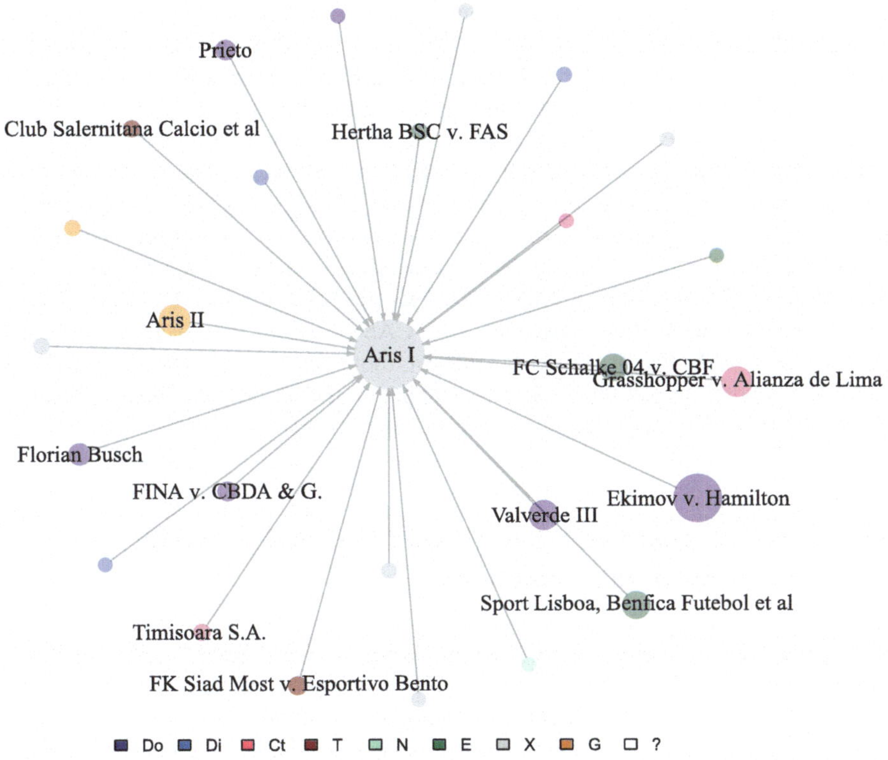

Fig. 5.4 Decisions Referring to *Aris I*. [*Source* The author]

international federations and the hierarchy between these actors' rules in case of conflict.[67]

These are issues of fundamental importance and the decision establishes principles that can be and below will be likened to constitutional principles.[68] However, based on how CAS in subsequent cases has relied upon *UCI & CONI*, the decision's main impact on CAS's jurisprudence and on sports law more generally does not relate to division of regulatory power but on the establishment of the principle of *lex mitior*[69] as a binding principle in international sports by merit of being a "fundamental principle in all democratic regimes."[70] Since the principle of *lex*

[67] Ibid., paras 11–23. There was also the complicating fact that the Italian federation was obligated by Italian law to comply with CONI's rules. Ibid., paras 24–30.

[68] See further Sect. 7.2.

[69] Meaning that "if the law relevant to the offence of the accused has been amended, the less severe law should be applied." ECtHR's decision 17 September 2009 in *Scoppola v. Italy* (no. 2), appl. no 10249/03, para 81.

[70] CAS 94/128, *UCI & CONI*, para 33 (my translation).

mitior is an issue in many CAS decisions, *UCI & CONI* is an often-cited decision. *UCI & CONI* is also important on a systemic level because in declaring that the principle of *lex mitior* must be respected, CAS also paved the way for a number of important subsequent decisions regarding setting appropriate sanctions.[71]

The difference between *UCI & CONI*'s importance as measured by indegree and PageRank can in part be explained by the fact that CAS sometimes, intentionally or unintentionally, fails to cite the principle's point of origin in CAS's jurisprudence. For example, some CAS decisions refer to *UCI v. FFC*[72] in support for the rule that the principle of *lex mitior* is applicable in disciplinary matters in sport.[73] However, if we read CAS's decision in *UCI v. FFC* we find that the panel's conclusion is explicitly based on *UCI & CONI* and other CAS decisions that, in turn, are based on *UCI & CONI*. PageRank is capable of more accurately measuring *UCI & CONI*'s extended impact on CAS jurisprudence in the absence of direct references by considering "indirect references" through such decisions as *UCI v. FFC*.[74]

5.4 Good or Just Old? The Example of Strict Liability and Proportional Sanctions

So far, the discussion about CAS's landmark decisions has been based on a static, snapshot image of the CAS case law network as it appears at the end of the studied period. But law is not static. It changes continuously and the law is not today what it was yesterday, nor will it be tomorrow what it is today; "all things move and nothing remains still."[75] This is not least true in legal orders where the law develops extensively through decisions and relevant for the present discussion regarding landmark decisions.

For example, a decision may have been an important decision initially, and was therefore cited frequently and by other important decisions, but has since declined in relevance because it was overruled or the law changed in a way that made the decision less relevant. Such changes will eventually be reflected in the decision's indegree and PageRank will eventually pick up on this decline, but it may take significant time before it is evident in the data.

---

[71] An illustrative example is CAS 96/156, *Foschi*, para 15.1, where CAS discusses the principles of lex mitior and proportionality as alternative grounds for departing from the written rules when it comes to setting a sanction.

[72] CAS 2000/A/289.

[73] See e.g. CAS 2001/A/318, *Virenque*, para 29; CAS 2008/A/1471 & 1486, *Tagliaferri*, para 9.6.1.

[74] See also Sect. 1.6.

[75] Plato 1921, secs. 401d, 402a (citing Heraclitus).

A straightforward and good illustration of this is the indegree centrality of some key CAS decisions concerning sanctioning athletes for doping violations in the absence of any (proven) individual fault. Many of CAS's early decisions concerned doping. Besides the above discussed *Quigley*, two such decisions were *Chagnaud* and *Foschi* that both concerned strict liability and proportional sanctions for doping violations.

Chagnaud concerned a French swimmer, Anne Chagnaud, who tested positive for a banned stimulant, etilephrine, during an international competition. Chagnaud's coach admitted that he had "accidentally" given her a capsule containing the substance in direct connection with the competition. Chagnaud pointed out that during the time period immediately surrounding a competition she had effectively no control over the supplies that she consumed or came in contact with and that she had to rely on her coach ensuring that the supplies do not contain banned substances.[76]

These claims were not disputed and the main issues in the case was whether Chagnaud in the absence of fault should be held responsible for a doping violation and, if so, what would constitute an appropriate sanction. The French federation and the international federation (FINA) concluded that accident or ignorance was not a defense under the applicable rules and suspended Chagnaud for two years. CAS noted that FINA's rules were based on the principle of strict liability under which fault is not a requisite for athletes' liability.[77] CAS concluded that a requirement for fault would, if applied strictly, make it practically impossible to police doping and that athletes that test positive for banned substances must be disqualified for the sake of fairness to other athletes.[78] While the panel believed that SGBs and sports rules ought to take the level of guilt into consideration when setting disciplinary sanctions in doping cases,[79] it acknowledged that it must be allowed under the applicable sports rules and that the applicable rules contained an irrefutable presumption of guilt.[80] However, CAS concluded that the governing bodies had actually not applied these rules rigorously and that the rules therefore, contrary to a literal interpretation, could be interpreted as allowing to vary the sanction by the degree of fault.[81]

In *Chagnaud*, CAS stopped short of establishing that the principle of proportionality applies as a general principle, that is regardless of the rules applicable in a particular sport, although it does mention the principle in passing. However, in *Foschi*, decided one and a half years later, CAS went further. Examining the very

---

[76] CAS 95/141, *Chagnaud*.

[77] Ibid., paras 8, 12.

[78] Ibid., paras 13, 15. The reasoning in *Chagnaud* in this manner shares many similarities with that of *Quigley*, decided one month later by a different set of arbitrators and without referring to *Chagnaud*.

[79] Ibid., paras 16, 19.

[80] Ibid., paras 19–20.

[81] Ibid., paras 20–24. The panel ultimately found that the suspension served at the time of its decision, thirteen and half months, was sufficient. Ibid., para 30.

same rules as in *Chagnaud*,[82] CAS declared that "[t]he general principle that a penalty must not be disproportionate to the fault or guilt of the accused must also be observed in doping cases";[83] that it had "serious doubts whether such a mandatory sanction of two years can be *legally justified*" in an extreme case;[84] and that CAS "must have flexibility to reduce a sanction" when the applicable rules are unclear.[85]

Quigley, *Chagnaud*, and *Foschi* show CAS's willingness to uphold the principle of strict liability or, viewed from a different perspective, set aside the principle of presumption of innocence because doing so would severely limit the efficacy of the anti-doping system. However, these decisions also show CAS's discomfort with the strict liability rule and willingness to avoid applying it in a way that leads to disproportionate sanctions,[86] for example through various means of interpretation.[87] In previous decisions, CAS had been able to infer setting a sanction that was proportional to the level of guilt from the applicable written rules.[88] The text of the rules applicable in *Chagnaud* were more rigid than in those previous cases and the panel's interpretation more extensive, even directly contrary to the letter of the rules, and in *Foschi* CAS showed a willingness to go even further.[89]

Between 1995 and 2004, *Quigley*, *Chagnaud,* and *Foschi* were some of the main sources used by CAS in subsequent cases to settle these sensitive issues.[90] As shown in the figure below, until 2005, *Quigley* and *Chagnaud* were cited equally frequently, most frequently among all CAS decisions, and *Foschi* was not far behind.

Whereas *Quigley* is still frequently cited by CAS, *Chagnaud* and *Foschi* have rarely been cited after 2005. As far as I have been able to determine, CAS has not cited *Chagnaud* a single time since 2009.[91] This cannot be explained by a shift in the type of cases that come before CAS. CAS has seen a significant increase in the number of doping-related disputes over time, particularly after 2005, and the doping-related disputes' portion of all decisions has remained largely the same over time.[92] Also, CAS still frequently refers to some of its decisions concerning doping

---

[82] Rule 4.17.4.1 of FINA's Medical Rules.

[83] CAS 96/156, *Foschi*, para 13.2 (emphasis omitted). Cf. CAS 2004/A/690, *Hipperdinger*, para 50 ("the principle of proportionality is a general principle of law that must also be observed in applying a sanction for a doping offence.").

[84] CAS 96/156, *Foschi*, para 13.2 (emphasis added).

[85] Ibid, para 15.1 (emphasis omitted), citing, *inter alia*, CAS 95/141, *Chagnaud.*

[86] Cf. Wise & Meyer 1997, p. 246; Nafziger 2006, p. 415.

[87] Erbsen 2006, p. 447.

[88] CAS 92/63, *Gundel*, para 13; CAS 92/86, *W. v. FEI.*

[89] For some examples of the subsequent development, see e.g. CAS 2004/A/690, *Hipperdinger*, para 50.

[90] See e.g. CAS 98/208, *Wang et al.*; CAS 98/214, *Bouras*; CAS 99/A/246, *Ward*; CAS 2001/A/317, *Aanes*.

[91] CAS 2008/A/1583 & 1584, *Benfica & Vitória*, para 42; CAS 2009/A/1768, *Hansen*, para 15.5.

[92] See Fig. 3.10 *CAS Decisions Over Time - Football, Doping, and the Rest.*

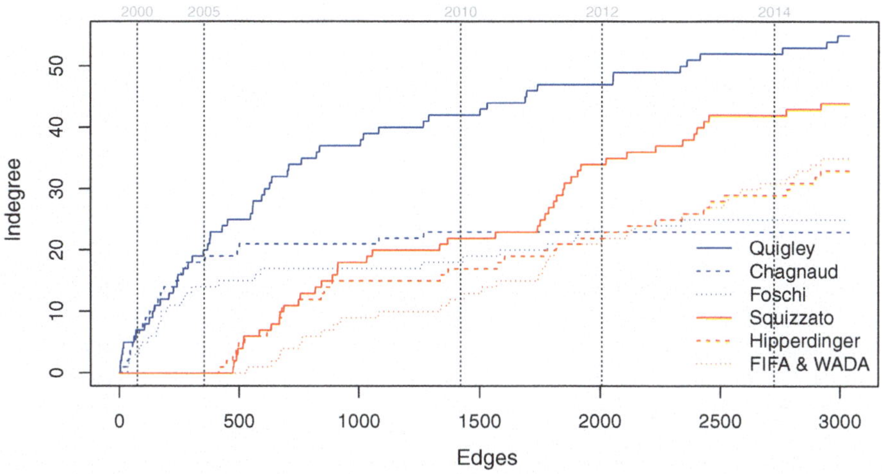

Fig. 5.5 Indegree of Strict Liability and Proportionality Decisions Over Time. [*Source* The author]

violations.[93] The more important trend is that some of the classic CAS decisions discussed above have been replaced by other, newer CAS decisions, many of which were decided around 2005.

One of the top cases in the 2005 group is *Hipperdinger*.[94] The case concerned a Spanish tennis player, Diego Hipperdinger, who tested positive for cocaine in connection with a tournament in Chile. The athlete claimed that he had consumed a tea and chewed on some leaves for the purpose of relieving altitude sickness without knowing that the products came from the coca plant.[95] When discussing the proportionality of the sanction in *Hipperdinger*, CAS strongly distanced itself from its previous decisions on the matter:

> [I]n the past, CAS case law took considerable care in measuring a sanction to the individual offence and the situation of the offender. However, the CAS case law of the past is based on anti-doping rules of different [International federations] and other institutions. Those anti-doping regulations were not necessarily harmonised and indeed varied considerably, in particular regarding sanctions. The [World Anti-Doping Code] has changed this situation.[96]

Thus, according to the *Hipperdinger* panel, the implementation of the World Anti-Doping Code (WADC) had made previous case law irrelevant – although it is unclear exactly which previous decisions were no longer good law – by replacing the standards used under various sport rules with common ones, including specifically rules for ensuring proportional sanctions. Also, in its ruling in *Wang*

93 See above Fig. 5.5 *Indegree of Strict Liability and Proportionality Decisions Over Time.*

94 See above Table 5.1 *Top Decisions by Indegree* and below Table 5.2 *Top Decisions by PageRank.*

95 CAS 2004/A/690, *Hipperdinger.*

96 Ibid., para 50.

Table 5.2 Top Decisions by PageRank. [*Source* The author]

Case	PageRank
CAS 94/129, *Quigley*	0.01053
CAS 94/128, *UCI & CONI*	0.00508
CAS 96/149, *Cullwick*	0.00442
CAS 98/208, *Wang et al.*	0.00420
CAS 2005/A/830, *Squizzato*	0.00394
OG 04/003, *Edwards*	0.00383
CAS 98/211, *Smith de Bruin*	0.00378
CAS 93/109, *FFTri & ITU*	0.00359
CAS 2000/A/274, *Susin*	0.00356
CAS 96/156, *Foschi*	0.00353
CAS 2005/A/847, *Knauss*	0.00351
CAS 2005/C/976 & 986, *FIFA & WADA*	0.00350
CAS 2005/A/899, *Aris I*	0.00328
CAS 2006/A/1025, *Puerta*	0.00324
CAS 95/141, *Chagnaud*	0.00323
CAS 98/200, *AEK Athens*	0.00317
CAS 2004/A/690, *Hipperdinger*	0.00317
CAS 2001/A/317, *Aanes*	0.00312
OG 96/003 & 004, *Korneev & Gouliev*	0.00311
CAS 2004/A/574, *Associacao Portuguesa de desportos v. Club Valencia*	0.00289
CAS 97/169, *Menegotto*	0.00281
CAS 2005/A/983, *Club Atletico Penarol et al.*	0.00276
CAS 2009/A/1920, *FK Pobeda et al.*	0.00273
CAS 2006/A/1180, *Ribery*	0.00258
CAS 2007/A/1370 & 1376, *Lucas Dodo*	0.00252
CAS 98/214, *Bouras*	0.00248
CAS 2003/A/484, *Vencill*	0.00247
CAS 2006/A/1119, *UCI v. L. & RFEC*	0.00243
CAS 2005/A/952, *Ashley Cole*	0.00240
CAS 2009/A/1870, *Hardy*	0.00239

et al. the Swiss Federal Tribunal (SFT) held that it will rarely set aside a CAS decision for reasons of the proportionality of the sanction. Only if the sanction constitutes "an attack on personal rights which was extremely serious and totally disproportionate to the behaviour penalised" would it motivate the SFT's intervention.[97] In doing so, the SFT in practice gave CAS its blessing to apply the

[97] SFT's decision of 31 March 1999 in Case 5P.83/1999 (*Wang et al. v. FINA*), para 3.c (as translated in Digest of CAS Awards II). This was a review of the decision in CAS 98/208, *Wang et al.* See also CAS 2005/C/976 & 986, *FIFA & WADA*, para 143 ("only if the sanction is

WADC's sanction-setting scheme as it appears unlikely that the SFT will override a sanction set in accordance with the WADC.[98] This decision also had an impact on the development of the WADC and was, in a manner, codified.[99] These explanations help us understand why the precedential power of decisions like *Chagnaud* and *Foschi* decreased around 2004–2005.

Another important decision settled by CAS in 2005 is *Squizzato*. Like *Hipperdinger, Squizzato* concerned athletes' duty of diligence to ensure that they are not exposed to a banned substance. The case concerned Giorgia Squizzato, an Italian swimmer and at the time of the incident a minor, who faced a one-year ban for testing positive for traces of a steroid.[100] Squizzato had unknowingly exposed herself to the substance by using an over-the-counter foot ointment that her mother had given her to treat a skin affliction.[101] The applicable anti-doping rules allowed the standard sanction to be adjusted based on the athlete's degree of fault or negligence,[102] but CAS took a stand for also upholding the principle of proportionality as a general principle. The panel found that the principle of proportionality is "a widely accepted general principle of sports law"[103] and under Swiss law.[104] In its reasoning in *Squizzato*, CAS showed a greater degree of independence from the sports rules than it had in many previous decisions:[105]

> [T]he Panel holds that the mere adoption of the WADA Code… by a respective Federation does not force the conclusion that there is no other possibility for greater or lesser reduction of a sanction than allowed by DC 10.5. The mere fact that regulations of a sport federation derive from the World Anti-Doping Code does not change the nature of these rules. They are still – like before – regulations of an association which cannot (directly or indirectly) replace fundamental and general legal principles like the doctrine of proportionality a priori for every thinkable case.

The *Squizzato* panel then turned to interpreting the rule for a lower than standard sanction: no fault or negligence or no significant fault or negligence. CAS found that she did not bear no fault or negligence; it is negligent for an athlete, even a minor, not to check the content of a medical cream. But CAS also emphasized that Squizzato had not intended to gain a competitive advantage and that her failure was "mild in comparison with an athlete that is using doping products in order to gain such advantage" and therefore concluded that she was not guilty of significant fault

---

evidently and grossly disproportionate in comparison with the proved rule violation and if it is considered as a violation of fundamental justice and fairness, would the Panel regard such a sanction as abusive and, thus, contrary to mandatory Swiss law.").

98 Cf. Duffy 2013, p. 37.

99 CAS 2005/A/830, *Squizzato*, para 47. Cf. Nafziger 2006, p. 415; Mitten 2014, p. 70.

100 The facts of *Squizzato* in this regard bear some resemblance to those in 96/156, *Foschi*.

101 CAS 2005/A/830, *Squizzato*.

102 Ibid., para 26.

103 Ibid., para 44, quoting CAS 1999/A/246, *Ward*, para 31.

104 CAS 2005/A/830, *Squizzato*, para 45.

105 Ibid., para 48. Compare CAS 95/141, *Chagnaud*, para 19 ("la Formation observe qu'un tel développement n'est possible que si les règlements applicables le permettent").

or negligence.[106] In this manner, *Squizzato* made intent a relevant factor when assessing the level of fault or negligence and, consequently, when setting the sanction, even though there was nothing in the wording of the anti-doping rules supporting this at the time. It was also held in *Squizzato*, in accordance with what was explained above, that "the principle of proportionality would apply if the award were to constitute an attack on personal rights which was serious and totally disproportionate to the behaviour penalized,"[107] but CAS did not consider a one-year ban to violate this standard.

Squizzato disturbed CAS's existing jurisprudence.[108] It has been used in many subsequent cases, many of which were quite difficult or controversial, as a reference point for assessing doped athletes' level of fault or negligence.[109]

5.5 Strategically Placed Decisions

As discussed above, indegree centrality and PageRank represent two ways to think about and measure how individual decisions' impact case law on a systemic level. Indegree and PageRank are distinctly different from each other but they are also similar in that they measure a decision's importance in terms of how extensive, in a quantitative sense, its effect is on subsequent decisions.

There is a natural, but not absolute, connection between, on the one hand, how frequently the issues decided in a decision are the subject of adjudication and, on the other, the decision's indegree and PageRank. For example, the fact that a large portion of all CAS jurisprudence concerns doping violations increases the likelihood that CAS will refer to its previous conclusions regarding the application of the principle of strict liability in doping cases like *Quigley* and *Squizzato*. Although PageRank is calculated in a different way than indegree centrality, it still reflects this relationship.[110]

This does not mean that indegree and PageRank are invalid or flawed measurements for measuring the importance of decisions. When comparing two decisions that each settle a point of law one might on good grounds argue that the one establishing the legal rule on the more frequently adjudicated issue is the more important one, all else being equal. However, this is not the only way to think about decisions' structural impact and in this section we shall consider two alternatives.

A first alternative approach is to consider to what extent decisions may have a substantial systemic impact on case law by connecting otherwise disconnected or weakly-connected decisions. Using this approach, which emphasizes breadth over

---

106 CAS 2005/A/830, *Squizzato*, paras 34–39.

107 Ibid., para 50.

108 Duffy 2013, p. 44.

109 See e.g. CAS 2005/A/951, *Cañas*; CAS 2006/A/1025, *Puerta*; CAS 2007/A/1252, *Mellouli*.

110 See above Sect. 5.3.

depth, a decision is considered important because it functions as an important intermediate. This can be measured using betweenness centrality. A decision's betweenness centrality in the CAS case law network is equal to the number of shortest paths from all vertices to all vertices that pass through that decision.[111] Betweenness can be described as measuring to what extent a particular decision influences the spread of information across the network.[112]

When we calculate betweenness centrality for all decisions in the CAS case law network, we find that the decisions with the highest betweenness centrality are quite different than those with high indegree or PageRank. However, there are some decisions that score high on all three measurements, for example *Squizzato*[113] and *FIFA & WADA*.[114,115]

Many references made in CAS decisions tend to be to other previous CAS decisions concerning the same subject matter.[116] Consequently, CAS decisions that have a high betweenness centrality tend to be decisions that are cited on issues that are relatively unrelated to any particular subject matter. Differently phrased, decisions with high betweenness centrality tend to be cases cited on legal issues whose relevance transcend subject matter. Prominent examples of such issues are jurisdictional, procedural, and evidentiary issues.

This can be exemplified with *Valverde II*.[117] *Valverde II* is the second of three CAS decisions involving Alejandro Valverde, a Spanish cyclist.[118] All three decisions concern various issues relating to Valverde's involvement in a Spanish police investigation into doping in cycling in 2004 (Operación Puerto). The Spanish police discovered that a Spanish doctor, Fuentes, was assisting a large number of athletes with doping and one of the athletes implicated in this investigation was Valverde.[119] The Spanish cycling federation decided not to open disciplinary proceedings against Valverde. However, CONI, supported by the World Anti-Doping Agency (WADA) and UCI, initiated anti-doping proceedings against Valverde in the Italian Tribunale Nazionale Antidoping, which subsequently issued Valverde a two-year ban "from participating in or attending athletic events organized under the auspices of CONI or related national sport organizations in

---

[111] See Freeman 1979. Regarding shortest paths, see further Sect. 3.2.

[112] See e.g. Puig 2014, p. 408.

[113] CAS 2005/A/830.

[114] CAS 2005/C/976 & 986.

[115] See Table 5.3 *Top Decisions by Betweenness*.

[116] This is also evident in that vertices tend to cluster based on subject matter. See Sect. 6.2.

[117] CAS 2009/A/1879.

[118] The first decision is CAS 2007/O/1381, *Valverde I*, and the third is CAS 2007/A/1396 & 1402, *Valverde III*.

[119] More specifically, the case against Valverde turned on whether the so-called "Blood Bag no. 18", which Spanish police had collected in Fuentes's office, contained Valverde's blood.

Table 5.3 Top Decisions by Betweenness. [*Source* The author]

Case	Betweenness
CAS 2009/A/1879, *Valverde II*	5096
CAS 2001/A/317, *Aanes*	3852
CAS 2005/C/976 & 986, *FIFA & WADA*	3087
CAS 2009/A/1880 & 1881, *FC Sion & El-Hadary*	2773
CAS 2007/A/1396, *Valverde & RFEC*	2761
CAS 2004/A/748, *Ekimov v. Hamilton*	2577
CAS 2008/A/1574, *D'Arcy II*	2382
CAS 2011/A/2384, *Contador*	2167
CAS 2005/A/830, *Squizzato*	1951
CAS 2007/A/1370 & 1376, *Lucas Dodo*	1863
CAS 2004/A/777, *ARcycling AG v. UCI*	1793
CAS 2005/A/983, *Club Atletico Penarol et al.*	1726
CAS 2008/A/1545, *Anderson et al.*	1672
CAS 2008/A/1583, *Sport Lisboa, Benfica Futebol et al.*	1578
CAS 99/A/234, *Meca-Medina I*	1523
CAS 98/208, *Wang et al.*	1486
CAS 2011/A/2615, *Fauconnet*	1459
CAS 2003/O/486, *Fulham FC v. Olympique Lyonnais*	1455
CAS 2008/A/1705, *Grasshopper v. Alianza de Lima*	1408
CAS 2006/A/1025, *Puerta*	1391
CAS 2000/A/274, *Susin*	1346
CAS 2001/A/337, *Bray*	1324
CAS 2009/A/1920, *FK Pobeda et al.*	1256
CAS 2007/A/1394, *Landis*	1233
CAS 2003/A/452, *IAAF v. MAR & B*	1163
CAS 2007/A/1433, *Di Luca*	1141
CAS 2008/A/1718, *Yegorova et al.*	1131
CAS 2006/A/1175, *International DanceSport Federation*	1117
CAS 2008/A/1519, *Metuzalem*	1072
CAS 2008/A/1594, *Sheykhov v. FILA*	1067

Italy."[120] Valverde appealed the decision to CAS which in *Valverde II* ended up upholding it.[121]

Valverde II is not a particularly frequently cited CAS decision.[122] However, the decision contains some key conclusions that CAS has since relied upon in

[120] CAS 2007/A/1396 & 1402, *Valverde III*.

[121] CAS 2009/A/1879.

[122] With 15 citations, the decision falls outside the top 30 by indegree, see above Table 5.1 *Top Decisions by Indegree*.

subsequent decisions, some of which concern doping but also others that involve distinctly different factual circumstances, including cases concerning contract violations[123] and corruption[124] in football. The reason that *Valverde II* has such broad relevance is that the decision deals with important issues concerning procedural fairness. Valverde argued that the evidence had been collected illegally and that it should therefore be inadmissible. In *Valverde II,* CAS concluded that it is not bound by the rules of state courts and that in the absence of more specific rules governing matters of procedure and evidence it has broad discretion to fill the gaps, subject only to the limitation that the decision must be compatible "with the values recognized in a State governed by the rule of law."[125] Also, with regard to claims of violations of procedural fairness more generally, *Valverde II* is frequently cited as a source of the principle that any procedural failures in the lower instances are "healed" through a *de novo* hearing by CAS.[126]

5.6 Characteristics of Landmark Decisions

There is empirical support for the existence of landmark decisions in CAS jurisprudence. However, it follows from the discussion above that it is impossible to identify one single standard for what constitutes a landmark decision or, consequently, to establish a definitive list of CAS landmark decisions. Rather, there are different reasonable ways to think about and identify landmark decisions. As discussed in this chapter, a strong case can be made that *Quigley,*[127] *UCI & CONI,*[128] *Squizzato,*[129] and *Valverde II*[130] are all landmark decisions, although in different ways. The findings and discussion above reveal the complexity of the term landmark decisions but also, at the same time, allows for some general observations about what characterizes CAS decisions that can be considered important using different approaches.

First, under all measurements considered, many of the important CAS decisions concern disciplinary actions in general and doping violations in particular. If we consider centrality score by subject matter, we see that CAS decisions involving doping violations have higher centrality scores, both in terms of indegree centrality

123 See e.g. CAS 2009/A/1880 & 1881, *El-Hadary*, para 21.

124 CAS 2011/A/2426, *Adamu*, para 76.

125 CAS 2009/A/1879, *Valverde II*, paras 69–70, as translated in CAS 2011/A/2426, *Adamu*, para 76. Subsequently cited in e.g. CAS 2011/A/2425, *Fusimalohi*, para 80; CAS 2011/A/2426, *Adamu*, para 76; CAS 2011/A/2384 & 2386, *Contador*, para 20.

126 See e.g. CAS 2011/A/2433, *Diakite*, para 7; CAS 2012/A/2922, *Fernandes*, para 102; CAS 2013/A/3264, *Achhakir*, para 95. Regarding this principle, see also further Sect. 7.4.

127 CAS 94/129.

128 CAS 94/128.

129 CAS 2005/A/830.

130 CAS 2009/A/1879.

and PageRank, than decisions concerning other subject matters across the board.[131] This is hardly surprising. The great majority of all cases that come before CAS concerns these matters and CAS jurisprudence is particularly dominated by doping-related disputes. Even though there has been some development in recent years, doping cases still make up roughly half of CAS's collected jurisprudence.[132] It is thus natural, even inevitable, that many of the principles established and subsequently relied upon in CAS decisions will concern these substantive areas.[133]

As discussed above, a static examination may be deceiving. Until the mid-1990s, nearly all references made by CAS to its previous decisions concerned decisions involving doping matters. CAS's doping-related decisions' relative dominance in terms of received references subsequently declined until 2009 but has since stabilized on still dominant levels. Considering that doping as a subject matter continues to dominate CAS's docket and jurisprudence, it is interesting to note that CAS's top decisions include relatively many non-doping-related cases.[134]

Second, many of the CAS decisions identified as particularly important above were decided in the earlier years of CAS. Again, this is natural. Early on, CAS had to deal with a number of important, unregulated, complicated, and important issues for the first time, for example as it did in *Quigley* and *UCI & CONI*. It makes natural sense that CAS, when it in subsequent cases faced those same issues again, relied upon and referred back to those decisions. But not all landmark decisions are old decisions. As discussed in this chapter, there are some, more recent CAS decisions that are quite central in the CAS case law network.[135] CAS decisions decided in 2005 appear to do particularly well in this regard, which to a great extent can be explained by the adoption of the WADA Code and the need for CAS to (re-) examine many legal issues as a consequence.

One way of confirming these impressions is to track the average indegree and PageRank of all CAS decisions decided in a particular year.[136] Doing so suggests that 1995 was a real "super year" with regard to CAS establishing landmark decisions. However, the importance of the class of 1995 is probably exaggerated by the fact that CAS only issued eight decisions that year,[137] six of which are included in the dataset. Mean scores are easily distorted when dealing with a small sample. If we look at the cases decided by CAS in 1995, we find that most of the centrality score of that year's decisions come from two decisions: *UCI & CONI*[138] and *Quigley*.[139] These are certainly important decisions, arguably some of the most

131 See above Sect. 5.3 and Sect. 6.3.1.

132 See Sect. 2.4.

133 See also Chap. 7.

134 This is studied in greater detail in Chap. 7.

135 See above Sect. 5.4.

136 See Fig. 3.15 *Indegree Centrality Over Time*.

137 See CAS, Statistics 2016.

138 CAS 94/128.

139 CAS 94/129.

important, but the difference between 1995 and the immediately surrounding years is probably less distinct than the numbers suggest.

Tracking mean indegree centrality by year lends some support to the impression that CAS decisions issued in 2005 have had greater impact on CAS's case law compared to the decisions in many other years. 2005 represents a break in the trend compared to preceding and subsequent years, but the difference is not as distinct as one might perhaps have expected.

References

Agnoloni T (2014) Network Analysis of Italian Constitutional Case Law. Semantic Processing of Legal Texts (SPLeT) 2014:24–28

Anderson J (ed) (2013) Leading Cases in Sports Law. T.M.C. Asser Press, The Hague

Barabási A-L, Albert R (1999) Emergence of Scaling in Random Networks. Science 286:509–512

CAS (2016) Statistics 2016. http://www.tas-cas.org/fileadmin/user_upload/CAS_statistics_2016_.pdf. Accessed 7 September 2018

David R, Brierley J (1985) Major Legal Systems in the World Today. Stevens and Sons, London

Derlén M, Lindholm J (2015) Characteristics of Precedent: The Case Law of the European Court of Justice in Three Dimensions. German Law Journal 16(5):1073–1098

Derlén M, Lindholm J (2016a) Bosman: A Legacy Beyond Sports. In: Duval A, Van Rompuy B (eds) The Legacy of Bosman. T.M.C. Asser Press, The Hague, pp. 31–49

Derlén M, Lindholm J (2016b) Judiciell aktivism eller prejudikatbildning? En empirisk granskning av Högsta domstolen. Svensk Juristtidning 2016:143–158

Derlén M, Lindholm J (2017) Peek-a-boo, It's a Case Law System. German Law Journal 18 (3):647–686

Duffy J (2013) Proportionality of sanctions under the WADA Code: CAS jurisprudence and the need for a strict approach. Australasian Dispute Resolution Journal 24(1):26–40

Erbsen A (2006) The Substance and Illusion of Lex Sportiva. In: Blackshaw I, Siekman R, Soek J (eds) The Court of Arbitration for Sport 1984–2004. T.M.C. Asser Press, The Hague, pp. 441–454

Foster K (2006) Lex Sportiva and Lex Ludica: The Court of Arbitration for Sport's Jurisprudence. Entertainment and Sports Law Journal 3(2)

Fowler J, Jeon S (2008) Authority of Precedent. Social Network 30:16–30

Freeman L (1979) Centrality in Social Networks: Conceptual Clarification. Social Networks 1:215–239

Geist A (2010) The Open Revolution: Using Citation Analysis to Improve Legal Text Retrieval. European Journal of Legal Studies 2(3):137–145

Komárek J (2011) Judicial Lawmaking and Precedent in Supreme Courts. LSE Law, Society and Economy Working Papers 4/2011. http://ssrn.com/abstract=1793219. Accessed 6 July 2018

Louw A M (2012) Ambush Marketing and the Mega-Event Monopoly: How Laws are Abused to Protect Commercial Rights to Major Sporting Events. T.M.C. Asser Press, The Hague

Lupu Y, Voeten E (2011) Precedent in International Courts: A Network Analysis of Case Citations by the European Court of Human Rights. British Journal of Political Science 42:413–439

Maduro M P, Azoulai L (2010) Introduction. In: Maduro M P, Azoulai L (eds) The Past and Future of EU Law: The Classics of EU Law Revisited on the 50th Anniversary of the Rome Treaty. Hart, Oxford, pp. xiii–xx

Martens D-R (2006) CAS Landmark Decisions. In: Blackshaw I, Siekman R, Soek J (eds) The Court of Arbitration for Sport 1984–2004. T.M.C. Asser Press, The Hague, pp. 235–245

Mitten M (2014) The Court of Arbitration for Sport and its Global Jurisprudence: International Legal Pluralism in a World Without National Boundaries. CAS Bulletin 2014(2):48–79
Nafziger J (2006) Lex Sportiva and CAS. In: Blackshaw I, Siekman R, Soek J (eds) The Court of Arbitration for Sport 1984–2004. T.M.C. Asser Press, The Hague, pp. 409–419
Neale T (2013) Citation Analysis of Canadian Case Law. Journal of Open Access to Law 1(1):1–60
Plato (1921) Cratylus. In: Fowler H (transl) Twelve Volumes 12. Harvard University Press, Cambridge
Puig S (2014) Social Capital in the Arbitration Market. The European Journal of International Law 25(2):387–424
Redner S (1998) How Popular is Your Paper? An Empirical Study of the Citation Distribution. European Physical Journal B4:131–134
Siems M (2014) Comparative Law. Cambridge University Press, Cambridge
Strömholm S (2000) General Features of Swedish Law. In: Bogdan M (ed) Swedish Law in the New Millenium. Norstedts Juridik, Stockholm, pp. 31–47
Tarissan F, Nollez-Goldbach R (2014) The Network of the International Criminal Court Decisions as a Complex System. In: Sanayei A, Zelinka I, Rössler O (eds) ISCS 2013: Interdisciplinary Symposium on Complex Systems. Springer, Berlin pp. 255–264
van Opijnen M (2012) Citation Analysis and Beyond: In Search of Indicators Measuring Case Law Importance. Frontiers in Artificial Intelligence and Applications 250:95–104
Vauchez A (2016) What is a Classic in Law? Methodological Notes on Grandes arrêts at the European Court of Justice. In: Davies B, Nicola F (eds) EU Law Stories: Contextual and Critical Histories of EU Jurisprudence. Cambridge University Press, Cambridge, pp. 21–34
Watts D, Strogatz S (1998) Collective Dynamics of 'Small-World' Networks. Nature 393:440–442
Wild A (ed) (2012) CAS and Football: Landmark Cases. T.M.C. Asser Press, The Hague
Wise A, Meyer B (1997) International Sports Law and Business. Kluwer Law International, Boston

Chapter 6
Structure of CAS's Jurisprudence

Abstract Lawyers are accustomed to organizing the law into distinct fields or areas that serve as a framework for understanding and approaching a legal order. The case law of the Court of Arbitration for Sport (CAS) is no exception in this regard, but because of the nature of the disputes that are adjudicated by CAS, traditional areas of law such as criminal or family law carry little relevance and can arguably be replaced by issues that are prominent in CAS's case law, for example doping and eligibility. By applying and comparing different approaches, this chapter explores the empirical existence of distinct communities of CAS decisions, the connections between these communities, and whether CAS decisions' role as a source of law differ between these communities.

6.1 The Importance of Structure

In this chapter, we continue exploring the jurisprudence of the Court of Arbitration for Sport (CAS). Whereas the previous chapter studied individual CAS decisions, this chapter seeks to identify and analyze the structure of CAS jurisprudence on a more general level. While individual CAS decisions constitute the basic building blocks of this structure, this chapter analyzes CAS jurisprudence from a broader perspective where the role of individual CAS decisions is largely limited to being used as illustrative examples. For the purpose of exploring the structure of CAS jurisprudence it is broken down into two components: communities and connections. It is necessary to clarify the meaning of these terms and the value of the distinction.

The term *community* is here used broadly to refer to a group of CAS decisions. From a legal perspective, the most obvious basis for classifying and grouping decisions is based on the issues addressed in those decisions. When issues and relevant rules and principles are grouped together based on some shared characteristic, lawyers might refer to these as areas. In this manner, a community of CAS decisions can be said to roughly correspond to an area of sports law. As explored in greater detail in the next section, there is no single, objectively superior method for

J. Lindholm, *The Court of Arbitration for Sport and Its Jurisprudence*,
ASSER International Sports Law Series,
https://doi.org/10.1007/978-94-6265-285-9_6

identifying communities. One can apply different approaches for identifying communities in CAS jurisprudence and each approach will produce a slightly different picture of the communities.

The term *connection* refers to how such communities of decisions relate to each other. One way that communities (and individual decisions) relate to each other is by relying on each other as a source of law or, to view that relationship from the opposite perspective, by being relied upon as a source of law. Together with identifying communities, identifying to what extent communities rely on and is relied on by other communities exposes fundamental information about the structure of CAS jurisprudence.

There are several reasons why identifying and analyzing the structure of CAS jurisprudence is important. Identifying communities of decisions and connections between communities reduces the otherwise overwhelming complexity of a large number of decisions to a manageable but fundamentally accurate model. The need for identifying structures is arguably particularly strong when it comes to orders that are largely based on case law and where the risk of getting lost in the specific circumstances of individual cases are higher. It also has a pedagogical value. Identifying communities can greatly assist in understanding and navigating a (supposedly) transnational legal order, similar to how the division of law into areas of law assists understanding and navigating national and international legal orders. Finally, it is relevant for assessing the existence of a case law-based transnational legal order. If we can determine that CAS jurisprudence follows a coherent and foreseeable structure, this would support the existence of a transnational legal *order*. To put it simply, in a well-functioning case law-based legal order we expect to find decisions dealing with the same issue citing each other.

6.2 Communities

6.2.1 Three Approaches to Community Detection

As described above, the dataset covering CAS jurisprudence includes certain information about the decisions (metadata) provided by CAS or, when no such data was provided, reconstructed using CAS's example. One such type of metadata found in the CAS jurisprudence database is CAS's classification of all its decisions as dealing with one (and exactly one) of eight subject matters:

(i) transfers (T);
(ii) non-transfer-related contractual disputes (Ct);
(iii) doping (Do);
(iv) non-doping-related disciplinary disputes (Di);
(v) nationality (N);
(vi) non-nationality-related eligibility (E);

(vii) governance (G); and
(viii) other matters (X).

CAS's subject matter classification constitutes a natural element for exploring the structure of its jurisprudence where these eight subject matters can be treated as the eight main communities of the jurisprudence. CAS has selected these eight subject matters to describe its jurisprudence and because the categorization is created by humans it reflects how those humans perceive the structure of the jurisprudence. We can safely assume that CAS is capable, rational, and intends to be helpful to those who seek to explore its jurisprudence, and these categories more specifically would seem to reflect what CAS perceives as being the main subject matters that it encounters.[1] Because it reflects the understanding of CAS, CAS's subject matter classification is likely to provide valuable insight.

However, we should be careful about approaching these subject matters as absolute truths for the purpose of dividing CAS's jurisprudence into communities.[2] Human knowledge can be and tends to be imperfect, for example because it is based on imperfect data or because it is outdated. The institutional knowledge of CAS of its own jurisprudence is no exception in this regard. For this reason it is worthwhile to question established theories and models. For example, are the cases before CAS dealing with nationality actually distinct from the cases concerning eligibility as CAS's classification seems to suggest?

To test established models such as subject matter taxonomies, we need to use neutral methods that, as far as possible, are neither based on nor affected by human biases. One approach for empirically testing for the existence of such groups is to search for clusters or communities in the CAS case law network.[3] There are various methods that can be used for identifying such communities in case law.

Using such approaches to detect communities is not merely a tool for testing CAS's own subject matter classification. Previous studies of the jurisprudence of judicial bodies have been successful in identifying communities of case law. For example, using Newman's algorithm,[4] Lupu and Voeten were able to prove the existence of communities in the case law of the European Court of Human Rights (ECtHR).[5] Similarly, using the Mapequation algorithm[6] we were in a previous study able to detect communities in the case law of the Court of Justice of the European Union (CJEU).[7] If similar methods fail to detect communities in CAS

[1] The fact that each case is only assigned one subject matter could arguably suggest that CAS perceives these subject matters as clearly distinct and that each case can only deal with one subject matter.

[2] Peel et al. 2017.

[3] See generally Newman 2006.

[4] Newman 2004.

[5] Lupu and Voeten 2011, pp. 434–438.

[6] Rosvall et al. 2009.

[7] Derlén et al. 2013. See also ibid., Fig. 6.3.

jurisprudence, this could constitute a reason for questioning the existence of a case law-based legal order, or at least of the maturity of such an order.

In this section, we will use two, quite different such approaches for community detection: LDA topic modelling and co-citation clustering. Together with the CAS's own subject matter classification, these three different models will be compared and analyzed. For pedagogical reasons, I will below refer to the different communities identified using these three approaches as *subject matters*, *topics*, and *clusters* respectively.

6.2.2 LDA Topic Modelling

The first method to be addressed is topic modelling. In examining CAS jurisprudence in search of communities, we are departing from the assumption that CAS deals with a certain number of topics. This is an assumption that is reasonably safe and one that we share with CAS itself; CAS's list of subject matters is nothing but a list of topics.

Over the last decades, research in the intersection between computer science and linguistics has developed statistical methods, referred to as topic modelling, for summarizing a text collection (corpus) in terms of a number of themes or topics or, more precisely described, "probabilistic models for uncovering the underlying semantic structure of a document collection based on a hierarchical Bayesian analysis of the original texts…"[8]

A leading method for topic modelling is Latent Dirichlet Allocation or LDA topic modelling.[9] LDA topic modelling is based on the assumption that underneath a corpus there is an unknown structure of topics. This structure is reflected in the individual documents, each of which may and frequently will address several topics. Also, the same word may mean different things when used in different contexts. In trying to identify that underlying structure, LDA topic modelling takes a bag-of-words-approach where the order of words is irrelevant. Instead, LDA topic modelling uses a repeated, multi-step process using unsupervised machine learning to cluster words based on the hypothesis that words that have similar meaning will cluster together in the documents. In this manner, LDA topic modelling seeks to provide the best description of the different topics appearing in the entire corpus (in our case the entire text of all collected CAS decisions) and in the individual documents of which it consists (in our case the individual CAS decisions). Each topic is essentially a list of all words found in the corpus along with the relative probability that a word appears together with the other words.[10]

---

[8] Blei and Lafferty 2009, p. 71.

[9] Blei et al. 2003.

[10] Blei et al. 2003; Blei 2012.

LDA topic modelling has previously been successfully applied in the field of law. For example, in studying the content of the Yale Law Journal, Blei and Lafferty identified topics that roughly correspond to established areas of law and legal issues such as criminal law, labor law, gender discrimination, and contract law.[11] Another example is a study by Panagis et al. of the jurisprudence of the CJEU which indicates that LDA topic modelling can be used to detect "the dynamic properties of case-law."[12]

The process began by creating a corpus consisting of the full text of all collected CAS decisions.[13] This corpus contained a total of 101,095 unique words. However, some of these words carry no information about the topics addressed, such as words relating to CAS itself,[14] articles,[15] numbers, months, pronouns,[16] and prepositions.[17] 243 such words, many of which are very common, were removed from consideration to facilitate the process of identifying topics. The remaining words, which appear 2,733,132 times in the corpus, were analyzed using LDA topic modelling,[18] identifying the main twelve topics in the corpus.[19] Additionally, the prevalence of each topic in each CAS decision was calculated, information that was subsequently used to group decisions by topic.

6.2.3 Understanding Topics

The next step in the process is to analyze these topics in order to better understand and describe the nature of each topic. Topic modelling essentially reveals the most natural topics by clustering words. By analyzing these words, we can understand

---

11 Blei and Lafferty 2009, Fig. 6.3.

12 Panagis et al. 2016, p. 165.

13 Some of the decisions collected and considered in full text, see Sect. 1.5, were either in print or not in a machine-readable format. The corpus therefore ended up consisting of the text of 785 CAS decisions for a total of 6,189,300 tokens (words). The corpus was preprocessed to facilitate analysis, primarily by removing punctuation and converting all text to lower case.

14 E.g. "tribunal", "arbitration", and "tas".

15 E.g. "the", "la", and "le".

16 E.g. "she", "her", and "elle".

17 E.g. "à", "on", and "for".

18 More specifically this study employed the implementation of LDA topic modelling incorporated in the Mallet machine learning package for R.

19 See below Table 6.1 *Topic Model, Topic Description*. LDA topic modelling does not identify an optimal number of topics. Rather, the number of topics in the corpus is a parameter to be set in the LDA algorithm. Because CAS has identified eight subject matters, this was used as a starting point for deciding the number of topics. However, manual analysis confirmed that, due to the multilingual nature of CAS jurisprudence, many of the topics initially identified were essentially different language versions of the same topic. The number of topics was therefore increased accordingly.

Table 6.1 Topic Model: Topic Description. [*Source* The author]

Label	Topic 1	Topic 2	Topic 3	Topic 4	Topic 5	Topic 6	Topic 7	Topic 8	Topic 9	Topic 10	Topic 11	Topic 12
	Contractual breaches	German	Doping procedure	Doping sanction	Non-contractual breaches	Doping obligations	French	Australia	Eligibility	Italian	Doping and medical treatment	Contractual obligations
Top words (probability of occurrence in parenthesis)	fifa (3.07), contract (1.76), law (0.72), football (0.69), employment (0.63), fc (0.57), amount (0.53), players (0.48), compensation (0.47), dispute (0.47)	wada (1.46), der (0.89), die (0.8), mfa (0.57), und (0.41), w (0.36), antidoping (0.32), qfa (0.32), 19 (0.29), von (0.29)	doping (1.21), laboratory (1.06), analysis (0.89), test (0.84), samples (0.75), results (0.71), evidence (0.62), iaaf (0.59), hearing (0.52), urine (0.49)	doping (2.12), prohibited (1.51), substance (1.48), anti (1.09), period (0.96), wada (0.89), ineligibility (0.84), sanction (0.75), fault (0.7), use (0.63)	uefa (2.53), match (1.03), disciplinary (0.79), football (0.6), clubs (0.44), law (0.44), statutes (0.43), evidence (0.4), fenerbahçe (0.38), sanction (0.35)	doping (2.88), anti (1.75), uci (1.43), wada (1.14), code (0.85), violation (0.71), law (0.65), period (0.56), hearing (0.56), disciplinary (0.54)	appel (0.57), droit (0.56), joueur (0.48), fifa (0.46), uci (0.45), procédure (0.44), contrat (0.42), selon (0.39), sont (0.39), ont (0.38)	iaaf (1.37), fei (1.28), evidence (0.68), aiba (0.56), hearing (0.55), australian (0.43), australia (0.36), usatf (0.33), horse (0.33), law (0.33)	olympic (1.8), ioc (1.09), games (1.03), team (0.75), law (0.64), international (0.57), application (0.49), national (0.45), ad (0.44), hoc (0.44)	coni (2.06), ie (1.95), si (0.58), ama (0.52), con (0.51), dell (0.51), upa (0.5), delle (0.45), antidoping (0.44), dal (0.43)	fat (0.9), election (0.71), electoral (0.69), ioc (0.64), fide (0.57), appellants (0.53), pinter (0.52), fis (0.49), medical (0.48), blood (0.47)	training (1.84), transfer (1.64), fifa (1.39), compensation (1.37), agreement (1.25), amount (1), eur (0.82), fc (0.63), football (0.57), payment (0.49)
Number of decisions[a]	216	47	92	165	78	125	153	73	172	19	25	88
Portion of all decisions[a]	25.7	5.6	10.9	19.6	9.3	14.9	18.2	8.7	20.5	2.3	3	10.5

[a]Decisions with at least 20% topic occurrence

and find a descriptive and appropriate label for each topic.[20] To assist this process, we can also consider how the known characteristics of individual decisions, including the subject matters assigned by CAS, the type of action, the sport involved, and the language of the case.[21]

Language-Based Topics

In doing this, we find that for three of the topics the main shared characteristic is language.[22] The most commonly occurring words in Topic 7 are all *French* and the topic represents 95 percent of all CAS decisions written in French. Topic 2 is similarly dominated by *German* and Topic 10 by *Italian*. The role of language in CAS and its jurisprudence is an exciting topic which we will explore further below.[23] However, these three language-based topics are fundamentally distinct from the other nine topics which all consist of English words and instead distinguish themselves from each other with regard to substance.

Doping-Related Topics

Several of the topics share the same most frequently occurring words. The most obvious example concerns "doping" which is the most common word for Topics 3, 4, and 6. Thus, topic modelling indicates that what CAS refers to as single subject matter, doping, in fact constitutes three distinct topics.[24] Is this an indication that topic modelling erroneously over-distinguishes between cases that are fundamentally similar? One indication of this would be if there is a lot of overlap in the sense that decisions dealing with one of these topics also deal with one of the other. While there is some such overlap between these three topics, it is not particularly high but limited to between 13 and 27 percent.[25] But if there really is three doping-related topics, what is it that distinguish them from each other? In order to answer this question we need to study the other words, besides doping, that describe each of the three topics.

Many of the words strongly associated with Topic 3 relate to procedure, either the doping testing procedure or the procedure in subsequent disciplinary actions,

---

[20] See above Table 6.1 *Topic Model: Topic Description*.

[21] See below Table 6.2 *Topic Model: Decision Characteristics*. The documents in the corpus were matched with data from the main dataset through an automatic process of reading the case name from the full text decision. Because of technical difficulties, reliable matching was not possible for 155 decisions and these were therefore excluded from consideration from the analysis in this part.

[22] This outcome is a rather strong indication of the capacity and consistency of LDA topic modelling.

[23] See Sect. 9.4.

[24] CAS decisions that are coded "Do" for subject matter are primarily split between these three topics: 15.1% for Topic 3, 25.3% for Topic 4, and 16.1% for Topic 6. Of the remaining CAS decisions, most (25.4%) are distributed across the three language-based topics discussed above. See below Table 6.2 *Topic Model: Decision Characteristics*.

[25] See below Fig. 6.1 *Topic Co-Occurrence*. As a point of comparison, the overlap between Topic 12 and Topic 1 is 73.9%.

Table 6.2 Topic Model: Decision Characteristics. [*Source* The author]

	Topic 1	Topic 2	Topic 3	Topic 4	Topic 5	Topic 6	Topic 7	Topic 8	Topic 9	Topic 10	Topic 11	Topic 12
	Contractual breaches	German	Doping procedure	Doping sanctions	Non-contractual breaches	Doping obligations	French	Australia	Eligibility	Italian	Doping and medical treatment	Contractual obligations
Subject matter by topic (%)												
Ct	69.7	0.1	0.4	0.8	2	0.1	19.2	0.7	1.3	0	0	5.8
Di	21.2	1.5	0.7	2.1	20.5	2.5	29.7	4.6	14.1	0.1	0.2	2.7
Do	2.6	4.4	15.1	25.3	1.2	16.1	18.7	4.3	8.5	2.3	1.3	0.1
E	12.1	0	1.6	0.9	8.5	4.2	7	17.2	46.4	0.1	0.4	1.5
G	12	0	0.4	0.3	12.7	3.5	34.6	3.2	32.3	0	0.9	0.1
N	7	0	0.2	0.7	2.8	0.5	12.1	3.5	72.1	0	0	1
T	35.8	0.2	0.2	0.3	3.9	0.1	14	0.1	1.5	0	0	44
X	17.5	0.8	1.6	0.7	19.9	5.4	14	7	26.3	0.4	2.4	3.9
Case type by topic (%)												
A	20.6	2.3	7.5	12.2	6.5	8.8	17.9	4.6	10.3	1.1	0.9	7.2
C	6.7	0	0.5	9.6	1.7	5	36.4	1	37.8	1.2	0	0
H	0.5	0	2.5	6.6	0.9	3.1	2.8	3.7	78.9	0.2	0.6	0.2
O	15.4	1.9	3.8	2.8	9.1	2.6	33.2	6.7	15.2	0.9	1.3	7.1
Sport by topic (%)[a]												
Alpine skiing	3.6	0.5	9.6	20.4	0.7	2.3	0	6.6	53.2	0	2.5	0.6
Athletics	0.6	1.5	25.9	16.1	1.3	16.1	9.9	13	14.2	0.5	1.1	0
Basketball	7.4	1.1	0.5	8.3	15.9	6.2	14.8	1.9	41.7	0.7	0	1.5
Boxing	2.7	2.6	2.3	13.4	9.8	6.9	11.9	20.6	28.6	1	0	0.1
Canoeing	4.1	0	0	2.1	0.1	6.8	0	40.7	45.9	0	0	0.2
Cross-country skiing	0.3	4	34.8	18.9	1.9	4.8	0	4	24.9	0	6.2	0.1

(continued)

Table 6.2 (continued)

	Topic 1	Topic 2	Topic 3	Topic 4	Topic 5	Topic 6	Topic 7	Topic 8	Topic 9	Topic 10	Topic 11	Topic 12
	Contractual breaches	German	Doping procedure	Doping sanctions	Non-contractual breaches	Doping obligations	French	Australia	Eligibility	Italian	Doping and medical treatment	Contractual obligations
Equestrian	2.7	0	5.7	12.4	1	6.9	41.9	21.1	8.2	0	0	0
Football	44.3	1	0.5	3.2	11.9	2.6	16.2	0.2	3.2	0.1	0.5	16.3
Gymnastics	0	0.2	4.8	23.1	0.4	5.7	62.5	0.1	3.2	0	0	0.1
Hockey	0.1	0	1.2	1.1	2.5	13.8	19.7	0	61.5	0	0	0
Ice Hockey	3.6	0.7	0.6	4.6	1.1	10.4	54.6	0	24.1	0.2	0	0.1
Judo	1.3	3	5.3	18.8	2.6	6.1	37.4	16.1	9.5	0	0	0
Skiing	0.7	0.2	36.8	18.5	2.7	9.5	0	0	10	0	21.4	0.1
Snowboard	4.4	0	1.1	8	1.4	0.2	0	1.4	81.6	1.4	0	0.4
Swimming	2.4	3.7	15.4	24	1	8	7.8	5.9	29.9	0.1	1.8	0.1
Tennis	1.8	1.6	5.6	63	3.9	4.3	6.6	1.5	10.4	1.3	0	0
Weightlifting	0.5	7.8	16.4	22.1	1	28.1	0.1	2.8	18.2	1.1	1.6	0.2
Wrestling	1	8.1	9.9	19	3.9	20.1	0.4	0.9	36.3	0	0	0.3
Language by topic (%)												
English	23.8	2	8.6	14.1	7.8	10.1	0.3	5.8	17.7	0.3	1.1	8.3
French	0.2	0.5	0.3	0.5	0.2	0.2	94.7	0.2	0.9	2.2	0	0.1
German	0.1	99.2	0	0	0.2	0.5	0	0	0.1	0	0	0
Italian	0	0	0	0.3	0	0.5	0	0	0	99.1	0	0

[a]At least 5 decisions

...% also deal with Topic...

Of decisions that deal with Topic...

	1	2	3	4	5	6	7	8	9	10	11	12
1		2.3		3.7	11.1	4.6	1.4	0.9	3.7			30.1
2	10.6		4.3	46.8	2.1	40.4	2.1	2.1	4.3		4.3	2.1
3		2.2		23.9	3.3	27.2		12	14.1		1.1	1.1
4	4.8	13.3	13.3		0.6	18.8		12.1	15.2	1.2	4.8	1.2
5	30.8	1.3	3.8	1.3		2.6		6.4	15.4		5.1	7.7
6	8	15.2	20	24.8	1.6			7.2	13.6	2.4	0.8	0.8
7	2	0.7							1.3	5.9		
8	2.7	1.4	15.1	27.4	6.8	12.3			32.9	1.4		1.4
9	4.7	1.2	7.6	14.5	7	9.9	1.2	14			4.1	1.2
10				10.5		15.8	47.4	5.3			10.5	
11		8	4	32	16	4			28	8		8
12	73.9	1.1	1.1	2.3	6.8	1.1		1.1	2.3		2.3	

Minimum 20% topic occurence

Fig. 6.1 Topic Co-Occurrence. [*Source* The author]

including before CAS.[26] CAS decisions that deal extensively with Topic 3 concern such key procedural issues as CAS's power to hear a case *de novo*,[27] the burden and standard of proof,[28] and proper doping testing procedure,[29] but also many fundamental procedural principles, including the right to be heard, the principle of non-retroactivity, and the presumption of innocence.[30] Thus, Topic 3 can be understood as concerning *Doping Procedure*.

While Topic 3 primarily deals with the process leading to a finding that a doping violation has occurred, the words most strongly connected to Topic 4 relate to what happens after such a finding, that is suspensions and other *Doping Sanctions*. CAS decisions that predominantly include Topic 4 address the proportionality of the sanction and related issues such as the athlete's level of negligence or fault.[31] Based on this observation, it is understandable and reasonable that almost one in four CAS decisions that to a significant extent discuss *Doping Procedure* also discuss *Doping*

[26] See above Table 6.1 *Topic Model: Topic Description*.

[27] See e.g. CAS 98/211, *de Bruin*; CAS 2001/A/345, *Meier*.

[28] See e.g. CAS 98/208, *Wang et al.*; CAS 98/211, *de Bruin*; CAS 2004/A/607, *Boevski*.

[29] See e.g. CAS 2001/A/337, *Bray;* CAS 2001/A/345, *Meier*; CAS 2004/A/607, *Boevski*; CAS 2007/A/1394, *Landis*; CAS 2009/A/1752 & 1753, *Devyatovskiy & Tsikhan*.

[30] See e.g. CAS 2000/A/274, *Susin*; CAS 2001/A/317, *Aanes*.

[31] See e.g. OG 04/003, *Edwards*; CAS 2005/A/830, *Squizzato*; CAS 2005/A/847, *Knauss*; CAS 2006/A/1025, *Puerta*.

Sanctions.[32] However, the distinction between the two is fairly clear and, in my opinion, provides a better understanding of CAS's jurisprudence and international sports law generally than treating these as a single topic.

The main theme of Topic 6 is less clear than for Topics 3 and 4. Many of commonly occurring words in Topic 6 are names of sports governing bodies (SGBs) and seemingly general terms in the area of doping, such as "letter", "control", "statement", "suspension", and "code". To better understand if there is a common theme to Topic 6 that distinguishes it from Topics 3 and 4, I have manually examined CAS decisions that had a high content of Topic 6 to see what, if anything, they have in common.[33] In doing so, I found that CAS decisions that to a large extent involve Topic 6 can clearly be placed in one of two groups.

The first group consists of CAS decisions concerning other types of doping violations than those that involve a positive doping sample,[34] which are the most common in CAS jurisprudence, such as failure to submit a sample,[35] failure to comply with the whereabouts system,[36] and possession of a prohibited substance.[37] While this description fits many CAS decisions that contain a large portion of Topic 6, it is not true for all decisions. Almost all of the remaining decisions,[38] which thereby constitute a second group, have in common that they concern the applicability of and the duty to comply with anti-doping rules, including both the duties of individual athletes,[39] SGBs,[40] or both.[41] The smallest common denominator of these two groups seems to be that they concern *Doping Obligations.*[42]

The word "doping" does not appear very frequently in Topic 11, which is a very rare topic in CAS jurisprudence.[43] However, it does contain many common terms that relate to *Doping and Medical Treatment.* Many of the CAS decisions

---

[32] See above Fig. 6.1 *Topic Co-Occurrence.* The reverse, i.e. the portion of Topic 4 cases that also include Topic 3, is limited to 13.3%.

[33] This approach was taken based on the idea that the nature of a topic will be most obvious in decisions that have a high content of that topic, here defined as excess of 70%.

[34] Article 2.1 WADA Code.

[35] Article 2.3 WADA Code. See e.g. CAS 2008/A/1551, *Cherubin*; CAS 2009/A/1892, *Slay & Diaz Gonzalez*; CAS 2012/A/2791, *Jamaludin et al.*; CAS 2013/A/3077, *Casas Buitrago.*

[36] Article 2.4 WADA Code. See e.g. CAS 2011/A/2499, *Subirats*; CAS 2011/A/2671, *Rasmussen.*

[37] Article 2.6 WADA Code. See e.g. CAS 2011/A/2678, *Fernández Peláez.*

[38] One CAS decision was difficult to clearly place in either of these two categories: CAS 2011/A/2435, *Thys.* However, the decision deals extensively with the obligation of a national anti-doping body to render a timely decision and can therefore, perhaps, be placed in the second category.

[39] See e.g. CAS 2002/A/378, *Simeoni*; CAS 2008/A/1458, *Vinokourov.*

[40] See e.g. CAS 98/192, *UCI v. DCU & DIF*; CAS 2010/A/2226, *Brito Leal Queiroz.*

[41] See e.g. CAS 2008/A/1564, *Busch.*

[42] With a larger number of topics, it is possible that these two groups of cases would split into two distinct topics.

[43] Only 3% of all CAS decisions studied contain at least 20% of Topic 11. Only Topic 10, *Italian*, is less common. See above Table 6.1 *Topic Model: Topic Description.*

containing a high degree of Topic 11 fit this description,[44] many of which concern essentially the same factual circumstances.[45]

Contract-Related Topics

There are other topics, besides these doping-related topics, that share several of the key terms. Topics 1, 5, and 12 all share several keywords that relate to football, most importantly the word "football", but also the names of several SGBs engaged in the governance of football. Topics 1 and 12 also share many words related to contractual obligations and monetary compensation.[46] They are also the two topics that are most likely to appear in the same CAS decision.[47]

For the purpose of understanding Topics 1 and 12 it is interesting to determine what separates the two. Here we find that Topic 1 frequently includes words associated with players and the contractual relationships between clubs and players,[48] whereas Topic 12 more frequently includes words associated with clubs and contractual relationships between clubs.[49]

CAS decisions that exclusively or nearly exclusively concern Topic 1[50] involve (i) player breach of employment contract[51] and compensations for such breaches, including the liability of the player's new club when it induced the breach,[52] (ii) club breach of employment contract,[53] and (iii) failure of clubs to pay their debts and the possibility of bringing disciplinary actions against such clubs.[54] There is a clear pattern here: Topic 1 concerns *Contractual Breaches* and to some extent related procedural issues.

CAS decisions dealing with Topic 12, by comparison, concern what can be characterized as good faith disagreement regarding contractual obligations. These decisions, which do not include claims for damages for breaches, primarily concern disagreements between football clubs regarding the calculation of training

[44] See e.g. CAS 94/129, *Quigley*; CAS 2008/A/1511, *O'Hara*.

[45] CAS 2007/A/1286, 1288 & 1289, *Eder et al.*; CAS 2007/A/1434 & 1435, *Pinter*; CAS 2008/A/1513, *Hoch*.

[46] "Agreement", "contract", "compensation", "amount", and "payment".

[47] 73.9% of all decisions that deal with Topic 12 also deal with Topic 1. This is the highest of all topic co-appearance rates. However, that 30.1% of all cases dealing with Topic 1 also deal with Topic 12 is also quite high. See above Fig. 6.1 *Topic Co-Occurrence*.

[48] "Player" and "employment".

[49] "Training", "compensation", "transfer", and "fc".

[50] More than 98%.

[51] Referred to by CAS as "unilateral termination of the employment contract by a player without just cause."

[52] See e.g. CAS 2004/A/780, *Henning*; CAS 2007/A/1429 & 1442, *Sall*; CAS 2008/A/1568, *Mica*; CAS 2012/A/2750, *Shakhtar Donetsk v. Real Zaragoza*.

[53] CAS 2007/A/1251, *Aris II*; CAS 2008/A/1518, *Rebelo Lopes*; CAS 2012/A/3033, *Pešić*.

[54] CAS 2006/A/1008, *Rayo Vallecano de Madrid v. FIFA*; CAS 2012/A/2981, *Desportivo Nacional v. FK Sutjeska*.

compensation,[55] solidarity contribution,[56] and transfer fees,[57] but also other issues related to contractual obligations.[58] Thus, Topic 12 deals with *Contractual Obligations* – and possibly more specifically interpretation of contractual obligations – as compared to *Contractual Breaches* which is the common factor of decisions addressing Topic 1.

Non-contractual Disciplinary Cases

As discussed above, Topic 5, like Topics 1 and 12, involves many frequently used football-related words. However, unlike Topics 1 and 12, words relating to contractual obligations do not frequently occur in Topic 5.[59] The fact that CAS decisions classified as dealing with the subject matter *Contracts* rarely deal extensively with Topic 5 supports the relative absence of a contractual dimension in Topic 5.[60] By comparison, decisions classified as dealing with the subject matter of (non-doping related) *Discipline* are strongly overrepresented in Topic 5.[61] Similarly, words associated with disciplinary cases are common in Topic 5.[62] This is also true for Topic 1, but not for Topic 12.[63]

Thus, Topics 1 and 5 have in common that they frequently address both football-related and discipline-related issues. Cases that deal with Topic 5 also quite often deal with Topic 1.[64] The key difference between the Topics 1 and 5 is the contractual dimension. As discussed above, CAS decisions that deal extensively with Topic 1, including those that involve disciplinary action, concern breaches of contractual obligations. By comparison, decisions that contain a large portion of Topic 5[65] exclusively concern disciplinary matters without connection to

---

55 See e.g. CAS 2003/O/527, *Hamburger Sport-Verein v. Odense Boldklub*; CAS 2004/A/594, *Hapoel Beer-Sheva v. Real Racing Club de Santander*; CAS 2006/A/1029, *Maccabi Haifa FC v. Real Racing Club Santander.*

56 See e.g. CAS 2006/A/1018, *CA River Plate v. Hamburger SV*; CAS 2012/A/2707, *AS Nancy-Lorraine v. FC Dynamo Kyiv.*

57 See e.g. CAS 2005/O/985, *Feyenoord Rotterdam NV v. Cruzeiro Esporte Club*; CAS 2011/A/2557, *FC Dynamo Kyiv v. AS Nancy-Lorraine*; CAS 2012/A/2875, *Helsingborgs IF v. Parma FC.*

58 See e.g. CAS 2011/A/2646, *Club Rangers de Talca v. FIFA* (regarding whether the purchaser of a bankrupted club's assets incurred an obligation to pay outstanding wages to the latter club's player); CAS 2012/A/3035, *Parma FC v. VFL Wolfsburg* (regarding when contractual obligations must be performed).

59 See above Table 6.1 *Topic Model: Topic Description.*

60 See above Table 6.2 *Topic Model: Decision Characteristics.*

61 Ibid.

62 "Disciplinary" and "sanction".

63 See above Table 6.2 *Topic Model: Decision Characteristics.*

64 See above Fig. 6.1 *Topic Co-Occurrence* (30.8%). This overlap is likely attributable to the issue of disciplinary sanctions.

65 More than 75%.

contractual obligations. The latter cases primarily concern match-fixing,[66] but also other types of collusion and corruption,[67] and cases relating to violence and disorder.[68] Topic 5 thus seem to concern various forms of *Non-contractual Breaches* of obligations.[69]

Other Topics

This leaves Topics 8 and 9 to be examined. Topic 9 is interesting in that it is the only topic that appears disproportionally frequently in certain types of CAS procedures, more specifically in ad hoc procedures:[70] almost two out of three CAS decisions that contain a large amount of Topic 9 were decided by a CAS Olympic Game ad hoc tribunal and many of the remaining decisions concern the eligibility to compete in the Olympic Games.[71] It appears that eligibility to compete is the common factor shared by CAS decisions dealing heavily with Topic 9, including eligibility-related disputes concerning such varied issues as when entries must be made,[72] the qualification and selection process,[73] and athlete nationality.[74] However, while there is thus a close connection between Topic 9 and eligibility to compete in the Olympic Games, there are also several CAS decisions that heavily include Topic 9[75] and that do not concern eligibility to compete in Olympic Games but the right of athletes more generally to represent a nation in international

66 See e.g. CAS 2009/A/1920, *FK Pobeda et al. v. UEFA*; CAS 2010/A/2172, *Oryekhov*; CAS 2013/A/3062, *Sammut*; CAS 2013/A/3256, *Fenerbahçe v. UEFA II*; CAS 2014/A/3625, *Sivasspor Kulübü v. UEFA*. This explains why the word "match" frequently occurs in Topic 5.

67 CAS 98/200, *AEK Athens* (concerning the prevention of collusion by banning multi-club ownership); CAS 2011/A/2425, *Fusimalohi*; CAS 2011/A/2625, *Bin Hammam*.

68 CAS 2007/A/1217, *Feyenoord Rotterdam v. UEFA*; CAS 2012/A/2699, *Al-Birair*; CAS 2013/A/3139, *Fenerbahçe v. UEFA I*.

69 Of course, the individuals' duty not to engage in corruption or violence and the SGBs' power to discipline such behavior has a contractual basis, in e.g. an agreement or license. The term contractual is here used more narrowly to refer to transfer agreements, employment contract, and other contracts of a more commercial nature.

70 See above Table 6.2 *Topic Model: Decision Characteristics*. The table also reveals that consultation procedures are disproportionally common in connection with Topic 9. However, because there is a very limited number of consultation procedures, the correlation in that relationship is more uncertain.

71 See e.g. CAS 94/132, *PRABF v. USAB*; CAS 98/215, *IBA*; CAS 2008/A/1615, *Darby*; CAS 2009/A/1752, *Devyatovskiy & Tsikhan*.

72 OG 96/001, *US Swimming v. FINA*.

73 See e.g. OG 02/005, *Billington*; OG 02/006, *NZOC v. SLOC;* OG 06/002, *Schuler*.

74 See e.g. OG 00/005, *Perez*; OG 08/002, *Simms*; OG 08/006, *MNOC v. IOC*.

75 More than 90%.

competitions.[76] Topic 9 thus appear to concern *Eligibility* to represent a nation, primarily but not exclusively with regard to the eligibility to compete in the Olympic Games.

Topic 8 is more difficult to understand. The words that commonly occur in the topic is a strange mixture of abbreviations for SGBs and rather general terms that are not obvious connected to each other.[77] There are however two words that are common for Topic 8 and that stand out: "Australia" and "Australian". Among CAS decisions that score high for Topic 8 there is a surprisingly large number of decisions that concern the failure of Australian federations and the Australian Olympic Committee to include particular athletes in the Australian Olympic team to compete in various Olympic Games.[78] In this regard, Topic 8 could be characterized as a sub-topic to Topic 9. However, Topic 8 is also extensively found in a number of CAS decisions without any direct connection to the Olympics or the issue of eligibility but with a strong connection to Australia.[79] Many of these decisions also have in common that they were handled by the CAS's Oceania Registry.[80] Thus, although it is not a characteristic that is universal shared by all decisions that score high for Topic 8,[81] the best label for Topic 8 appears to be *Australia*.

6.2.4 Co-citation Clustering

As explained above, the use of topic modelling to detect communities in CAS jurisprudence relies on full-text analysis and textual similarity. A second, alternative approach used here to identify communities independently of CAS's subject matter classification is to use network analysis and a clustering algorithm.[82]

---

[76] See e.g. CAS 2001/A/357, *Nabokov* (regarding nationality requirement for representing a national ice hockey team); CAS 2009/A/1988, *Belize Basketball Federation v. FIBA* (regarding nationality requirement for representing a national basketball team). But see CAS 2003/A/461, 471 & 473, *WCM-GP v. FIM* (regarding technical requirements for eligibility to compete in international motorcycle road racing championship). These cases do not concern the right to compete in the Olympic Games, at least directly. However, it is possible that they could affect the latter.

[77] "Evidence", "hearing", "horse", and "law".

[78] CAS 96/153, *Watt*; CAS 2000/A/260, *Beashel & Czislowski*; CAS 2002/A/361, *Berchtold*; CAS 2008/A/1549, *Michael*; CAS 2008/A/1574, *D'Arcy*; CAS 2008/A/1605, *Jongewaard*; CAS 2012/A/2837, *Beresford*.

[79] See e.g. CAS 2004/A/651, *French* (regarding doping violations by an Australian cyclist); CAS 2007/A/1201, *Baggaley* (regarding doping violations by an Australian canoer); CAS 2008/A/1652 & 1664, *Troy* (regarding doping violations by an Australian rugby player).

[80] See CAS 2000/A/305, *CPC v. IPC* (neither the parties nor the facts had any direct connection to Australia but the case was handled by the Oceania Registry and all three arbitrators were from Australia).

[81] See e.g. CAS 2012/A/2917, *BPA v. IFDS & NIF*.

[82] See Peel et al. 2017.

We will cluster based on co-citation. This approach departs from the rather intuitive proposition that two sources are likely to deal with the same issue or belong to the same area if they are frequently co-cited, that is cited together in the same document. Conversely, the more rarely two sources are cited together, the less likely it is that they deal with the same issue or belong to the same area.[83] Co-citation clustering relies on the work of the persons behind the citations and their knowledge and ability to find and cite sources that are relevant on a particular issue. Previous research in the field of network analysis has demonstrated that co-citation clustering can for example be used to identify distinct research fields.[84] We will here use the same technique to identify distinct communities in CAS jurisprudence.

Departing from the CAS case law network, we first create a co-citation network where each cited CAS decision is treated as a vertex. The network is then constructed by inferring edges between two decisions if they are cited in the same CAS decision. In this manner, we create an undirected weighted co-citation network where CAS decisions that are frequently cited together in the same decisions are strongly connected and, conversely, CAS decisions that are infrequently co-cited are weekly connected or unconnected.[85] This network is then analyzed to identify communities of decisions that are more strongly connected to each other through co-citation than to other decisions.[86]

There are many different algorithms that can be used for community detection, each with its own advantages and disadvantages.[87] Here, we use the so-called Louvain method.[88] Like most other commonly used clustering algorithms,[89] the Louvain method is a modularity optimization algorithm. Modularity is a measurement used in network analysis to describe the quality of a particular clustering.[90] The Louvain method initially places each vertex in its own community and then moves vertices to other communities if this results in improved

---

83 See generally Newman 2011, pp. 70, 72, 115–118.

84 See e.g. McCain 1986 (author co-citation); Small 1973 (article co-citation).

85 It should be noted that this co-citation network differs from the directed citation CAS case law network examined elsewhere in this book.

86 As discussed above, a single CAS decision will frequently contain multiple issues and may therefore also cite CAS decisions dealing with different issues, for example a procedural issue and a substantive issue. Because of this, the co-citation network contains edges between CAS decisions that potentially have little or nothing in common. However, such incidental connections that a decision may have will be weak compared to its connections with decisions dealing with the same issues as itself and together with which it is more frequently cited.

87 For an excellent overview, see Newman 2012.

88 Blondel et al. 2008 (sometimes also referred to as the Blondel method).

89 Newman 2011, p. 373.

90 The goal of community detection is to minimize connections between communities or, differently phrased, maximize connections within communities (a "minimum cut" approach). Modularity reflects to what extent communities under a particular clustering are connected over what would be the result if vertices would be clustered randomly. Newman 2006, p. 8578. See also Newman and Girvan 2004.

modularity.[91] This continues until modularity cannot be improved further. These communities are then collapsed and treated as vertices connected with weighted edges. These new vertices are then again subjected to the first step, i.e. combined to the extent that it improves modularity. This process is repeated until no modularity improvement is possible.[92] This has shown to be one of the best-performing clustering methods.[93]

This approach identifies eight main clusters in CAS jurisprudence.[94] Although this model does not consist of the exact same CAS decisions as the other two,[95] it is both possible, interesting, and valuable to compare how these three approaches divide the CAS decisions that they share into communities. Unlike topic modelling, this community detection model does not provide a list of words that describe the different clusters and this makes it somewhat more difficult to determine what the clustered decisions have in common. However, it is relatively easy to explore how this approach differs from the other two by comparing community membership.

The structure identified using co-citation clustering in several ways resembles the one identified using topic modelling.[96] For instance, like topic modelling, co-citation clustering splits CAS's doping-related jurisprudence into four doping-dominated clusters.[97] Also, Cluster 2 consists of a mix of contract-, disciplinary-, and transfer-related CAS decisions that almost entirely belong to Topic 1, *Contractual Breaches*. A clear difference, however, is the absence of language-based communities. This can be explained by the fact that reference to previous decisions are to a great extent language independent.[98]

Two of the clusters, Clusters 3 and 10, are particularly interesting as they consist of a rather large[99] and, from the perspective of the other two approaches, heterogeneous group of decisions. CAS decisions belonging to these two clusters concern

---

[91] This is an example of hierarchical clustering.

[92] Blondel et al. 2008, pp. 3–4.

[93] Fortunato 2010, p. 150; Lancichinetti and Fortunato 2009. See also Newman 2012, p. 28; Wallace et al. 2009.

[94] Additionally, the method identifies two clusters, Clusters 8 and 9, each with two decisions. In both of these cases this is because the two decisions have only been cited once and only together.

[95] I.e. CAS decisions collected and considered in full herein. Because of how it is constructed, the co-citation network obviously fails to include CAS decisions that have never been cited in the same decision as another decision. Additionally, the network includes co-cited CAS decisions regardless of whether they belong to the main dataset.

[96] See below Fig. 6.2 *Clustering Methods Compared*. Regarding the special issues with community detection using topic modelling, see below Sect. 6.2.5.

[97] It should be noted, however, that there are some differences between how the two approaches divide CAS's doping-related decisions.

[98] It should be noted that for the purpose of this study, all references to previous decisions have been coded in a consistent way regardless of how they were written in the decision. All variances in style of reference, including language-related differences, have thereby been eliminated. Also, as discussed in greater detail in Sect. 9.4, it is possible that the arbitrators' language skills may affect which decisions they cite.

[99] 111 and 144 decisions respectively.

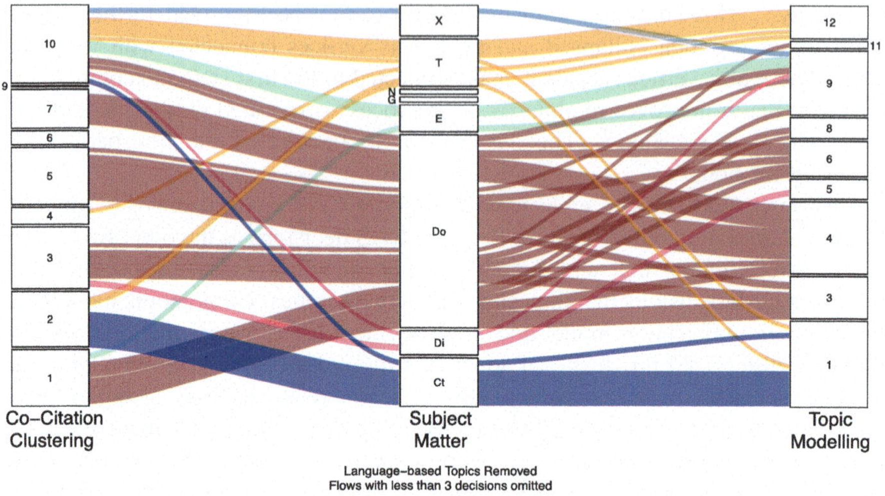

Fig. 6.2 Clustering Methods Compared. [*Source* The author]

most subject matters and topics. As these are clearly not something that these decisions have in common, it is interesting to explore what they have in common. Because the clustering is based on citations it is natural to seek such common characteristics in the points of law for which decisions belonging to these clusters are cited as authorities.[100]

Beginning with Cluster 3, CAS decisions belonging to this cluster are primarily cited on points of law that can broadly be considered procedural and administrative, or possibly constitutional.[101] The clustered decisions are for example cited in support for (i) that the standard of proof in disciplinary actions is "comfortable satisfaction";[102] (ii) that when sitting under appeals jurisdiction, CAS can conduct a full *de novo* hearing of the case and that because this hearing comes with all due process guarantees it cures any procedural defects or procedural rights violations that may have previously occurred;[103] and (iii) that disciplinary rules cannot apply retroactively[104] and what constitutes a disciplinary rule for the purpose of defining

---

[100] On the topic of citations and points of law, see further Sect. 7.1.

[101] See further Sect. 7.2.

[102] E.g. CAS 2009/A/1920, *Zabrcanec & Zdraveski* para 85; CAS 2010/A/2172, *Oryekhov*, para 53, co-cited in e.g. CAS 2012/A/2699, *Al-Birair*, para 88; CAS 2013/A/3323, *Deportivo Petare FC v. FIFA*, para 75. Other, older decisions in the cluster that deal with this issue include CAS 98/211, *De Bruin*; CAS 2005/A/908, *Wium*; CAS 2000/A/310, *Leipold I*.

[103] E.g. CAS 2003/O/486, *Fulham FC v. Olympique Lyonnais*, para 50; CAS 2004/A/549, *Deferr*; para 31; CAS 2006/A/1153, *Lopes de Almeida*, para 53, co-cited in e.g. CAS 2009/A/1880–1881, *El-Hadary*, paras 19–21; CAS 2010/A/2178, *Caucchioli*, para 25; CAS 2013/A/3264, *Achchakir*, para 95.

[104] Also known as the principle of *tempus regit actum*.

this prohibition's scope.[105] This helps explain why Cluster 3 contains decisions that are diverse in terms of subject matters and topics: procedural and administrative issues such as these can arise in a very broad range of cases.

It is however not clear what distinguishes Cluster 3 from Cluster 10. CAS decisions belonging to Cluster 10 is cited on issues such as (i) CAS's jurisdiction under the Appeals Arbitration Procedure, particularly what constitutes an appealable decision,[106] and the conditions for reviewing a so-called field-of-play decision;[107] (ii) the hierarchy of norms and compliance with the principle of legality;[108] and (iii) that CAS proceedings are based on an adversarial system where the burden of proof lies with the party asserting facts to support a claim or a right.[109] These issues, of which there are more examples, must reasonably also be broadly defined as procedural or administrative.

Because there are no clear and obvious differences between Clusters 3 and 10 that can be used to distinguish them from each other, they will in the continued discussion simply be referred to as *Administrative and Procedural Principles I* (Cluster 3) and *Administrative and Procedural Principles II* (Cluster 10).

6.2.5 Subjects, Topics, and Clusters Compared

Topic modelling and co-citation clustering produces two models for dividing CAS jurisprudence into communities that supplement CAS's own subject matter classification. In this context, it is worth pointing out that the goal of this exercise is not to find the one, true categorization of CAS jurisprudence or to assess whether the CAS's subject matter classification is correct in an absolute sense. Rather, these three community-detection models represent three different approaches to grouping decisions based on commonalities. The approaches differ in that they focus on

[105] E.g. CAS 2000/A/274, *Susin*, para 208; CAS 2004/A/635, *Barcelona v. Velez Sarsfield*, para 44; CAS 2005/C/841, CONI, paras 51, 80, co-cited in e.g. CAS 2005/C/841, CONI, paras 51, 80; CAS 2008/A/1545, *Anderson et al.*, paras 10–11; CAS 2009/A/1912 & 1913, *Pechstein*, para 40.

[106] E.g. CAS 2004/A/748, *Ekimov & Hamilton*, para 86; CAS 2005/A/899, *Aris I*, para 63; CAS 2008/A/1633, *FC Schalke 04 v. Confederaçã Brasileira de Futebol*, para 31, co-cited in e.g. CAS 2009/A/1869, *La Chaux-de-Fonds v. SFL*, para 7; CAS 2010/A/2315, *Netball New Zealand v. IFNA*, para 7.4; CAS 2013/A/3380, *Club Atlético Independiente v. FIFA*, paras 100–109.

[107] E.g. OG 96/006, *Mendy*, para 13; OG 00/013, *Segura*, para 17; CAS 2001/A/354 & 355, *IHA v. LHF & FIH & LHF v. FIH*, para 16; co-cited in e.g. CAS 2008/A/1641, *NAOC v. IAAF & USOC*, para 24; CAS 2010/A/2090, *Saarinen*, para 7.3; CAS 2012/A/2731, *Ferreira*, para 104.

[108] E.g. CAS 2004/A/794, *Unknown*; CAS 2006/A/1181, *FC Metz v. FC Ferencvarosi*; CAS 2008/A/1705, *Grasshopper v. Alianza Lima*, co-cited in e.g. CAS 2008/A/1708, *IRIFF v. FIFA*; CAS 2015/A/4153, *Fedor*, para 154.

[109] E.g. CAS 2003/A/506, *Unknown*, para 54; CAS 2009/A/1810 & 1811, *V Wilhelmshaven v. Club A. Excursionistas & Club A. River Plate*, para 46, co-cited in e.g. CAS 2009/A/1908, *Parma FC SpA v. Manchester United FC*, para 42; CAS 2011/A/2681, *KSV Cercle Brugge v. FC Radnicki*, para 118; CAS 2013/A/3297, *FC Metalist v. UEFA & PAOK FC*, para 8.33.

slightly different characteristics when looking for commonalities and differences between decisions, but each of these characteristics are, in my opinion, relevant and reasonable to consider. Thus, the main value of the three models lies in comparing and analyzing them for the purpose of gaining a deeper understanding of CAS jurisprudence.[110]

As discussed above, topic modelling rests on the theory that a single document may deal with several topics and the ability to measure the relative presence of different topics in a single document is also one of the advantages of topic modelling. However, in order to identify and analyze the existence of communities in CAS jurisprudence, we must group together individual decisions. For the purpose of enabling comparison, CAS decisions are grouped based on main topic, i.e. each decision is placed in a community based on the topic for which it has received the highest score together with other decisions that have scored highest for the same topic.[111] While this is a simplification of the model, it does not appear to significantly affect the overall results.[112]

An initial observation is that none of the three models is fundamentally and completely different from the others. The fact that the models have much in common makes it both manageable and meaningful to analyze the parts where the models differ from each other. One can also observe that CAS's subject matter classification appears to be a quite reasonable classification on a general level. Most topics and clusters primarily consist of decisions concerning a single subject matter. Also, in several cases, decisions concerning a particular subject matter are grouped together in a cluster or topic. Several subject matters fit both of these descriptions and there is only one that fits neither: the subject matter *Other*. This is hardly surprising considering that the subject matter *Other* is a community that is defined negatively, i.e. that consists of decisions that do not fit any other subject matter, rather than positively, i.e. that consists of decisions that are seen as having something in common.[113]

The subject matter *Other* illustrates the value that approaches such as topic modelling can add when classifying case law. CAS decisions belonging to the subject matter *Other* are, by definition, decisions that fit the CAS classification system poorly, in other words decisions that were difficult to classify using that system. Topic modelling, by comparison, was capable of classifying an

[110] For a graphical representation of this comparison, see above Fig. 6.2 *Clustering Methods Compared*.

[111] For example, two decisions that among all topics have the largest content of Topic 9 are clustered together, regardless of whether a majority of the documents concern that topic. In this regard, compare below Sect. 6.3.

[112] To test the impact of this method, two samples of decisions whose highest topic score were at least 0.75 and 0.9 respectively, and thus more reliably can be clustered together, were analyzed. The relationships between the clustering models were essentially the same under both samples and under the main approach.

[113] These decisions are so evenly spread between different topics and clusters that they have largely been omitted above in Fig. 6.2 *Clustering Methods Compared*.

overwhelming majority of all *Other*-decisions with a high degree of certainty.[114] A manual examination confirms the reasonableness of these categorizations. For example, CAS's decision in *AEK Athens*, concerning a violation of a multi-club ownership ban[115] belong to the subject matter *Other* but was clearly classified as concerning the topic *Non-contractual Breaches*.[116] Similarly, the decision of *Perez III*, concerning the eligibility of Angel Perez to compete in the 2000 Sydney Olympic Games,[117] was with an even higher degree of probability classified as dealing with the topic *Eligibility*.[118] The point I am trying to make here is not that CAS should have done a better job classifying its decisions, but that human-created classification systems, even those created with great care by knowledgeable and well-intending individuals, have certain limitations that methods such as those used here can help identify and overcome.

While there are many similarities between the three models, topic modelling and co-citation clustering produce pictures of the main themes in CAS jurisprudence that differ in some regards from CAS's own subject matter classification. First, many of CAS's subject matters, including the ones that are most common in the dataset, are split between several topics and clusters. As discussed above, CAS decisions concerning the subject matter *Doping* is split into three topics – *Doping Obligations*, *Doping Procedure*, and *Doping Sanctions* – and four principle clusters.[119] The fact that most doping cases end up together in doping-dominated topics suggests that doping is in many ways distinct from other issues that CAS deals with. Reasonable minds can also differ regarding how to best divide doping cases into smaller units. However, it seems clear that the doping as an overarching label is too broad to accurately capture the breadth of the field and obscures distinct sub-fields.[120] Topic modelling and co-citation clustering produce slightly different answers to what exactly those sub-fields are. For example, the topic *Doping Sanctions* is split into two clusters when we use co-citation rather than the text itself as the basis for identifying communities and Cluster 3 brings together doping decisions dealing with a number of different topics.[121]

[114] 74% of all *Other*-decisions scored higher than 50% for one topic and 37% scored higher than 75%.

[115] See also Sect. 7.2.

[116] 78% probability.

[117] OG 00/009.

[118] 96% probability.

[119] 1, 3, 5, and 7. See above Fig. 6.2 *Clustering Methods Compared.*

[120] For example, as will be discussed in greater detail below in Sect. 6.3, there are distinct differences in the roles and influences of these different sub-fields.

[121] Clusters 5 and 7. See above Fig. 6.2 *Clustering Methods Compared.*

Decisions concerning the subject matter *Contracts* are largely, as one might expect, found in the topic *Contractual Breaches*. However, this topic also includes many decisions concerning the subject matters *Transfers* and *Discipline*. This makes good sense. Many of the cases concerning breach of contract that end up before CAS concern player transfers and where such breaches are egregious the breaching party will frequently be the subject of a disciplinary sanction.[122]

That they have different subject matter labels obscures the fact that these decisions deal with fundamentally similar issues. Those cases are also different from contract- and transfer-related cases where there are good faith disagreements about the financial obligations arising from a player transfer, decisions belonging to the topic *Contractual Obligations*. Similarly, decisions dealing with the subject matter *Discipline* involve two topics: *Contractual Breaches* and *Non-contractual Breaches*.[123] In this sense, the topics provide a more detailed picture of CAS jurisprudence than CAS's subject matter classification. Not only are the topics numerically superior to the subject matters, but, as revealed by the examination above, there are real and legally sensible differences between the different topics that subject matter classification fails to reflect.

The differences between subject matters and topics is however not limited to the latter being more detailed. Topic modelling also raises some more fundamental questions regarding how to understand CAS jurisprudence. For example, the two topics *Contractual Obligations* and *Contractual Breach* include, in almost equal shares, almost all CAS decisions classified as dealing with the subject matter *Transfers*. While it is true that those decisions concern player transfers, this finding raises the doubt concerning the value of the subject matter *Transfers*. If CAS decisions concerning the subject matter *Transfers* are, on one hand, closely connected with decisions concerning (other types of) *Contracts*, and, on the other hand, are almost equally split between decisions concerning the topics *Contractual Obligations* and *Contractual Breaches*, as the analysis above suggests, does the subject matter *Transfers* obscure more than it reveals? It appears so.

Similarly, finally, and opposite to the case with *Doping* and *Contracts*, topic modelling suggests that the distinction between the subject matters *Eligibility* and *Nationality* is not very strong as CAS decisions concerning both of these subject matters primarily form part of the topic *Eligibility*. Co-citation clustering, on the other hand, suggests that many decisions concerning the subject matter *Eligibility* are primarily cited together with decisions involving different subject matters on administrative or constitutional issues. Both models thus indicate that the subject matter *Eligibility* is not particularly distinct.

---

[122] See e.g. CAS 2005/A/899, *Aris I*; CAS 2006/A/1180, *Ribéry*.

[123] See above Sect. 6.2.3.

6.3 Connections

6.3.1 Precedential Power: Leader of the Pack?

Having identified key communities in CAS's jurisprudence we shall now consider whether these communities relate to each other and, if so, how. By determining how different communities relate to each other we also illuminate what position they occupy in CAS jurisprudence. In the discussion above it was demonstrated that CAS decisions differ with regard to how structurally important they are to CAS overall jurisprudence.[124] It is possible, even likely, that similar differences can be observed between communities of decisions.

Studying relevant differences between communities of CAS decisions is however not limited to identifying "landmark communities". By understanding how communities of decisions are connected to each other and how they influence or fail to influence each other, we can reach a better understanding of the issues that drive CAS jurisprudence. It is obviously true that there are some important differences between CAS decisions that deal with different issues. However, as will be explored in this section, decisions belonging to different communities are connected in complex ways that are not immediately obvious.

We have previously introduced the concept of precedential power, discussed how it can be measured using network analysis, and applied it to identify CAS landmark decisions.[125] The same techniques can also be applied to communities of decisions and, in doing so, assist our understanding of precedential power on a community level. In examining this, we are essentially exploring whether there are communities of CAS decisions that have a systemic impact on CAS jurisprudence that is particularly broad and/or deep.[126]

To answer this question, we must look beyond individual CAS decisions and study groups of cases whose precedential power may vary significantly compared to each other. For example, as discussed above, *Quigley* is a reasonable candidate for the position as CAS's premier landmark decision.[127] CAS's subject matter classification tells us that *Quigley* concerns *Doping* and topic modelling has revealed that *Quigley* primarily concerns *Eligibility*. However, we cannot, just based on this, deduce that the subject matter *Doping* or the topic *Eligibility* have a significantly strong systemic impact on CAS jurisprudence.

We should instead examine which communities of CAS decisions have a precedential power that is significantly higher or lower than the overall body of CAS jurisprudence. As previously, we will be using two alternative centrality measurements to measure precedential power: indegree, which is the same as the

---

[124] See Chap. 5.

[125] Regarding the last point, see Chap. 5.

[126] See also Sect. 5.1. While it is not an established term, we can in a sense say that this is the question of identifying "landmark clusters".

[127] See Sect. 5.3.

total number of times a decision or, in this context, a group of decisions have been cited, and PageRank, which reflects not only direct citations but also the indirect influence that a decision or a group of decisions has on CAS jurisprudence.[128] However, as shown below, these two measurements largely tend to follow each other and show the same general tendencies.

For the purpose of examining the precedential power of different communities of CAS decisions, we will use and compare the subject matter grouping provided by CAS and the topic grouping produced using topic modelling. With regard to subject matters and clusters the grouping is determined and fixed. Grouping decisions based on topics is somewhat more complicated. Because centrality is measured for each CAS decision as a single entity and each of these decisions may (and in fact do) include multiple topics, we must decide to what extent decisions must include a particular topic in order to count towards that topic's centrality score. It is a question of setting an appropriate threshold. A natural starting point is to include CAS decisions where the majority of the content concerns a particular topic.[129] However, in a model with twelve topics, not all decisions will meet this criterion and those that fail to do so will thus be entirely exempt from consideration.[130] We will therefore also, additionally, consider a model where an individual decision's centrality score counts towards a topic's centrality score as long as at least 20 percent of the decision's content belongs to the topic.[131] It turns out that which of these thresholds is used has a marginal impact on the outcome: while the mean scores vary somewhat between the models, the statistically significant findings are largely the same under both models.[132]

CAS decisions included in the dataset on average cite 2.7 previous decisions and have a mean PageRank of 0.00089.[133] This can serve as a measuring stock when determining whether communities of CAS decisions have a precedential power that is comparatively low or high.

While several subject matters have significantly low precedential power, like *Eligibility, Governance,* and *Nationality,*[134] none have significantly high

128 See Sect. 1.6.

129 This means that each decision's score can, at most, be counted towards one topic's score.

130 22.9% of the CAS decisions studied here do not consist of at least 50% of any single topic.

131 This threshold is set below the lowest maximum topic content of any studied decision, which means that every studied decision counts towards at least one topic's centrality score. However, this also means that a single decision's score may count towards several topics' score. 40.4% of the studied decisions count towards two topics, 3.9% towards three topics, and the remainder towards only one topic.

132 See below Table 6.3 *Precedential Power of Communities: Subject Matters.*

133 As discussed above, this has varied over time and is significantly greater in recent years. Thus, communities with a greater number of recent decisions will tend to have a greater mean score that is unrelated to the basis on which they have been clustered. For this reason, it is important to focus on means that are statistically significant.

134 This is also true for the subject matter *Other* but because of its special nature it is difficult to say anything concrete about what this means for CAS's jurisprudence or sports law more generally.

precedential value. Among all subject matters, only decisions concerning *Doping* have a mean precedential power that is clearly above the rest. However, these values are not statistically significant.[135] It is somewhat surprising that not even decisions concerning *Doping* have significantly high precedential power. A large portion of the CAS jurisprudence concerns doping and when deciding doping cases CAS panels seem to frequently rely on and cite previous CAS decisions.[136]

A comparison of the different community detection models reveals that this can be explained by the fact that doping cases can be and arguably ought to be further divided into distinct sub-groups and that these sub-groups vary significantly in terms of precedential power. CAS decisions belonging to the topics *Doping Sanctions* and *Doping Procedure* have significantly high precedential power. By comparison, decisions concerning the topics *Doping Obligations* and *Doping and Medical Treatment* have insignificant or significantly low precedential power.[137] These statistically significant differences do not appear attributable to topic modelling as such; similar differences can be observed between the doping-related communities detected using co-citation clustering.[138] Thus, it seems clear not only that CAS decisions concerning doping differ greatly in terms of precedential power, but that such difference are connected to specific aspects or issues, here expressed as topics and clusters. The broad subject matter *Doping* thus obscures important distinctions that the alternative community models reveal.

It is interesting to note that not a single non-doping-related community of CAS decisions have significantly high precedential power under any of the three models. That doping-related decisions are common in CAS jurisprudence is well-known. As previously discussed, nearly half of all CAS decisions in the dataset concern doping.[139] The findings made here show, however, that doping-related decisions are not merely common, but that they also dominate CAS jurisprudence in the sense that they have higher precedential power than other decisions. One might perhaps think that these two things are naturally connected in the sense that the former leads to the latter: if there are many cases on a particular issue, there are reasonably more opportunities for decisions on that topic to be cited. However, when studying the precedential power of CAS jurisprudence there is no clear correlation between the size of a community and its precedential power.[140]

---

[135] See Table 6.3 *Precedential Power of Communities: Subject Matters*. Statistical significance is here determined using resampling. See further Sect. 1.6.

[136] See below Table 6.6 *Persuasive Power of Communities: Subject Matters*.

[137] As seen below in Table 6.4 *Precedential Power of Communities: Topic Modelling*, these observations are even clearer under the majority occurrence model.

[138] Whereas Clusters 1 and 5 have significantly high precedential power, the precedential power of Clusters 3 and 7 does not significantly distinguish themselves from the general set. See below Table 6.5 *Precedential Power of Communities: Co-Citation Clustering*.

[139] See Sect. 2.4.

[140] For example, the topics *Doping Procedure* and *Contractual Obligations* have roughly the same number of decisions, but whereas the former has the highest or second highest precedential power among all topics (depending on model and measurement), the latter has among the lowest.

Table 6.3 Precedential Power of Communities: Subject Matters. [*Source* The author]

	All	Ct	Di	Do	E	G	N	T	X
n	844	95	87	384	76	21	17	87	77
Indegree	2.7	2.8	2.2	4.0	1.6*	1.2*	1.1*	2.1	1.6*
PageRank	0.00089	0.00086	0.00086	0.00103	0.00078*	0.00076*	0.00075*	0.00084	0.00077*

* $p < 0.05$

Table 6.4 Precedential Power of Communities: Topic Modelling. [*Source* The author]

	Topic 1	Topic 2	Topic 3	Topic 4	Topic 5	Topic 6	Topic 7	Topic 8	Topic 9	Topic 10	Topic 11	Topic 12
	Contractual breaches	German	Doping procedure	Doping sanction	Non-contractual breaches	Doping obligations	French	Australia	Eligibility	Italian	Doping and medical treatment	Contractual obligations
Large occurrence[a]												
n	216	47	92	165	78	125	153	73	172	19	25	88
Indegree	2.8	2.4	4.8*	5.3*	2.5	2.5	2.7	1.7*	3.3	0.8*	1.9*	1.6*
PageRank	0.00086	0.00080*	0.00110	0.00116*	0.00084	0.00082*	0.00097	0.00078*	0.00099	0.00070*	0.00088	0.00082*
Majority occurrence[b]												
n	125	3	41	72	39	47	145	23	96	5	3	49
Indegree	3.3	0.7*	6.0*	6.0*	3.5	2.1*	2.8	1.2*	2.8	2.7	5.0*	1.6*
PageRank	0.00089	0.00066*	0.00122*	0.00116*	0.00090	0.00080*	0.00097	0.00074*	0.00100	0.00083	0.00144*	0.00081*

*$p < 0.05$
[a]Decisions with at least 20% topic occurrence
[b]Decisions with at least 50% topic occurrence

Table 6.5 Precedential Power of Communities: Co-citation Clustering. [*Source* The author]

	Cluster 1 Doping 1	Cluster 2 Con/Adm 1	Cluster 3 Doping 2	Cluster 4??	Cluster 5 Doping 3	Cluster 6??	Cluster 7 Doping 4	Cluster 8 Irrelevant	Cluster 9 Irrelevant	Cluster 10 Con/Adm 2
n	122	123	111	30	111	35	40	2	2	144
Indegree	5.3*	3.8	4.4	1.8*	5.6*	2.1	3.8	1.0*	1.0*	3.2
PageRank	0.0013*	0.00098	0.00096	0.00078*	0.00108	0.00082	0.00084	0.00081*	0.00080*	0.00092

*$p < 0.05$

Table 6.6 Persuasive Power of Communities: Subject Matters. [*Source* The author]

	All	Ct	Di	Do	E	G	N	T	X
n	844	95	87	384	76	21	17	87	77
Outdegree	2.7	4.0	3.4	4.1	1.9*	2.9	1.3*	2.8	3.5
Hub score	0.055	0.032*	0.060	0.117*	0.022*	0.037*	0.015*	0.026*	0.051

*$p < 0.05$

These findings show that not all issues that CAS comes in contact with are equal in terms of precedential power, that decisions addressing certain issues are more likely to develop into important precedents, and that doping sanctions and procedural aspects of doping cases are two such issues. By comparison, decisions addressing other doping-related issues, for example the substantive obligations under anti-doping rules and relationship between anti-doping rules and medical treatment, are significantly less likely to develop into important precedents.

What factors affect the precedent potential of a particular issue? A plausible explanation that is consistent with these findings is that issues with high precedential potential concern or are governed by broad general rules and principles. Complex concepts, such as strict liability, significant fault or negligence, and fundamental rights, require more extensive interpretation and elaboration before they can be applied to the facts of a specific case. CAS provides such interpretation in its case law and it is natural that decisions dealing with such issues are extensively considered and relied upon in subsequent decisions. By comparison, decisions dealing with issues that are governed by clear and detailed rules or agreements tend to focus on factual circumstances and are less likely to provide valuable guidance for future disputes. It is however worth pointing out that the fact that certain groups of decisions have a comparatively limited role in establishing precedents for future cases does not, of course, diminish or detract from their important function in deciding the individual disputes.[141]

This could also explain differences in precedential power between contract-related CAS decisions. CAS decisions concerning *Contractual Obligations* are relatively rarely cited and have a limited structural impact.[142] This is not true, however, for CAS decisions concerning *Contractual Breaches*. This difference between the two topics seems to suggest that the likely structural impact of a CAS decision, as a source of law, in subsequent contractual disputes varies significantly depending on whether they concern an alleged breach. If the case concerns a breach of contract, CAS's decision is likely to have an average impact on future decisions. If, however, the decision concerns the interpretation of contractual obligations its impact on CAS jurisprudence is likely to be lower than average.

[141] Nor does this mean that there are no significant precedents among CAS decisions involving these subject matters. An example of such a case is CAS 94/132, *PRABF v. USAB* (concerning dual nationality and with a PageRank of 0.00107). The data does however show that these subject matters are generally negatively correlated with precedential power.

[142] That is, they have significantly low mean indegree and PageRank score. See above Table 6.4 *Precedential Power of Communities: Topic Modelling*.

6.3.2 *Persuasive Power: With a Little Help from My Friends?*

In discussing precedential power above we have examined to what extent communities of decisions *are relied on* by CAS decisions. One can similarly but oppositely study to what extent communities of decisions *rely on* CAS decisions and whether communities of decisions differ significantly in this regard. This, which is here referred to as *persuasive power*,[143] is the subject of this section.

Like precedential power, persuasive power can be usefully examined both when it comes to individual decisions and to communities of decisions. As discussed above, precedential power can be used to identify landmark decisions as decisions with high precedential power occupying central positions in a case law network.[144] In a similar manner, persuasive power can be used to determine how well-connected a decision is to the overall body of jurisprudence. A decision with high persuasive power is well-connected or well-embedded in existing case law compared to other decisions. When applied to communities of decisions, as the case is here, persuasive power reflects whether communities of CAS decisions significantly differ with regard to how well-embedded they are in jurisprudence. Such differences reveal the relative importance of jurisprudence in different communities of CAS decisions. Since these communities, as discussed above, represent different issues that CAS deals with, persuasive power also reveals to what extent different issues are driven by case law compared to each other.

The approach used to analyze persuasive power closely resembles the one used above to determine precedential power.[145] As with precedential power, different measurements can be used to measure persuasive power. We will here be considering two: outdegree and hub score. Outdegree is simply equal to the number of decisions cited.[146] Thus, a finding that a community has a significantly low or high mean outdegree reveals that CAS decisions belonging to that community cite fewer prior decisions than the average CAS decision and that this is correlated with the issue concerned.[147] In addition to outdegree, we will use hub score to measure persuasive power. While it is calculated in a different way, hub score fills a similar role as PageRank here in that it reflects not only how many decisions are cited but also the relative importance of the cited decisions.[148] In this way, hub score supplements outdegree by including a qualitative element. A low or high hub score can be attributed either to many decisions being cited or to many important decisions

---

[143] For further discussion, see also Derlén and Lindholm 2015.

[144] See Chap. 5. What more specifically defines the "center" depends on what measurement is used.

[145] See above Sect. 6.3.1.

[146] See also Sect. 1.6. Compare indegree centrality used for measuring precedential power above.

[147] The mean outdegree of all decisions in the dataset is 2.7.

[148] A decision's hub score depends on the authority of all decisions it cites. See also Sect. 1.6.

being cited.[149] However, to what extent a community's hub score is attributable to one or both of these factors can be determined by comparing a community's outdegree and hub score.[150]

A first observation is that there are some clear similarities between precedential and persuasive power. For example, the subject matters *Eligibility*, *Governance*, and *Nationality* have significantly low both precedential and persuasive power, and essentially regardless of what measurement is used to measure these.[151] Similarly, the topics *Doping Procedure* and *Doping Sanctions* have significantly high precedential and high persuasive power, even though the persuasive power of these decisions is somewhat lower than their precedential power.[152]

But there are some clear differences between precedential and persuasive power for certain communities. First, there are communities that have high precedential power but low persuasive power. This is most obvious with regard to the doping-related communities. CAS decisions belonging to clusters 1 and 5, *Doping 1* and *Doping 3*, have been cited on average 5.3 and 5.6 times respectively, i.e. roughly twice as often as the average CAS decision in the dataset. However, decisions belonging to those clusters on average only cite 2.2 and 2.0 previous decision respectively, significantly less than the average CAS decision.[153] Contract-related decisions follow essentially the same pattern, albeit not as extensively and in a slightly more complex way. The subject matter *Contracts* and the topic *Contractual Breaches* have no significant score for precedential power,[154] but significantly low hub scores. Thus, CAS decisions belonging to these communities distinguish themselves negatively among CAS decisions in terms of how well-embedded they are in important existing case law.[155] There are also communities that have high persuasive power but low precedential power. The most obvious example of this is decisions concerning the topic *Doping Obligations*.[156]

---

149 The mean hub score of all decisions in the dataset is 0.055.

150 Take, for example, a community that has an insignificant mean outdegree but a significantly high hub score. This means that CAS decisions belonging to this community does not cite previous decisions distinctly frequently but that the decisions cited are strong precedents.

151 The only exception is *Governance* which has a significantly low hub score but not outdegree. Thus, decisions involving *Governance* cite an average number of decisions but those decisions have relatively low precedential power.

152 As seen below in Table 6.7 *Persuasive Power of Communities: Topic Modelling*, their mean outdegree is somewhat lower than their mean indegree. Also, using the majority occurrence model, *Doping Procedure* scores significantly high for PageRank but not for hub score.

153 *Doping 3* follows the same pattern for PageRank and hub score. See below Table 6.7 *Persuasive Power of Communities: Topic Modelling*.

154 See above Table 6.3 *Precedential Power of Communities: Subject Matters*. Its mean indegree and PageRank scores are very close to the overall means for the entire dataset.

155 See above Table 6.6 *Persuasive Power of Communities: Subject Matters.*

156 Compare above Table 6.4 *Precedential Power of Communities: Topic Modelling* and below Table 6.7 *Persuasive Power of Communities: Topic Modelling*. This is the only community with significant but opposite scores. There are others that only score significantly high for persuasive power, for example the topic *Non-contractual Breaches*.

Table 6.7 Persuasive Power of Communities: Topic Modelling. [*Source* The author]

	Topic 1	Topic 2	Topic 3	Topic 4	Topic 5	Topic 6	Topic 7	Topic 8	Topic 9	Topic 10	Topic 11	Topic 12
	Contractual breaches	German	Doping procedure	Doping sanction	Non-contractual breaches	Doping obligations	French	Australia	Eligibility	Italian	Doping and medical treatment	Contractual obligations
Large occurrence[a]												
n	216	47	92	165	78	125	153	73	172	19	25	88
Outdegree	3.6	3.6	4.7*	4.7*	4.7*	4.1	2.6*	3.4	3.0	3.7	3.3	3.0
Hub score	0.039*	0.096	0.097	0.170*	0.089	0.117*	0.048	0.059	0.061	0.108	0.109	0.0250*
Majority occurrence[b]												
n	125	3	41	72	39	47	145	23	96	5	3	49
Outdegree	4.0	1.7*	5.4*	5.1*	5.4*	4.3	2.6*	2.5*	1.6*	8.3*	3.5	2.8
Hub score	0.034*	0.006*	0.108	0.207*	0.108	0.112*	0.047	0.054	0.024*	0.336*	0.070	0.018*

*$p < 0.05$
[a]Decisions with at least 20% topic occurrence
[b]Decisions with at least 50% topic occurrence

Table 6.8 Persuasive Power of Communities: Co-citation Clustering. [*Source* The author]

	Cluster 1 Doping 1	Cluster 2 Con/Adm 1	Cluster 3 Doping 2	Cluster 4??	Cluster 5 Doping 3	Cluster 6??	Cluster 7 Doping 4	Cluster 8 Irrelevant	Cluster 9 Irrelevant	Cluster 10 Con/Adm 2
n	122	123	111	30	111	35	40	2	2	144
Outdegree	2.2*	3.6	3.7	2.3*	2.0*	1.6*	0*	0*	5.6*	2.3*
Hub score	0.047	0.089	0.146*	0.027*	0.023*	0.015*	0*	0*	0.167*	0.031*

* $p < 0.05$

These differences in precedential and persuasive power show that CAS on some issues quite frequently cites decisions belonging to a different community than the case before it. This is the only possible explanation for how certain communities end up with large differences in precedential and persuasive power. This conclusion, along with the findings above, quite clearly shows that different communities of CAS decisions occupy different positions or, differently phrased, play different roles in the overall structure of CAS jurisprudence. Some communities of decisions appear to "lead" jurisprudential development in the sense that decisions concerning these issues are cited by decisions concerning other issues. Conversely, there appears to exist "follower communities" consisting of decisions that heavily rely on previous decisions concerning other issues than themselves. These relationships between communities are explored in greater detail below.[157]

A community that has significantly high both outdegree and hub score is a community where previous decisions are an unambiguously important source of law. The constituent decisions of such a community cite both many and important previous decisions. There is only one such community: the topic *Doping Procedure*. By comparison, there are several communities with significantly low scores for both outdegree and hub score. In such communities, previous decisions can be regarded as a relatively unimportant source of law. This includes the subject matters *Eligibility* and *Nationality* and some of the doping-related clusters. A third, clear category is communities that do not significantly distinguish themselves from the overall set in terms of persuasive power, neither positively nor negatively.[158]

The role of previous decisions as a source of law in remaining communities is more complex. First, there are communities that have a high hub score but not a high mean outdegree. Such communities can be described as dominated by quality, citing important decisions, over quantity, citing many decisions. This description fit the subject matter *Doping*, the topic *Doping Obligations*, and the cluster *Doping 2*.[159]

Similarly, there are several communities that have a higher outdegree than hub score. This suggests that decisions belonging to these communities cite a greater number of previous decisions than the average CAS decisions, but that the decisions cited are not particularly important. One possible explanation for this observation is that decisions belonging to these communities spread references more evenly rather than concentrating on a few landmark decisions.

---

157 See below Sect. 6.3.3.

158 This includes the subject matters *Disciplinary* and *Others*, the topic *Doping and Medical Treatment*, and the cluster *Constitutional/Administrative 2*.

159 A related type of pattern is significantly low outdegree coupled with insignificant hub score. This is for example true for the topic *Australia* and the cluster *Doping 1*.

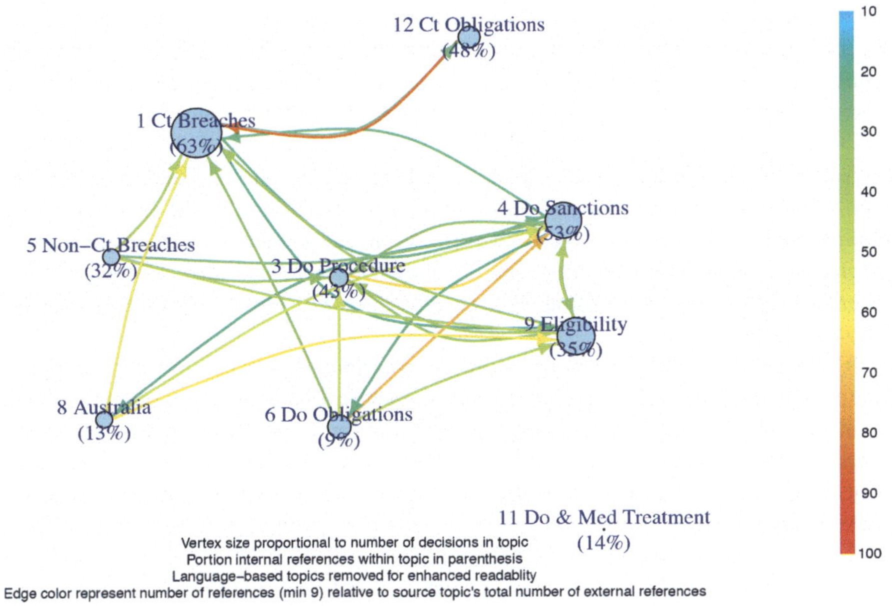

Fig. 6.3 References Within and Between Topics. [*Source* The author]

6.3.3 *Inter-Community Influence: All by Myself?*

The approach used above has led to the identification of communities of CAS decisions that are strongly connected, either in terms of discussing the same topic or in terms of frequently being cited together. However, differences in individual communities' precedential and persuasive power observed above indicate that CAS decisions rather frequently cite decisions belonging to other communities, a practice that can be referred to as *inter-community references*, and that the extent and direction of such inter-community references varies greatly between individual communities and between individual community-to-community relationships. We shall now examine more closely whether and to what extent this suspicion is correct.

In doing so, we would expect that communities dealing with related issues or areas, for example doping-related or contract-related communities, more frequently cite each other's decisions than less obviously related communities, for example a doping-related and a contract-related community.

This is confirmed in several cases,[160] and is perhaps most obvious with regard to contract-related topics. Almost a third of all references made in decisions predominantly concerning the topic *Contractual Breaches* are within that community

[160] See above Fig. 6.3 *References Within and Between Topics.*

(*intra-community references*). When references are made outside the community it is predominantly to decisions concerning the related topic of *Contractual Obligations* and the same is also true vice versa. Thus, based on this, one can describe contract-related CAS jurisprudence as rather distinct and self-contained.

Doping-related communities exhibit a similar pattern. CAS decisions dealing with *Doping Obligations* and *Doping Sanctions* rely heavily on decisions dealing with *Doping Procedure*. This observation can be explained by the fact that many doping-related disputes involve both procedural and substantive issues to a great extent. Decisions predominantly dealing with *Doping Procedure* to a significant extent cite decisions concerning *Doping Sanctions* but not decisions that concern *Doping Obligations*.[161]

It is also clear that decisions addressing certain topics occupy a particularly central position in CAS jurisprudence in the sense that they are frequently relied upon not only by decisions concerning the same topic but more broadly across all types of cases that come before CAS. One clear example of this is decisions concerning the topic *Contractual Breaches* which are extensively cited in decisions concerning almost all other topics. Thus, while *Contractual Breaches* as discussed constitutes a rather distinct and homogenous collection of CAS decisions that almost uniformly concern football and contracts and predominately cite each other, it appears that those decisions are relevant as a source of law across most of the issues that CAS encounters.

An example of a decision concerning *Contractual Breaches* that has this type of impact is *Aris I* presented and discussed above.[162] Another example is *Ribéry*.[163] The case concerned the French football player Franck Ribéry who entered an employment contract with and began playing for the Turkish football club Galatasaray. Four months later, the player terminated the contract on the basis that Galatasaray had failed to pay the remuneration agreed upon and shortly thereafter joined the French football club Olympique de Marseille. This lead to a dispute that was decided first by the FIFA DRC and thereafter CAS regarding whether either party had acted in breach of the contract and owed the other damages. In *Ribéry*, CAS formulated general principles that have been relied upon by subsequent CAS panels. First, CAS held that not every breach of a contract obligation constitutes "just cause" required under FIFA's regulations for terminating the contract. In order to meet this standard, the breach must according to CAS have "a certain

[161] This is consistent with the finding above that unlike *Doping Procedure* and *Doping Sanctions*, *Doping Obligations* have significantly low precedential power. See above Table 6.4 *Precedential Power of Communities: Topic Modelling*.

[162] See further Sect. 5.3.

[163] CAS 2006/A/1180.

seriousness."[164] By this it meant that the breach "causes the confidence, which the one party has in future performance in accordance with the contract, to be lost."[165] CAS continued by applying this sufficiently-serious-breach test to the more specific issue of non-payment of salary.[166] The more specific test has, for obvious reasons, been relied upon in cases concerning non-payment of salaries,[167] but the concept of a sufficiently serious breach has broader application and has also been relied upon by CAS in other types of disputes.[168] *Ribéry* is also frequently cited for CAS's reasoning regarding what law the parties have selected to govern their relationship and public policy limitations to that power. This element of the decision has been subsequently relied upon in other contractual disputes,[169] but for example also to determine the law governing doping-related disputes.[170]

Aris I and *Ribéry* are two examples that help explain why CAS's jurisprudence regarding *Contractual Breaches* is frequently relied upon in CAS decisions that mainly concern other topics. In deciding the former disputes, CAS has decided issues that are relevant across many of the areas touched by CAS.

In a similar way, decisions concerning *Doping Procedure* are frequently cited in CAS decisions concerning the topics *Eligibility* and *Non-contractual Breaches*. This can be explained by the fact that in settling doping-related decisions CAS has decided many important issues that come up in other types of disputes, such as jurisdictional issues, evidentiary issues, and fundamental procedural principles.[171]

Thus, decisions concerning *Contractual Breaches* and *Doping Procedure* have a central position in CAS jurisprudence, not because these topics as such are particularly relevant or important outside their own field, but because decisions addressing these issues contain broadly applicable principles. Consequently, it appears that decisions concerning these topics have a central role in the development of general principles and in this sense also a central role in the development of lex sportiva in the broad sense of the term.

---

[164] Ibid., para 21.

[165] Ibid., para 26.

[166] Ibid., para 26 ("Firstly, the amount paid late by the employer may not be 'insubstantial' or completely secondary. Secondly, a prerequisite for terminating the contract because of late payment is that the employee must have given a warning. In other words, the employee must have drawn the employer's attention to the fact that his conduct is not in accordance with the contract…").

[167] See e.g. CAS 2007/A/1320 & 1321, *Feyenoord Rotterdam v. Clube de Regatas do Flamengo*, para 23 (regarding training compensation in football); CAS 2008/A/1448, *Razek*, para 26.

[168] See e.g. CAS 2008/A/1517, *Pajuelo Chávez*, para 56.

[169] See e.g. Ibid., paras 16–17; CAS 2009/A/1919, *Costa*, para 16; CAS 2009/A/1960 & 1961, *Sylva*, para 15.

[170] See e.g. CAS 2009/A/1782, *Volandri* (regarding doping in tennis); CAS 2009/A/1926 & 1930, *Gasquet*, para 11.

[171] See above Sect. 6.2.3.

6.4 What We Might Have Missed

The examination carried out in this chapter has allowed us to identify and explore the structure of CAS jurisprudence, both in terms of which major issues can be found in CAS jurisprudence, what role they play in CAS's overall body of jurisprudence, and how they relate to each other.

This approach has produced an image of the issues dealt with by CAS that nuances and complements CAS's own subject matter classification. One important finding concerns contract-related disputes, which constitute a large and important part of CAS jurisprudence. The findings above show that it is relevant to distinguish between disputes concerning a claimed breach of contract and disputes where there is disagreement about the nature and extent of the contractual obligation. Decisions dealing with the former issue are closely connected to other, non-contract-related decisions, including doping-related disputes and other disciplinary cases. Using co-citation clustering we were also able to detect groups of decisions dealing with constitutional and/or administrative issues that do not fit squarely in any of CAS's subject matters but that have broad application across its jurisprudence. These issues serve as a backbone of CAS jurisprudence and are of fundamental importance when establishing a legitimate legal order.[172]

While many of CAS's decisions concern doping, the examination has shown that doping-related decisions are not a large, isolated group within CAS jurisprudence, but also that they are relevant for the development of CAS jurisprudence in non-doping-related issues and areas. Also, the findings suggest that doping as a category is too broad and too diverse and that it makes sense to separate it into at least three sub-categories: obligation, procedure, and sanction.

References

Blei D (2012) Probabilistic Topic Models. Communications of the ACM 55(4):77–84

Blei D, Lafferty J (2009) Topic Models. In: Srivastava A, Sahami M (eds) Text Mining: Classification, Clustering, and Applications. Chapman and Hall, Boca Raton, pp. 71–93

Blei D, Ng A, Jordan I (2003) Latent Dirichlet Allocation. Journal of Machine Learning Research 3:993–1022

Blondel V, Guillaume J-L, Lambiotte R, Lefebvre E (2008) Fast unfolding of communities in large networks. Journal of Statistical Mechanics 2008(10):P10008

Derlén M, Lindholm J (2015) Characteristics of Precedent: The Case Law of the European Court of Justice in Three Dimensions. German Law Journal 16(5):1073–1098

Derlén M, Lindholm J, Mirshahvalad A, Rosvall M (2013) Coherence Out of Chaos: Mapping European Union Law by Running Randomly Through the Maze of CJEU Case Law. Europarättslig Tidskrift 16(3):517–535

Fortunato S (2010) Community Detection in Graphs. Physics Reports 486:75–174

[172] The constitutional and administrative law issues and principles that can be identified in CAS jurisprudence are described and discussed in greater detail in Chap. 7.

Lancichinetti A, Fortunato S (2009) Community detection algorithms: A comparative analysis. Physical Review E 80(5):56117

Lupu Y, Voeten E (2011) Precedent in International Courts: A Network Analysis of Case Citations by the European Court of Human Rights. British Journal of Political Science 42:413–439

McCain K W (1986) Co-cited author mapping as a valid representation of intellectual structure. Journal of the American Association for Information Science 37:111–122

Newman M (2004) Fast algorithm for detecting community structure in networks. Physical Review E 69:066133

Newman M (2006) Modularity and community structure in networks. Proceedings of the National Academy of Sciences 103(23):8577–8582

Newman M (2011) Networks: An Introduction. Oxford University Press, Oxford

Newman M (2012) Communities, modules and large-scale structure in networks. Nature Physics 8:25–31

Newman M, Girvan M (2004) Finding and evaluating community structure in networks. Physical Review E 69(2):026113

Panagis Y, Christensen M L, Sadl U (2016) On top of topics: Leveraging topic modeling to study the dynamic case-law of international courts. In: Bex F, Villata S (eds) Legal Knowledge and Information Systems. Frontiers in Artificial Intelligence and Applications 294, pp. 161–166

Peel L, Larremore D, Clauset A (2017) The ground truth about metadata and community detection in networks. Science Advances 3:e1602548

Rosvall M, Axelsson D, Bergstrom C T (2009) The Map Equation. European Physics Journal Special Topics 178:13–23

Small H (1973) Co-citation in the scientific literature: A new measure of the relationship between two documents. Journal of the American Association for Information Science 24:265–269

Wallace M, Gingras Y, Duhon R (2009) A new approach for detecting scientific specialties from raw co-citation networks. Journal of the American Society for Information Science and Technology 60(2):240-246

Chapter 7
CAS's Normative Contribution

Abstract It is frequently claimed, both by the Court of Arbitration for Sport (CAS) and by others, that CAS jurisprudence contains a number of principles. By identifying and expressing such principles CAS contributes to the body of norms that govern sports. The extent and nature of this contribution is however not immediately obvious, nor is the method or methods used to determine the existence of a principle. This chapter seeks to add to the existing knowledge on this topic by studying what norms CAS itself finds in its jurisprudence, the nature of those norms, and the reasoning put forth by CAS in support of their existence.

7.1 Norms, Rules, and Principles, in and from CAS

Legal orders are normative orders and norms are thus a necessary and basic element of all legal orders.[1] Transnational legal orders are no exception in this regard.[2] Norms prescribe what ought to happen or not happen, including, in particular, how people ought to behave.[3] In this way, norms guide behavior and this is also one of the distinctive features of a legal order.[4] By merit of the authority that distinguish legal orders from other normative orders, legal norms, when interpreted and applied, constitute the basis for determining the legality of a particular act. In this manner, the existence of norms is a necessary (but not sufficient) condition for the existence of a legal order.[5]

There is no shortage of norms governing sports-related activities. Like all societal activities, sports-related activities must take place within the space defined by national and international law. Such norms may be of a general nature or

---

[1] Kelsen 1970, pp. 4–5.
[2] Cf. Lagarde 1982, p. 128 (regarding *lex mercatoria*). See also Sect. 1.3.
[3] Kelsen 1970, pp. 4–5; Kramer 1999, p. 80 (describing a norm as a "general directive that lays down a standard with which conformity is required and against which people's conduct can be assessed." Discussing Raz).
[4] Kelsen 1970, pp. 4–5.
[5] As pointed out by Hart, to understand law as a collection of rules is a common oversimplification. Hart 2012, pp. 8–17.

J. Lindholm, *The Court of Arbitration for Sport and Its Jurisprudence*,
ASSER International Sports Law Series,
https://doi.org/10.1007/978-94-6265-285-9_7

specifically target sports-related activities. They may be found in statute or case law and they may be what some would refer to as general principles. When studying the norms governing a particular societal activity, the starting point and primary object of examination is often norms found in national and international legal orders, those which we might call "legal norms".[6] To focus too narrowly on the legal norms may frequently lead to an incomplete or even erroneous understanding of the normative framework governing the studied activity. However, there are few societal activities that a person can engage in where the legal norms are more extensively supplemented by other norms than when it comes to sports.

This most obviously includes written, formalized norms established by sports governing bodies (SGBs). Such norms may be found in documents such as statutes, charters, rules, codes, and regulations, but are essentially a variety of private agreements connected through a rather complex web or matrix.[7] Such norms will for the sake of simplicity here collectively be referred to as "sports rules". There is no definitive list or classification of sports rules, but a few of the major types of rules are *playing rules* defining a sport, including its aims and activities; *safety rules* ensuring that the sport can (as far as possible) be carried out in a (reasonably) safe manner; *eligibility rules* governing who may participate in competition; *competition rules* defining the conditions for competitive sports; *transfer rules* dictating the terms for athletes' movements between teams and clubs; *disciplinary rules* defining punishments for those who violate other rules; *procedural rules* regulating disciplinary actions and other forms of dispute resolution; and *organizational rules* governing membership in clubs, teams, and SGBs, as well as the relationship between such entities, including the allocation of regulatory competence. Sports rules make up a significant part of the norms governing sports-related activities, they regulate essential areas, and sports would not be able to function without sports rules.

While legal norms and sports rules are two clear and important categories of norms, the entire body of norms governing sports-related activities cannot be adequately and accurately captured using just those two categories. In order to form a coherent system capable of answering all questions that arise in sports-related activities and disputes,[8] reflecting their complex nature,[9] gaps left by legal norms and sports rules must be filled. It is largely uncontroversial to claim that the Court

[6] The term "legal norms" as used here can be seen as a practical shorthand for "state law" or "state-based legal norms", not as a position on the possibility or existence of transnational legal orders. See Sect. 1.3.

[7] Cf. Anderson 2010, pp. 257–276; Beloff et al. 2012, pp. 35–43.

[8] Cf. Lagarde 1982, p. 130 (regarding lex mercatoria).

[9] Casini 2011, p. 1318 ("sports law is now far from being amenable to an exhaustive explanation based on structures of private law alone, but rather presents a mixed nature, in which a regulatory framework based on private autonomy interacts constantly with public law norms.").

of Arbitration for Sport (CAS) plays an important role in filling those gaps,[10] and in doing so makes a normative contribution to the field of sports.[11]

There is however more uncertainty and disagreement regarding the extent and nature of CAS's normative contribution.[12] One perspective, expressed for example in CAS's decision in *AEK Athens*, is that CAS establishes or defines certain "unwritten legal principles":[13]

> [A]ll sporting institutions, and in particular all international federations, must abide by general principles of law. Due to the transnational nature of sporting competitions, the effects of the conduct and deeds of international federations are felt in a sporting community throughout various countries. Therefore, the substantive and procedural rules to be respected by international federations cannot be reduced only to its own statutes and regulations and to the laws of the country where the federation is incorporated or of the country where its headquarters are. Sports law has developed and consolidated along the years, *particularly through the arbitral settlement of disputes*, a set of unwritten legal principles – a sort of lex mercatoria for sports or, so to speak, a lex ludica – to which national and international sports federations must conform, regardless of the presence of such principles within their own statutes and regulations or within any applicable national law…

The exact content and nature of these unwritten legal principles is not obvious. As pointed out by Foster, the principles developed by CAS are of varying nature and further distinctions are productive.[14] Others advocate understanding CAS's normative contribution using an approach that is both broader, in the sense of relating CAS's contribution to applicable legal norms and sports rules, and more nuanced.[15]

In this chapter we will explore CAS's normative contribution and the methods used by CAS in making such normative contributions. This will be achieved by studying CAS's reference to its own, previous decisions. It was concluded above that CAS extensively and regularly relies upon and adheres to its previous decisions as precedent in deciding subsequent disputes.[16] In this chapter we will focus on the particular points of law for which CAS refers to its previous decisions as a source or authority. These references will be used to identify norms established by CAS, in

---

[10] Cf. Erbsen 2006, p. 454 ("CAS's jurisprudence fills what until recently was a disturbing vacuum in international sports."); Rigozzi 2005, pp. 635–636.

[11] Latty 2007, p. 357. What is here referred to as a "normative contribution" appears for all purposes the same as what von Bogdandy and Venzke refer to as "judicial lawmaking" or "[t]he creation and development of legal normativity in judicial practice…", von Bogdandy and Venzke 2012, p. 12.

[12] See Sect. 1.3. See also e.g. Vieweg and Staschik 2015.

[13] CAS 98/200, *AEK Athens*, para 156 (emphasis added). The case is discussed in greater detail below in Sect. 7.3.

[14] Foster 2006, p. 2.

[15] See e.g. Erbsen 2006 (challenging the usefulness of the term lex sportiva).

[16] See Chap. 4.

other words its normative contribution.[17] To illustrate, take as an example the following section from CAS's decision in *Besiktas v. UEFA* where CAS recognized that it has in previous decisions established a norm governing the standard of proof required in disciplinary cases:[18]

> UEFA must establish the relevant facts "to the comfortable satisfaction of the Court having in mind the seriousness of allegation which is made" (CAS 2005/A/908).

Existing research on CAS commonly refers to norms recognized and developed in CAS jurisprudence as principles.[19] The term principle is somewhat ambiguous and is used with different meanings in different context. There is certainly pedagogical value in using the term principle broadly when studying CAS's normative contribution. However, at the same time, doing so risks obscuring some relevant differences between different types of norms. When studying CAS jurisprudence we find that some of the norms that CAS refers to can be characterized as rules in the sense that they are "fixed point" that "are always either fulfilled or not,"[20] "applicable in an all-or-nothing fashion," and where a particular outcome must be accepted under certain circumstances.[21] But not all norms found in CAS jurisprudence are of this type. Other norms can better be characterized as principles in the sense that they are "optimization requirements" that require that "something be realized to the greatest extent possible given the legal and factual possibilities."[22] It is not always easy to uphold this distinction. However, an attempt will be made below.

Researchers have previously aimed to describe and categorize the normative principles established in CAS jurisprudence and this research provides valuable findings that will be considered as we explore the question below.[23] Researchers have used slightly different approaches and focused on somewhat different things and, as a consequence, propose slightly different models for understanding the principles found in CAS jurisprudence. While the models differ quite considerably,

---

[17] It should be pointed out that such references form part of a method for identifying norms, not a criterion for the existence of norms. A norm articulated in a decision is a norm regardless of whether it has (yet) been referred to in a subsequent decision. Thus, while references point to a norm, not all norms are pointed to by way of a reference. However, it can be difficult to determine with a reasonable degree of certainty whether a statement made in one decision constitutes a general norm unless one sees that CAS treats it as such. In this way, references are a resource for identifying norms.

[18] CAS 2013/A/3258, *Besiktas Jimnastik Kulübü v. UEFA*, para 119. Cf. Rigozzi 2005, p. 228. See further below Sect. 7.4.

[19] See e.g. Beloff et al. 2012, pp. 11–16; Casini 2011, p. 1319; Foster 2006; Latty 2007, pp. 301–332; Rigozzi 2005, pp. 643–652; Vieweg and Staschik 2015, pp. 25–34.

[20] Alexy 2002, pp. 47–48.

[21] Dworkin 2013, pp. 40–41.

[22] Alexy 2002, pp. 47–48. Cf. Dworkin 2013, pp. 38–45 (using the term principle for non-rule standards that ought to be followed for moral reasons, such as justice or fairness). Cf. Buy et al. 2015, p. 142.

[23] Besides the ones discussed below, the presentation of CAS's landmark decisions in Martens 2006 provides a good overview of some of CAS's key normative contributions.

they are rarely in direct conflict with each other. Rather, by focusing on slightly different things, the different models supplement each other to produce a more nuanced and complete understanding.

Foster divides the principles developed in CAS jurisprudence into five main categories.[24] The first category consists of *rules of the game* (*lex ludica*). CAS jurisprudence in this area, Foster argues, reflect CAS's great respect for the autonomy and expertise for sport actors, including most obviously federations and match officials, and a reluctance to intervene. In this context, Foster recognizes a principle of autonomy and a "zone of autonomy for match officials and federations in so far as they are dealing with the rule of the game."[25] The second category is *good governance* that consists of principles laying down the standard that SGBs must follow in exercising disciplinary power over athletes and other members, such as the requirement that rules are clear, foreseeable, and transparent. Somewhat relatedly, a third category of principles provides the minimum standard of *procedural fairness* that applies in disciplinary matters. The fourth category of principles relate to the *harmonization of standards* across different sports, focusing on contributing to consistency, promoting "best practice", and upholding the primacy of international sports federations. The fifth and final category encompasses principles that seek to ensure *fairness and equitable treatment*, including the principle of proportionality and the principle of protection of legitimate expectations.[26]

McLaren's categorization of the principles emerging from CAS jurisprudence has certain similarities with Foster's.[27] McLaren's first category, *fairness of rules and procedure*, seem to cover Foster's second and third categories as they both pertain to fairness in a broader sense.[28] McLaren also recognizes *rules governing CAS's power to review* as a separate category and this category seems to cover largely the same principles as Foster's first category. However, McLaren's categorization also differs from Foster's. McLaren groups together all *principles pertaining to doping offenses*, such as the legality of strict liability, the standard of review, and the proportionality of sanctions, into one category. McLaren also recognizes *rules for resolving jurisdictional disputes* between national and international federations as a distinct category.[29]

Latty takes a slightly different approach and distinguishes between CAS's principles based on their origin. Latty distinguishes between, on one hand, general principles that have their origin in state-based legal orders (general legal principles) and, on the other, endogenous general principles that arise within the sport system

[24] Foster 2006.

[25] Ibid., pp. 3–5, 11 (quoted).

[26] Ibid.

[27] It is not entirely clear whether McLaren's categorization is intended to cover all principles established in CAS jurisprudence. See McLaren 2011, p. 54.

[28] It is not clear whether this category also includes the principles covered by Foster's fifth category. To the extent that they are applied to doping offenses, they appear to belong to a different category.

[29] These principles do not seem to fit in any of Foster's categories.

(principles of sports law).[30] The former category includes, among others, the principles of protection of legitimate expectations, *lex mitior*, and *nulla poena sine culpa*.[31] The latter category of principles that by merit of being generally and commonly recognized in sports rules have become "principles of customary law," such as principles seeking to uphold the fairness, integrity, and equality of sports competitions.[32]

Rigozzi identifies three major categories of principles. The first is *general legal principles that apply (directly) to sports-related disputes*, comprised of the principles of legality, equality, good faith, and protection of legitimate expectations. The second is *fundamental principles of criminal procedure applicable by analogy*, such as the principles of proportionality, *lex mitior*, and *nulla poena sine culpa*. The third and final category is *fundamental sports principles*, including principles governing responsibility and consequences in doping matters and principles relating to fair play.[33]

Erbsen, finally, proposes a different and "more subtle account of how CAS has tailored general legal principles to" sports-related disputes that is based on "the extent to which a written contract or rule governs the outcome of the dispute."[34] Erbsen presents a five-graded scale for classifying the nature of this "tailoring" depending on the nature of the underlying text that ranges from "clear and sufficiently just" to "silent".[35] One of Erbsen's key points is that the normative contribution of CAS jurisprudence is largely limited to filling gaps in the texts of sports rules and contracts and that the principles declared by CAS in fact rarely overrule sports rules.[36]

This review reveals, first, that commentators largely agree on what constitutes CAS's main normative contributions. Most of the norms that will be discussed in this chapter have been discussed extensively. This review also reveals that there are several possible ways of systematizing CAS's normative contribution. The presentation in this chapter is divided into five sections, each dealing with norms with, what I consider, a common theme. The first two sections cover general constitutional and administrative norms and the more specific issue of respect for fundamental rights respectively. We then turn to norms governing CAS itself and the procedure before CAS. These can also be described as procedural norms in a broad sense and methodological norms for identifying and interpreting the law governing

---

30 Latty 2007, pp. 303–332 (in his terminology "principes géneraux de droit" and "principia sportiva" respectively). See also Casini 2011, pp. 1327–1330; Beloff 2005, pp. 52–53; Beloff et al. 2012, p. 308. Cf. Erbsen 2006, p. 443.

31 Latty 2007, esp. pp. 316–323. Cf. CAS 98/200, *AEK Athens*, para 156 ("general principles of law drawn from a comparative or common denominator reading of various domestic legal systems … can be deemed to be part of such *lex ludica*.").

32 Latty 2007, pp. 323–332.

33 Rigozzi 2005, pp. 643–652.

34 Erbsen 2006, p. 441.

35 Ibid., p. 442.

36 Ibid., pp. 452–453.

a dispute. The fifth and final section covers norms governing sanctions and other remedies. Each of these sections seeks to both succinctly present some of the central norms within each theme and, to the extent that it can be ascertained, the reasoning and arguments presented by CAS in support of their existence.

7.2 Constitutional and Administrative Norms: Allocation and Exercise of Power

First, CAS has developed norms governing the allocation of power and the relationship between SGBs and between, on the one hand, SGBs and, on the other, clubs and individuals. These norms serve a similar function that, from the perspective of national law, warrants referring to them as constitutional or administrative norms.[37]

There is hardly any sport where the regulatory power rests exclusively with one actor or institution,[38] and in most sports there are several national, regional, and international actors making a claim for regulatory power. This is fertile ground for disputes over regulatory power. Occasionally these disputes end up before CAS who must resolve them, for example in a situation where an issue raised in a particular case is subject to incompatible regulation.

In its early case law, CAS appeared willing to provide national federations with significant regulatory power to regulate national competitions.[39] However, an exception from this general rule is the area of doping where, in case of conflict, international federations' anti-doping rules take precedence over the rules of national federations and national Olympic committees.[40] This exception has lost some of its practical relevance after the adoption of the World Anti-Doping Code (WADC). However, in settling this issue, CAS established a more general principle of "independence and autonomy of International Federations in the administration of their sports," that includes but is not limited to the area of doping.[41] In formulating this principle of independence and autonomy, CAS initially emphasized the values of uniformity – in the sense that sports competitions must be subject to the

---

[37] Cf. Casini 2011, pp. 1327–1328; Latty 2007, pp. 320–321 (discussing CAS's adoption of public law principles). This category includes many of the principles discussed by Foster, including good governance, primacy of international sporting federations, and the protection of procedural rights and other fundamental rights. See above Sect. 7.1.

[38] Besides the sports-specific SGBs, most sports are, if nothing else, subject to WADA and IOC rules.

[39] CAS 94/128, *UCI v. CONI*, para 11. A "national competition" in this regard was a competition that was not included in the international federation's calendar.

[40] Ibid, paras 21 et seq., cited with approval in e.g. CAS 95/144, *COE*; CAS 97/169, *Menegotto*, para 1. See also Nafziger 1999, p. 233 (commenting on this in the context of the globalization of sports law).

[41] CAS 94/128, *UCI v. CONI*, para 21; OG 02/001, *Prusis*, para 9 (quoted).

same conditions regardless of where they are taking place – foreseeability, certainty, and legitimate expectations, particularly in relation to affected athletes.[42] Later case law anchors the principle in the freedom of associations which, CAS emphasizes, is respected in many legal traditions.[43]

It is important to distinguish between who has regulatory power and the consequences of one actor violating the regulatory power of another actor. CAS has established that the superior rulemaker's rules are not directly applicable and cannot in case of conflict take precedent over an inferior rulemaker's rules. Even in the face of a blatant conflict, the inferior rulemaker's rules remain valid and binding in relation to governed clubs, individuals, and other members. The superior rulemaker's only recourse is to impose sanctions against the inferior rulemaker.[44] Only if the superior rulemaker's rules are incorporated by the inferior rulemaker do they become directly applicable.[45] CAS extrapolates this principle from the fact that sports rules are civil in nature and that regulatory power in sports rests on a contractual basis.[46] This is an example of CAS taking a private law principle and adopting it to govern what in a state-based legal context would be categorized as a public law issue.

The relationship between SGBs is in this regard fundamentally different from the relationship between SGBs and national and regional lawmakers. CAS has recognized the supremacy of law over sports rules and the obligation of national SGBs to abide by the law in the face of a conflict, for example when a federation is unable to comply with both national law and sports rules governing doping and doping violations. In these situations, CAS has instead called for cooperation among states and SGBs and urged states to exercise their regulatory power in a way that allows their nationals to compete.[47] The situation is complicated by the fact that most legal orders allow individuals considerable freedom to select the law that governs their relationships, including non-state-based norms like sports rules. The parties' freedom to choose the applicable law is, however, subject to the limitation that they must not violate *ordre public*, which is understood as universal values that form the basis of every legal system. All sports rules are in this manner subject to *ordre*

---

[42] CAS 94/128, *UCI v. CONI*, paras 19–20; OG 02/001, *Prusis*, paras 10–15; CAS 2005/A/983 & 984, *Suarez*, para 58 ("Ce besoin d'uniformité juridique est au demeurant l'une des plus évidentes 'spécificités du sport'"). See also CAS 95/144, *COE*.

[43] CAS 2005/A/830, *Squizzato*, para 50.

[44] OG 02/001, *Prusis*, para 10 (regarding conflicts between international federations' rules and the Olympic Charter); CAS 2012/A/2900, *Ionel*, paras 86–88 (regarding conflicts between national federations' rules and international federations' rules), citing CAS 2009/A/1889, *Unknown*, paras 77–78, 146–149; CAS 2008/A/1600, *Unknown*, para 5.19.

[45] See CAS 2008/A/1576 & 1628, *Grech*, paras 62–67.

[46] CAS 2009/A/1889, *Unknown*, paras 146–149 ("FIFA regulations do not constitute imperative State Law but private regulations which apply based on a contractual or similar basis."), quoted in CAS 2012/A/2900, *Ionel*, para 88.

[47] CAS 94/128, *UCI v. CONI*, para 29, cited with approval in e.g. CAS 95/144, *EOC*, para 3; CAS 2002/A/431, *Roux*, para 21.

public, including the unwritten principles expressed in CAS jurisprudence.[48] For example, EU competition law and the fundamental rights to free movement under EU law constitute mandatory rules that must be considered when the dispute has a close connection to the geographic territory of the EU.[49] The concept of *ordre public* and the need for sports rules to respect it has been expressed in CAS jurisprudence,[50] but an examination of that case law reveals that this is directly and closely connected to Swiss private international law.[51]

As discussed in further detail below, the concept of *ordre public* has had far-reaching normative consequences in CAS jurisprudence. Take, for example, the case of *Wang et al.* and its subsequent normative consequences. *Wang et al.* concerned four members of the China Swim Team who tested positive for a banned substance, Triamterene, and were subsequently suspended by the international federation (FINA) for a period of two years. FINA's suspension was upheld by CAS on appeal.[52] The athletes then challenged CAS's award in the Swiss Federal Tribunal (SFT) on a number of grounds, including that the sanctions were disproportionally strict given that the quantity of the banned substance found in the test was low and that a two-year suspension would have very serious consequences for them, including permanently ending their careers. The SFT concluded that the sanctions confirmed in CAS's award would only be incompatible with public policy and reviewable by the SFT if they constituted "an attack on personal rights which was *extremely serious and totally disproportionate* to the behaviour penalized," a level not reached in that particular case.[53] Similarly, five years later in *Hipperdinger* CAS concluded that "[i]n light of the jurisprudence of the Swiss Federal Supreme Court [in *Wang et al.*], the Panel is of the opinion that a two year suspension is not *totally disproportionate* to the behaviour of the Appellant, and the limitation of his freedom to practice his sport during that period can not be characterised as '*extremely serious*'."[54]

In this manner, the standard for what violates *ordre public* was effectively used as the standard for what constitutes a disproportionate sanction in sport. This is not entirely unproblematic. The *ordre public*-exception intends to protect against the most egregious outcomes and the bar for what constitutes *ordre public* is therefore intentionally set very high. If that bar, which is intended to function as a basic

[48] CAS 98/200, *AEK Athens*, para 156 ("Sports law has developed… a set of unwritten legal principles… to which national and international sports federations must conform… provided that they do not conflict with any national 'public policy'…").

[49] Ibid., paras 9–12.

[50] CAS 2005/A/983 & 984, *Suarez*, paras 20–30, cited with approval in e.g. CAS 2006/A/1180, *Ribéry*, paras 6–7; CAS 2007/A/1424, *FEB v. FIQ*, para 11; CAS 2008/A/1705, *Grasshopper v. Alianza Lima*, para 13.

[51] Article 187 PILA.

[52] CAS 98/208, *Wang et al.*

[53] SFT's decision 31 March 1999 in case 5P.83/1999 (*Wang et al. v. FINA*), para 3.c (translation in Digest of CAS Awards vol. II, p. 780 quoted, emphasis added).

[54] CAS 2004/A/690, *Hipperdinger*, para 55. Regarding the facts in *Hipperdinger*, see Sect. 5.4.

protection for human rights and other fundamental values, is used as a benchmark for evaluating the appropriateness of sports rules there is a clear risk for the development of a *de facto* standard that balance competing interests in a less than optimal way.

Finally, CAS has established the applicability of the principle of legality in sports law,[55] as well as norms that by content and function help to uphold the principle of legality and, in a broader sense, the rule of law.[56] A key source for this in CAS jurisprudence can be found in its seminal decision in *Quigley*:[57]

> The fight against doping is arduous, and it may require strict rules. But the rule-makers and the rule-appliers must begin by being strict with themselves. Regulations that may affect the careers of dedicated athletes must be predictable. They must emanate from duly authorised bodies. They must be adopted in constitutionally proper ways. They should not be the product of an obscure process of accretion. Athletes and officials should not be confronted with a thicket of mutually qualifying or even contradictory rules that can be understood only on the basis of the de facto practice over the course of many years of a small group of insiders.

This paragraph contains several of the key elements included in the legal principle of legality, from which CAS has claimed to have drawn inspiration.[58] First, it lays down the two principal conditions of *formal legality*: that the rules "emanate from duly authorised bodies" and "are adopted in constitutionally proper ways." These conditions are part of the fundamental requirements of a constitutional democracy. In order for a rule to be valid the rulemaker must have the authority to establish the rule and must have done so following the proper procedure.[59] In national and international legal orders, the rules governing when a body is "duly authorized" to make a rule and what constitutes the "proper" rulemaking process are some of the core elements of constitutional law.[60]

CAS does not clearly spell out why formal legality constitutes a general principle of sports law. However, it is easy to understand why the conditions of formal legality apply in the context of sports and in any other contract-based association: a body can only enact a rule that is valid and binding within the association if the basic agreement governing the association – which, depending on the association, even may be entitled "constitution" – provides it with rulemaking powers. The principle of formal legality is rather obvious in a relationship based on contract law

---

[55] See e.g. CAS 2007/O/1381, *Valverde I*, para 61.

[56] See also Latty 2007, pp. 319–321.

[57] CAS 94/129, *Quigley*, para 34, cited with approval in e.g. CAS 95/150, *Volkers*, paras 14–15; CAS 2002/A/363, *Pastorello*, paras 5.7–5.9; CAS 2008/A/1557, *FIGC et al. v. WADA*, para 6.15; CAS 2009/A/1768, *Hansen*, para 15.2. For a summary of the facts in *Quigley*, see Sect. 5.3.

[58] Cf. CAS 2008/A/1545, *Anderson*, para 30 (interpreting the Olympic Charter in accordance with the principle of legality, citing CAS 94/129, *Quigley*, para 34).

[59] See e.g. CAS 98/185, *RSC Anderlecht v. UEFA*, para 5 ("La violation de ses propres statuts et règlement par l'UEFA et les conséquences de cette violation constitue un vice suffisamment grave pour que la décision attaquée soit considérée comme nulle et de nul effet.").

[60] Barak 2012, pp. 107–109 (referring to this as the "authorization chain").

as physical and legal entities in that relationship are only bound by what they agree to be bound by. Thus, a player is not bound by rules that he or she did not consent to, through membership or some other form of agreement. In this manner, the principle of formal legality can be understood as closely related to the principle of hierarchy of norms.[61]

An illustrative example of this reasoning and its consequences can be found in *Rebagliati*. In the 1998 Winter Olympic Games in Nagano, Canadian athlete Ross Rebagliati was initially awarded the Olympic Gold medal in the snowboard giant slalom competition, but the International Olympic Committee (IOC) subsequently rescinded that medal after Rebagliati tested positive for a marijuana metabolite.[62] CAS found that this measure could not be based on the IOC Medical Code, which did apply to the athlete, and that there was therefore no agreement between the IOC and the international federation (FIS) to treat marijuana as a banned substance. The panel therefore concluded that the IOC's decision lacked basis and that it "must decide within the context of the law of sports, and cannot invent prohibitions or sanctions where none appear."[63]

In addition to these formal elements, the above-quoted paragraph in *Quigley* contains the key elements of *qualitative legality*, that is that the rules must be accessible, predictable, and clear,[64] and that they must also not be applied in a retroactive[65] or arbitrary manner.[66] Qualitative legality does not however require perfect predictability and clarity and CAS has refrained from applying it too strictly.[67] These qualitative requirements are closely connected to the rule of law which requires that rules must be fixed and announced beforehand and "make it possible to foresee with fair certainty how the authority will use its coercive powers in given circumstances and to plan one's individual affairs on the basis of this knowledge."[68]

---

[61] See below Sect. 7.5.

[62] It can be noted that in the same year Rebagliati established a brand for medical marijuana, Ross' Gold. See http://rossgold.com (accessed April 17, 2017).

[63] OG 98/002, *Rebagliati*, para 26 quoted ("Our own decision is not difficult… It is clear that the sanctions against [Rebagliati] lack requisite legal foundation." Ibid., para 27).

[64] See e.g. CAS 2001/A/330, *Reinhold*, para 17, citing CAS 94/129, *Quigley*, para 34. Also referred to as the predictability test.

[65] See e.g. CAS 2000/A/274, *Susin*, para 72. The principle of non-retroactive application is discussed further below in Sect. 7.5.

[66] See e.g. CAS 96/157, *FIN v. FINA*, para 22.

[67] See e.g. CAS 95/122, *NWBA v. IPC*, para 12 ("It is true that the ICC [International Coordinating Committee of World Sports Organizations for the Disabled] Rules do not contain a provision that clearly calls the reader's attention to the establishment of the strict liability principle… It may well be desirable for such a provision to be articulated. Nevertheless, the Panel is satisfied that no one subject to the ICC Rules could come to the conclusion that they would excuse the inadvertent ingestion of banned substances."); CAS 95/150, *Volkers*, paras 14–15.

[68] Hayek 2007, p. 112 (describing the rule of law as an ideal rather than a requirement). Cf. Council of Europe, Venice Commission, CDL-AD(2011)003rev-e, Report on the rule of law - Adopted by the Venice Commission at its 86th plenary session (Venice, 25-26 March 2011).

As CAS clearly explained in *Anderson*, *Quigley* should not be understood narrowly as a requirement of actual notice. *Anderson* concerned who should be awarded the gold medals for the Men's 4 × 400 m relay competition during the 2000 Olympic Games in Sydney.[69] The American team finished the race first and its members were initially awarded the gold medals. Four years later, however, CAS found that one of the team members, Jerome Young, had committed a doping offence prior to the Olympic Games and that he therefore should not have been allowed to participate in the Games.[70] On this basis, the International Association of Athletics Federations (IAAF) decided to annul the result of the American team, a decision the validity of which Young's team members challenged before CAS. In its decision in *Anderson* CAS explained that the holding in *Quigley* was the result of principles that are relevant not only to the individual athletes involved, but to the system as a whole:[71]

> The rationale for requiring clarity of rules extends beyond enabling athletes in given cases to determine their conduct in such cases by reference to understandable rules. As argued by the Appellants at the hearing, clarity and predictability are required so that the entire sport community are informed of the normative system in which they live, work and compete, which requires at the very least that they be able to understand the meaning of rules and the circumstances in which those rules apply.

Raz explains why these requirements are important in a way that is both simple and convincing: "if the law is to be obeyed it must be capable of guiding the behaviour of its subjects."[72] Conversely, if the rules applicable in sports are inaccessible, unpredictable, or unclear, we cannot reasonably expect physical and legal persons to follow them. As explained by CAS in *Cullwick*, athletes should know clearly where they stand and it is unfair to punish someone for doing something that he or she could not reasonably have known was wrong.[73]

Thus, the qualitative elements of legality are well-based in fairness and reasonableness, two important values that we obviously should strive to uphold. However, that qualitative legality supports values that *ought* to be respected in sports does not necessarily mean that the qualitative elements of legality forms part of a principle of legality that *must* be respected in sports. To go back to the language used by CAS in *Quigley*: why *must* sports rules be clear and predictable?

Neither *Quigley* nor the subsequent CAS decisions repeating the principles expressed in *Quigley* explicitly and clearly address this issue.[74] However, the most

---

These criteria correspond if not perfectly at least quite well to Fuller's basic criteria for what constitutes a legal order, i.e. that there must be rules and that those rules must be accessible, understandable, coherent, and otherwise capable of being complied with. Fuller 1969, p. 39.

[69] The case was also discussed Sect. 4.2.1.

[70] CAS 2004/A/628, *Young*.

[71] CAS 2008/A/1545, *Anderson*, paras 19–20.

[72] Raz 2009, pp. 213–214.

[73] CAS 96/149, *Cullwick*, para 31.

[74] See e.g. CAS 2007/A/1363, *TTF Liebherr Ochsenhausen v. ETTU*, para 16, cited with approval in e.g. CAS 2008/A/1545, *Anderson*, para 34.

likely explanation, which also has some support in CAS jurisprudence,[75] lies in the concept of *ordre public* discussed above. There is a strong chance that decisions that apply and enforce rules that are incompatible with the values recognized in states governed by the rule of law will be set aside on grounds of violating *ordre public*.[76]

In addition to the requirements of the Swiss PILA as *lex arbitri*, Swiss law contains other requirements that apply when Swiss law governs the substantive matters of the disputes. In cases governed by Swiss law, which are common as many of the disputes before CAS involve a SGB governed by Swiss law,[77] other provisions under Swiss law may, in a similar way as the requirements found in the PILA, lead to sports rules or decisions being set aside. The Swiss Civil Code contains two important requirements in this regard: a person may not "surrender his or her freedom or restrict the use of it to a degree which violates the law or public morals"[78] and associations are prohibited from having articles of association that are contrary to mandatory law.[79] As illustrated by CAS jurisprudence, these provisions can be and are applied to uphold general principles and fundamental values in situations that would otherwise violate *ordre public* under the PILA.[80] When applicable, the latter provisions can potentially impose more far-reaching requirements,[81] but in many cases these provisions are closely connected.[82]

Regardless of why the principle of legality forms part of the principles applicable in sports, its inclusion is of great value to the validity, legitimacy, and, by extension, autonomy of global sports law. If the international sports community, including CAS, seeks to argue for the existence of a transnational *legal* order, certain basic requirements must be met. Using the term "law" obligates.[83] Difficult as it may be

---

75 CAS 2013/A/3256, *Fenerbahçe v. UEFA II*, paras 190–191.

76 Cf. CAS 2007/A/1392, *FPJ & FVJ v. IJF*, para 89 (stating that the principle of legality, at least in a narrow sense, is "clearly part of international public policy and have to be qualified as transnational principles of international public order."); CAS 2009/A/1879, *Valverde II*, para 102; CAS 2011/A/2425, *Fusimalohi*, para 71 (discussing procedure rules).

77 See Geeraert et al. 2014, p. 292 (finding this to be true for 77% of all Olympic SGBs). See also Article R58 CAS Code.

78 Article 27(2) of the Swiss Civil Code ("Nul ne peut aliéner sa liberté, ni s'en interdire l'usage dans une mesure contraire aux lois ou aux mœurs.").

79 Article 63(2) of the Swiss Civil Code ("Les statuts ne peuvent déroger aux règles dont l'application a lieu en vertu d'une disposition impérative de la loi.").

80 See e.g. CAS 2005/C/976 & 986, *FIFA & WADA*, paras 133–142 (discussing the application of Article 27 of the Swiss Civil Code to sanctions under the WADC, including the system of strict liability); CAS 2014/A/3628, *Eskişehirspor v. UEFA*, paras 51–52 (examining whether UEFA rules establishing a system of strict liability is consist with Article 63(2) of the Swiss Civil Code).

81 Kaufmann-Kohler and Rigozzi 2015, pp. 382–383.

82 See e.g. SFT's decision 27 March 2012 in case 4A_558/2011 (*Matuzalem v. FIFA*), paras 4.1–4.3 (finding that sports rules that too extensively limited the athlete's fundamental freedom were incompatible with Article 27(2) of the Swiss Civil Code and a CAS award enforcing a sanction on the basis of those rules was contrary to public policy under Article 190(2) PILA).

83 Schultz 2014, pp. 8, 23–31.

to identify, "law" has certain characteristics or features that distinguishes it from "non-law". Consequently, whether something constitutes "law" can be evaluated on the basis of whether it exhibits these characteristics or not.[84] This topic was touched upon initially in this book as part of the underlying theoretical framework.[85] In addition to their use as a theoretical framework, the characteristics of law have concrete relevance. To earn and maintain its character as a legal order, a system of governance must establish certain basic legal principles that seek to ensure that the system retains its legal character, principles that broadly relate to the rule of law and, as discussed, the principle of legality.

The principle of legality can be understood broadly to encompass all matters. It is however particularly important to respect the principle of legality in disciplinary matters and matters that have disciplinary-like consequences for those concerned.[86] In law there are certain principles that closely relate to the principle of legality but specifically apply to criminal matters, captured in the maxim *nullum crimen, nulla poena sine lege certa*. CAS has stressed that these principles must be strictly respected in disciplinary proceedings, even though these proceedings are not criminal per se.[87]

Finally, CAS has established a general prohibition of arbitrary or unreasonable rules and measures. A seminal case in this regard is *AEK Athens*. AEK Athens was a Greek football team that qualified to play in the 1997/1998 UEFA Cup.[88] However, UEFA subsequently adopted a rule to prevent multi-club ownership and on the basis of this new rule decided that AEK Athens would not be allowed to compete since it was controlled by the same legal entity as another participating team, SK Lavia Praha. AEK Athens and SK Lavia Praha challenged UEFA's rule on a number of different grounds, including that UEFA contrary to general principles of law had abused its regulatory power.[89]

CAS concluded in *AEK Athens* that the prohibition of rules and measures that are substantively arbitrary or unreasonable is one of the principles included in sports law.[90] While CAS found no infringement of the principle in the case at hand it indicated that it would have done so if it had found that UEFA had abused its regulatory power to protect its monopoly power.[91] Thus, the principle appears to involve a substantive examination of the reasons underlying a rule or measure and of the legitimacy of those reasons. It is not clear how CAS would determine whether a particular reason is legitimate or, by extension, whether a rule or measure

---

[84] See e.g. Kramer 2007, pp. 101–109.

[85] See Sect. 1.3.

[86] See e.g. CAS /156, *Foschi*, para 13.3.

[87] See e.g. CAS 2007/A/1392, *FPJ & FVJ v. IJF*, para 89; CAS 2009/A/1935, *Fédération Royale Marocaine de Football v. FIFA*, para 98; CAS 2009/A/1823, *PJU v. IJF*, para 9.5.

[88] Since replaced by the UEFA Europa League.

[89] CAS 98/200.

[90] Ibid., para 156.

[91] Ibid., para 157.

is reasonable. The basis of this principle appears to be "drawn from a comparative or common denominator reading of various domestic legal systems," but it is not clear from *AEK Athens* what legal systems were considered in this case or how the comparison was carried out.[92]

7.3 Respect for Fundamental Rights

As discussed above, CAS has defined the outer limits within which SGBs must act and this includes respecting certain fundamental rights, also known as principles of natural justice. One of the most important limbs of CAS jurisprudence on the respect for fundamental rights concerns the protection of procedural rights, sometimes also referred as the principle of procedural fairness, the right to a fair hearing, or the right to due process.[93] Procedural rights are sometimes explicitly included in sports rules,[94] but in the words of CAS they are also "surely among the unwritten principles of sports law to be complied with by international federations."[95] As such, basic procedural rights are to be respected not just by CAS and disciplinary bodies but in all procedures where subjects have an interest in the outcome.[96] A basic level of respect for fundamental rights is also an inherent element of the rule of law. CAS acts as a guardian of procedural rights. It exerts the power to review and overrule actions by SGBs that fail to respect or afford due process.[97] CAS can also heal any violations of procedural rights that may have occurred by providing a full hearing *de novo*.[98]

---

[92] CAS 98/200, *AEK Athens*, para 156.

[93] Without any clear substantive differences.

[94] See e.g. CAS 96/129, *Quigley*, para 54 (regarding the IOC Charter Against Doping in Sport); CAS 98/211, *de Bruin*, para 4 (regarding FINA Guidelines for doping control).

[95] CAS 98/200, *AEK Athens*, para 158. See also CAS 2004/A/777, *ARcycling AG v. UCI*, para 20 ("It is undisputable that the [right to be heard and the right to a fair proceeding] are fundamental and that the CAS has always endeavored to protect them.").

[96] See e.g. CAS 91/53, *G. v. FEI*, para 11; CAS 2001/A/317, *Aanes*, para 6 ("the CAS has always considered the right to be heard as a general legal principle which has to be respected also during internal proceedings of the federations"); CAS 2004/A/777, *ARcycling AG v. UCI*, para 20 (concerning the licensing of a pro cycling team); CAS 2010/A/2275, *CGF v. EGA*, para 29 ("The right to be heard is a fundamental and general principle which derives from the elementary rules of natural justice and due process... CAS has always protected the principle audiatur et altera pars in connection with any proceedings, measures or disciplinary actions taken by an international federation vis-à-vis a national federation, a club or an athlete..."). Of course, a precondition for CAS to exercise that power is that those affected bring a case and this is in practice far from always the case.

[97] OG 04/009, *Kaklamanakis*, para 24 ("CAS will always have jurisdiction to overrule the Rules of any sport federation if its decision making bodies conduct themselves with a lack of good faith or not in accordance with due process.").

[98] See e.g. CAS 96/129, *Quigley*, para 54; CAS 98/211, *de Bruin*, para 8 ("The virtue of an appeal system which allows for a full rehearing before an appellate body is that issues relating to the

The concept of procedural rights is broad,[99] and it can be subdivided into a number of smaller, more concrete rights. One group of rights can be grouped under the common heading of the right to be heard (*audiatur et altera pars*).[100] This for example includes the right to access claims made by the opposing party, to examine and submit evidence, to cross-examine witness, and to present arguments and evidence.[101]

The protection of procedural rights is a general legal principle and the more specific, related norms expressed in CAS jurisprudence can be described as legal norms applied in the context of sports.[102] The protection of procedural rights is to some extent a mandatory or forced normative element as failure to respect certain fundamental procedural rights constitutes a violation of *ordre public* and grounds for legal challenge.[103] The protection of the rights stemming from these principles forms part of Swiss procedural public policy but is in turn informed by a broader set of norms, including Article 6 of the European Convention of Human Rights (ECHR).[104] This can at least be traced back to 1992 when CAS declared in *Gundel* that athletes accused of doping as a consequence of the application of general principles have a right to rebut the presumption of guilt.[105] This forms part of the right to be heard which constitutes an element of the fundamental principle of due process that is binding *inter alia* on sports federations.[106] The situation in *Gundel* and other cases that involve a "quasi-penal" disciplinary hearing can be compared to a criminal procedure and a parallel can therefore be made to the criminal

fairness of the hearing before the tribunal of first instance fade to the periphery"); CAS 2002/A/378, *Simeoni*, para 13; CAS 2011/A/2426, *Adamu*, para 47. The fact that it is a full review means that CAS is free to reconsider issues that were decided in the appellant's favor. See e.g. CAS 99/A/223, *Korda*, para 3.

99 Its full breadth is for example represented in the European Court of Human Rights' (ECtHR's) extensive jurisprudence on the right of a fair trial under Article 6 ECHR.

100 See e.g. CAS 91/53, *G. v. FEI*, para 11; OG 96/005, *Andrade et al. II*, paras 7–9; CAS 2007/A/1392, *FPJ & FVJ v. IJF*, para 90.

101 See e.g. CAS 2004/A/777, *ARcycling AG v. UCI*, para 20 ("the applicants should be allowed to present their case at such stage in an adversarial proceeding, i.e. having the right to know the allegations of the UCI representatives and of the UCI consultants, to examine in advance all the evidence submitted by the UCI to the Licence Commission and to question it or refute it with its own counter-evidence. Otherwise, the right to be heard and the right to a fair proceeding would be breached."); CAS 2008/A/1545, *Anderson*, para 15 ("a CAS appeal arbitration procedure allows a full de novo hearing of a case with all due process guarantees, granting the parties every opportunity not only to submit written briefs and any kind of evidence, but also to be extensively heard and to examine and cross-examine witnesses or experts during a hearing. The Panel harbours no doubt that in the present CAS procedure the Appellants were given ample latitude to fully plead their case and be heard…").

102 See e.g. CAS 91/53, *G. v. FEI*, para 11.

103 See e.g. CAS 2007/A/1392, *FPJ & FVJ v. IJF*, paras 89–90; CAS 2009/A/1879, *Valverde II*, paras 70–71.

104 See e.g. CAS 2013/A/3139, *Fenerbahçe v. UEFA I*.

105 CAS 92/63, *Gundel*, para 13.

106 CAS 2001/A/317, *Aanes*, para 6.

procedural right to be heard. However, CAS has extended the principle of procedural fairness to other, non-disciplinary situations.[107]

Another consequence of the Swiss legal requirement that general principles and fundamental values are respected, and that has a close connection to the respect for fundamental rights, is the inclusion of the principle of proportionality as a general principle of sports law.

The principle of proportionality appears in various legal contexts and with slightly different meanings.[108] For example, in European Union law it is possible to distinguish three possible uses of the principle of proportionality: it (i) limits the Union's use of its regulatory competence to what is necessary to achieve the intended objectives;[109] (ii) determines whether a Member State may restrict rights under Union law, including the right to free movement of people, goods, services, and capital,[110] and (iii) governs whether a limitation of a fundamental right is justified.[111] While there are differences between these three functions, the principle of proportionality essentially requires the same thing: a measure must be both appropriate and necessary for the purpose of achieving a legitimate aim and a proper balance must be struck between the aim of the measure and the right or interest that it infringes upon (proportionality in *strictu sensu*).[112] Unlike the case of European Union law, CAS has not, at least as far as I have been able to detect, recognized and applied the principle of proportionality to govern the division and exercise of power within sports. It has however applied the principle of proportionality as a general principle to determine if a limitation of the fundamental rights of athletes is justified, particularly in the context of doping sanctions.

CAS has a relatively long history of modifying disproportional sanctions. In many of the earliest cases, it did so on the basis of the sports rules applicable to the specific case.[113] However, a situation where the applicable sports rules expressly included a proportionality element[114] is of course different from applying a

---

[107] See e.g. CAS 96/153, *Watt*, para 10 (regarding selection decision).

[108] The principle is considered to be most well-developed in German law. Craig 2006, p. 656.

[109] Article 5(4) of the EU Treaty. See also Tridimas 2006, pp. 135–174.

[110] See e.g. Case 120/78, Rewe-Zentral AG v Bundesmonopolverwaltung für Branntwein (*Cassis de Dijon*), EU:C:1979:42, paras 10–11; Tridimas 2006, pp. 193–241.

[111] Article 52(1) of the Charter of Fundamental Rights of the European Union. This is a codification of a principle that was first expressed in the CJEU's decision in Case 11/70, *Internationale Handelsgesellschaft mbH v. Einfuhr- und Vorratsstelle fur Getreide und Futtermittel*, EU: C:1970:114, para 12.

[112] Cf. Barak 2012, p. 3.

[113] See e.g. CAS 92/63, *Gundel*, para 13 (FEI's rules provided that the extent of the sanctions, a monetary fine and a suspension, could and should vary depending on the degree of fault); CAS 95/141, *Chagnaud*, paras 23–24 (FINA's application of its own sanction rules revealed the possibility to set a sanction that was proportionate to the athlete's level of fault); CAS 96/149, *Cullwick*, para 26 (operation of the principle of *lex mitior* allowed CAS to apply rules that provided some discretion in setting an appropriate sanction).

[114] See e.g. CAS 2011/A/2681, *KSV Cercle Brugge v. FC Radnicki* (examining the proportionality of training compensation governed by FIFA rules).

requirement of proportionality as a general principle and it is debatable whether those early CAS decisions can be seen as recognizing a general principle of proportionality.[115] However, step-by-step, CAS's proportionality review became less connected to the specific rules applicable to the case at hand.

One of the earliest decisions where it is quite clear that CAS applied a requirement of proportionality as a general principle is *FIN v. FINA* where CAS held "that it can intervene in the sanction imposed only if the rules adopted by the FINA Bureau are contrary to the general principles of law, if their application is arbitrary, or if the sanctions provided by the rules can be deemed excessive or unfair on their face."[116] The case concerned CAS's power to review a decision, rather than proportionality as a general principle per se. Nevertheless, the decision in *FIN v. FINA* contributed to a development where it became gradually clear that the norms applicable in sports include a general principle of proportionality. There was little doubt of this after CAS's decision in *Ward* where it confidently declared that "it is a widely accepted general principle of sports law that the severity of a penalty must be in proportion with the seriousness of the infringements."[117]

CAS's early case law on proportionality does not clearly identify the basis for this principle. Some of the decisions can even be seen as suggesting that CAS enjoys a general discretion to review and set a proportional sanction, regardless of the applicable rules or the extent of the disproportionality.[118] However, later CAS decisions make it quite clear that the principle of proportionality is connected to Swiss law. According to the jurisprudence of the SFT it can overturn an award if it imposes a sanction that is "evidently and grossly disproportionate to the offence" and this has in turn been adopted by CAS as the proportionality test.[119] Thus, the principle of proportionality must be viewed through the lens of what constitutes *ordre public* according to Swiss law.

The development of the principle of proportionality as applied to doping sanctions and leading up to the SFT's decision in *Wang et al.* was previously

---

[115] CAS's reluctance to rely on these decisions more broadly is for example evident in CAS 96/156, *Foschi*, para 15.1.

[116] CAS 96/157, *FIN v. FINA*, para 22.

[117] CAS 99/A/246, *Ward*, para 31, citing *inter alia* CAS 92/63, *Gundel* (quoting the decision in part but leaving out the reference to the specific rules in question); CAS 95/141, *Chagnaud*; CAS 96/157, *FIN v. FINA*.

[118] See e.g. CAS 2000/A/310, *Leipold I*, para 26; CAS 2000/A/312, *Leipold II*, para 35; CAS 2001/A/337, *Bray*, para 78. One way of possibly reconciling these seemingly inconsistent strands of case law is that they address different types of review. As discussed below, CAS hears all cases on appeal *de novo* and therefore enjoys the same discretion to set an appropriate sanction as the body whose decision it is reviewing. Where that body had discretion to set a proportional sanction, so does CAS. Oschütz 2002, p. 699. However, even if the applicable sports rules are strict and inflexible with regard to the sanction, CAS must be able to review a sanction that would violate *ordre public*.

[119] See e.g. CAS 99/A/234 & 235, *Meca Medina & Majcen*, para 11.3; CAS 2004/A/690, *Hipperdinger*, para 55; CAS 2005/A/830, *Squizzato*, paras 45–50; CAS 2009/A/1870, *Hardy*, para 48 (quoted).

discussed.[120] While doping sanctions are the type of measures in sport that most commonly have been challenged for being disproportional, it would be a mistake to believe that the principle of proportionality only applies to such measures. This is illustrated by the case of *Matuzalem*. Matuzalem was a football player that terminated his employment contract with one football club, FC Shakhtar Donetsk, without cause, in order to enter into an employment relationship with another club. The FIFA Dispute Resolution Chamber (FIFA DRC) decided that Matuzalem owed Shakhtar Donetsk € 6.8 million plus 5 percent interest until the amount was paid, a decision that was subsequently confirmed by CAS.[121] Matuzalem appealed the CAS award to the SFT and argued that the award should be annulled on the grounds that it violated public policy. The SFT agreed. The SFT concluded that if Matuzalem was unable to pay the entire amount the award would prevent him from playing football, earning an income, and repaying his debt. This "unlimited career ban"[122] constituted a severe limitation of Matuzalem's fundamental right to personal freedom, which includes economic freedom, that was disproportional in relation to the aim of ensuring that players honor their employment contracts.[123]

There are multiple examples of CAS protecting the interests of parties that acted in reasonable reliance on a particular rule or practice. One such example can be found in *Quigley*:[124]

> If he had been subject to a fundamentally different regime, i.e. that of strict liability, his understanding would have been different and his conduct might therefore have been different. He might have summoned the fortitude to eschew medications prescribed by a stranger. In other words, his conduct may have been responsive to his perception of a greater risk of sanction. This is a matter of legitimate expectations, and it is crucial to any decent system of laws.

For example, in *US Swimming v. FINA* CAS held that FINA would not be allowed to suddenly depart from a flexible practice to the detriment of "unsuspecting and blameless athlete" and against national federations that "acted in a manner which they reasonably believed was acceptable under the Rules."[125]

The protection of one party's legitimate expectations may be in conflict with the protection of the other party's right to be heard. CAS has adopted a Swiss legal doctrine, *venire contra factum proprium*,[126] under which a party may be prohibited to change a previously adopted position when it would cause detriment to another party that has acted in reliance.[127]

---

[120] See Sect. 5.4.

[121] CAS 2008/A/1519-1520, *Matuzalem*.

[122] "unbegrenzten Berufsverbots".

[123] SFT's decision 27 March 2012 in case 4A_558/2011 (*Matuzalem v. FIFA*), paras 4.3.4–4.3.5.

[124] CAS 94/129, *Quigley*, para 33.

[125] CAS OG 96/001, *US Swimming v. FINA*, paras 15–16.

[126] In a common law context this would likely be considered a form of estoppel.

[127] See e.g. CAS 98/200, *AEK Athens*, para 60; CAS 2000/A/274, *Susin*, para 37; CAS 2001/A/357, *Nabokov*, para 23.

7.4 Procedural Norms: CAS on Being Before CAS

Many of the norms found in CAS jurisprudence concern proceedings before CAS and many of these norms are directed to CAS itself. A first category in this regard concerns CAS's jurisdiction. While the CAS Code contains rules governing jurisdiction,[128] it leaves many issues open, issues that CAS has the power to determine according to Swiss law.[129] CAS has used this power taking procedural rights into consideration: CAS has justified its own involvement when failure to do so would in violation of general principles constitute denial of justice,[130] for example to grant jurisdiction when an "authority refuses without reason to make a ruling or to delay a ruling beyond a reasonable period."[131]

A large portion of CAS jurisprudence regarding CAS's appellate jurisdiction concerns interpretation of the conditions provided in the CAS Code according to which appellate arbitration jurisdiction requires a decision by an SGB, exhaustion of internal legal remedies, and an arbitration agreement between the parties.[132] What for this purpose constitutes a "decision" is one of the issues for which CAS most frequently refers to its own case law. The term was initially defined in *Felipe II*, a dispute concerning the transfer of a Brazilian footballer between two football clubs, Vasco Da Gama and Galatasaray, where the latter asked the international federation (FIFA) to investigate who had received the transfer fee.[133] FIFA responded to Galatasaray by letter stating that it lacked the necessary competence to conduct such an investigation. Galatasaray subsequently brought an action against FIFA before CAS whose jurisdiction depended on whether FIFA's letter constituted an appealable decision. Relying on the definition under Swiss law, CAS defined a decision as "a unilateral act, sent to one or more determined recipients and is intended to produce legal effects."[134] While providing this since often-repeated[135] definition constitutes a normative contribution, it is more limited than many other norms discussed in this chapter. This and other similar normative contributions can perhaps best be described as authoritative rule interpretations.

---

[128] Articles R39 (ordinary jurisdiction) and R47 (appellate jurisdiction) CAS Code.

[129] See e.g. CAS 2004/A/748, *Ekimov v. Hamilton*, para 6; CAS 2005/A/952, *Cole*, para 3; CAS 2010/A/2091, *Lachter v. Boateng Owusu*, para 3. A determination of jurisdiction is however subject to review by the SFT who in this sense has the ultimate competence.

[130] See e.g. CAS 97/169, *Menegotto*, para 7; CAS 2005/A/899, *Aris I*, para 13; CAS 2011/A/2479, *Sinkewitz*, para 20.

[131] CAS 2004/A/659, *Felipe II*, para 11.

[132] Article R47 CAS Code.

[133] CAS 2004/A/659. CAS 2003/O/453, *Felipe I*, concerned the player's termination of his contract with Galatasaray.

[134] CAS 2004/A/659, *Felipe II*, paras 9–10 (para 10 quoted). See also CAS 2005/A/899, *Aris I*, paras 9–12.

[135] See e.g. CAS 2008/A/1705, *Grasshopper v. Alianza Lima*, para 3; CAS 2012/A/2731, *Ferreira v. Valadez*, para 34; CAS 2013/A/3112, *Chernova*, para 40.

This can be compared to the issue of standing (*locus standi*), another jurisdiction-related issue on which the CAS Code provides little guidance. In order for a party to have standing CAS has required a showing of legal interest in the dispute. Only those who are harmed by a decision or have some other particular, protection-worthy interest in a decision have standing to appeal it (the aggrievement requirement).[136] On the other side of the dispute, one that has "nothing at stake" in the dispute lacks standing to be sued.[137] As explained by CAS in *El-Hadary*, this follows from "the well-known general procedural principle that if there is no legal interest there is no standing ('*pas d'intérêt, pas d'action*'),"[138] but it can also be deduced from the purpose behind CAS's ordinary and appellate jurisdiction, which is to solve actual disputes, not to deliver advisory opinions.[139]

A related issue is the extent of CAS's power to review. Much like SGBs enjoy considerable independence and autonomy vis-á-vis each other,[140] CAS must "respect the freedom of associations to establish their own rules."[141] CAS grounds this duty on the existence of a similar, constitutional right in many national legal orders and under EU law.[142] The strength of this argument is however questionable,[143] and other CAS decisions suggest that it is actually based on Swiss law.[144]

While there is nothing in the CAS Code mandating it, CAS has self-restricted its appellate jurisdiction over field-of-play decisions, that is decisions on "technical matters" by sports officials entrusted with applying the rules-of-the-game, unless they are manifestly unfounded or there is evidence of bad faith.[145] This is not a legal principle but a norm that rests on three, rather pragmatic arguments: the practical infeasibility of reviewing all decisions, the interest of finality, and that sports officials are better equipped than CAS to make these types of decisions.[146]

---

136 See e.g. CAS 2004/A/727, *De Lima*, para 3.

137 CAS 2006/A/1189, *IFK Norrköping v. Trinité Sports FC & FFF*, para 5; CAS 2007/A/1329 & 1330, *Chiapas FC v. Cricuma Esporte Clube*, para 3.

138 CAS 2009/A/1880 & 1881, *El-Hadary*, para 28.

139 Ibid., para 30. There was previously a now revoked consultation procedure for that purpose. See Sect. 2.2. CAS later, additionally, finds support for this interpretation in the term "*against* a decision". OG 12/005, *Sterba*, para 7.8.

140 See above Sect. 7.2.

141 CAS 2005/A/830, *Squizzato*, para 50.

142 Ibid.

143 CAS does not provide any specific examples of such national constitutional rights. It does refer to the General Court's decision in Case T-313/02, *Meca-Medina & Igor Majcen v. Commission*, EU:T:2004:282. However, the validity of this has been seriously called into question when the CJEU in its review of the same case subsequently significantly narrowed the scope for any special exception for sports rules. See Case C-519/04 P, *Meca-Medina & Igor Majcen v. Commission*, EU:C:2006:492, paras 25–28. See e.g. Rincon 2007, esp. pp. 233–235.

144 CAS 2001/A/330, *Reinhold*, para 19.

145 Nafziger refers to this as the non-interference rule. Nafziger 2011, pp. 28–30.

146 See e.g. OG 96/006, *Mendy*, paras 5–13; CAS 2001/A/354 & 355, *IHA v. LHF & FIH*, paras 16–17; OG 02/007, *KOC v. ISU*, paras 11–12, 16–17; CAS 2012/A/2731, *Ferreira v. Villa Valadez*, paras 104–105; CAS 2012/A/2912, *Murofushi*, para 87.

CAS has also established a number of evidentiary norms. First, CAS has established that as a general principle it is the party that makes a claim that has the burden of proof, i.e. that must establish the facts on which it relies, in both disciplinary cases[147] and in contractual disputes.[148] CAS has taken this principle, more or less directly, from Swiss law.[149]

Second, in doping cases[150] and other disciplinary disputes[151] the standard of proof to be used is "established to the comfortable satisfaction of the Court having in mind the seriousness of the allegation which is made."[152] The initial basis for this standard is uncertain as the decision where it was first established, *Korneev & Gouliev*,[153] is not publicly available.[154] However, it is clear from subsequent decisions that this standard of proof is intentionally designed to be higher than the ordinary civil standard ("balance of probability"), but lower than the ordinary criminal standard ("proof beyond a reasonable doubt"), since "[t]o adopt a criminal standard... is to confuse the public law of the state with the private law of an association..."[155] It is also supported by the principle of proportionality as "the more serious the allegation and its consequences, the higher certainty (level of proof) the Panel would require to be 'comfortable satisfied'."[156]

7.5 Methodological Norms: Norms for Determining Norms

The CAS Code gives the parties extensive power to decide the applicable rules governing their dispute. There are nevertheless a number of issues relating to the applicable rules that are governed by norms developed by CAS.

---

147 See e.g. CAS 98/208, *Wang et al.*, para 12; CAS 98/211, *de Bruin*, para 25; CAS 2009/A/1920, *Zabrcanec & Zdraveski*, para 84.

148 See e.g. CAS 2009/A/1810 & 1811, *SV Wilhelmshaven v. Club A. Excursionistas & Club A. River Plate*, para 18; CAS 2009/A/1908, *Parma FC S.p.A. v. Manchester United F.C.*, para 42; CAS 2009/A/2014, *AMA v. RLVB & Keisse*, para 34 (all citing CAS 2003/A/506, para 54).

149 Article 8 of the Swiss civil code. See e.g. CAS 2009/A/1810 & 1811, *SV Wilhelmshaven v. Club A. Excursionistas & Club A. River Plate*, para 18; CAS 2011/A/2616, *UCI v. Rivera & RFEC*, paras 21–22; CAS 2014/A/3628, *Eskisehirspor Kulübü v. UEFA*, para 121.

150 See e.g. CAS 98/208, *Wang et al.*, para 13; CAS 98/211, *de Bruin*, para 2; CAS 2002/A/385, *Tchachina*, para 10; CAS 2005/A/908, *Wium*, para 6.2.

151 See e.g. CAS 2009/A/1920, *Zabrcanec & Zdraveski*, para 85; CAS 2011/A/2426, *Adamu*, para 88.

152 OG 96/003-004, *Korneev & Gouliev*, quoted in CAS 98/208, *Wang et al.*, para 13.

153 Ibid.

154 See Sect. 4.5.

155 CAS 98/208, *Wang et al.*, para 13.

156 CAS 2014/A/3628, *Eskisehirspor Kulübü v. UEFA*, para 123. See also e.g. CAS 2001/A/345, *Meier*, para 22.

Following Swiss law, CAS has adopted the principle of *tempus regit actum* according to which "any deed should be regulated in accordance with the law in force at the time it occurred."[157] This means that an action will be governed by the substantive rules applicable when the facts at issue took place and that new rules do not generally apply retroactively.[158] However, pursuant to the fundamental principle of *lex mitior*, found in several national legal orders, disciplinary rules will be applied retroactively if they are beneficial to the accused.[159] Procedural aspects, by comparison, are governed by the law applicable at any given time.[160]

All norm systems of sufficient complexity face the very real risk of having valid and applicable norms that are in conflict with each other and that cannot be applied, fully and simultaneously, in a particular case. Sports is no exception in this regard and in several cases CAS has been required to determine how to resolve conflicts between sport norms. In doing so, CAS has declared several principles.

First, where CAS has found that one of the conflicting norms is hierarchically superior to the other it has resolved the conflict by applying the superior norm over the inferior norm. CAS has expressed this principle, which can be referred to either as *the principle of hierarchy of norms* or *the principle of lex superior (derogat inferior)*, as that "rules and resolutions enacted by an association must be in compliance with the highest regulatory framework, i.e. the statutes of the associations."[161] CAS has explained that the principle of hierarchy of norms follows from the principle of legality.[162]

In determining which rules are superior, CAS has looked to the internal rules and workings of the rulemaking body; rules established by a properly constituted body acting in a "legislative capacity" under the statutes cannot be amended, contradicted, or expanded by an inferior body unless the statutes expressly authorize it. As far as I am aware, all CAS decisions explicitly addressing the issue have concerned the relationship between regulations and circulars in football. However, the principle can reasonably be applied to other circumstances considering CAS's reasoning that the hierarchical order between norms regulating a sport are governed by the most fundamental documents and that the rules established by "legislative" sports bodies cannot be set aside by "administrative" sports bodies.[163] The basis of

[157] CAS 2004/A/635, *Barcelona v. Velez Sarsfield*, para 8; CAS 2005/C/841, *CONI*, para 51.

[158] See e.g. CAS 2000/A/274, *Susin*, para 72; CAS 2010/A/2041, *Chepalova*, para 11; CAS 2014/A/3488, *Lallukka*, para 111.

[159] CAS 94/128, *UCI & CONI*, para 33.

[160] CAS 2000/A/274, *Susin*, para 73; CAS 2004/A/635, *Barcelona v. Velez Sarsfield*, para 11.

[161] See e.g. CAS 2008/A/1705, *Grasshopper v. Alianza Lima*, para 26; CAS 2011/A/2612, *Hui*, para 102; CAS 2011/A/2563, *CD Nacional v. FK Sutjeska*.

[162] CAS 2008/A/1705, *Grasshopper v. Alianza Lima*, para 25. See further above Sect. 7.2.

[163] See CAS 2005/A/835 & 942, *Bomfim*; CAS 2006/A/1125, *Hertha BSC Berlin v. Stade Lavallois Mayenne FC*, para 27; CAS 2005/A/889, *Mathare United FC v. Al-Arabi SC*, para 8 (citing CAS 2003/O/506, *Unknown*, paras 51–52). As far as I am aware, all CAS cases dealing with this issue have concerned the relationship between regulations and circulars within FIFA.

this principle is not entirely clear from CAS jurisprudence.[164] However, this principle regarding intra-federation norm conflicts is similar in nature to the principle governing inter-federation norm conflicts and like the latter the former can be explained on contractual grounds: sports rules' binding nature rests on a contractual basis and rules that lack a clear connection to the foundational agreements are therefore not binding.[165] To resolve conflicts between hierarchically equivalent norms CAS will, when possible, use the principle of *lex specialis* based on the reasoning that the more specific rule is the better expression of the rulemaker's intent.[166]

CAS has emphasized that unlike SGBs, it is not a rulemaker: "CAS cannot rewrite but can only interpret rules set forth by sports authorities in the light of general principles of law."[167] CAS has adopted a purposive approach as the overarching principle when interpreting sports rules.[168] CAS expresses this in terms of employing an approach to interpretation that "seeks to discern the intention of the rule-maker, and not to frustrate it."[169] It will take a broad approach in determining the rulemaker's intention. While CAS does not consider itself bound by SGBs' practice, clarifications, circulars, commentaries, and other rules-related communications, it will use them to interpret the rules,[170] particularly when it is favorable to an athlete facing disciplinary action.[171] The reasons for this is not well-explained in the case law, perhaps because CAS considers it obvious.

As discussed above, an inferior rule cannot be applied in case of conflict with a superior rule and the former is in this sense not applicable. However, it follows from CAS jurisprudence that as long as the inferior rule does not contradict or change the superior rule, the former can be used to complement and concretize the latter. In this manner, the inferior rule can be used as an aid when interpreting the superior rule.[172]

When it comes to interpreting disciplinary rules that have multiple possible interpretations, CAS will, as a matter of principle, choose the interpretation that favors the party facing the sanction.[173] CAS has also declared that when rules are

---

164 It should in this context be noted that the original CAS authority on this point, CAS 2003/O/506, is not publicly available.

165 See above Sect. 7.2.

166 See e.g. CAS 2002/O/373, *Scott*, para 38; CAS 2004/A/748, *Ekimov v. Hamilton*, 31; CAS 2010/A/2170 & 2171, *Iraklis & OFI v. HFF*, para 32.

167 CAS 2009/A/1910, *Telecom Egypt Club v. EFA*, para 33.

168 An early, clear example of this can be found in OG 00/014, *FFG v. SOCOG.*

169 See e.g. CAS 96/149, *Cullwick*, para 22; CAS 2001/A/317, *Aanes*, para 23; CAS 2009/A/1910, *Telecom Egypt Club v. EFA*, para 33.

170 See e.g. CAS 2005/C/976 & 986, *FIFA & WADA*; CAS 2003/O/527, *Hamburger Sport-Verein e.V. v. Odense Boldklub*, para 17; OG 04/001, *RNOC v. FEI*, para 19.

171 CAS 2002/A/383, *Dos Santos*, para 129.

172 CAS 2006/A/1125, *Hertha BSC Berlin v. Stade Lavallois Mayenne FC*, para 27, cited with approval in e.g. CAS 2008/A/1705, *Grasshopper v. Allianz Lima*, para 25.

173 See e.g. CAS 98/222, *Bernhard*, para 31, cited in CAS 2009/A/1768, *Hansen*, para 15.2; CAS 2002/A/363, *Pastorello*, para 5.9.

unclear, but not so unclear that enforcing them would violate the requirements of qualitative legality,[174] it will interpret any uncertainties against the party that formulated the rules (*contra proferentem*), in practice normally an SGB.[175] CAS will also seek to interpret sports rules in a way that avoids conflicts with mandatory national law.[176]

7.6 Sanctions and Remedies

The fifth and final major theme in CAS's normative contribution concerns the end result of legal actions: sanctions and remedies. This includes disciplinary sanctions, most commonly for doping violations and match-fixing and other corruption-related disputes.

First, more generally, CAS has established that its own power to review is to some extent protected as a matter of general principle. As discussed above, CAS's jurisdiction to hear a dispute is grounded in arbitration agreements, found either in contracts or, as is frequently the case, sports rules established by an SGB that has subsequently taken a decision that is being appealed to CAS.[177] The arbitration agreement constitutes the foundation for CAS's power to adjudicate and, as is frequently the case, power to review the decision. However, CAS has established that it will not accept agreements that restrict CAS's review to a greater extent than the review that would be afforded by national courts, including in particular restricting its power to review breaches of fundamental rights. As explained by CAS, to allow such restrictions would "lead to possible abuse of process and of authority, which would be absolutely unacceptable and would represent a substantial and special danger to sporting spirit,"[178] violate Swiss *ordre public*, and "leave the door open to a review of a higher standard by State courts."[179]

Like for what constitutes a punishable offence, what sanction should follow must be and is governed by sports rules.[180] The SGBs' power to regulate sanctions and disciplinary bodies' power to apply such rules in individual cases is however subject to certain general principles.[181] CAS has found that it follows from Swiss

---

174 See above Sect. 7.2.

175 See e.g. CAS 91/53, *G. v. FEI*, para 7; CAS 2000/A/317, *Aanes*, para 18.

176 CAS 2001/A/317, *Aanes*, para 23; CAS 2001/A/337, *Bray*, para 21. It can however be discussed if this is a process of interpretation or if it would be more correct to refer to it as disapplication.

177 See Sect. 2.2.

178 CAS 2009/A/1782, *Volandri*, para 70.

179 CAS 2012/A/3031, *Katusha Management SA v. UCI*, para 69.

180 See e.g. CAS 2005/C/976 & 986, *FIFA & WADA*, para 142; OG 98/002, *Rabagliati*, paras 26–27. As discussed above in Sect. 7.2, it would violate the principle of legality to punish an action without support in previously established, clear, and foreseeable rules.

181 See e.g. CAS 2010/A/2172, *Oryekhov*, para 47.

law that "sport-related disciplinary proceedings conducted by a sport federation against an athlete are qualified as civil law disputes and not as criminal law proceedings."[182] Consequently, disciplinary sanctions are not criminal but civil in nature and principles of criminal law therefore do not apply.[183]

However, as discussed in numerous CAS decisions, the principle of proportionality applies to disciplinary actions and is particularly relevant when it comes to assessing the sanctions.[184] CAS jurisprudence on the requirement of proportional sanctions has varied over time. As discussed above, pre-2005 CAS jurisprudence suggested that the principle of proportionality could be used relatively broadly and in flexible manner to achieve proportional doping sanctions.[185] If we consider the extent by which CAS relies on its previous decisions to constitute a reasonable proxy for its normative contribution, this case law was for some time its most important.[186] However, the application of the principle of proportionality to doping sanctions changed following the adoption of the WADC, from the application of a more vague and general notion to a standard mandated by Swiss law. It has been confirmed by both CAS and the Swiss courts that a CAS decision would violate the rights of those affected and thereby *ordre public* if it imposes a disciplinary sanction that is "extremely serious and totally disproportionate to the behaviour penalized."[187] This standard, which can be said to govern when CAS *must* set aside a doping sanction for reasons of proportionality, has also become the standard for when CAS *may* do so. Doping sanctions will be upheld unless they are "evidently and grossly disproportionate."[188] Thus, the principle of proportionality has in this regard narrowed in scope over time and become more closely attached to Swiss law.

As described, this development took place in the context of doping sanctions and the adoption of the WADC played an important role. In *Daniute*, CAS expressed this as a self-imposed restriction on its review powers more generally.[189] However, it appears that CAS's review of the proportionality of sanctions for non-doping

[182] CAS 2010/A/2311 & 2312, *Stichting Anti-Doping Autoriteit Nederland & KNSB v. W*, para 7.6.

[183] See e.g. CAS 2006/A/1102 & 1142, *Eder*, para 52.

[184] See e.g. CAS 2007/O/1381, *Valverde I*, paras 61, 92–99.

[185] See e.g. CAS 95/141, *Chagnaud*, paras 29–30; CAS 96/149, *Cullwick*, para 29; CAS 96/156, *Foschi*, para 15.1; CAS 2000/A/281, *Haga*, para 45.

[186] See Sect. 5.4.

[187] CAS 2004/A/690, *Hipperdinger*, para 52, citing SFT's decision 31 March 1999 in case 5P.83/1999 (*Wang et al. v. FINA*), para 3C. See also CAS 2005/C/976 & 986, *FIFA & WADA*, para 143.

[188] See e.g. CAS 2005/A/690, *Squizzato*, para 50; CAS 2006/A/1175, *Daniute*, para 48 (quoted); CAS 2009/A/1817 & 1844, *WADA & FIFA v. CFA*, para 174; CAS 2012/A/2756, *Armstrong*, paras 8.31–8.33.

[189] CAS 2006/A/1175, *Daniute*, para 47 ("the Panel underlines that it is willing to enforce a strict approach in the definition of its power reviewing the exercise of the discretion enjoyed by the disciplinary body of an association to set a sanction. To the extent the exercise of such discretion does not run against the internal rules of the association, the mandatory provisions of the law applicable or even fundamental general principles of law, the Panel finds itself limited by the

offences, such as match-fixing, is more extensive in the sense that even punishments that are not "evidently and grossly disproportionate" may be set aside for reasons of proportionality.[190]

An athlete must realistically be able to pay awarded damages it this is a condition for continued economic sporting activity.[191] Much of CAS's jurisprudence on damages has concerned the issue of damages for breach of employment contracts without just cause, particularly in football and governed by the FIFA Regulations on the Status and Transfer of Players (RSTP).[192] CAS has held that such damages should be calculated such that the injured party is placed "in the position that the same party would have had if the contract was performed properly" (the positive or expectation interest).[193] To calculate the damages that a club in breach owes a player has been relatively straightforward,[194] at least compared to the damages that is owed to a club. The calculation of such compensation may include a number of factors, including the player's remuneration, the club's costs for acquiring the player, and other "replacement costs".[195] The FIFA RSTP instructs that the "specificity of sport" and "any other objective criteria" shall be taken into consideration when calculating the compensation,[196] and thereby provides the competent bodies considerable discretion in setting the damage.[197] CAS jurisprudence obviously plays a considerable role in clarifying how damages are to be

respect to be paid to the freedom of the association to set the way to secure observance by its associates of the association rules.").

190 See e.g. CAS 2013/A/3256, *Fenerbahçe v. UEFA II*, para 573 (finding that its power to review the case *de novo* includes making an independent evaluation of the sanction); CAS 2013/A/3297, FC *Metalist v. UEFA & PAOK FC*, paras 8.25–8.34 (expressing a broad principle of proportionality but requiring a showing that the sanction was "clearly disproportionate").

191 See SFT's decision 27 March 2012 in case 4A_558/2011 (*Matuzalem v. FIFA*).

192 Of particular relevance in this regard is Article 17(1) FIFA RSTP that governs the calculation of damages.

193 CAS 2008/A/1519 & 1520, *da Silva*, para 86. See also e.g. CAS 2009/A/1880 & 1881, *El-Hadary*, para 80; CAS 2010/A/2145–2147, *de Sanctis*, para 61; CAS 2013/A/3411, *Bresciano*, para 103.

194 See also de Weger 2016, pp. 286–294.

195 See e.g. CAS 2013/A/3411, *Bresciano*, paras 103–116.

196 Article 17(1) FIFA RSTP. See also CAS 2007/A/1298–1300, *Webster*, para 67 (finding "that the specificity of sport is a reference to the goal of finding particular solutions for the football world which enable those applying the provision to strike a reasonable balance between the needs of contractual stability, on the one hand, and the needs of free movement of players, on the other hand, i.e. to find solutions that foster the good of football by reconciling in a fair manner the various and sometimes contradictory interests of clubs and players."); CAS 2007/A/1358, *Lombe*, paras 40–41.

197 CAS 2008/A/1519 & 1520, *Matuzalem*, para 89.

calculated under these conditions,[198] and that constitutes a considerable normative contribution, even if CAS in doing so has partly relied on Swiss law.[199]

Besides sanctions and damages, which to a great extent are supported and governed by sports rules, what remedies CAS can provide and under what conditions is frequently governed by Swiss law "since Swiss law applies subsidiarily and Swiss law also defines the powers of adjudication of arbitration bodies having their seat in Switzerland."[200] As discussed above, when acting under appellate jurisdiction CAS has the power to reconsider all factual and legal aspects of individual decisions in their entirety.[201] Because CAS's review power is based on and governed by arbitration clauses it does not generally have a power to review or invalidate sports rules. At the same time, CAS will, as discussed above, test whether applicable sports rules run counter to superior norms, including mandatory law and fundamental legal principles. When this is the case, CAS is "bound not to apply" the sports rules.[202] This is functionally a type of judicial review and one could say that this form of "disapplication" constitutes a remedy.[203] However, CAS cannot as such invalidate violating rules.[204]

7.7 Method, Madness, and Magpies

Besides its important role in resolving the disputes that are brought before it, CAS is closely associated with the establishment of a transnational legal order for sport, which can be referred to as lex sportiva.[205] By providing and adhering to jurisprudence, CAS contributes to the formation of such a transnational legal order.[206] Whether, to what extent, and in what way it also substantively contributes to its normative content is more difficult to say.

---

198 The perhaps most important example of this is the issue of whether the compensation should include missed transfer fees. Compare CAS 2005/A/902–903, *Mexès*, paras 71–72; CAS 2008/A/1298–1300, *Webster*, paras 74–81; CAS 2009/A/1880-1881, *El-Hadary*, paras 92–100.

199 See e.g. CAS 2005/A/893, *Metsu*, paras 25–27.

200 CAS 2009/A/1870, *Hardy*, para 55 (regarding the availability of and conditions for a declaratory judgment).

201 See above Sect. 7.3. See also e.g. CAS 2008/A/1718–1724, *Yegorova et al.*, paras 165–167.

202 CAS 2009/A/1889, *Unknown*, paras 77–78, quoted in CAS 2012/A/2900, *Ionel*, paras 86–88. However, there are exceptions and it has happened that CAS has received actions for annulment. See e.g. CAS 97/168, *FFSA, FIC, FNSA v. FISA*.

203 Cf. van Gerven 2000, pp. 506–509 (on the remedy of disapplication of national law under EU law).

204 The difference between disapplication and invalidation may however in practice be limited.

205 See Sect. 1.3.

206 See Chap. 4. Cf. Rigozzi 2005, pp. 635–637.

Foster interprets CAS in *NOCCS et al. v. IOC*[207] as implying "that the lex sportiva is little more than the proper interpretation and application of the legislative codes of sports federations"[208] and correctly criticizes such a narrow understanding. The cursory but hopefully representative examination in this chapter has shown that CAS has established the existence of a quite substantial body of norms that cannot directly be found in sports rules. In doing so, CAS has undeniably made a significant normative contribution.

It is more difficult to describe with certainty and specificity the nature of that normative contribution. CAS has suggested that sports norms can be deduced from the existence of a "general consensus" or a "definite pattern" in international sports law.[209] However, there are few clear examples of CAS establishing "genuine" general principles of sports law using this method.[210] There are more examples of CAS explicitly referring to the advancement of key sports-related values, most commonly the advancement of fair play and competition on equal terms. However, in many situations this is presented as a supporting argument for reaching a particular outcome, frequently used together with references to specific rules and principles, and it is uncertain whether and to what extent such values can be said to constitute independent and invocable norms.[211] Of course, this does not mean that such values lack legal relevance or weaken the claim that sports rules are based on certain ethical or equitable principles.[212]

This type of mixed approach seems to be one of CAS's characteristic traits. The examination in this chapter confirms that CAS uses a variety of methods, sources, and arguments to establish the existence of norms, including mandatory application of legal principles related to *ordre public*; extensive, generalized, or analogous "voluntary" application of general legal principles; broad application of common principles of contract law; deducing general norms from fundamental sports values; and establishing authoritative interpretations of key sports rules. When CAS turns to state-based legal norms, applying them directly or by analogy, it sometimes relies primarily or exclusively on Swiss law,[213] other times on a comparative analysis of

---

207 CAS 2002/O/372. Despite being frequently cited, see e.g. Blackshaw 2011, p. 141, the decision in *NOCCS et al. v. IOC* is not publicly available and it seems as if the case was consolidated with CAS 2002/O/373, *Scott*. However, the latter case, para 14, contains the same quoted language.

208 Foster 2006, p. 2.

209 Cf. CAS 2005/C/841, *CONI*, para 44.

210 There are examples of CAS declaring that lex sportiva includes a particular principle without clearly explaining the origin of that principle, for example the principle that event organizers "have a right to use their official languages." CAS 2010/A/2268, *I v. FIA*, para 75.

211 See e.g. OG 96/005, *Andrade et al. II*, para 7; OG 00/004, *Kibunde*, para 11; CAS 2004/A/707, *Millar*, para 53; CAS 2009/A/1757, *MTK Budapest v. FC Internazionale Milano SpA*, paras 30–31. But see e.g. CAS 2008/O/1455, *Boxing Australia v. AIBA*, para 42.

212 See Foster 2003, pp. 5–6.

213 This is unsurprising given the construct of the CAS Code and that many SGBs are domiciled in Switzerland. See Articles R45 and R58 CAS Code.

multiple legal orders, sometimes with clear references, other times not. As aptly expressed by one of CAS's most experienced arbitrators, "[i]n locating these principles and rules, sports law borrows, magpie like, from private as well as public law, appropriately mixing Latinisms with French phrases, and from civilian and common law concepts."[214]

Taken one-by-one, most norms established by CAS are supported by clear and convincing reasons. However, when looking at CAS's normative contribution on a whole it is difficult to find any obvious patterns or explanations why one method rather than another was used to determine the existence and content of a particular norm. While there are normative contributions that clearly rest on a particular method, most do not. There are also many examples of CAS changing, or at least supplementing, the reasons supporting a particular norm over time.

The historical context can help us understand why this is. Some CAS decisions referring to and applying general principles, including several of the earliest examples, were issued in cases heard by Ad Hoc Divisions resolving disputes arising in connection with the Olympic Games. In such cases, the rules governing the procedure explicitly dictate that CAS shall apply "general principles of law."[215] But even in cases where CAS is not explicitly authorized to do so it considers general principles of law part of the law applicable to disputes that come before it. This is sometimes essentially unavoidable as compliance with the applicable norms is mandatory and failure to comply would give rise to well-founded grounds for challenging the award.[216] By comparison, for example, while the practice of interpreting ambiguous provisions against the author (*contra stipulatorem*) can perhaps be referred to as a general legal principle,[217] it is not a legal principle that is a mandatory part of the law applicable to the dispute in the sense that CAS must consider and apply it in order to produce a decision that can withstand a challenge before state courts. Thus, when CAS applies the principle it to some extent does so "voluntarily".

There are many examples of the basis of a norm shifting or becoming blurred over time. For example, in its early case law, CAS refused to apply doping rules imposing strict liability unless they were "absolutely crystal clear and unambiguous,"[218] a standard of relatively narrow scope that can be traced back to the principle of legality[219] or a more general interest of fairness.[220] However, over time, the line between that narrower norm and the broader norm of *contra stipulatorem*,

---

[214] Beloff 2011, p. 14. See also Buy et al. 2015, pp. 144–145 (describes the CAS's "vampirization" of general and common legal principles).

[215] Article 17 of the Arbitration Rules applicable to the CAS ad hoc division for the Olympic Games.

[216] See e.g. the discussion above Sect. 7.3.

[217] See CAS 91/53, *G. v. FEI*, para 7.

[218] CAS 96/156, *Foschi*, para 13.3. See also e.g. CAS 94/129, *Quigley*, para 17; CAS 98/211, *Bernhard*, para 31.

[219] See above Sect. 7.2, esp. with regard to CAS 94/129, *Quigley*.

[220] See CAS 96/149, *Cullwick*, para 31, quoted in CAS 96/156, *Foschi*, para 13.3.

which is a general legal principle of interpretation applied to the field of sports, became blurred.[221] This is natural as the distinction between refusing to apply an ambiguous onerous rule or protecting a subject from its application by means of interpretation is of limited practical value. The example does however illustrate the problem with determining the basis of a particular norm or whether it is a "general legal principle" or a "sports principle". Whereas someone studying the early case law might well conclude that CAS has established a sports principle, someone studying more recent decisions may find CAS applying a more general legal principle. This may have little to do with the norm changing its character or justification and more to do with the process of norm development through decisions by panels that are formally independent from each other and composed by international arbitrators that in several relevant respects differ from each other.

References

Alexy R (2002) A Theory of Constitutional Rights. Oxford University Press, Oxford

Anderson J (2010) Modern Sports Law. Hart, Oxford

Barak A (2012) Proportionality: Constitutional Rights and Their Limitations. Cambridge University Press, Cambridge

Beloff M (2005) Is there a lex sportiva? International Sports Law Review 3:49–60

Beloff M (2011) Is There Such a Thing as Sports Law? The Circuiteer 33:13–15

Beloff M, Kerr T, Demetriou M, Beloff R (2012) Sports Law, 2nd edn. Hart Publishing, Oxford

Blackshaw I (2011) Towards a "Lex Sportiva". The International Sports Law Journal 2011(3/4): 140–144

Buy F, Maramyou J-M, Poracchi D, Rizzo F (2015) Droit du Sport, 4nd edn. LGDJ, Paris

Casini L (2011) The Making of Lex Sportiva by the Court of Arbitration for Sport. German Law Journal 12(5):1317–1340

Craig P (2006) EU Administrative Law. Oxford University Press, Oxford

de Weger F (2016) The Jurisprudence of the FIFA Dispute Resolution Chamber. T.M.C. Asser Press, The Hague

Dworkin R (2013) Taking Rights Seriously. Bloomsbury, London

Erbsen A (2006) The Substance and Illusion of Lex Sportiva. In: Blackshaw I, Siekman R, Soek J (eds) The Court of Arbitration for Sport 1984–2004. T.M.C. Asser Press, The Hague, pp. 441–454

Foster K (2003) Is There a Global Sports Law? Entertainment Law 2(1):1–18

Foster K (2006) Lex Sportiva and Lex Ludica: The Court of Arbitration for Sport's Jurisprudence. Entertainment and Sports Law Journal 3(2)

Fuller L (1969) The Morality of Law, 2nd edn. Yale University Press, New Haven

Geeraert A, Alm J, Groll M (2014) Good governance in international sport organizations: An analysis of the 35 Olympic sport governing bodies. International Journal of Sport Policy and Politics 6(3):281–306

Hart H L A (2012) The Concept of Law, 3rd edn. Oxford University Press, Oxford

Hayek F A (2007) The Road to Serfdom. Chicago University Press, Chicago

Kaufmann-Kohler G, Rigozzi A (2015) International Arbitration: Law and Practice in Switzerland. Oxford University Press, Oxford

[221] Compare e.g. CAS 96/156, *Foschi*, para 13.3, CAS 98/211, *Bernhard*, para 31, and CAS 2009/A/1768, *Hansen*, para 15.2.

Kelsen H (1970) The Pure Theory of Law. Knight M (transl). University of California Press, Berkeley
Kramer M H (1999) In Defense of Legal Positivism: Law Without Trimmings. Oxford University Press, Oxford
Kramer M H (2007) Objectivity and the Rule of Law. Cambridge University Press, Cambridge
Lagarde P (1982) Approche critique de la 'lex mercatoria'. In: Le Droit des Relations Economiques Internationales: Etudes Offertes a Berthold Goldman. Litec, Paris, pp. 125–150
Latty F (2007) La lex sportiva: Recherche sur le droit transnational. Martinus Nijhoff, Leiden
Martens D-R (2006) CAS Landmark Decisions. In: Blackshaw I, Siekman R, Soek J (eds) The Court of Arbitration for Sport 1984–2004. T.M.C. Asser Press, The Hague, pp. 235–245
McLaren R (2011) The Court of Arbitration for Sport. In: Nafziger J, Ross S (eds) Handbook on International Sports Law. Edward Elgar Publishing, Cheltenham, pp. 32–64
Nafziger J (1999) Globalizing Sports Law. Marquette Sports Law Journal 9:225–238
Nafziger J (2011) International Sports Law. In: Nafziger J, Ross S (eds) Handbook on International Sports Law. Edward Elgar Publishing, Cheltenham, pp. 3–31
Oschütz F (2002) Harmonization of Anti-Doping Code Through Arbitration: The Case Law of the Court of Arbitration for Sport. Marquette Sports Law Review 12:675–702
Raz J (2009) The Authority of Law, 2nd edn. Oxford University Press, Oxford
Rigozzi A (2005) L'arbitrage international en matière de sport. Helbing & Lichtenhahn, Basel
Rincón A (2007) EC Competition and Internal Market Law: On the Existence of a Sporting Exemption and its Withdrawal. Journal of Contemporary European Research 3(3):224–237
Schultz T (2014) Transnational Legality: Stateless Law and International Arbitration. Oxford University Press, Oxford
Tridimas T (2006) The General Principles of EU Law, 2nd edn. Oxford University Press, Oxford
van Gerven W (2000) Of Rights, Remedies and Procedures. Common Market Law Review 37:501–536
Vieweg K, Staschik P (2015) The Lex Sportiva: The Phenomenon and its Meaning in the International Sporting Arena. In: Vieweg K (ed) Lex Sportiva. Duncker & Humblot, Berlin, pp. 17–58
von Bogdandy A, Venzke I (2012) Beyond Disputes: International Judicial Institutions as Lawmakers. In: von Bogdandy A, Venzke I (eds) International Judicial Lawmaking. Springer, Berlin, pp. 3–33

Part III
The Actors

Chapter 8
CAS Arbitrators and Their Relationships

Abstract The men and women that serve as arbitrators make up the essence of the Court of Arbitration for Sport (CAS) and have the power not only to decide individual disputes but also to shape international sports law more generally. To understand who serves on CAS panels is therefore important in order to understand CAS and its jurisprudence. As shown in this chapter, not just anyone gets to serve on CAS panels, not even anyone that appears on the list of CAS arbitrators. When studying a large number of CAS decisions it becomes clear that those who appoint arbitrators tend to appoint certain arbitrators. The chapter explores the nature and causes of such tendencies and their implications.

8.1 CAS as a Human Network

The examination has thus far largely focused on the jurisprudence of the Court of Arbitration for Sport (CAS). It comes quite natural to most lawyers to understand judicial bodies through their decisions. However, it is important to remember that CAS "is not a mechanical system" but "a network of human actors."[1] Understanding who those actors are, their backgrounds, what influence they exercise within CAS, and how they relate to each other is important for understanding the institution. These are the types of questions that this third Part of the book seeks to answer.

In doing so, we will at times explore some aspects of CAS that could perhaps be described as behavioral or sociological in nature. This book is in this regard inspired by and in part follows studies conducted by sociologists,[2] and even more so by the related, subsequent work of legal scholars, in particular legal scholars studying international arbitration.[3] The main focus of the examination is however legal in nature, looking at how these actors, their backgrounds, and their interactions

[1] Swigart and Terris 2015, p. 619 (commenting on international adjudication generally). Cf. Reeb 2004, p. xxxii ("The CAS performs its functions through the intermediary of arbitrators…").
[2] See e.g. Dezalay and Garth 1996; Latour 2010.
[3] See e.g. Drahozal 2005; Franck et al. 2015; Puig 2014.

J. Lindholm, *The Court of Arbitration for Sport and Its Jurisprudence*,
ASSER International Sports Law Series,
https://doi.org/10.1007/978-94-6265-285-9_8

influence the reasoning and outcome of individual cases, CAS as an institution, and CAS jurisprudence in the long term.

This examination is split into three chapters. Chapters 8 and 9 primarily focus on CAS arbitrators, Chap. 8 from a relational perspective focusing on arbitrators' connections to each other and to the parties that come before CAS and Chap. 9 with a focus on the arbitrators' backgrounds and other characteristics. The final chapter of the book, Chap. 10, shifts focus to the parties that come before CAS, their relationships to each other, the roles that CAS fills for different parties, and the success rate of different litigants.

8.2 The Appointable Arbitrator

As previously discussed, CAS panels can be formed in various ways. A panel can consist of a sole arbitrator or of three arbitrators including a panel president. The parties' influence over the formation of the panel also varies between the Ordinary Arbitration Procedure and the Appellate Arbitration Procedure.[4] All arbitrators that appear on CAS panels do however have in common that they have been appointed by the International Council of Arbitration for Sport (ICAS) to appear on the list of CAS arbitrators.[5] According to the CAS Code, the CAS list of arbitrators shall contain no less than 150 individuals,[6] but the actual number of arbitrators on the CAS list is significantly higher,[7] in recent years exceeding 300[8] and currently including 389 individuals.[9]

As demonstrated by the case of *Lazutina & Danilova*, it is important, even essential, that the list of approved arbitrators is kept reasonably extensive and diverse.[10] The circumstances behind this case, which we will have reason to return to below, began at the 2002 Olympic Winter Games in Salt Lake City where two Russian cross-country skiers, Larissa Lazutina and Olga Danilova, performed very well and were initially awarded two Olympic medals each. However, following random drug testing, the two Russians tested positive for NESP, an EPO-like substance that increases blood cell production. As a result of this, they were disqualified from the Olympic Games by the International Olympic Committee (IOC) and suspended for a period of two years. Lazutina and Danilova appealed

[4] See Sect. 2.3.

[5] Article S3 CAS Code.

[6] Article S14 CAS Code.

[7] See e.g. Reeb 2004, p. xxxii (noting that the list at that time included 241 arbitrators).

[8] Kaufmann-Kohler and Rigozzi 2015, p. 166; Mavromati and Reeb 2015, pp. 264–265.

[9] This statement is based on the list available at http://www.tas-cas.org/en/arbitration/list-of-arbitrators-general-list.html, accessed 11 October 2018.

[10] As Duval points out, it is also a question of the legitimacy of CAS arbitration. Duval 2013, p. 834.

these decisions to CAS that upheld both the disqualifications and the suspensions.[11] The two skiers subsequently appealed CAS's decision to the Swiss Federal Tribunal (SFT).[12] The key question before the SFT was whether CAS was sufficiently independent from the IOC in order for its jurisdiction and its decisions to be enforced by the Swiss legal order. In its decision *Lazutina & Danilova*, the SFT laid down and applied some basic institutional requirements that CAS must comply with.

There will be reasons to return to *Lazutina & Danilova* below, but we shall for now limit ourselves to the issue of CAS's closed list of eligible arbitrators. Following its previous decisions, the Swiss Federal Tribunal did not condemn the list as such but required that the use of such a list be justified, which it also found to be the case.[13] In this context, the SFT also noted that the list of approved arbitrators was extensive and diverse enough to offer parties that come before CAS a real possibility of choice.[14] Thus, conversely, if the list of approved arbitrators is so limited that parties before CAS lack a real choice in arbitrator, there is a very real risk that the SFT would no longer consider it a "real arbitration tribunal" which in turn would mean that its jurisdiction and decisions would not be upheld by the Swiss courts.[15]

However, having a large number of arbitrators involved in CAS's activities is not necessarily exclusively positive. One of CAS's aims and functions is to establish a consistent body of case law.[16] As is evident from the examples of many national and international legal orders, it is possible to establish a case law-based legal order through processes that involve many individuals. Indeed, any legal order that aims to exist and expand over time will by necessity involve multiple individuals. However, all else being equal, it is easier to develop and maintain a coherent body of jurisprudence if the number of individuals involved in the decision-making process is relatively small. The interest of having an extensive list of arbitrators must also be weighed against the aim of providing high-quality adjudication by arbitrators with expert knowledge in the field of sports and sports law.[17]

---

[11] CAS 2002/A/370, *Lazutina I* (regarding disqualification); CAS 2002/A/371, *Danilova* (regarding suspension); CAS 2002/A/397, *Lazutina II* (regarding suspension).

[12] SFT's decision 27 May 2003 in case 4P.267/2002, ATF 129 III 445 (*Lazutina & Danilova v. IOC*).

[13] Ibid., pp. 456–457.

[14] Ibid., pp. 457–458 ("Les arbitres figurant sur la liste sont au nombre de 150 au moins et le TAS en compte environ 200 à l'heure actuelle. La possibilité de choix offerte aux parties est ainsi bien réelle, quoi qu'en disent les recourantes, même si l'on tient compte de la nationalité, de la langue et de la discipline sportive pratiquée par l'athlète qui saisit le TAS.").

[15] See also the ECtHR's decision in *Mutu & Pechstein v. Switzerland*, app. no. 40575/10 and 67474/10, para 157 (finding that CAS exercises a "real influence" over the nomination procedure but that a violation of Article 6 ECHR also requires showing individual lack of independence and impartiality).

[16] See e.g. Reeb 2002, p. xxx.

[17] See also Article S14 CAS Code (requiring appointable arbitrators to have "recognized competence with regard to sports law and/or international arbitration" and "a good knowledge of

8.3 The Appointed Arbitrator

Against this background, we shall now consider to what extent individual arbitrators are selected to be included in CAS panels. It has been claimed in the literature that some arbitrators appear more frequently than others on CAS panels.[18] Most individuals that are familiar with CAS jurisprudence probably share the impression that certain arbitrators participate on CAS panels relatively frequently. Using the collected data, we can with a comfortable degree of certainty empirically test whether this is correct, more exactly what the distribution looks like, and what, if anything, characterizes and distinguishes arbitrators that are frequently appointed to CAS panels from those who are less frequently appointed.

In the CAS decisions collected and considered in full text there is a total of 2,195 instances where an arbitrator was appointed to sit on a CAS panel, either as one of the arbitrators on a three-arbitrator panel or, more rarely, as a sole arbitrator. This data includes the appointment of 232 unique individual arbitrators. This is obviously less than the 389 individual arbitrators that currently appear on the CAS list. However, the total number of individual arbitrators that have appeared on the CAS list, i.e. were appointable, but does not appear in the dataset, i.e. were appointed in the studied cases, is clearly higher and potentially significantly higher. It is difficult to produce an exact number of unique individuals that have ever appeared on the CAS list. However, it can be noted that roughly half of the arbitrators that participated in deciding any of the studied decisions no longer appear on the current CAS list.

It should be pointed out that these findings likely are affected by the data selection and that it is possible, even likely, that there are additional CAS arbitrators, beyond the 232 individuals identified here, that have actually participated on a CAS panel. However, considering the distribution of decisions per arbitrator in the data collected, we can say with a high degree of certainty that most arbitrators that are appointed by CAS and that appear on the list of CAS arbitrators have participated in rendering very few decisions, if any at all. There is a drastically inequitable distribution of appointments among CAS arbitrators: 28 percent of all unique arbitrators found to have participated in any of the studied decisions have participated in delivering only one decision and 42 percent of the arbitrators appeared in only one or two decisions.[19] Another way to describe this lower end of the inequitable distribution of panel appointments within CAS is that the 42 percent of all appointed CAS arbitrators with the fewest appointments received only

sport"). But see Cavalieros and Kim 2015, p. 249 ("It is debatable whether sports arbitration is specialized enough to justify the existence of a closed-list system.").

[18] See e.g. Gorbylev 2013, pp. 296–297; Latty 2007, p. 262; McAuliffe and Rigozzi 2013, pp. 16–17; Rigozzi 2010, p. 238.

[19] See below Fig. 8.1 *Decisions per Arbitrator*.

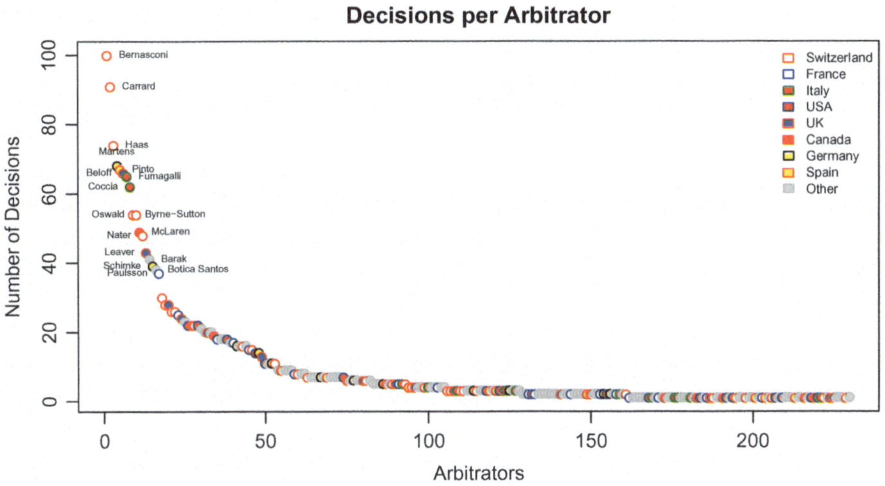

Fig. 8.1 Decisions per Arbitrator. [*Source* The author]

6 percent of all appointments,[20] and that does not even take into account the many arbitrators who never appear on a panel.

There is a similarly inequitable distribution of appointments at the high end of the scale. The distribution of appointments to CAS follows roughly a power law distribution where a small number of arbitrators are involved in delivering a disproportionally large number of CAS decisions.[21] While the distribution is relatively smooth and continuous, a quite clear distinction can be made between, on one hand, the seventeen arbitrators that appear most frequently in the collected decisions, which I will refer to as CAS's "super-arbitrators", and, on the other hand, the other 215 arbitrators found in the dataset.[22] As a group, the super-arbitrators have been appointed a total of 996 times in the data. To put this in perspective, the super-arbitrators, which make up 7 percent of the appointed arbitrators and an even smaller portion of all appointable CAS arbitrators, have received more than 45 percent of all appointments. The most extreme example of this is Swiss attorney Michele Bernasconi who appeared on the panel in more than one in eight of the collected decisions.

These findings clearly confirm the view that appointments to CAS panels are inequitably distributed among CAS arbitrators. At the same time, it should be pointed out that CAS is not unique in this regard. The distribution of arbitrator appointments in CAS is for example similar to that in International Centre for

[20] The 98 (unique) CAS arbitrators with the lowest number of appointments found in the collected data have collectively been appointed 130 times.

[21] Compare the distribution of references to case law discussed in Sect. 5.2.

[22] The members of this group are marked in Fig. 8.1 *Decisions per Arbitrator* above.

Settlement of Investment Disputes (ICSID),[23] and it seems that appointments of arbitrators to arbitration tribunals generally tend to follow a power law distribution. Because appointments tend to be distributed in this manner, the number of arbitrators that appear on the CAS list will have little impact on which arbitrators or how many different arbitrators actually end up serving on CAS panels. The fact that the average time that it takes CAS to deliver a decision has largely remained constant over time, despite a substantially increased case load,[24] suggests that the pool of available arbitrators is sufficiently large,[25] and that actual appointments are primarily governed by the interests and preferences of the actors involved in the selection process.[26]

So what can explain this distribution? Why are appointments to CAS not more equally distributed among all the arbitrators on the list? Latty offers three explanations for why certain arbitrators appear in CAS more frequently than other: (i) Swiss arbitrators tend to be nominated more frequently because of their geographic proximity to CAS, (ii) major sports governing bodies (SGBs), who frequently appear as litigant before CAS,[27] tend to repeatedly nominate the same arbitrators, and (iii) CAS Division Presidents place importance on previous experience when selecting which arbitrators to nominate as panel presidents.[28]

The empirical evidence supports that Swiss arbitrators are disproportionally frequently appointed to CAS panels. Swiss arbitrators are included in CAS panels almost three times as frequently as arbitrators of any other nationality, including arbitrators from much more populous nations.[29] This does not by itself necessarily mean that there is a preference for Swiss arbitrators as such. One possible explanation for the findings could be that a few, very popular individual arbitrators happen to be Swiss.[30] However, this does not appear to be the case as there are

[23] Puig 2014, pp. 419–420.

[24] See Fig. 3.13 *CAS Procedure Length Over Time*.

[25] Cf. Giordetti 2013, p. 481.

[26] Thus, one can argue that expanding the CAS list to include arbitrators that are in some regard different than those already included may be valuable even if adding more arbitrators as such is not.

[27] See Sect. 10.4.

[28] Latty 2007, p. 262.

[29] See below Fig. 8.2 *Arbitrator Appointments by Nationality*. In the data, there are 627 appointments of Swiss arbitrators. British is the second most common nationality of CAS arbitrators with a total of 220 appointments. The nationality of the arbitrators was decided on the basis of, in order, the nationality stated in CAS decisions, the nationality stated in the CAS arbitrator database, and other sources describing the arbitrators found on the Internet.

[30] For example, the appearance of Portuguese arbitrators in CAS is relatively common. With a total of 46 appearances it is the tenth most common nationality of CAS arbitrators. However, 38 of these appearances were made by a single individual: Lisbon-based attorney-at-law Rui Botica Santos.

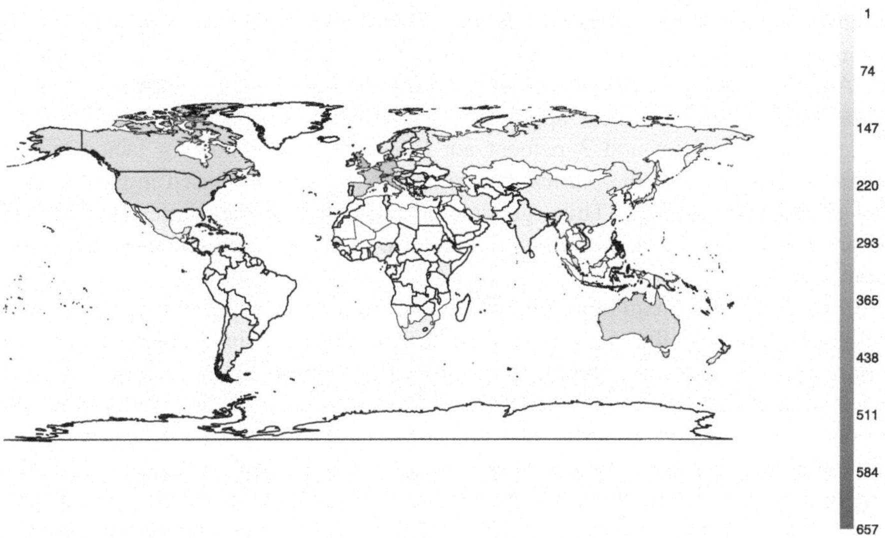

Fig. 8.2 Arbitrator Appointments by Nationality (Color figure online). [*Source* The author]

almost twice as many unique individual CAS arbitrators from Switzerland than from any other nation.[31]

It is more difficult to establish with certainty what may be the cause of this overrepresentation; there are other possible explanations besides geographic proximity to CAS. For example, Switzerland is generally considered an "arbitration-friendly" nation,[32] arbitration in Switzerland is relatively common, and, not unrelatedly, there are many experienced arbitrators living in Switzerland. Although it is difficult to quantify and compare the combined arbitrator experience by nation, this is unlikely to explain the massive dominance of Swiss CAS arbitrators. There are many other nations with experienced arbitrators, not least the United States, Canada, and the United Kingdom.[33] A factor supporting the theory that geographic proximity to CAS matters is the relatively high frequency of CAS arbitrators from nations bordering Switzerland; German, French, and Italian are all among the five most common nationalities of CAS arbitrators. By contrast, North American arbitrators are relatively uncommon in CAS considering these nations' population size, their level of sport commercialization, and the significant number

[31] In the data we find 38 different Swiss arbitrators. The second largest group is American of which there are 18 individuals.

[32] Cf. Duval 2015, p. 403 ("La Suisse semble être un paradis juridique pour l'arbitrage sportif.").

[33] See e.g. Franck 2007, pp. 77–78 (regarding investment arbitration tribunals), Puig 2014, p. 405 (regarding ICSID). Cf. Pauwelyn 2015, pp. 772–775 (noting that panelists from developing countries are more common in the WTO system).

of lawyers experienced in sports law and arbitration that are based there.[34] In this regard, CAS deviates quite strongly from ICSID where the majority of arbitrators are American and only 6.5 percent of the arbitrators are Swiss.[35] Similarly, Franck found that among arbitrators appointed in international investment arbitration 19 percent are American and 3 percent are Swiss.[36] A complicating factor in this regard is that many of the parties that come before CAS are based in Switzerland and neighboring nations. Thus, geographic proximity to the parties that litigate before CAS may be a contributing factor to the over-representation of Swiss arbitrators.[37]

In studying the inequitable distribution of arbitration appointments in ICSID, Puig makes findings that point toward another possible explanation for why certain arbitrators are appointed more frequently. Puig observes that arbitrators that received their first appointment to ICSID in the early stages of the institution would go on to receive a disproportionally high portion of the subsequent appointments compared to arbitrators that received their first appointment at a later stage. His explanation for this is that early appointees were able to establish a social and professional standing in the community that translated to subsequent appointments, which, in turn, solidified and enhanced their standing as parties value experience. In this manner, arbitrators that are early arrivals have an advantage compared to later arriving arbitrators when it comes to being appointed and that this advantage remains and even increases over time.[38]

Puig's observation and explanation are compatible with the theory that parties to arbitration avoid arbitrators whose views, opinions, and inclinations are unknown, and that parties conversely prefer arbitrators whose predispositions are known.[39] All else being equal, arbitrators that have been active in the community for a longer period of time are more well-known and therefore more attractive to the parties, and this should in turn translate into more appointments.

If these theories are correct, we should expect to see some correlation between, on the one hand, arbitrators' total number of appointments and, on the other hand, when in time they were first appointed to a CAS panel. Of course, arbitrators that were first appointed to a CAS panel in recent years can be expected to have appeared less frequently than arbitrators that have been active in CAS for a longer time simply as a consequence of the latter having had more opportunities to be appointed.[40] In order to compensate for the inequitable number of appointment

[34] In the cases collected and studied here there are a combined total of 220 appearances by American and Canadian arbitrators which can be compared to 176 appearances by German arbitrators.

[35] Puig 2014, p. 406.

[36] Franck 2007, p. 78.

[37] See below Sect. 8.8.

[38] Puig 2014, pp. 421–422 (commenting on ICSID "power-brokers").

[39] Giordetti 2013, p. 466 and sources cited.

[40] The impact of this effect is however reduced by the fact that the number of cases lodged with CAS was initially low and has since strongly increased. See Sect. 3.3.

opportunities, we will compare the actual number of times each individual has been appointed as a CAS arbitrator to the total number of CAS arbitrators appointed since the individual's first appearance. We can then see if, as predicted, arbitrators that received their first appointment to a CAS panel early received a greater than equitable share of the subsequent appointments and, conversely, if newcomers have received a smaller portion.[41]

Doing so reveals no clear and direct correlation between arbitrators' year of first appointment and their shares of subsequent appointments.[42] Like in ICSID, early appointees have generally fared quite well. However, if we focus on the super-arbitrators and other arbitrators that have received a disproportionally large share of appointments during their active time, we find that their debuts are quite evenly distributed over time, from CAS's earliest years until around 2006. In fact, many of the arbitrators that are appointed more frequently than predicted made their debut in CAS between 2000 and 2005 rather than in the 1980s and 1990s. Perhaps this reflects the inevitable process of older, established, and reputable members of the community leaving room for younger colleagues.

While there is thus no clear correlation in the data between debut year and share of appointments, it seems to take about seven or eight years before arbitrators that are new to CAS have a realistic chance to receive a proportional number of the subsequent appointments.[43] In some cases it goes faster,[44] but generally it seems to take almost a decade for an individual to fully build his or her reputation as a CAS arbitrator.

---

[41] For example, based on the collected decisions, Michael Beloff made his debut in CAS in the Ad Hoc Division for the 1996 Atlanta Olympic Games. If arbitration appointments were distributed randomly among all arbitrators that had appeared on a CAS panel at least once, Beloff would have been appointed in 0.6 percent of all CAS decisions that were decided in and after 1996. Had he been appointed exactly that many times, his ratio of actual to be expected appointments would be 1. If he had received a lower than expected number of appointments, that number would be less than 1. Conversely, if he had received a higher than expected number of appointments, that number would be greater than 1. Beloff actually appears as an arbitrator in 3 percent of all collected CAS decisions rendered since 1996. Beloff is thus "over-appointed" by a ratio of more than four to one (3/0.6) compared to an equal distribution of appointments among all appointed arbitrators.

[42] See below Fig. 8.3 *Appointments by First Decision Year*.

[43] See below Fig. 8.3 *Appointments by First Decision Year*. Contrary to this conclusion, arbitrators that were appointed for the first time in 2014 have received significantly more than their expected number of appointments. However, the results for the most recent years are skewed by the small sample size and are not reliable. For example, the three 2014 debutants with the highest ratio have only appeared in two decisions, all decided as part of the CAS Ad Hoc Division for the XVII Asian Games in Incheon. However, the collected data only includes 28 CAS decisions from 2014 and these two appointments therefore make up a large portion.

[44] For example, with his 16 appointments, including 10 as panel president, since his debut in 2006, Danish attorney Lars Hilliger has established a strong position quicker than expected.

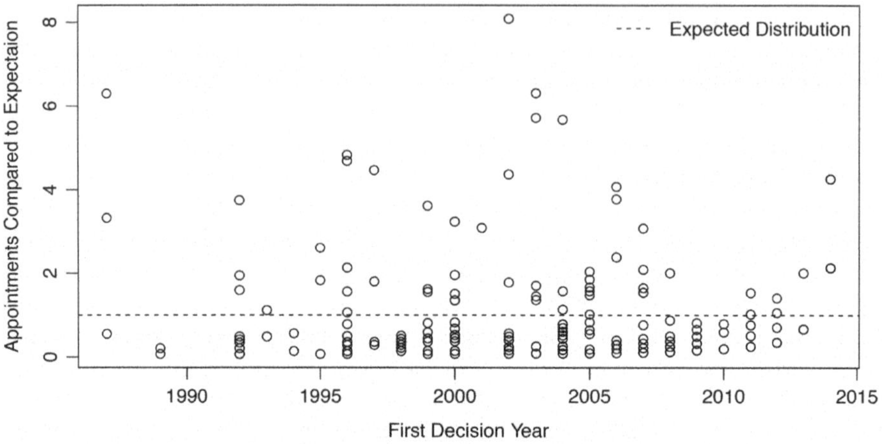

Fig. 8.3 Appointments by First Decision Year. [*Source* The author]

8.4 The Co-appearing Arbitrator

Because a small group of the arbitrators on CAS's list receive most of the appointments, a student of CAS jurisprudence will quickly become familiar with the names of the most frequently appointed arbitrators. Because CAS arbitrator appointments are inequitably distributed it is natural that two and sometimes even three frequently-appointed arbitrators will appear together on the same CAS panel. As a result, a person reading several CAS decisions will likely come away with the impression that some arbitrators appear together on CAS panels disproportionally frequently.

What legal significance, if any, would it have if this impression is true and that some arbitrators frequently appear together on CAS panels? The answer depends, first, on the strength of such clustering tendencies. To be appointed to sit on a CAS panel carries with it not just the power to settle the individual dispute at hand but also an opportunity to influence CAS jurisprudence and, by extension, sports law more generally,[45] both by selecting and applying rules and principles laid down in previous CAS decisions and by formulating new rules and principles that can and frequently will be relied upon when other cases are subsequently decided. Regardless of whether arbitrators intentionally and strategically use these opportunities, and regardless of whether they are aware of them, the more times an individual arbitrator is appointed, the greater his or her potential influence on CAS jurisprudence and on sports law.[46] If a group of arbitrators frequently appear on CAS panels together one can along similar lines think of them as exercising a

[45] See Chap. 4.

[46] See also Sect. 8.6.

significant collective influence on CAS jurisprudence. In other words, it is possible that there are particularly influential groups of arbitrators within CAS and identifying the existence of such groups is important to understand CAS and how it influences sports law. Depending on the extent to which certain arbitrators co-appear together there is also a risk of jurisprudential fractionalization as distinct groups of arbitrators may develop distinct approaches that differ from those of other clusters of arbitrators.[47]

It is difficult to accurately gauge whether certain arbitrators co-appear on CAS panels disproportionately frequently simply by reading individual CAS decisions. As touched upon above, it is natural, even inevitable, that the arbitrators with the highest number of appointments will frequently appear together considering the inequitable distribution of appointments. For example, Bernasconi and Carrard have 100 and 91 appointments respectively in the dataset. With such a large number of appearances it is all but inevitable that they will appear together on a number of panels. The relevant question is whether those instances are so frequent that this type of clustering affects CAS and its jurisprudence.

In order to have the type of effect that we are interested in here, the relationship between two arbitrators must fulfill two conditions. First, they must co-appear in a sufficiently large number of panels. For example, that two arbitrators have appeared on the same panel 100 percent of the time will not necessarily have a significant systemic impact on CAS and its jurisprudence if they, as almost half of all appointed CAS arbitrators, have only been appointed once or twice.[48] After all, unless an arbitrator has only been appointed as sole arbitrator – which is very rare – he or she will inevitably have appeared with some other arbitrators. We will therefore use five co-appearances as the minimum level in order for two arbitrators co-appearing to be considered relevant.[49]

Second, the number of co-appearances must also constitute a sufficiently large proportion of the individual arbitrator's appearances. The fact that Bernasconi and Carrard co-appear as arbitrators in five CAS decisions is unlikely to affect CAS and its jurisprudence on a structural level considering that for each of those instances there are 18–19 instances where they did not appear together. By comparison, it is more relevant that two arbitrators sat on five panels together if they each have been appointed a total of ten times. Thus, what constitutes a relevant relationship in the context discussed here also depends on the total number of panels each arbitrator has appeared on. We will here use 20 percent as the minimum level for "high

[47] This can be compared to how local courts within a national system of courts or independent chambers within a court may develop tendencies that differentiates them from other courts or chambers.

[48] See Sect. 8.3.

[49] This is equivalent to 0.6% of all decisions in the dataset.

co-appearance relationship", meaning that an arbitrator appears with another arbitrator on at least one out of five panels on which he or she appeared.[50]

In this context, it is worth noting that a relationship between two arbitrators can be, and frequently is, asymmetrical. For an arbitrator that has only served on eleven CAS panels, serving with a particular arbitrator in six out of those eleven panels represents a significant portion of her or his activities as a CAS arbitrator. However, if the latter arbitrator is considerably more experienced than the former arbitrator their relationship is less significant to the latter than to the former.[51]

There are several interesting observations we can make if we map these high co-appearance relationships.[52] First, there are relatively few examples of arbitrators frequently appearing together on CAS panels. There is a total of 1,276 unique co-appearances of CAS arbitrators in the CAS decisions included in the dataset. Only 26 or one in fifty of these relationships meet the criteria defined above. Second, most high co-appearance relationships involve individual arbitrator pairs and arbitrator "chains". 17 of the 29 CAS arbitrators that are involved in a high co-appearance relationship are only involved in one such relationship. The data thus indicates that arbitrators generally do not tend to cluster in groups.

Third, there seems to be a correlation between how many times an arbitrator has been appointed and the arbitrator's involvement in high co-appearance relationship, but to understand the underlying relationship is somewhat complex. Most of the CAS arbitrators with the highest number of appointments are involved in high co-appearance relationship.[53] However, it is rare that these relationships constitute a large portion of the most frequently appearing arbitrator's relationships.[54] An image of linked star-shaped constellations emerges. Many of the less frequently appointed arbitrators are connected to a super-arbitrator with whom they have appeared frequently together from their perspective. Most super-arbitrators are however involved in a relatively large number of such relationships.[55] Most of these are

[50] These proportions are calculated by dividing the number of times two particular arbitrators appear on the same panel with the number of times each of those arbitrators appear on a panel, thus disregarding all appointments as sole arbitrators.

[51] This is a description of the relationship between Martens and Ellicott. See below Fig. 8.4 *Co-Appearing Arbitrators.*

[52] See below Fig. 8.4 *Co-Appearing Arbitrators* (minimum 5 co-appearances representing at least 20% of all appearances). Vertex size is proportional to each arbitrators' number of non-sole arbitrator appointments, which is also given in the vertex label. Edge labels provide the number of co-appearances and vertex color represents percentage of arbitrators' appointments in football-related disputes.

[53] Most of the seventeen arbitrators with the highest number of decisions are included. See above Fig. 8.1 *Decisions per Arbitrator*. There are, however, notable exceptions such as Beloff, Coccia, Nater, and McLaren.

[54] 22% of all co-appearances involve two super-arbitrators. This is in line with what can be expected on three-arbitrator panels considering that super-arbitrators receive 42% of all appointments.

[55] For example, Carrard appears in the data on panels together with 70 different arbitrators.

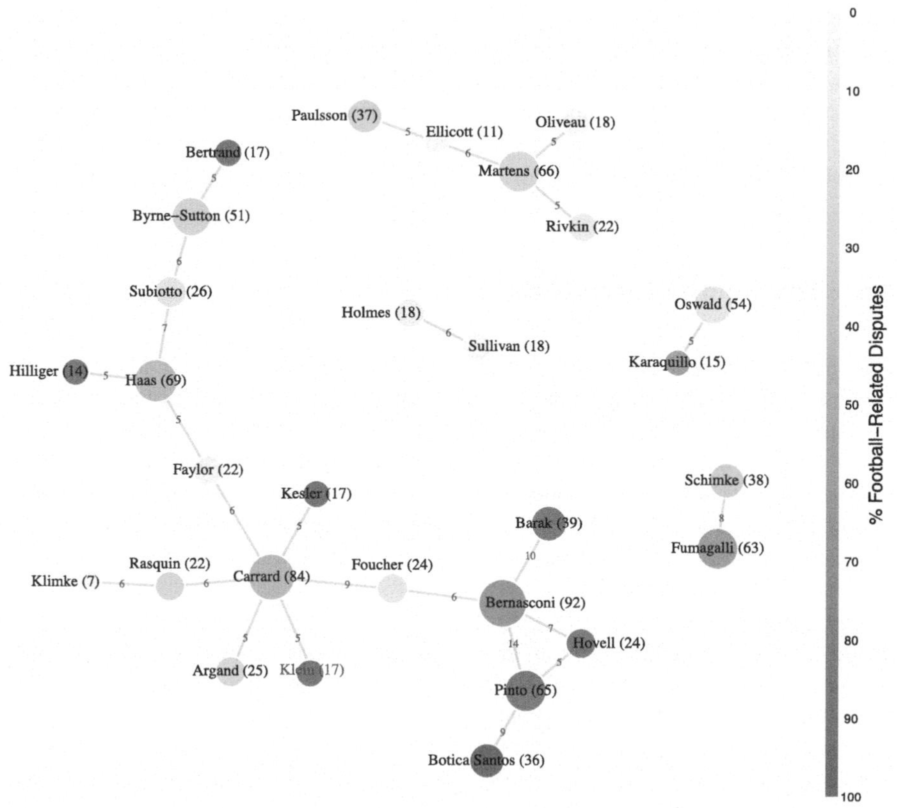

Fig. 8.4 Co-Appearing Arbitrators (Color figure online). [*Source* The author]

therefore relatively weak, but each super-arbitrator does however also generally have a strong connection to one or two other super-arbitrators.

These findings are not particularly surprising. Two of the three arbitrators sitting on a CAS panel are nominated by the parties involved in the dispute,[56] and there are no clear incentives for parties to select arbitrators that have previously served together. However, at the same time, we do not expect parties to appoint arbitrators randomly. If this was true, high co-appearance relationships, or for that matter super-arbitrators, would be extremely unlikely. On the contrary, as discussed, there are incentives for parties that come before CAS to select experienced arbitrators and this contributes to the development of a system where appointments follow a power law distribution, rather than for example an equal or normal distribution, and where the existence of some high co-appearance relationship are natural, even inevitable. The procedure used for appointing panel presidents contributes to this trend, particularly in cases that fall under the Ordinary Arbitration Procedure where the

[56] See Sect. 2.3.

party-appointed arbitrators play a significant role in selecting the panel president.[57] It would be natural if party-appointed arbitrators had a tendency to push for arbitrators that they have worked with previously as panel presidents, especially if those arbitrators are experienced and working with them was a positive experience.[58] Presidents and the impact of president appointments on CAS and its jurisprudence is explored more extensively below.[59]

8.5 The Football Arbitrator

One notable exception from the lack of clear clusters observed above is the Bernasconi-Pinto-Hovell triangle and its "satellites", Barak and Botica Santos.[60] This group includes five super-arbitrators and the only example of a triangular high co-appearance relationship. Perhaps most interesting is the relationship between Michele Bernasconi and Jose Juan Pinto. Considering that both of these arbitrators are among the five CAS arbitrators with the most appointments in the data, it is surprising that they appear on the same CAS panel in fourteen cases, the highest of any two arbitrators in the data.

One possible contributing factor may be that Bernasconi and Pinto made their debuts as CAS panelists around the same time and that their careers as CAS arbitrators in this sense coincide temporally.[61] However, time of debut as a CAS arbitrator is clearly not a decisive factor. For example, Quentin Byrne-Sutton is also a super-arbitrator that made his debut as a CAS arbitrator around the same time as Bernasconi and Pinto,[62] but he only co-appears with Bernasconi and Pinto three times[63] and one time[64] respectively.

The primary thing that these five arbitrators have in common and that distinguish them from most of the other arbitrators with high co-appearance relationships is the beautiful game: Bernasconi, Pinto, Hovell, Barak, and Botica Santos are all specialized in resolving football-related disputes.[65] This is supported by a closer examination of the fourteen CAS panels on which Bernasconi and Pinto appear together. The two arbitrators have worked together to resolve cases concerning

57 See Sect. 2.3.

58 Unfortunately, the available sample of CAS decisions in Ordinary Arbitration Procedures is too limited to empirically test this hypothesis.

59 See below Sect. 8.9.

60 See above Fig. 8.4 *Co-Appearing Arbitrators*.

61 They appear for the first time in the dataset in 2002 and 2003 respectively.

62 First appears in the data in 2002.

63 CAS 2008/A/1551, *Cherubin*; CAS 2008/A/1759 & 1778, *Jaben*; CAS 2011/A/2426, *Adamu*.

64 CAS 2007/A/1251, *Aris II*.

65 See above Fig. 8.4 *Co-Appearing Arbitrators*.

various subject matters, including transfers disputes,[66] other contractual disputes,[67] disciplinary matters,[68] eligibility issues,[69] and other matters.[70] However, all fourteen cases where the two arbitrators appeared together on the panel concerned a football-related dispute.

More generally, beyond the aforementioned five individuals, it appears that football is an important factor when it comes to explaining why certain CAS arbitrators commonly appear together on panels. If we map all co-appearances among all CAS arbitrators we can see that arbitrators who predominantly sit on football-related cases are relatively strongly connected to each other and relatively weakly connected to their colleagues that are infrequently involved in resolving football-related disputes.[71]

There are organizational factors that can explain the observed pattern. As has been discussed above, the composition of CAS is substantially different from both ordinary courts and many arbitration tribunals. Unlike in most national and international courts, the individuals that decide cases at CAS are not permanently attached to the institution but, for the most part and primarily, selected by the parties. At the same time, the parties' autonomy when it comes to selecting arbitrators is more limited than in many arbitration tribunals as these must be selected from a list of pre-approved arbitrators. The president of the panel is selected from the same list in a process where CAS's Division Presidents play a significant role, particularly in appeals cases.[72] Within this selection scheme there is an "extra-special" selection scheme for disputes concerning football. In 2002, the international football federation, FIFA, and ICAS entered into an agreement whereby CAS assumed the jurisdiction of the Arbitration Tribunal for Football. CAS has since functioned as the appellate body for decisions by the FIFA Dispute Resolution Chamber (FIFA DRC).[73] In order to facilitate this jurisdictional shift, CAS created a separate list of arbitrators particularly qualified to hear football-related disputes.[74]

Latty argues that the creation of a group of football-specialized arbitrators within CAS may affect the coherence and consistency of CAS jurisprudence.[75] In line with the discussion above, we can imagine that the creation of a smaller, more

---

[66] CAS 2010/A/2193, *Cagliari Calcio v. Olimpia Deportivo*; CAS 2011/A/2557, *Dynamo Kyiv v. Nancy-Lorraine*; CAS 2012/A/2707, *Nancy-Lorraine v. Dynamo Kyiv*.

[67] CAS 2005/A/893, *Metsu*; CAS 2005/A/902 & 903, *Mexes II*; CAS 2007/A/1358, *Lombe*; CAS 2007/A/1359, *Bete*; CAS 2008/A/1665, *J. v. Udinese Calcio SpA*; CAS 2010/O/2132, *Pereira Dias*; CAS 2011/A/2539, *Monchengladbach v. Boca Juniors*.

[68] CAS 2005/A/916, *AS Roma v. FIFA*.

[69] CAS 2008/A/1633, *FC Schalke 04 v. CBF*; CAS 2008/A/1634, *Hertha BSC v. FAS*.

[70] CAS 2008/O/1808, *KFF v. FIFA*.

[71] See below Fig. 8.5 *Co-Appearances and Football*.

[72] See Sect. 2.3.

[73] Blackshaw 2012, p. 9; de Weger 2016, pp. 106–107.

[74] Latty 2007, p. 261.

[75] Ibid.

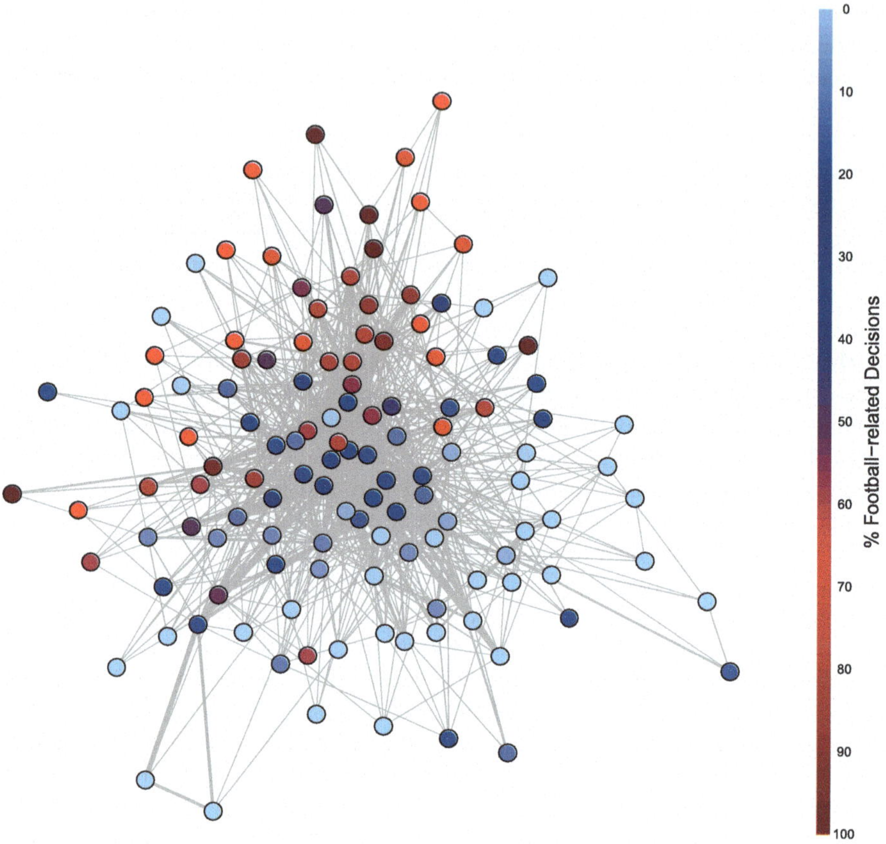

Fig. 8.5 Co-Appearances and Football. [*Source* The author]

specialized group of arbitrators can, on the one hand, create greater coherence and consistency among football-related CAS decisions but, on the other hand, at the same time give rise to differences between football-related and non-football-related CAS jurisprudence. This could have quite severe consequences considering that many of the subject matters that CAS deals with are dominated by football-related disputes.[76]

The data supports Latty's observation. Almost a quarter of all CAS arbitrators predominantly adjudicate football-related cases,[77] and many of these exclusively or primarily appear on CAS panels together.[78] On the other side of the spectrum there

[76] See Sect. 2.4.

[77] 22% of all arbitrators in the dataset (51 of 229) appear in cases that are football-related in 75% of the cases or more. See also above Fig. 8.5 *Co-Appearances and Football*. If we only consider arbitrators that appear in at least three cases that number is 17% (22 of 128).

[78] See above Fig. 8.5 *Co-Appearances and Football*.

is a large number of CAS arbitrators that never or rarely adjudicate football-related matters[79] and that never or rarely appear on CAS panels with arbitrators that predominantly adjudicate football-related disputes.[80] These two groups are thus quite distinct from each other.

CAS arbitrators also tend to cluster based on to what extent they are involved in the resolution of football-related disputes. CAS arbitrators that hear many football-related disputes tend to co-appear with other arbitrators that hear many football-related disputes. Similarly, CAS arbitrators that rarely hear football-related disputes tend to co-appear with other arbitrators that rarely hear football-related disputes.[81]

The distinction between football and other sports thus runs quite deep in CAS and has a clear observable impact on the clustering of its arbitrators. However, it is important to point out that this does not mean that the distinction between football and other sports is the only relevant factor. Nor does it mean that CAS arbitrators can be divided into two isolated groups, football-focused and non-football-focused. Finally, there are a number of CAS arbitrators that deal extensively with both football-related cases and non-football-related cases and that sit on CAS panels with arbitrators of varying degree of football focus.[82] These arbitrators are important when it comes to fighting a divergence of football-related and non-football-related CAS jurisprudence. By frequently serving on panels resolving both types of disputes, these individuals facilitate communication and transfer of knowledge within CAS and help ensure that comparable cases are decided the same regardless of what sport they concern.

8.6 The Influential Arbitrator

Do CAS arbitrators differ with regard to how much influence they exert over CAS jurisprudence? In order to answer this question, we must begin by clarifying what we mean by influence. As discussed on several occasions above, adjudicators influence legal orders on a normative and structural level by formulating general principles and establishing precedents in individual decisions that are considered,

[79] 45% of all arbitrators in the dataset (103 of 229) do not appear in any panel adjudicating a football-related dispute. See also below Fig. 8.6 *Football Arbitrators - Distribution and Correlation*. However, it should be noted that many of those arbitrators have participated in very few cases. Of the arbitrators that appear in at least three cases, i.e. the arbitrators represented above in Fig. 8.5 *Co-Appearances and Football*, 28% (36 of 128) have not adjudicated any football-related dispute.

[80] See above Fig. 8.5 *Co-Appearances and Football* and below Fig. 8.6 *Football Arbitrators - Distribution and Correlation*.

[81] See below Fig. 8.6 *Football Arbitrators - Distribution and Correlation*.

[82] See above Fig. 8.5 *Co-Appearances and Football* and below Fig. 8.6 *Football Arbitrators - Distribution and Correlation*.

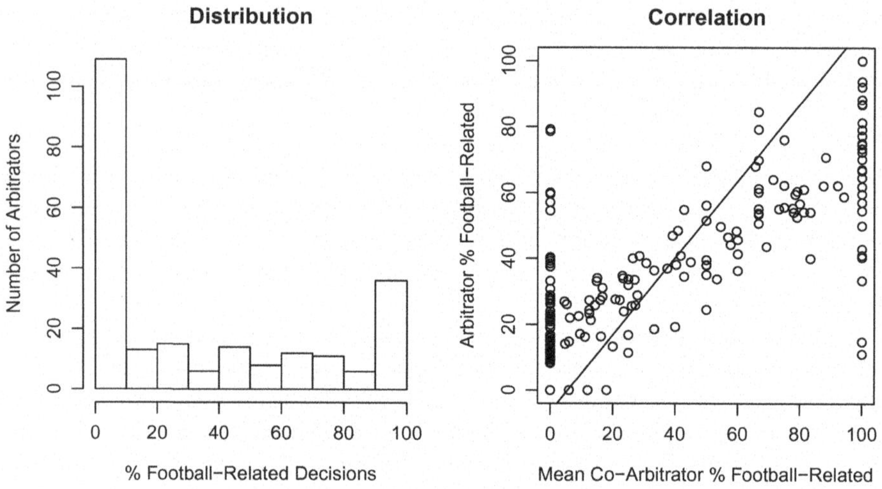

Fig. 8.6 Football Arbitrators - Distribution and Correlation. [*Source* The author]

followed, and developed in subsequent decisions and this normative influence increases with the importance of case law as a source of law.

Network analysis enables us to approximate the influence that individual arbitrators exert over CAS jurisprudence by treating a positive reference from one decision to an older decision as a proxy for the latter decision influencing the former. Unless we have reason to believe that CAS panels pick references at random or that they may have reason to obfuscate and deceive their audience, this is quite reasonable. This approach was used above to identify CAS's landmark decisions,[83] as well as areas or issues where previous decisions have particularly strong precedential power.[84] It can also be used to measure the influence that individual CAS arbitrators have exerted on CAS jurisprudence: the greater the role of a CAS arbitrator in setting a CAS precedent, the more influence he or she exerts on CAS jurisprudence.

This meaning of arbitrator influence is rather straightforward. However, accurately capturing this influence is a little more complicated and involves some methodological choices. First, it is not a given that all members of a CAS panel were equally influential in formulating the panel's decision and, consequently, should share equally in the precedential value of the decision (or the lack thereof). It is impossible to know with certainty to what extent individual panelists influenced the decision.[85] For example, it is possible that the more experienced arbitrators exert more influence in a panel, especially if its other members are comparatively

[83] See Chap. 5.

[84] See Chap. 6.

[85] CAS decisions are written in a way that provides little to no insight into the opinions of the individual panelists.

inexperienced. Thus, it is possible that an arbitrator may receive undue credit for a precedent that he or she had a smaller part in deciding relative to his or her panel colleagues. However, the risk that such false indicators distort the results decreases with numbers. A CAS arbitrator may by chance end up participating in delivering one or two important CAS decisions, but it is increasingly unlikely that this will happen five or ten times.

Second, network analysis offers different measurements for decisions' precedential value and, consequently, for individual arbitrators' influence. Following the approach used for individual decisions, we shall measure and compare two different measurements also used above: indegree, which in this context is equal to the number of times that a CAS decision has been cited in subsequent decisions, and PageRank, which also captures the decision's influence over decisions that do not directly cite it.[86]

There are two alternative approaches one can take when using these measurements as measurements for arbitrator influence. One approach is to study the sum of the indegree and PageRank of all decisions that different arbitrators have participated in delivering. These values are naturally dependent on the number of decisions an arbitrator has delivered; the more decisions an arbitrator has delivered, the greater the chance that those decisions have been cited in subsequent decisions. Thus, all else being equal, an arbitrator's influence – measured in this manner – can be expected to be significantly correlated to the number of CAS decisions that he or she has participated in delivering. This is nevertheless a quite defensible approach to measuring influence. Arbitrators that have participated in delivering a large portion of all CAS decisions can reasonably be expected to have had a large impact on its jurisprudence in an absolute sense.

An alternative approach would acknowledge and take into consideration that all decisions are not equal. As discussed above, CAS decisions differ quite strongly in precedential power.[87] Thus, a CAS arbitrator may have delivered relatively many decisions but if those decisions belong to the rather extensive group of CAS decisions that primarily cite and apply rules and principles established in other decisions without adding much that is relied upon in subsequent CAS decisions, the arbitrator's influence will be lower than the influence of some arbitrators that have participated in a similar number of decisions. Conversely, an arbitrator may have participated on a relatively limited number of CAS panels but if those panels delivered decisions that belong to the select group of landmark decisions that have an extensive systemic impact on CAS jurisprudence the arbitrator has had a higher influence on CAS's jurisprudence than a colleague that participated in an equal number of CAS decisions of average precedential power.

It would not be surprising if these types of differences between arbitrators were quite significant and that experienced CAS arbitrators would be more influential

[86] See also Sect. 1.6. As discussed immediately below, indegree centrality and PageRank are often strongly correlated, but there are situations where they differ significantly.

[87] See Sect. 5.2.

than less experienced colleagues even when correcting for the number of decisions delivered. An arbitrator that has delivered a large number of decisions is more knowledgeable and can, by merit of greater experience, act with greater confidence. Because experienced arbitrators receive more opportunities to sit on CAS panels they can also afford to be pickier and select cases of greater importance.

In light of this it is somewhat surprising that the relative difference in influence between CAS arbitrators, taking into account the number of decisions delivered, appears to be quite marginal. There is a clear correlation between, on the one hand, the number of decisions that a CAS arbitrator has participated in deciding and, on the other hand, the total indegree and PageRank of those decisions.[88]

This result is interesting as it suggests that there are small differences between individual arbitrators with regard to their ability to influence CAS jurisprudence. An arbitrator that has decided fifty cases has obviously wielded greater influence over CAS jurisprudence than a colleague that has settled one or two cases, but influence is strongly correlated to the number of cases decided with limited differences between individual arbitrators.

To measure arbitrators' total influence on CAS jurisprudence is a quite intuitive approach, but there are some possible problems with measuring accumulated influence in this manner. This approach benefits arbitrators that participate in delivering a large number of CAS decisions and applying it means that an arbitrator that is frequently appointed is almost unavoidably more influential than his or her less frequently appointed colleagues. While this is accurate in one sense, it can be questioned depending on how we think about influence. Let us assume that we are comparing two arbitrators, one that has participated in rendering ten decisions that are all frequently relied on as precedents and one that has participated in rendering a hundred decisions but none that have great precedential power. Which of these two arbitrators is the more influential one? The approach used above tends to benefit the latter, but a case could be made for the arbitrator that rarely appears on panels but when doing so consistently produces strong precedents.

We can capture this type of influential arbitrator by using mean indegree and PageRank instead of total indegree and PageRank. It can be argued that an arbitrator whose decisions have a significantly high mean indegree or PageRank can accurately be described as influential regardless of how many decisions he or she has delivered.[89] The figure below includes all 93 CAS arbitrators with at least five CAS decisions in the dataset and displays the mean indegree centrality and PageRank of all CAS decisions that each arbitrator participated in.

---

[88] See below Fig. 8.7 *Arbitrator Decisions and Indegree* and Fig. 8.8 *Arbitrator Decisions and PageRank.*

[89] A different issue is how many observations are needed to attain a reliable measurement. Because of how indegree centrality and PageRank is distributed across CAS jurisprudence (see Sect. 5.2) arbitrators' mean values can vary extensively at a low number of observations. For this reason, Fig. 8.9 *Mean PageRank and Indegree by Arbitrator* below only includes arbitrators with at least five CAS decisions in the dataset. In the discussion below, this is supplemented by a qualitative analysis of individual arbitrators.

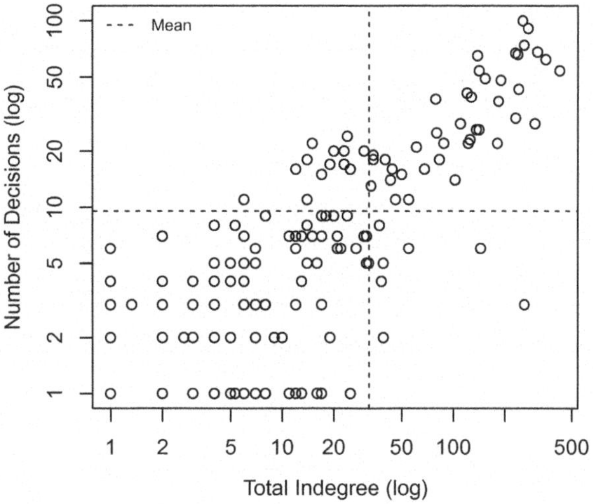

Fig. 8.7 Arbitrator Decisions and Indegree. [*Source* The author]

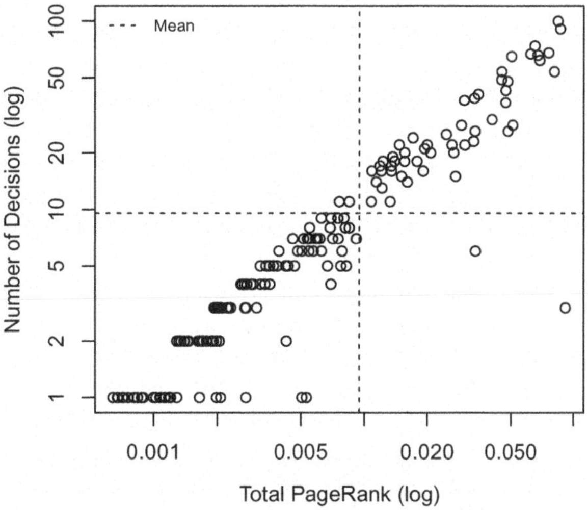

Fig. 8.8 Arbitrator Decisions and PageRank. [*Source* The author]

Two main conclusions can be drawn from this. First, there are clear differences between CAS arbitrators in terms of the mean indegree and PageRank of their decisions, differences that are not directly dependent on the number of decisions the arbitrators have rendered. None of the five arbitrators with the greatest number of decisions in the dataset[90] rank among the ten highest by either mean indegree or mean PageRank. Thus, the impact of some of the arbitrators that qualify in the latter

[90] Bernasconi, Carrard, Haas, Martens, and Pinto. See also above Fig. 8.1 *Decisions per Arbitrator*.

groups can easily be overlooked if one focuses too narrowly on number of appointments. For example, this approach suggests that the decisions that Canadian lawyer and diplomat Yves Fortier participated in writing have been particularly influential, placing him among the top five CAS arbitrators in terms of both mean indegree and mean PageRank, despite him appearing on a relatively low number of CAS panels.[91]

Second, there is a quite strong correlation between mean indegree and mean PageRank. However, there are also some interesting deviations from this rule. For example, CAS decisions delivered by Klimke are cited rather infrequently compared to many other CAS arbitrators (low mean indegree) but the extended effect of his decisions though subsequent case law is relatively high (high mean PageRank).

8.7 The Repeat Arbitrator

A fundamental principle of international arbitration is that the arbitrators are impartial and independent, both in relation to the parties and to the object of the dispute.[92] The composition of an independent tribunal is the foundation on which the arbitral award rests.[93] It is therefore crucial that CAS both actually is impartial and independent and that it is perceived as such, both in order for national courts to respect and enforce its jurisdiction and decisions,[94] and in order for CAS to maintain its legitimacy among those who are subject to its jurisdiction.[95] This is reflected in the CAS Code which provides that "[e]very arbitrator shall be and remain impartial and independent of the parties and shall immediately disclose any circumstances which may affect her/his independence with respect to any of the parties."[96]

One particular important issue in this regard is the relationship between arbitrators and parties and whether the nature and intensity of that relationship casts doubt over the arbitrators' impartiality and independence. As discussed above, one challenge to CAS's impartiality and independence is the influence that SGBs have over ICAS and the process through which arbitrators are included on the list of approved CAS arbitrators.[97] Another issue is the financial connections between certain parties and arbitrators. That certain financial connections exists between party-appointed arbitrators and the parties appointing them, for example that the

---

[91] With 22 decided cases, Fortier ranks forty-seventh among all CAS arbitrators by total number of decisions.

[92] Blackaby et al. 2015, p. 254.

[93] Slaoui 2009, p. 119.

[94] See e.g. Article 190.2(a) PILA.

[95] See e.g. Nafziger 2004, p. 8 ("Ultimately, the reputation of the CAS relies on the twin pillars of independence and impartiality."); Vaitiekunas 2014, pp. 110–111.

[96] Article 33 CAS Code. This conforms closely with the IBA Guidelines on Conflict of Interest (2014), general standards 1 and 3.

[97] See above Sect. 8.2.

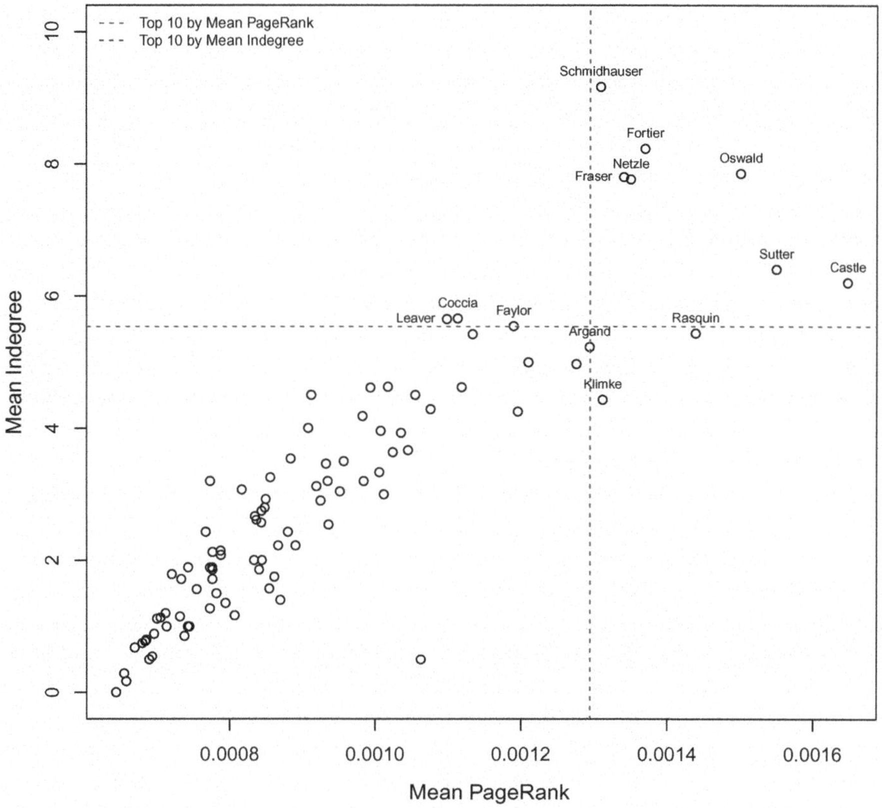

Fig. 8.9 Mean Indegree and PageRank by Arbitrator. [*Source* The author]

arbitrator receives remuneration for his or her services, is unavoidable in arbitration, but every financial connection does not detrimentally threaten the arbitrator's impartiality and independence. Rather, each such connection must be assessed on a case-by-case basis with consideration of the nature and intensity of the connection.[98] For example, if an arbitrator regularly advises one of the parties and thereby derives significant financial income from the party, this raises justified doubts about his or her impartiality and independence.[99]

The prevalence of repeat arbitrators, that is arbitrators that are repeatedly appointed by the same party in multiple arbitrations,[100] and whether such arbitrators are sufficiently impartial and independent from the parties appointing them are two

[98] See Blackaby et al. 2015, pp. 268–271 (explaining ICSID practise); Kaufmann-Kohler and Rigozzi 2015, pp. 190–191.

[99] The IBA Guidelines on Conflict of Interest (2014), Non-Waivable Red List, para 1.4. See also e.g. Puig 2016, pp. 15–16.

[100] Slaoui 2009, p. 109.

important issues in this context. The fact that a party has appointed an arbitrator for a previous arbitration tribunal does not as such disqualify the arbitrator from being appointed again by the same party,[101] nor do such repeat appointments necessarily imply an improper relationship between the party and the arbitrator. A party may for example choose to repeatedly appoint the same arbitrator because it has gained knowledge about his or her predisposition.[102]

Repeat arbitrators can however constitute a problem and if an arbitrator has been nominated sufficiently frequently by the same party he or she can be expected to disclose it.[103] In order for repeat arbitrators to be active at CAS there must be repeat parties, that is parties that frequently litigate before CAS, and this group consists of certain major SGBs.[104] It is in this regard problematic that SGBs through their influence over ICAS indirectly also exercise some influence over which arbitrators are included on the CAS list and, thereby, over which arbitrators are appointable. The SFT and ICAS have thus far never found a repeat arbitrator not to be sufficiently impartial and independent.[105]

This can be illustrated by the case of *Contador* that concerned Alberto Contador, a professional cyclist from Spain, who had been suspected of a doping violation but had been acquitted by the Spanish cycling federation's disciplinary body. The national decision was appealed to CAS by the international cycling federation, UCI, and the World Anti-Doping Agency (WADA) who nominated Quentin Byrne-Sutton as arbitrator. The respondent challenged Byrne-Sutton's independence and impartiality on the ground that WADA had nominated him in several previous arbitrations. This challenge was rejected by ICAS.[106]

Considering how important it is for CAS's actual and perceived impartiality and independence, it is well worth empirically exploring how common and extensive repeat arbitrators are in CAS. As discussed above, it is clear that some arbitrators appear much more frequently than others and that appointments are not distributed equally among all arbitrators on the CAS list.[107] That does not, however, necessarily mean that arbitrators that are frequently appointed are also repeat arbitrators in the way that the term is used here, that is, that they are frequently appointed by the same party.

As discussed, repeat CAS arbitrators can for obvious reasons only be appointed by repeat CAS parties. This attempt to map the extent of the phenomenon will

---

[101] Kaufmann-Kohler and Rigozzi 2015, p. 193 (discussing Swiss law); Slaoui 2009, p. 105.

[102] Giordetti 2013, p. 466. See above Sect. 8.3.

[103] What in this context constitutes "sufficiently frequent" may vary depending on the circumstances, but one standard of possible conflict is two appointments in a three-year period. The IBA Guidelines on Conflict of Interest (2014), Orange List, para 3.1.5. See also Slaoui 2009.

[104] See also Sect. 10.4. Some football clubs also appear before CAS noticeably frequently.

[105] Kaufmann-Kohler and Rigozzi 2015, pp. 198–199.

[106] CAS 2011/A/2384 & 2386, *Contador*. See also Kaufmann-Kohler and Rigozzi 2015, pp. 198–199 (describing and criticizing ICAS's ruling). Byrne-Sutton belongs to the group of CAS arbitrators that appear most frequently in CAS. See above Sect. 8.3.

[107] See above Sect. 8.3.

therefore focus on the parties that most commonly appear in the collected CAS decisions. I have selected to study the twenty actors that most frequently appear before CAS in disputes decided by three-arbitrator panels.[108] These are all national and international SGBs. In the CAS decisions collected and considered herein, those twenty parties have, by themselves or together with joining parties, nominated a total of 110 unique arbitrators 488 times.[109] Already from the relatively large number of unique arbitrators nominated we can tell that SGBs do not generally select arbitrators from a small pool. Thus, the data suggests that on a systemic level there are no strong and obvious ties between individual CAS arbitrators and SGBs generally.

This does not however necessarily mean that there are no strong ties between individual SGBs and individual arbitrators. The best way to explore this issue is to consider how each party distributes its nominations between individual CAS arbitrators. We can think of each unique relationship between a particular party and a particular arbitrator that the party has nominated to sit on a CAS panel as a *party-arbitrator relationship*. The data contains 270 unique party-arbitrator relationships between the top-twenty most frequently appearing CAS parties and different arbitrators. The strength of each such relationship can be measured as the number of times the party has nominated the arbitrator as a percentage of the party's total number of nominations.[110] If a repeat-party SGB nominates the same arbitrator disproportionally frequently, this reduces CAS's actual and/or perceived impartiality. Conversely, if the party spreads its nominations fairly equally among a larger group of arbitrators, this suggests that it is not systematically building relationships with particular arbitrators and that arbitrators are less likely to receive business based on past performance.

In examining all party-arbitrator relationships, we find that in general repeat-party SGBs spread their nominations among a fairly large number of individual arbitrators: the median party-arbitrator relationship represents little more than 5 percent of the nominating party's total number of nominations,[111] more than nine out of ten party-arbitrator relationships represent 1–20 percent of the party's nominations, and the median number of unique arbitrators nominated by repeat-party SGBs is twelve.[112] One could argue that all repeat appointments contribute to the erosion of

[108] The total number of disputes included in the data that the individual parties are involved in drop quickly below these top twenty. Sole arbitrators are decided by mutual agreement or by the CAS Division President and can therefore not reliably be connected to a particular party. See Sect. 2.3. See also Mavromati and Reeb 2015, p. 269.

[109] See below Fig. 8.10 *Repeat Parties and Arbitrators: All Relationships*.

[110] I.e. the percentage of a party's total number of nominations that are made to each individual nominated arbitrator.

[111] See below Fig. 8.10 *Repeat Parties and Arbitrators: All Relationships*. The median proportion of all party-arbitrator relationships relative to the sum of the nominating party's nominations is 5.26.

[112] It should be noted that this number varies a lot between different parties but that it follows quite closely the total number of CAS disputes that the party has been involved in. This makes

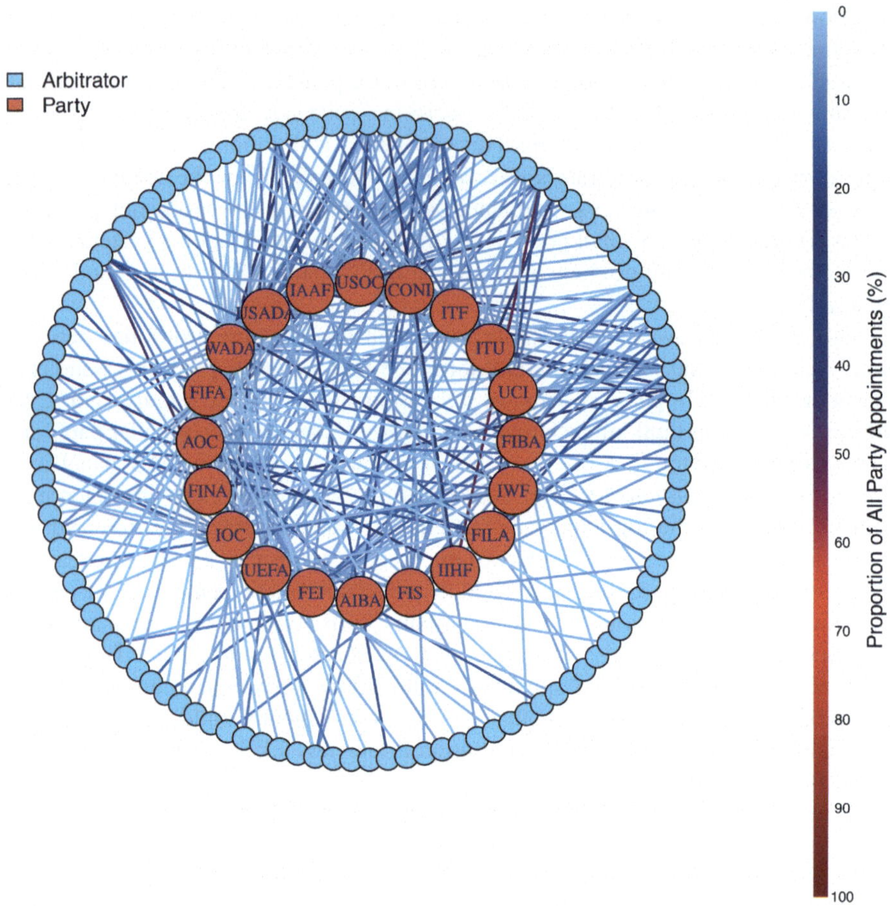

Fig. 8.10 Repeat Parties and Arbitrators: All Relationships. [*Source* The author]

CAS's actual and perceived impartiality. It is also true that repeat appointments are unnecessary considering that ICAS has approved almost 400 different CAS arbitrators,[113] and that SGBs – as a collective – have identified more than 110 CAS arbitrators that are sufficiently competent and experienced to be nominated to sit on a CAS panel. However, the data shows that, overall and on a general level, repeat arbitrator appointments are not very common in CAS, nor something that SGBs engage in on a broad and systematic level. It is also evident from the data that repeat party SGBs do not generally tend to frequently appoint the same individual arbitrators as each other as the median CAS arbitrator has only been selected by two of

natural sense as the more disputes a party has been involved in, the more opportunities it has had to appoint different arbitrators.

[113] Cf. Coccia 2013, p. 8.

the SGBs belonging to this group.[114] Thus, there do not appear to be arbitrators that are favored by SGBs more generally.

Another way to explore this issue is to consider to what extent different classes of CAS litigants tend to appoint certain arbitrators or, differently stated, whether certain arbitrators are predominantly appointed by certain classes of CAS litigants. CAS litigants can be divided into three main classes: individuals (predominantly athletes), clubs, and SGBs.[115] We can examine how CAS parties belonging to these classes distribute their appointments between individual arbitrators,[116] and examine to what extent different classes appoint different arbitrators.

This reveals that there are some differences in appointment tendencies between different classes of CAS litigants, but these differences are not primarily found, as one might perhaps have expected, between individuals and SGBs but between clubs and the other two classes.[117] Some arbitrators are slightly favored by either individuals or SGBs, but these differences are quite small and all but a few arbitrators receive comparable shares of these classes' appointments.[118] There are, however, noticeable differences between arbitrators with regard to what share of the clubs' appointments they receive: roughly one-third are hardly ever appointed by clubs, one-third receive a more or less equal portion of all three classes' appointments, and one-third are predominantly appointed by clubs. This pattern can likely to a significant extent be explained by the conditions surrounding the resolution of football-related disputes: clubs' appearing as litigants in CAS is predominantly frequent in football-related disputes and some CAS arbitrators are specialized in resolving football-related disputes.[119]

The fact that repeat arbitrators are not a general and systematic problem does not however mean that there are no individual, potentially problematic party-arbitrator relationships. One way of identifying such potentially problematic relationships is to focus only on the strongest party-arbitrator relationships. If we focus on the 11 percent of all party-arbitrator relationships that cover more than 15 percent of the

[114] The average number of party-arbitrator relationships for all nominated arbitrators is 2.45.

[115] See also Sect. 10.1.

[116] Although all three classes are well represented in the data, they are not equally represented: individuals have participated in 506 appointments, clubs in 312 appointments, and SGBs in 819 appointments. The arbitrators' absolute number of appointments by party class is irrelevant and can be misleading when determining party class preferences. We therefore instead consider what share of each classes' appointments each arbitrator has received. For example, Beloff has received 2.2% of the individuals' appointments, 1.6% of the clubs' appointments, and 3.5% of the SGBs' appointments.

[117] See below Fig. 8.11 *Arbitrators' Appointments by Party Class*. It is difficult to assess party class preferences for the large number of arbitrators who have only received one or two appointments. See above Sect. 8.3. They have therefore been excluded from the figure.

[118] As seen in Fig. 8.11 *Arbitrators' Appointments by Party Class* there are a few outliers. However, it should be noted that these outliers disappear if one increases the minimum number of appointments provided. It is thus possible that these outliers may have more to do with the underlying data than any actual, general differences in preference.

[119] See above Sect. 8.5.

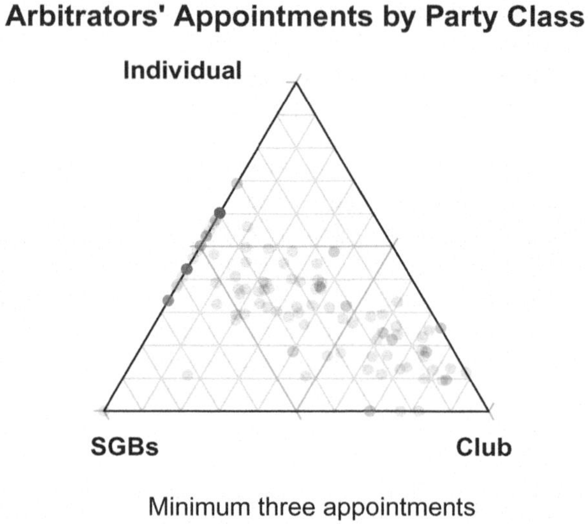

Fig. 8.11 Arbitrators' Appointments by Party Class (Color figure online). [*Source* The author]

nominating party's appointments,[120] we find some patterns worthy of closer examination.[121]

There is no obvious correlation between a particular party being involved in many disputes and it appointing the same arbitrator in several disputes. Some of the SGBs that are involved in the largest number of CAS disputes have a low concentration of arbitrator appointments. For example, in the decisions studied here, WADA is involved in 90 decisions but has appointed 31 different arbitrators and only one arbitrator was nominated by WADA in more than 15 percent of the disputes it was involved in.[122] Similarly, the IOC is a party in 39 disputes, it has appointed 20 different arbitrators, and has also only appointed one arbitrator in more than 15 percent of all disputes.[123] This distribution of nominations must overall be considered acceptable. Nor does there appear to be a natural connection between an arbitrator being frequently appointed to sit on CAS panels and he or she being a repeat arbitrator. Of the ten arbitrators with the largest number of appointments in the data, half have been appointed by at least one repeat party in more than 15 percent of the party's cases,[124] half have not.[125,126]

---

120 32 out of 270.

121 See below Fig. 8.12 *Repeat Parties and Arbitrators - Strong Relationships.*

122 This is the aforementioned Quentin Byrne-Sutton who WADA nominated in 15.6% of all CAS disputes included in the dataset.

123 The IOC nominated Dirk-Reiner Martens in 20.5% of all disputes.

124 Bernasconi, Carrard, Martens, Oswald, and Byrne-Sutton.

125 Haas, Beloff, Pinto, Fumagalli, and Coccia.

126 Compare above Fig. 8.1 *Decisions per Arbitrator* and below Fig. 8.12 *Repeat Parties and Arbitrators - Strong Relationships*

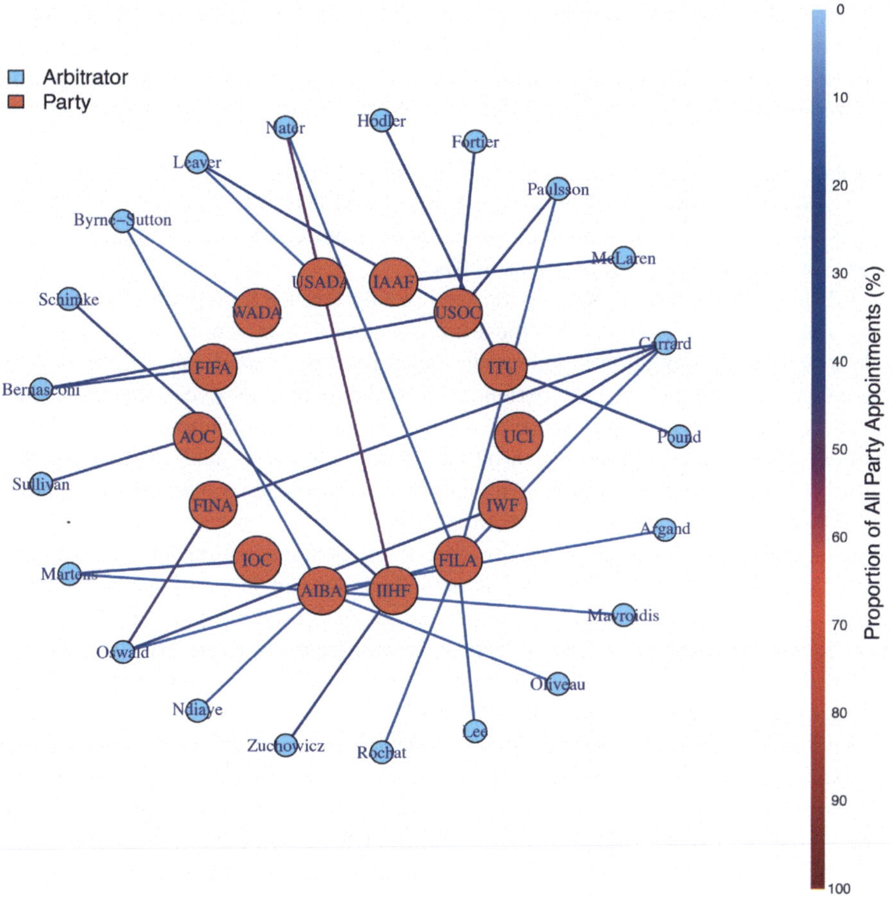

Fig. 8.12 Repeat Parties and Arbitrators - Strong Relationships. [*Source* The author]

Upon closer scrutiny, we find that some of the arbitrator-party relationships are perhaps not as strong as they appear at first glance. Even among what is here considered repeat-party SGBs, some are involved in a relatively low number of cases and for these parties the appointment of the same arbitrator in a few cases may have a large effect and it might be misleading to infer from this that the party has a strong preference for a particular arbitrator.[127]

[127] The most obvious example of this is the relationship between the International Ice Hockey Federation (IIHF) and the Swiss attorney Hans Nater who has received half of all IIHF's nominations. This is the strongest party-arbitrator relationship in the data. However, this may not mean much considering that in the collected data IIHF is only involved in four decisions and Nater has only been appointed twice.

There are however some party-arbitrator relationships that warrant closer scrutiny. For example, while UCI has appointed 21 different arbitrators it appointed Olivier Carrard in 37 percent of its disputes. Similarly, the international swimming federation, FINA, has appointed Denis Oswald in 45 percent of the disputes it was involved in. Both UCI and FINA are repeat CAS litigants with a relatively high number of disputes in the collected data.[128] Thus, it appears from the data that they have a relatively strong preference for Carrard and Oswald respectively. UCI and FINA are not alone in having such preferences. Both Carrard and Oswald are also quite frequently appointed by other SGBs.

It is important to clarify that a party having a preference for a particular arbitrator does not prove or even imply that the arbitrator cannot be or is not actually impartial and independent in relation to the appointing party. For example, the arbitrator may have a particular expertise or experience that make them attractive to the appointing party. It has also been suggested that when selecting which arbitrator to nominate, parties may want to appoint an arbitrator that understands and can explain the party's "culture" to the rest of the tribunal.[129] This may encourage SGBs to appoint arbitrators that have experiences inside SGBs.[130]

It is however worth emphasizing that there is harm in repeat nominations, regardless of whether the arbitrator is actually biased in favor of the nominating party. It is sufficient that they are perceived as biased or possibly biased.[131] Considering that the CAS list of approved arbitrators is relatively extensive, it seems that certain parties repeatedly nominating the same arbitrators unnecessarily damages the perceived impartiality of CAS.[132]

Thus far we have approached the phenomenon of repeat arbitrator appointments by examining to what extent parties reappoint the same arbitrator in multiple cases. However, an alternative approach is to examine when parties *do not* reappoint the same arbitrator. When selecting which arbitrator to nominate, a litigant that come before CAS is making a strategic decision, often after careful consideration and with the guidance of counsel. If we assume that parties are rational, they will want to select an arbitrator that improves their chances of success.[133] In making this decision, many CAS litigants will have limited information about different candidates' tendencies. One source of such information is however how panels that included a particular arbitrator ruled in previous cases. Repeat parties can in these situations draw on their experiences with individual arbitrators in previous

[128] The data contains 52 and 29 decisions where they appeared as parties respectively.

[129] Paulsson 2010, pp. 350–351.

[130] For example, both Denis Oswald and Olivier Carrard have extensive experience with working in SGBs.

[131] Vaitiekunas 2014, p. 196.

[132] Cf. Coccia 2013, p. 8; Kaufmann-Kohler and Rigozzi 2015, p. 199.

[133] Puig 2016, p. 16.

cases,[134] and it would be natural if repeat parties tended to re-appoint arbitrators that participated in deciding a case in their favor compared to those who sat on cases where the outcome was favorable to the opposing side. Such a tendency would not necessarily be an expression of a conscious, strategic process. It is natural and efficient to continue to behave in the same way, including when nominating arbitrators, as long as it leads to the desired outcome and to reconsider and shift behavior if the outcome was undesirable.

One way of testing for such tendencies is to compare the likelihood of the nominating party reappointing an arbitrator following a decision that was a "win" compared to a decision that was a "loss". Whether a CAS decision constitutes a win or loss is not always easy to determine, particularly in cases heard under the Ordinary Arbitration Procedure. However, in cases heard under the Appeals Arbitration Procedure it is reasonable to treat decisions that result in the appealed decisions being overturned as a win for the appellant and as a loss for the respondent. Conversely, CAS upholding the appealed decision should clearly be considered a loss for the appellant and a win for the respondent.[135]

The dataset includes information about 346 instances where a repeat-party SGB[136] was involved in an Appeals Arbitration Procedure, either as an appellant or as a respondent, that had a clear win/loss-outcome delivered by a panel consisting of three arbitrators, including one arbitrator nominated by the SGB. For each of these instances, we can examine whether that SGB reappointed the arbitrator in a subsequent case and, if so, how many other arbitrators that same SGB appointed before the arbitrator was reappointed, if any.[137] The latter measurement, which we can refer to as *reappointment distance*, is a measurement of how long it takes for an arbitrator to be reappointed. With this data, we can compare if repeat-party SGBs' tendencies to reappoint arbitrators vary depending on whether the panel on which he or she served delivered a decision that was favorable to the nominating SGB.

If we, first, treat all SGBs as a collective there does appear to be such a tendency, although only a rather weak one. SGB-appointed arbitrators that delivered SGB-advantageous decisions were subsequently reappointed by the same or another SGB in 72 percent of the cases. By comparison, arbitrators that delivered SGB-disadvantageous decisions were reappointed 65 percent of the time. It would also take the latter on average 50 percent longer than the former to be reappointed.[138] This finding is consistent with the proposition advanced above that

---

[134] The information is imperfect in both cases as the party-appointed arbitrator is only one of three members on a panel that issues a common decision.

[135] See also Chap. 10.

[136] These are the same SGBs presented above in Fig. 8.10 *Repeat Parties and Arbitrators - All Relationships.*

[137] It should be noted that because the dataset is incomplete, this information is also incomplete. This does not however impair the ability to compare the tendency towards repeat appointments after wins and losses within the dataset.

[138] See below Table 8.1 *Winning, Losing, and Reappointing.*

Table 8.1 Winning, Losing, and Reappointing. [*Source* The author]

	Decisions			Chance of reappointment (%)			Reappointment distance (Cases)		
	All	Wins	Losses	After win (%)	After loss (%)	Loss diff (%)	After win	After loss	Loss diff
All SGBs	346	219	127	72.1	64.6	−6.5	22.4	33.6	+11.2
ASADA	2	2	0	50					
AOC	4	3	1	0	0	0			
CONI	11	5	6	0	16.7	+16.7		1	
FIFA	64	41	23	46.3	47.8	−1.5	9.5	10	+0.5
FINA	22	12	10	83.3	60	−23.3	2.3	1	−1.2
FILA	5	2	3	0	0	0			
FIBA	5	2	3	0	0	0			
FEI	25	7	18	14.3	27.8	+13.5	6	2.4	−3.6
FIS	10	6	4	16.7	0	−16.7	1		
IAAF	17	12	5	25	0	−25	5		
IOC	20	14	6	35.7	33	−2.5	3	7	+4
ITF	13	5	8	20	25	+5	9	3.5	−5.5
IWF	5	1	4	0	0	0			
IIHF	3	1	2	0	0	0			
UCI	42	32	10	59.4	30	−29.4	2.8	1.3	−1.5
UEFA	28	16	12	18.8	41.7	+22.9	7	2.6	−4.4
USOC	2	2	0	50					
USADA	13	12	1	25	0	−25	5		
WADA	73	57	16	56.1	68.8	+12.7	5.8	12.8	+18.6

SGBs, like other parties, use their power to nominate arbitrators strategically to maximize their chances to win based on arbitrators' tendencies in the past.

However, the data does not clearly support the expectation that individual SGBs disfavor arbitrators that have previously participated in rendering decisions that were disadvantageous to them. Some repeat-party SGBs follow the SGBs overall tendency and show a slight tendency towards reappointment for arbitrators that have given them wins, some of them follow no clear tendency, and some repeat-party SGBs tend to favor reappointing arbitrators or to reappoint quicker after a loss than after a win.[139] The findings of this approach are thus essentially the same as the previous one: while some individual cases are worth looking into, there is little evidence of serious, systemic problems with repeat reappointments within CAS.

[139] Ibid.

8.8 The Compatriot Arbitrator

We previously concluded that arbitrators from certain nations are more frequently appointed to CAS panels,[140] and further below we will examine what this means for CAS jurisprudence.[141] In this section, we will explore another aspect of arbitrators' nationality, namely the issue of party-arbitrator nationality identity, that is the phenomenon of arbitrators having the same nationality as the parties to the dispute.

While some commentators believe that nationality ought not to be an important factor when selecting an arbitrator,[142] many researchers studying arbitration believe that parties to arbitration are in fact likely to appoint arbitrators of the same nationality as themselves, if given the opportunity.[143] Few seem to believe that arbitrators actually are partial towards parties of the same nationality as themselves,[144] or, conversely, impartial simply because they are of a different nationality than the parties.[145] There is however a concern that an arbitration panel will be perceived as less impartial if it contains arbitrators of the same nationality as one of the parties. To avoid unnecessary harm to the panel's perceived impartiality, many arbitration rules therefore contain rules that seek to support the "national neutrality" of the panel.[146] The scope of such national neutrality rules varies between systems, but many systems have rules that prevent or discourage the appointment of a sole arbitrator or panel president that is of the same nationality as either party.[147]

The CAS Rules contain no national neutrality rule,[148] and an arbitrator that is included on the CAS list can sit on a panel regardless if he or she is of the same nationality as either or both of the parties, including a nominating party, and this extends to sole arbitrators and panel presidents as well. Thus, if CAS parties tend to nominate arbitrators of the same nationality as themselves, this should be quite evident in the collected data. It is generally quite easy to define the geographical center of interest for natural persons (whether they are parties or arbitrators), clubs,

---

140 See above Sect. 8.3 and Fig. 8.2 *Arbitrator Appointments by Nationality.*

141 See Sect. 9.2.4.

142 Blackaby et al. 2015, p. 250; LaLive 1984, p. 25. For the sake of brevity, the term "nationality" is in this section used in a broad sense to include not only the citizenship and country of birth of natural persons, but also where they reside and the nation of incorporation and primary activity of legal persons.

143 See Lee 2008, p. 603 and sources cited. Cf. Bond 1991, p. 56 (expressing an unsupported impression that there may be regional differences in this regard). But see Franck 2007, p. 79 (finding no obvious correlation in investment Treaty arbitrations).

144 Cf. Blackaby et al. 2015, p. 250; LaLive 1984, p. 25.

145 Paulsson 2010, p. 352.

146 Blackaby et al. 2015, pp. 250–251; LaLive 1984, pp. 24–25; Zuberbühler et al. 2013, pp. 100–101.

147 See e.g. Article 6(7) UNCITRAL Rules; Article 6.1 LCIA Arbitration Rules; Article 13 ICC Rules of Arbitration; Article 20(b) WIPO Arbitration Rules; Article 1(3) ICSID Arbitration Rules.

148 See Article R40 CAS Code. Nor is this required under Swiss law. Zuberbühler et al. 2013, p. 100.

and national SGBs.[149] It is more difficult to place international SGBs geographically. They will therefore be disregarded when examining this issue.[150] The data allows us to test to what extent party-nominated arbitrators are of the same nationality as the party that nominated them or, if they are from different nations, the geographic distance between the two.[151]

In doing so, we find that CAS parties frequently tend to appoint arbitrators from the same nation as themselves: 27 percent of all CAS parties appoint an arbitrator from the same nation as themselves and there is no discernable difference in this regard between applicants and respondents. However, a closer examination of the data suggests that CAS parties' appointment preferences in this regard may be tied to distance rather than nationality per se. The data reveals that CAS parties tend to appoint arbitrators that are geographically near. Half of all arbitrators appointed to CAS were situated within 1,376 km of the party that nominated them,[152] and the likelihood that a party will nominate a particular arbitrator decreases quickly as the geographic distance between them increases.[153]

That CAS parties seemingly tend to appoint arbitrators based on distance rather than nationality is important if we want to understand why parties exhibit these tendencies. We can to some extent put ourselves in the minds of the appointing parties if we make the rather safe assumption that each party is self-interested and will as far as possible and to the best of its abilities use its appointment power to maximize its chances of success in the dispute at hand.[154] Not even the appointing parties appear to believe that a compatriot arbitrator will be biased in the party's favor or that appointing an arbitrator of the same nationality as themselves would in some other sense give them a distinct advantage in the adjudication of the dispute.[155] If parties do not believe that it helps them to appoint an arbitrator of the same nationality as themselves, it seems unlikely that they perceive arbitrators of the same nationality as the opposing party to be biased in the opposing party's favor. This casts some doubt over the necessity of national neutrality rules in international arbitration.

---

149 For the purpose of this study, this is for parties that are natural persons the nation of their citizenship (normally as designated by CAS in its decision); for clubs the nation where they are established; and for national federations the nation where they are active in organizing sport.

150 Switzerland is the nation with which most international SGBs have their closest connection, having either their seat or their principal activity in Switzerland.

151 In cases where several parties cooperate in appointing an arbitrator, e.g. as co-applicants, the shortest distance between any of the appointing parties and the appointed arbitrator was used. Google Maps Geocoding API was used to define the geographic position of and measure the distance between two actors.

152 I.e. the median distance. See also below Fig. 8.13 *Party-Arbitrator Distance*.

153 See below Fig. 8.13 *Party-Arbitrator Distance*.

154 Cf. Paulsson 2010, p. 350.

155 Cf. LaLive 1984, p. 26 ("If the nationality (or, to a lesser extent, the residence) is deemed relevant at all, it is because of its supposed implications: by an instinctive reaction, parties will generally assume without much further thought that a prospective arbitrator is likely, or even bound, to share his country's ideology and common values, if any.").

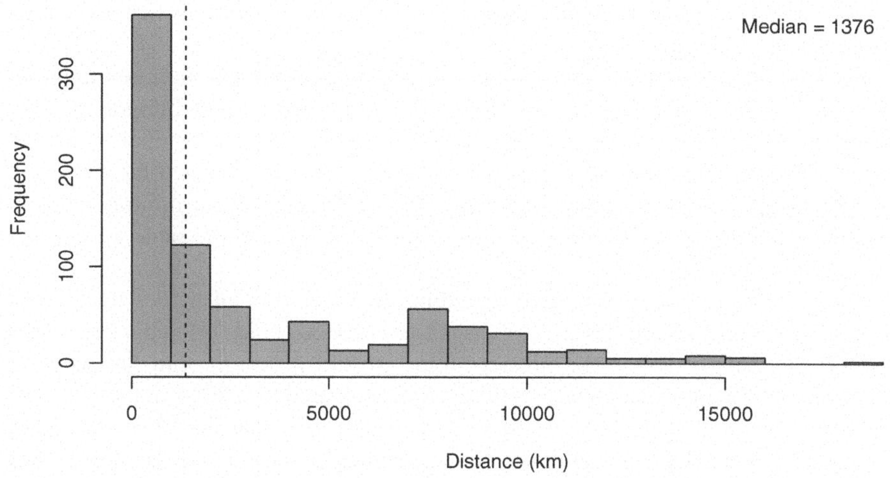

Fig. 8.13 Party-Arbitrator Distance (Color figure online). [*Source* The author]

The findings can also be read to suggest that national neutrality rules are by themselves insufficient to ensure completely equal, actual and perceived, opportunities of success as the parties seem to believe that there is a strategic advantage in appointing arbitrators that are geographically near them. The dominant explanation for why parties tend to appoint arbitrators of the same nationality is that they want to have at least one arbitrator on the panel that is familiar with the cultural, economic, and legal context in which the party is operating.[156] One commentator has expressed this as the nominating party hoping that "the party-appointed arbitrator serves as a cultural intermediary and translator."[157]

The findings above provide some support for this explanation. CAS parties tend to prefer arbitrators that are geographically proximate to themselves and this tendency applies not only to arbitrators from the same nation as the party but also, albeit to a decreasing extent, to arbitrators from nearby nations. The explanation above can explain this observation if we assume that geographically proximate nations are in general more similar in terms of culture, economics, and law than geographically distant nations. For example, it seems plausible that a CAS party from Sweden might view a Danish, Norwegian, or Finnish arbitrator as a "cultural intermediary" whose knowledge and insight on the panel would benefit the party. From this it follows that the current order, under which each party is given the opportunity to select one "cultural intermediary" on the tribunal, enhances CAS's

[156] See e.g. Bond 1991, p. 6; Franck 2007, p. 78; LaLive 1984, p. 26; Lee 2008, pp. 603–604; Paulsson 2010, pp. 350–351.

[157] Lee 2008, p. 604.

actual and perceived impartiality in a way that would be difficult to compensate through other measures.[158]

An obvious, alternative, and combinable explanation for the observed appointment tendencies is that CAS parties are more familiar with CAS arbitrators that are geographically proximate to themselves. Most parties will not be familiar with most of the arbitrators on the CAS list, particularly those that are situated far away, but they or their counsel are more likely to have knowledge of an arbitrator, or an institution that he or she is affiliated with, if they are active in the same geographic area as the party.

Finally, a comment is warranted regarding the tendencies of parties in different parts of the world of appointing compatriot arbitrators. Bond has suggested that a "non-Western party will make greater efforts to find a person with the requisite expertise and the same nationality as that party" compared to a Western party.[159] His argument for this, which follows the reasoning above, is that non-Western parties have a greater need for an arbitrator that understand their cultural, economic, and legal background than Western parties.[160] If Bond is correct, the average party-arbitrator distance would be lower for non-Western parties than Western parties. Although there is some variance between CAS parties of different nationalities, the opposite, if anything, appears to be true for CAS. The further away a party is from CAS, the more likely it is that the party will pick an arbitrator that is situated far away from the party. Thus, it appears as if European parties are less prone than other parties to appoint arbitrators from far away. This does not, however, necessarily mean that European parties are more culturally biased. One possible explanation that is consistent with these empirical observations is that CAS parties regardless of nationality favor qualified and experienced CAS arbitrators but that European CAS parties generally do not need to search as far away to find such arbitrators.[161]

8.9 The President Arbitrator

According to the CAS Code, if a CAS panel is to be composed of three arbitrators it shall be headed by an arbitrator acting as the panel's president. Under the Ordinary Arbitration Procedure, the general rule is that the two party-appointed arbitrators mutually agree on the third and final arbitrator that will act as the panel president.[162] The appointment process is slightly different under the Appeals Arbitration

[158] Adopting national neutrality rules would be insufficient and to create broader rules that ensure cultural neutrality seems, to me, quite difficult.

[159] Bond 1991, p. 6.

[160] Ibid. Cf. LaLive 1984, p. 26.

[161] The veracity of this explanation could perhaps be tested by comparing CAS to an arbitration tribunal where the seat and the arbitrators are less centred in Europe.

[162] Article R40.2 CAS Code. If the party-appointed arbitrators fail to reach an agreement, the third arbitrator is appointed by the president of the CAS Division. See also Sect. 2.3.

Procedure as the arbitrator appointed by the respondent nominates a panel president that is appointed by the CAS Division President after consulting both arbitrators.[163] Thus, the CAS Division President has more influence over the appointment of panel presidents under the appellate arbitration procedure, but under both procedures the party-appointed arbitrators wield significant influence over who is appointed as panel president.[164] One can consequently described CAS panel presidents as to some extent peer-selected.

But what factors guide arbitrators when selecting another arbitrator to sit as president in a panel on which they themselves serve? The fact that panel president appointments are not distributed equally but, like CAS arbitrator appointments generally,[165] follow a power law distribution clearly shows that certain arbitrators are more attractive than others when it comes to serving as panel presidents. Only about 100 unique arbitrators were appointed as panel presidents and barely 50 have been appointed more than twice. The distribution at the top end of the spectrum is also similar to CAS arbitration appointments with seventeen individuals receiving 52 percent of all president appointments.[166] Thus, CAS arbitrators and CAS Division Presidents seem to favor particular arbitrators when it comes to selecting panel presidents.

So, what is it about certain arbitrators that make them particularly attractive as panel presidents in the opinion of other arbitrators and CAS Division Presidents? It is highly unlikely that the preference for particular presidents are based on the outcome of the dispute since there are multiple factors that enhance the neutrality of the arbitrator.[167] Moreover, the efficacy of an outcome-based president appointment strategy is reduced by the fact that both the Division President and both party-appointed arbitrators are involved in the selection process. Thus, factors that cause other actors to prefer particular arbitrators as panel presidents most likely relate to personal qualities that can contribute to the arbitration procedure. That arbitrators prefer arbitrators that they view, simply put, as "high quality arbitrators" is not a radical proposal, but it is difficult to capture which factors affect the quality of an arbitrator as panel president in the opinion of his or her colleagues.

One factor that may conceivably contribute to the arbitrator's perceived quality is the extent of his or her experience as arbitrator. One could reasonably expect that

---

[163] Article R54 CAS Code. See also Sect. 2.3.

[164] It is difficult to say with certainty how frequently CAS departs from the general procedure described above. The matter has not been commented on in existing literature and in all of the 830 CAS decisions examined I only found a handful of cases where the Division President's role in the panel president appointment procedure was explicitly addressed. For example, in CAS 2011/A/2364, *Butt*, the parties agreed that CAS would appoint the panel president. Another example is the decision in CAS 2002/A/2731, *Ferreira*, para 22, where it appears that the CAS Division President was the one nominating the panel president. From the scarcity of such examples it appears that the general rules normally apply.

[165] See above Sect. 8.3.

[166] See below Fig. 8.14 *President Appointments and Other Appointments*.

[167] Cf. Paulsson 2010, pp. 350–351.

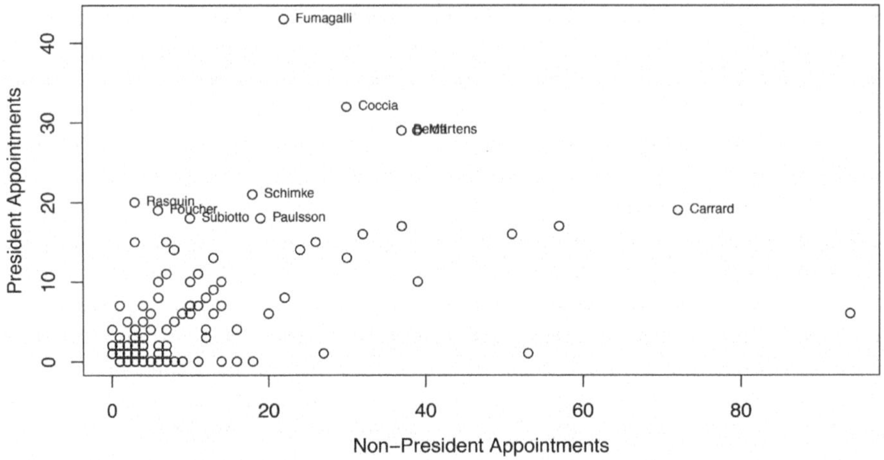

Fig. 8.14 President Appointments and Other Appointments. [*Source* The author]

there is a correlation between, on the one hand, the total number of panels that a CAS arbitrator have sat on and, on the other, the likelihood that he or she will be appointed as panel president. For example, it is clearly positive from the perspective of party-appointed arbitrators if the panel president, who directs the hearing,[168] has extensive prior experiences with arbitration, particularly if the party-appointed arbitrators are less experienced, and CAS Division Presidents are likely to share this sentiment.

One way to test whether this is correct is to compare how many times particular arbitrators have sat on CAS panels and how many times they have been appointed panel presidents.[169] There are some arbitrators that compared to other CAS arbitrators are frequently appointed to both president and non-president panel positions.[170] However, there is no clear correlation in the data between how many times a particular arbitrator has sat on CAS panels and how many times they have been appointed panel presidents. For example, whereas the CAS arbitrator with the most president appointments, Milanese law professor Luigi Fumagalli, has a significant but not quite outstanding number of non-president appointments, the arbitrator with the most non-president appointments, Michele Bernasconi, has a quite modest number of presidential appointments.[171] It also seems quite possible to become a leading CAS panel president without almost ever appearing in a non-president capacity. For example, Gérard Rasquin, an attorney from Luxembourg with an

[168] Article R58 CAS Code.

[169] To measure this, we compare how many times each arbitrator appears in a panel as the panel president to how many times they appear in another capacity.

[170] This is for example true for Carrard, Coccia, Martens, and Beloff.

[171] 93 non-president and 6 president appointments. The same is for example true for Oswald with 54 and 1 appointments respectively.

active involvement in sports generally,[172] was one of the most frequently appointed panel presidents for many years and is the sixth most frequently appointed panel president in the data overall. However, Rasquin only appeared twice in a non-president position.[173]

Thus, the correlation between presidential and non-presidential appointments appears weak. This also suggests that the qualities that make an individual arbitrator attractive as a party-appointed arbitrator are not necessarily the same qualities that makes one attractive as a party president and vice versa.

As discussed above, previous research conducted on other arbitration tribunals has shown that arbitrators' reputation and expertise have a significant impact on the selection process.[174] Many of the prominent panel presidents were involved in multiple early CAS cases that were high profile and/or had great impact on CAS jurisprudence,[175] often as panel presidents. While it is difficult to prove empirically, it seems quite reasonable that this may have contributed to increasing their reputation in the CAS arbitration community.[176] It has also been suggested that because of how arbitration tribunals work, arbitrators that work well with other arbitrators and that are willing to conform and compromise will have greater reputation in the arbitration community.[177] Unfortunately, it would require other methods and data than those used here to empirically test whether this can explain why certain arbitrators are appointed as panel presidents more frequently than others.

It can be noted, however, that some of the high co-appearance relationships identified above[178] are consistent with the thesis that arbitrators tend to re-nominate certain panel presidents. One clear example of this is the co-appearance of German arbitrator Reiner Klimke and the aforementioned Gérard Rasquin. In the decisions included in the dataset, Klimke appears on seven panels. In the first six, Rasquin was appointed panel president.[179] It can also be noted that in all but two of those cases,[180] the third arbitrator was Hans Ulrich Sutter. We should be careful not to

---

[172] Rasquin was an active athlete who, among other things, participated in the 1952 and 1956 Summer Olympic Games. He later became the president of the Luxembourg NOC (Comité Olympique et Sportif Luxembourgeois).

[173] See above Fig. 8.14 *President Appointments and Other Appointments*.

[174] See above Sect. 8.3.

[175] See Chap. 5.

[176] For example, Rasquin participated in e.g. CAS 92/63, *Gundel*, CAS 95/141, *Chagnaud*, and CAS 94/128, *UCI & CONI*; Coccia participated in e.g. CAS 98/200, *AEK Athens*, CAS 99/A/246, *Ward*, CAS 2000/A/274, *Susin*, CAS 2004/A/748, *Ekimov v. Hamilton*, and CAS 2005/A/830, *Squiazzato*; Martens participated in e.g. CAS 96/158, *Foschi* and CAS 2001/A/317, *Aanes*; Beloff participated in e.g. CAS 96/149, *Cullwick*, CAS 98/208, *Wang et al.*, CAS 98/211, *de Bruin*, CAS 99/A/234 and CAS 2000/A/270, *Meca-Medina I and II*, and CAS 2002/O/273, *Scott*.

[177] Puig 2016, p. 33 and sources cited.

[178] See above Sect. 8.4.

[179] CAS 91/56, *S v. FEI*; CAS 92/71, *SJ v. FEI*; CAS 92/73, *N v. FEI*; CAS 92/63, *Gundel*; CAS 92/86, *W v. FEI*; CAS 94/123, *Brandt Hagen*.

[180] CAS 92/71, *SJ v. FEI*; CAS 94/123, *Brandt Hagen*.

infer causation from correlation but considering the role of the party-appointed arbitrators in selecting the panel president and the high degree of overlap it seems very likely that Klimke and Sutter developed a preference for Rasquin as panel president.

The CAS Code allows for ICAS to "identify the arbitrators with a specific expertise to deal with certain types of disputes."[181] One possible use of this rule that has been seriously discussed is to create a list of presidents, that is a closed list of arbitrators that can be selected to sit as presidents on CAS panels. The main purpose of such a shift would be to promote consistency.[182] The fact that in practice only a quite exclusive group of arbitrators are appointed panel presidents suggests that the gain in consistent jurisprudence that such a reform may bring about may be quite limited. However, depending on how such a reform is carried out it may help enhance the perceived and actual impartiality of CAS panels.

8.10 The Sole Arbitrator

Under all forms of procedure before CAS it is possible to form a panel that only consists of one arbitrator, a so-called sole arbitrator. However, the rules suggest that the presumption for a three-arbitrator panel is stronger under the Appeals Arbitration Procedure compared to the Ordinary Arbitration Procedure.[183] Consequently, one would expect decisions by sole arbitrators to be more common in cases brought under the Ordinary Arbitration Procedure than in cases brought under the Appeals Arbitration Procedure. However, there is no significant difference based on procedure in the data: 13 percent of the decisions issued under Ordinary Arbitration Procedure were decided by a sole arbitrator and the same was true for decisions issued under Appellate Arbitration Procedure.

The procedure for appointing a sole arbitrator differs under the Ordinary and Appellate Arbitration Procedures. Under the Ordinary Arbitration Procedure, the sole arbitrator is, as a general rule, selected by the parties by mutual agreement,[184] whereas under the Appellate Arbitration Procedure it is the President of the Appellate Division that appoints the sole arbitrator.[185] This difference in appointment procedure provides an opportunity to examine whether there is a difference

[181] Article S6 CAS Code.

[182] Rigozzi et al. 2013, p. 5; Mitten 2014, pp. 78–79.

[183] Rules R40.1 (Ordinary Arbitration Procedure) and R50 (Appeal Arbitration Procedures) CAS Code.

[184] Article R40.2 CAS Code. However, if the parties cannot agree on a Sole arbitrator, one will be selected by the CAS Division president.

[185] Article R54 CAS Code.

between arbitrators that constitute good sole arbitrators in the opinion of CAS parties and in the opinion of CAS Division Presidents. Unfortunately, because the number of publicly available CAS decisions in Ordinary Arbitration Procedure cases is quite limited and only 13 percent of those were decided by a sole arbitrator, the size of the data sample is too limited to draw any empirically supported conclusions. It would however be a valuable study to conduct if more CAS decisions become publicly available in the future.

References

Blackaby N, Partasides C, Redfern A, Hunter M (2015) Redfern and Hunter on International Arbitration, 6th edn. Oxford University Press, Oxford

Blackshaw I (2012) Introductory Remarks. In: Wild A (ed) CAS and Football: Landmark Cases. T.M.C. Asser Press, The Hague, pp. 5–10

Bond S (1991) The International Arbitrator: From the Perspective of the ICC International Court of Arbitration. Northwestern Journal of International Law and Business 12(1):1–22

Cavalieros P, Kim J (2015) Can the Arbitral Community Learn from Sports Arbitration? Journal of International Arbitration 32(2):237–260

Coccia M (2013) The jurisprudence of the Swiss Federal Tribunal on challenges against CAS awards. CAS Bulletin 2013(2):2–17

de Weger F (2016) The Jurisprudence of the FIFA Dispute Resolution Chamber. T.M.C. Asser Press, The Hague

Dezalay Y, Garth B (1996) Dealing in Virtue: International Commercial Arbitration and the Construction of a Transnational Legal Order. The University of Chicago Press, Chicago

Drahozal C (2005) Behavioral Analysis of Arbitral Decision Making. In: Drahozal C, Naimark R (eds) Towards a Science of International Arbitration: Collected Empirical Research. Kluwer Law International, The Hague, pp. 319–337

Duval A (2013) Lex Sportiva: A Playground for Transnational Law. European Law Journal 19(6):822–842

Duval A (2015) La Lex Sportiva Face au Droit de l'Union Européenne: Guerre et Paix dans l'Espace Juridique Transnational. Academic thesis, European University Institute, Florence

Franck S (2007) Empirically Evaluating Claims About Investment Treaty Arbitration. North Carolina Law Review 86:1–88

Franck S, Freda J, Lavin K, Lehmann T, van Aaken A (2015) Diversity Challenge: Exploring the 'Invisible College' of International Arbitration. Columbia Journal of Transnational Law 53:429–506

Giordetti C (2013) Who Decides Who Decides in International Investment Arbitration? University of Pennsylvania Journal of International Law 35:431–486

Gorbylev S (2013) A short story of an athlete: Does he question independence and impartiality of the Court of Arbitration for Sport? The International Sports Law Journal 13:294–298

Kaufmann-Kohler G, Rigozzi A (2015) International Arbitration: Law and Practice in Switzerland. Oxford University Press, Oxford

LaLive P (1984) On the Neutrality of the Arbitrator and of the Place of Arbitration. In: Reymond C, Bucher E (eds) Swiss Essays on International Arbitration. Schulthess, Zürich, pp. 23–33

Latour B (2010) The Making of Law: An Ethnography of the Conseil d'Etat. Brilman M, Pottage A (transl). Polity, Cambridge

Latty F (2007) La lex sportiva: Recherche sur le droit transnational. Martinus Nijhoff, Leiden

Lee I (2008) Practice and Predicament: The Nationality of the International Arbitrator (with Survey Results). Fordham International Law Journal 31:603–633

Mavromati D, Reeb M (2015) The Code of the Court of Arbitration for Sport: Commentary, Cases and Materials. Wolters Kluwer, Alphen aan den Rijn

McAuliffe W, Rigozzi A (2013) Sports Arbitration. The European, Middle Eastern and African Arbitration Review 2013:15–22

Mitten M (2014) The Court of Arbitration for Sport and its Global Jurisprudence: International Legal Pluralism in a World Without National Boundaries. CAS Bulletin 2014(2):48–79

Nafziger J (2004) Lex Sportiva. The International Sports Law Journal 2004(1–2):3–8

Paulsson J (2010) Moral Hazard in International Dispute Resolution. ICSID Review 25(2): 339–335

Pauwelyn J (2015) The Rule of Law Without the Rule of Lawyers? Why Investment Arbitrators Are From Mars, Trade Adjudicators Are From Venus. The American Journal of International Law 109(4):761–805

Puig S (2014) Social Capital in the Arbitration Market. The European Journal of International Law 25(2):387–424

Puig S (2016) Blinding International Justice. Virginia Journal of International Law 56(3):647–700

Reeb M (2002) The Court of Arbitration for Sport: History and Operation. In: Reeb M (ed) Digest of CAS Awards II. Kluwer Law International, The Hague, pp. xxiii–xxx

Reeb M (2004) The Court of Arbitration for Sport: History and Operation. In: Reeb M (ed) Digest of CAS Awards III. Kluwer Law International, The Hague, pp. xxvii–xxxv

Rigozzi A (2010) Challenging Awards of the Court of Arbitration for Sport. Journal of International Dispute Settlement 1(1):217–265

Rigozzi A, Hasler E, Quinn B (2013) The 2011, 2012 and 2013 revisions to the Code of Sports-related Arbitration. Jusletter 3 June 2013

Slaoui F-Z (2009) The Rising Issue of 'Repeat Arbitrators': A Call for Clarification. Arbitration International 25(1):103–119

Swigart L, Terris D (2015) Who are International Judges? In: Romano C, Alter K, Shany Y (eds) The Oxford Handbook of International Adjudication. Oxford University Press, Oxford, pp. 619–638

Vaitiekunas A (2014) The Court of Arbitration for Sport: Law-making and the question of independence. Stämpfli Verlag, Bern

Zuberbühler T, Müller C, Habegger P (2013) Swiss Rules of International Arbitration, 2nd edn. Schulthess, Zürich

Chapter 9
The Characteristics of CAS Arbitrators

Abstract The Court of Arbitration for Sport (CAS) exercises considerable influence, not only over the outcome of individual disputes that come before it, but also over the development of international sports law, and because they wield this influence, it matters who the arbitrators are. It is important for CAS's legitimacy that it involves a diverse set of arbitrators that is representative of those who are affected by it. In an international adjudicatory institution like CAS, that uses arbitrators from around the world, it is also important to consider if and to what extent the legal tradition in which they are trained or the languages that they understand affect how they behave as CAS arbitrators. This chapter explores the arbitrators' characteristics and how they affect CAS.

9.1 Who the Arbitrators Are and Why It Matters

In the previous chapter, we studied arbitrators through a relational lens, focusing on how they interact with each other, directly by serving on the same panels and indirectly by reading and referring to each other's decisions, and with the parties that come before the Court of Arbitration for Sport (CAS). This chapter continuous the examination of the arbitrators by focusing on their backgrounds and personal characteristics.

Why should we care about the characteristics of CAS arbitrators? A first reason why the issue is worth exploring is that it is both possible and likely that the arbitrator's characteristics influence how he or she behaves when deciding cases in CAS, at least in some ways and to some extent. Lawyers generally value objectivity and do their best not to be colored by their personal experiences and views. However, lawyers are not machines and few would seriously challenge that the background and personal characteristics of a judge has an impact on his or her behavior in the judicial role.[1] While personal background matters in all forms of

[1] Swigart and Terris 2015, pp. 620–621.

J. Lindholm, *The Court of Arbitration for Sport and Its Jurisprudence*,
ASSER International Sports Law Series,
https://doi.org/10.1007/978-94-6265-285-9_9

adjudication, difference in personal background can be particularly strong and important in international dispute resolution institutions.[2]

Second, this raises some related, complex, and sensitive questions such as whether the judge's personal characteristics is or can be a strength or a liability and whether actions should be taken to curb or control such tendencies. If we acknowledge that background and individual characteristics may impact how a person acts as a judge or arbitrator, this raises some potentially serious concerns regarding the objectivity, consistency, and foreseeability of the adjudicatory system.[3] Because law is interpreted and applied by humans we must accept that the judicial process is not and cannot be perfectly consistent and objective. This is true in sports law as well as in other sectors.

Third, one aspect of arbitrator characteristics is diversity or, more precisely, the potential lack of diversity. Who has a voice in CAS and who does not is an important question because it affects which perspectives and views are considered and which are not.[4] It also seriously impacts the perceived legitimacy of the institution.[5] That European arbitrators in general and Swiss arbitrators in particular are heavily overrepresented in CAS is an example of a diversity problem.[6] The fact that the lack of diversity among CAS arbitrators is in part related to a lack of diversity among CAS parties does not mitigate these problems.[7] CAS establishes precedents of international sports law with a global impact and "arbitrators who make decisions of public importance should reflect the make-up of those affected by their decisions."[8]

Arbitration tribunals are frequently criticized for lacking diversity, seemingly not entirely without basis.[9] International arbitrators, particularly those active in commercial arbitration, have been described as a homogenous group of elite, capitalist, male, and "white-shoe" lawyers;[10] an "old boys club";[11] and "pale, male, and stale."[12] There are however indications that the characteristics of the typical international arbitrator more recently has started shifting and that they are becoming younger, less male, and less Western.[13] It is relevant to explore to what extent CAS has followed these trends and achieved real "democratization of the invisible

[2] See Terris et al. 2007, pp. 207–209.

[3] Schachter 1977, pp. 218–219.

[4] Cf. Swigart and Terris 2015, p. 622.

[5] Franck et al. 2015.

[6] See Sect. 8.3.

[7] See Sect. 10.5. See also Sect. 8.8.

[8] Van Harten 2012, p. 1.

[9] See e.g. Giordetti 2013, esp. pp. 458–461; Franck et al. 2015.

[10] Puig 2016, p. 655 (quoting Elizabeth Warren).

[11] Swigart and Terris 2015, p. 635.

[12] Franck et al. 2015, p. 452 (quoting Sarah Francois-Poncet).

[13] Swigart and Terris 2015, pp. 636–637.

college."[14] Regardless of whether diversity among arbitrators actually contribute to making the decisions that come out of CAS qualitatively better, a CAS that is perceived by other actors as inclusive and representative is more likely to be viewed as legitimate, credible, and authoritative.[15] Presenting the demography of CAS arbitrators, the characteristics of the individuals that are involved in CAS's activities, is thus an important task in and of itself.[16]

There is an infinite number of factors that can be said to describe arbitrators' characteristics and to study the characteristics of the arbitrators necessarily requires selecting certain relevant factors to examine. The examination in this chapter focuses on seven factors: gender, age, experience working in CAS, professional background, geographical origin, the dominant legal tradition in that region, and language. The relevance of these factors will be discussed in greater detail below.[17]

For the vast majority of all CAS arbitrators, the data for the first five factors were extracted from the description of the arbitrators available on CAS's website.[18] In some cases the relevant data was not available from that website. In those cases, the information was extracted from other publicly available sources, two primary sources being news articles and presentations on websites of law firms where the arbitrators work. The database of legal systems and legal traditions compiled by the University of Ottawa JuriGlobe research group was used as the basis for the final two factors.[19]

Another methodological issue in this context is deciding which arbitrators to consider. One possible approach would be to study all CAS arbitrators that are included on the CAS list. Who is included on the CAS list is of course important as only individuals that are on the list can appear on CAS panels. However, the issues that were outlined above and that this chapter seeks to explore concern the actual composition of CAS rather than its potential composition and as discussed many CAS arbitrators rarely or never actually participate on CAS panels. We will therefore study the appointed arbitrators rather than the appointable arbitrators.[20]

As described above, one of the primary objectives of this chapter is to describe to what extent individuals with different backgrounds and characteristics are represented in CAS, but we will also in some regards be exploring the question of whether those backgrounds and characteristics impact their judicial behavior. This is a difficult question that cannot be definitively answered within the framework of this study, among other reasons because "judicial behavior" is an ambiguous and

---

[14] See Alvarez 2007.

[15] See e.g. Schachter 1977, pp. 222–223; Swigart 2010.

[16] For examples from arbitration generally, see Dezalay and Garth 1996; Franck et al. 2015.

[17] It can be noted that this follows existing research of international judges, see e.g. Swigart and Terris 2015, and international arbitrators, see e.g. Franck et al. 2015.

[18] http://www.tas-cas.org/en/arbitration/list-of-arbitrators-general-list.html, accessed 7 September 2018.

[19] Fathally and Mariani 2008.

[20] See Sects. 8.2–8.3.

elusive concept. The collected data does however offer an opportunity to test whether there is a correlation between, on the one hand, the above-stated characteristics of CAS arbitrators and, on the other hand, certain quantifiable characteristics of the decisions that they participated in delivering. Thus, it is possible to test if there are significant differences between CAS decisions authored by CAS arbitrators having different characteristics and to explore whether and to what extent certain arbitrator characteristics is evident in their decisions. However, it is important to note that findings made in that context must be understood against this particular backdrop, and it is worth emphasizing that this text does not purport to make general descriptive claims about the judicial behavior of individuals belonging to particular groups or, even less, about the appropriateness or advantageousness of such tendencies.

9.2 Demographics of CAS Arbitrators

9.2.1 Age

A common stereotype of international arbitrators is that they are relatively old.[21] For example, in 1996 Dezaley and Garth described "generational warfare" among international arbitrators where a dominant group of "grand old men" were challenged by "young technocrats".[22] According to the authors, this process started in the late 1970s and 1980s.[23] CAS properly established itself at the turn of the last century,[24] thereby presumably largely by-passing the generational shift in international arbitration described by Dezaley and Garth. Indeed, Jan Paulsson, who Dezaley and Garth describe as "a leading member of the new generation,"[25] is one of CAS's most experienced and established arbitrators.[26]

The fact that a new generation of arbitrators have gradually taken over does not however necessarily mean that they are particularly young. In 2015, Franck et al. surveyed 548 members of the International Council for Commercial Arbitration (ICCA) and found that the median respondent was 54 years old, which made them six years older than the median arbitration counsel.[27] It is not a given that those who specialize in commercial arbitration and sports arbitration are of similar age, but the findings by Franck et al. can nevertheless serve as a sort of benchmark against which we can compare CAS arbitrators.

---

[21] See e.g. Giordetti 2013, p. 458.

[22] Dezaley and Garth 1996, pp. 20, 34–41.

[23] Ibid., pp. 36–37.

[24] See Sect. 3.3.

[25] Dezaley and Garth 1996, p. 37.

[26] See Fig. 8.1 *Decisions per Arbitrator*.

[27] Franck et al. 2015, pp. 452–453.

Due to differences in underlying data and methodology it is difficult to perfectly replicate the study of Franck et al. for CAS. A close alternative however is to consider how the age of the CAS arbitrators that appear in the data was distributed at the end of the period studied.[28] In doing so, we find that CAS arbitrators are even older than the respondents of Franck et al. with a median age of 63.[29]

A reasonable methodological objection that can be raised against this approach is that the data includes arbitrators that are no longer active. Relatedly but more generally, one could argue that when studying the demographics of CAS arbitrators we should consider not just the age of the arbitrators as such but also take into consideration how frequently they actually appear on CAS panels. Both of these points can be resolved by using the age of each appointed arbitrator at the time of appointment.

This confirms that the first approach includes arbitrators that are no longer active. It is very rare that arbitrators that sit on CAS panels are more than 70 years old at the time when the panel makes its decision. However, it also reveals that it is rare that arbitrators making decisions in CAS are younger than 40 years old and that the age of participating CAS arbitrators at the time of the decision clusters quite closely around a median age of 54 years.[30] This approach suggests that sports arbitrators are comparable in age to commercial arbitrators based on the findings of Franck et al.

Finally, it has been suggested that the membership of the college of international judges and arbitrators have become increasingly younger over time.[31] There is no

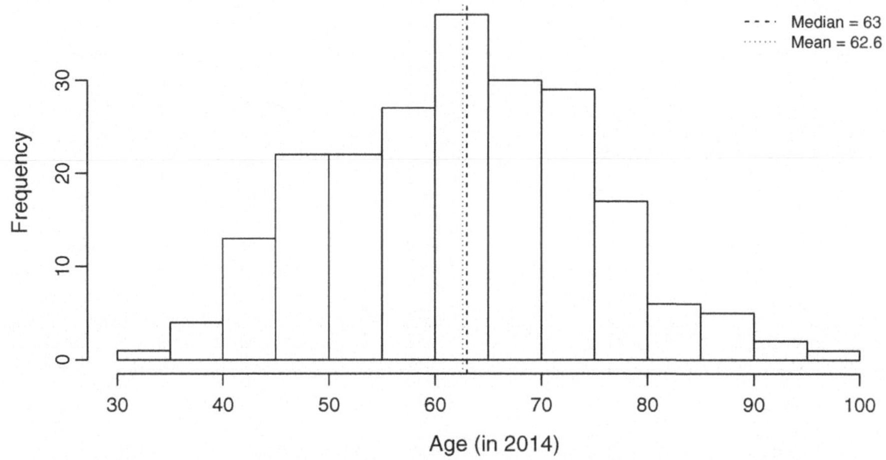

Fig. 9.1 Age Distribution of Appointed Arbitrators. [*Source* The author]

[28] This would essentially represent taking a survey among all CAS arbitrators in 2014 and having all those who had ever been appointed in a published CAS decision answer the survey.

[29] See above Fig. 9.1 *Age Distribution of Appointed Arbitrators.*

[30] See below Fig. 9.2 *Age Distribution of Arbitrators When Deciding.*

[31] Swigart and Terris 2015, p. 637.

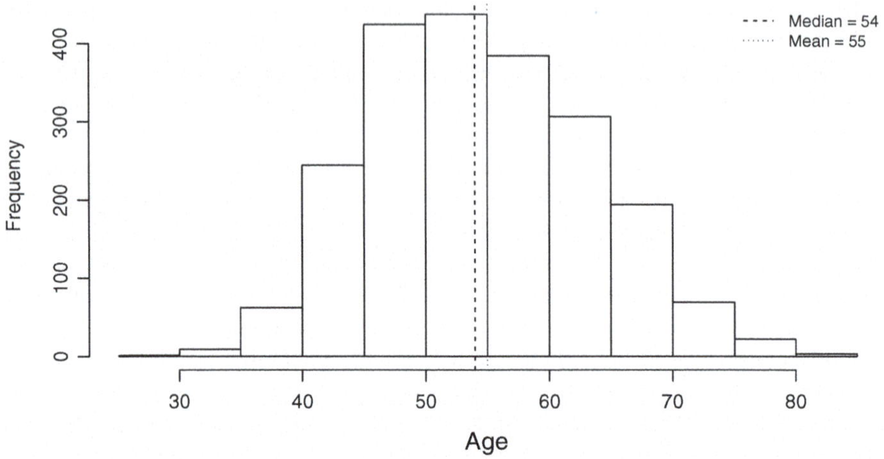

Fig. 9.2 Age Distribution of Arbitrators when Deciding. [*Source* The author]

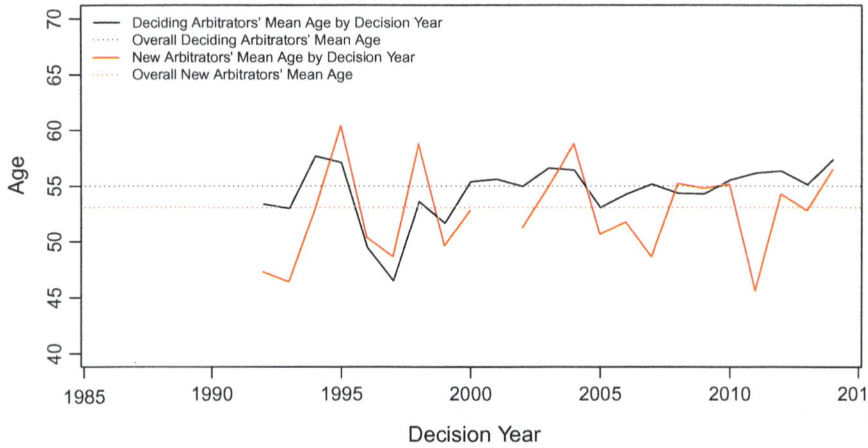

Fig. 9.3 Mean Age of Deciding CAS Arbitrators Over Time. [*Source* The author]

clear support in the data for such a trend among CAS arbitrators. The average age of a CAS arbitrator at the time of a CAS decision on a year-to-year basis has remained rather stabile around 55 over time. There are no clear indications of a significant influx of younger arbitrators, nor is there a clear tendency that new arbitrators that are joining CAS are significantly younger than their more experienced colleagues or that they have become younger over time.[32]

[32] See above Fig. 9.3 *Mean Age of Deciding CAS Arbitrators Over Time.*

9.2.2 Gender

As described in the preceding section, international arbitrators are viewed as being predominantly male, particularly so when it comes to the top arbitrators that receive the majority of all appointments. When it comes to commercial arbitration, this view has been substantiated by empirical evidence. Around 5 percent of the arbitrators that resolve investments disputes within the International Centre for Settlement of Investment Disputes (ICSID) are women and this has not increased significantly over the last decade.[33] However, in some arbitration institutions female arbitrators have over time received an increased portion of all appointments and in some institutions about 15 percent of the appointed arbitrators are women. While the portion of female judges in the national judiciaries vary considerably between nations, they are almost universally significantly higher than the portion of female arbitrators in international arbitration tribunals.[34]

Sadly, the gender representation among arbitrators in CAS is not only comparable to that of other arbitration tribunals, it is arguably worse. Only 20 of the 230 unique arbitrators that appear in the collected decisions, or less than 9 percent, are women. However, these 20 women have overall also received a smaller share of the appointments than their male colleagues as evidenced by the fact that only 3.5 percent of all arbitrator appointments in CAS went to female arbitrators. That female arbitrators will receive a smaller than proportional share of all appointments is not a given. For example, one study showed that while 5 percent of all appointed ICSID arbitrators were female they received 7 percent of the appointments.[35]

There appears to be a general trend to increase the number of female judges in national and international courts, often driven by a deliberate movement,[36] and studies have found that more than a quarter of all judges in international courts are women.[37] As outlined above, arbitration tribunals are lagging behind international courts when it comes to achieving gender-equal representation,[38] but at least some

[33] Franck 2007; Giordetti 2013, pp. 459–460; Puig 2014, p. 405; Van Harten 2012; Greenwood and Baker 2015.

[34] For example, the percentage of female judges varies significantly between countries, between 61 and 74% in France depending on the stage of the career (Boigeol 2013, p. 126 (2009 numbers)), 51–57% in Sweden depending on the stage of the career (statistics from Domstolsverket (2014 numbers)), 23–30% in Switzerland depending on the stage of the career (Ludewig and LaLlave 2013, p. 235 (2000 numbers)), 30% in Australia (Mack and Roach Anleu 2013, p. 212 (2009 numbers)), and 26% in the United States (Kenney 2013, p. 426 (2009 numbers)).

[35] Puig 2014, p. 406.

[36] See e.g. Kenney 2013 (regarding e.g. Canada); SOU 2003:102, p. 411 (regarding Sweden); Swigart and Terris 2015, p. 624 (regarding international courts).

[37] Swigart and Terris 2015, p. 624.

[38] Van Harten 2012, p. 2.

institutions appear to make real improvements. Again sadly, CAS does not appear to be among those institutions. While female arbitrators appear in the collected decisions in every year since 2002, there is no clear trend towards an increased share of female arbitrators delivering decisions during the studied period.[39]

While structural factors may cause women to be underrepresented in international arbitration,[40] these findings cannot be explained by a lack of willing and active female CAS arbitrators in the arbitrator pool as the number of unique appointed female arbitrators in the data increased from four to twenty individuals between 2004 and 2014. If arbitrator appointments were distributed equitably with regard to gender, those twenty individuals would have received 9 percent of the appointments during the latter parts of the period.[41] Researchers point to the arbitration parties' lack of interest in increased diversity as an important factor when explaining the limited improvement.[42] It is true that ICAS has included a greater share of female arbitrators on the CAS list and that CAS as an institution has very limited influence over which arbitrators the parties decide to appoint. CAS does however, through its Division Presidents, exert significant influence over the

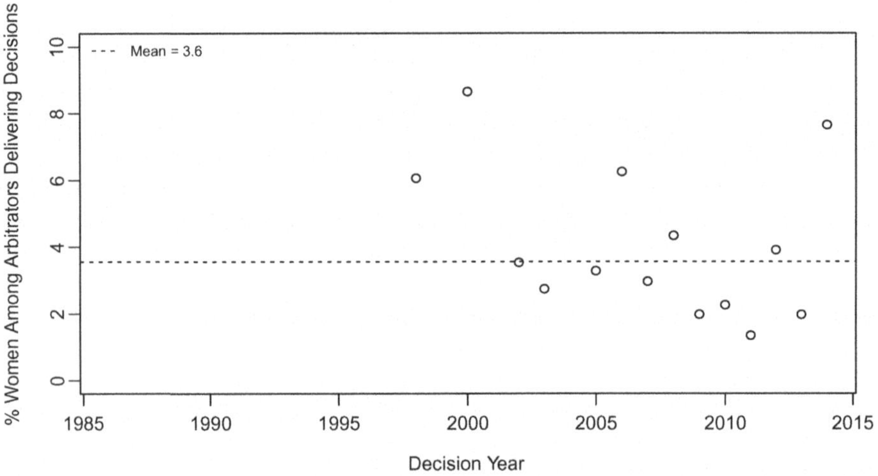

Fig. 9.4 Female Arbitrators Over Time. [*Source* The author]

---

[39] See above Fig. 9.4 *Female Arbitrators Over Time*. For example, a total of 148 (non-unique) arbitrators participated on the panels that delivered the 54 CAS decisions that were decided in 2011 included in the dataset. Of those 148 arbitrators only 2, or 1.4%, were female.

[40] Greenwood and Baker 2015, pp. 418–420; Van Harten 2012, p. 2.

[41] The inequitable distribution of appointments could allow this group to potentially receive a higher share of the appointments. By comparison, the twenty most frequently appointed male CAS arbitrators have received 49.3% of all appointments in the data.

[42] Giordetti 2013, pp. 459–460; Greenwood and Baker 2015, p. 420.

appointment of panel presidents, particularly in appeals cases, and yet only 2.6 percent of all panel presidents in the dataset were women. Thus, the share of panel president appointments that are given to female CAS arbitrators is even smaller than their share of the party appointments. CAS also exerts considerable influence over the appointment of sole arbitrators and of the CAS decisions decided by a sole arbitrator included in the data, only a single one was decided by a female sole arbitrator.[43] There is thus significant room for improvement.

9.2.3 Professional Background

The typical CAS arbitrator is, unsurprisingly, a practicing attorney that works in a law firm and offers his or her legal services to the public. While some are arbitration specialists, almost all CAS arbitrators extensively combine their work as CAS arbitrators with other business, including serving as arbitrators in other arbitration tribunals and as arbitration counsels.

Perhaps somewhat more surprising is the quite prominent presence of legal academics among CAS arbitrators. 30 percent of CAS arbitrators have a substantial background in academia and many of these hold permanent university positions.[44] CAS arbitrators with a legal academic background are also slightly overrepresented in terms of appointments, receiving 39 percent of all appointments in the studied decisions. Differently phrased, CAS arbitrators with an academic background on average receive about 32 percent more appointments than the average CAS arbitrator.[45] Since most CAS arbitrators are party-appointed, this could indicate that parties that come before CAS have a preference for arbitrators with an academic background. If so, there are several possible explanations, including that they appear particularly knowledgeable, that their academic status provides them with a certain legitimacy, or that these arbitrators' scholarly work increases their name recognition among CAS litigants.

By comparison, CAS arbitrators that have a background as a judge[46] or a public official[47] receive a lower than average number of appointments. CAS decisions delivered by arbitrators that have such backgrounds also cite fewer and/or less important previous CAS decisions. Practicing attorneys cite more previous decisions, but not necessarily more important previous decisions.[48] In all other regards,

---

43 CAS 2014/A/3861, *Izaguirre*.

44 Sometimes in combination with being practicing attorneys.

45 See below Table 9.1 *Arbitrator Professional Background*.

46 In most cases as judges in national courts.

47 E.g. serving as ministers of national governments or high-level bureaucrats.

48 Importance here defined using network centrality. See also Sect. 5.3.

Table 9.1 Arbitrator Professional Background. [*Source* The author]

	Individuals	Appointments		Persuasive power		Precedential power	
		Total	Mean	Mean outdegree	Mean HubScore	Mean indegree	Mean PageRank
All arbitrators	229	2,195	9.5	3.32	0.065	2.40	0.00088
Attorneys	184	1,795	9.8	3.52*	0.066	2.36	0.00085
Academics	68	855	12.6	3.12	0.065	2.29	0.00093
Judges	39	270	6.9	2.59*	0.047**	1.86	0.00089
Public officials	16	105	6.5	2.22*	0.053	1.91	0.00083
Sport officials	69	662	9.6	3.05	0.053	1.90	0.00084

$*p \leq 0.05$, $**p \leq 0.01$, $***p \leq 0.001$

the professional background of the participating arbitrators does not appear to significantly impact the persuasive or precedential power of the decision.[49]

9.2.4 Geographic Origin

CAS is and has since its creation been characterized as an international arbitration tribunal.[50] One aspect of the international character of CAS is that it is intended to resolve what can broadly be referred to as “international disputes”, but a dispute can be “international” in different regards. CAS is undoubtedly an international arbitration tribunal in the sense that it resolves disputes in connection with or arising during international sporting events, such as the Olympic Games. A different aspect, which will be explored in greater detail below, is whether disputes adjudicated by CAS involve litigants based in different nations.[51] A third aspect is to what extent CAS can be characterized as an international arbitration tribunal in the sense that it is composed of a geographically diverse group of arbitrators. This last aspect is the object of examination in this section.

ICAS has sought to ensure geographic diversity. In creating the list of CAS arbitrators, “ICAS tries to ensure fair representation of continents and different legal cultures.”[52] This ambition has resulted in a situation where there are several CAS-eligible arbitrators from every continent appearing on the CAS list.[53] However, CAS appointments are not distributed equally among all eligible individuals and in

[49] See above Table 9.1 *Arbitrator Professional Background.*

[50] See e.g. Reeb 1998, pp. xxiii–xxxiv.

[51] See further Sect. 10.5.

[52] Mavromati and Reeb 2015, p. 266.

[53] 24 from Africa, 53 from North America, 7 from Central America and the Caribbean, 17 from South America, 43 from Asia, 195 from Europe, and 30 from Oceania. http://www.tas-cas.org/fileadmin/user_upload/Liste_des_arbitres_par_nationalite__2017_.pdf (accessed 26 May 2017).

practice a relatively small group of CAS arbitrators receive the vast majority of all appointments whereas most CAS arbitrators receive few or no appointments.[54] Thus, while a geographically diverse list of eligible arbitrators is necessary to achieve real geographic diversity on CAS panels, it is not necessarily sufficient.

The data reveals that there is significant room for improving the geographic diversity when it comes to appointments at CAS. Of the 2,194 arbitrator appointments found in the studied CAS decisions, more than 77 percent went to arbitrators based in Europe,[55] and arbitrators from Europe, Oceania, and North America collectively received 94 percent of all CAS appointment. By comparison, less than 4 percent of the appointments went to arbitrators based in Asia.[56] This disparity comes across as particularly strong when one considers that Asia has nearly ten times the population of Europe. There is thus clearly no correlation between how many people live in a particular part of the world and their representation among appointed CAS arbitrators.[57]

This is potentially problematic. As discussed above, lack of diversity generally risks damaging the legitimacy of CAS and its jurisprudence.[58] A lack of geographic diversity is potentially particularly damaging as it risks creating a perception in the rest of the world of CAS adjudication as a Western-imposed process over which non-Western nationals have limited influence.[59]

However, a closer examination of the data cautions against simply describing CAS as a "Western judiciary". Reality is a little more complex. For example, while the number of appearances by American CAS arbitrators seems disproportionally high compared to the number of appearances by Chinese and Indian CAS arbitrators, it seems surprisingly low compared to the number of appearances by Canadian, British, and German arbitrators. This is particularly unanticipated considering that American arbitrators dominate many other international arbitration tribunals.[60]

Also, focusing too much on population size may be misleading. In order to better understand why arbitrators from certain nations appear particularly frequently on CAS panels it is reasonable to take into consideration the nationality of the parties that come before CAS. After all, as discussed above, parties that come before CAS has a tendency to appoint arbitrators that are geographically proximate to themselves.[61] If we compare the number of appearances of arbitrators from a particular nation to the number of appearances of parties from the same nation, there appears to be some

[54] See Sect. 8.3.

[55] 1,706 of 2,194.

[56] 84 of 2,194. Israeli arbitrator Efraim Barak, who is one of CAS's most frequently appointed arbitrators, see Sect. 8.3, received 41 of those 84 appointments.

[57] See below Fig. 9.5 *Arbitrator Appearances by Nation and Nation Population*.

[58] See above Sect. 9.1.

[59] Cf. Franck et al. 2015, pp. 468–469; Swigart and Terris 2015, p. 623 (discussing international arbitration generally).

[60] Franck et al. 2015, p. 459; Puig 2014, p. 406.

[61] See Sect. 8.8.

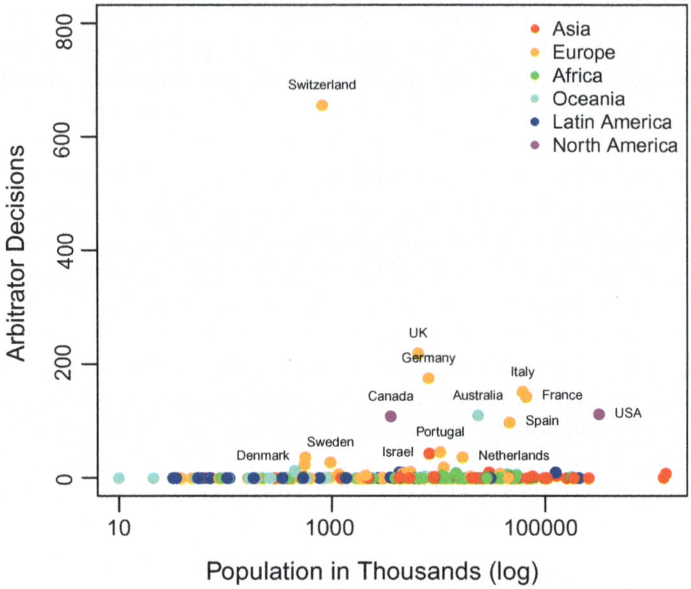

Fig. 9.5 Arbitrator Appearances by Nation and Nation Population. [*Source* The author]

correlation between the two,[62] particularly if we for these purposes treat Switzerland as the home of international sports governing bodies (SGBs).[63]

That there is a high number of appearances of CAS arbitrators from Europe, America, Canada, and Australia relative to population size can thus, at least in part, be attributed to the fact that most of the litigants that come before CAS are from there. This finding is in one way redeeming for CAS since to describe it as an institution where Western arbitrators decide cases concerning non-Western parties would be unfounded, at least in general and on an aggregate level. If we for the purposes of this analysis treat international SGBs as European entities, European and Oceanian arbitrators are slightly overrepresented and Asian arbitrators slightly underrepresented relative to parties from those continents, but the remaining differences are significantly less stark than they first appear.

That is not to say that the inequitable geographic distribution of CAS arbitrator appointments is unproblematic. North American arbitrators are still heavily overrepresented and Latin American and African arbitrators heavily underrepresented.[64] For example, the dataset includes 53 decision in cases where at least one of the

---

[62] See below Fig. 9.6 *Arbitrator and Party Appearances by Nation - No International.*

[63] See below Fig. 9.7 *Arbitrator and Party Appearances by Nation - International as Swiss.* While this is the most accurate designation for most international SGBs, it should be noted that it is not true for all.

[64] It can be noted that they receive about 10% of all appointments.

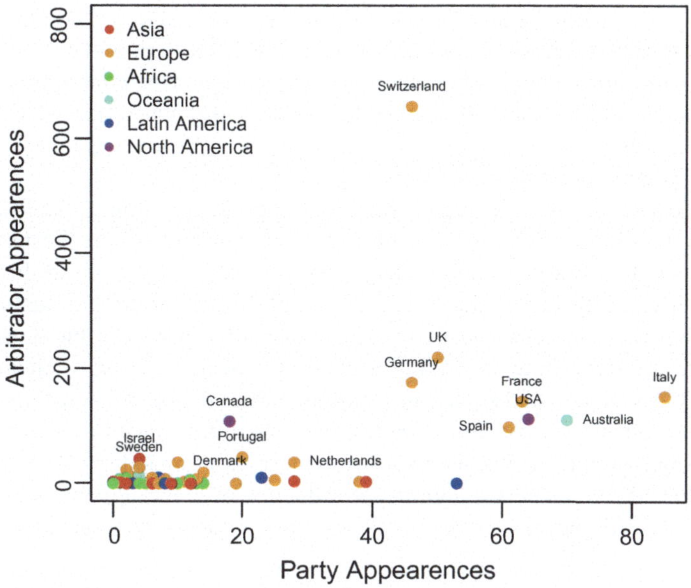

Fig. 9.6 Arbitrator and Party Appearances by Nation - No International. [*Source* The author]

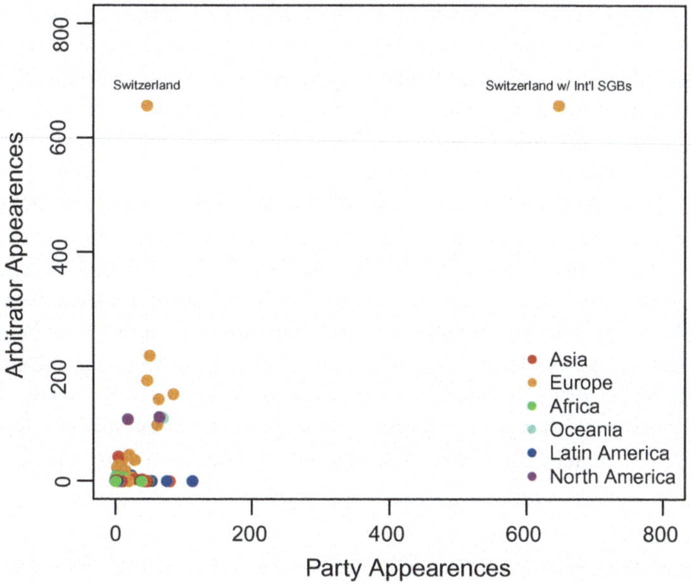

Fig. 9.7 Arbitrator and Party Appearances by Nation - International as Swiss. [*Source* The author]

parties was from Brazil but where the deciding panels did not contain a single Brazilian arbitrator. Moreover, while the fact that CAS is dominated by Western parties may to some extent explain the strong presence of Western arbitrators, this is problematic in and of itself. It is easy to see how the perception of CAS as an international adjudication body may be damaged by a high geographic concentration of arbitrators and parties.

The observations above begs a chicken-and-egg-like question: is the low number of non-Western CAS arbitrators a result of the low number of non-Western parties, or vice versa? It is not possible to adequately answer this question in this context. However, it is worth noting that the CAS list of eligible arbitrators includes individuals from most nations and that parties from all nations are therefore able to appoint an arbitrator from the same or at least a nearby nation as themselves.[65] ICAS and CAS cannot, and should not, require parties to appoint non-European and non-Western arbitrators, but this does not mean that they have no power over this situation. For example, as discussed above with regard to gender, CAS, through its Division Presidents, exercises significant influence over the appointment of panel presidents and sole arbitrators and could use this influence strategically.

9.2.5 Towards Increased Diversity and Representativeness

The findings above paint a picture of CAS as a not particularly diverse institution. Most CAS arbitrators are in their 50s, on par with commercial arbitrators and significantly older than most athletes.[66] Non-Western CAS arbitrators[67] are rare with 6.5 percent of all appointment and female CAS arbitrators are even rarer. CAS thus unfortunately fits the traditional stereotype of an international arbitration tribunal and the data shows no clear indications of this changing over time.[68] While CAS to some extent matches the dominant characteristics of CAS parties, it is not representative of athletes and other sports stakeholders around the globe.

That conscious efforts have been taken to increase the diversity and representativeness of the arbitrators included on the CAS list of arbitrators is obviously very positive. However, the composition of the list does not appear to be the main problem. The CAS list already includes many younger arbitrators, female arbitrators, and non-Western arbitrators, and this has been the case for some time. The problem rather lies with which arbitrators are selected from the list and appointed to appear on CAS panels. Proposals for coming to grip with this type of problem

[65] For example, the CAS list of arbitrators currently contains four Brazilian arbitrators.

[66] As a point of reference, the mean CAS arbitrator is thirty years older than the mean Olympic champion. IOC, "8 unusual facts about Olympic athletes". https://www.olympic.org/athlete365/news/8-unusual-facts-about-olympic-athletes/. Accessed 7 September 2018.

[67] Here defined as arbitrators based outside of Europe, North America, and Oceania.

[68] See above Sect. 9.2.1.

include everything from increased information and transparency[69] to selecting arbitrators using a mandatory roster system.[70] Considering that those who make appointment decisions seem to value previous experience,[71] one potentially promising approach would be for CAS Division Presidents to consciously prioritize younger, female, and non-Western arbitrators when exercising their power to appoint panel presidents and sole arbitrators. It has been argued that "[o]nce the appointing authority tests new and diverse arbitrator appointments, the confidence and reliance of new arbitrators will trickle down to party appointments."[72]

9.3 The Role of Legal Tradition

In the preceding section the geographical origin of arbitrators was examined using what can be described as a descriptive demographical approach. Geography is also closely connected with tradition and language, two factors of considerable importance in international adjudication institutions like CAS. In this section, we will focus on the role of the legal tradition of CAS arbitrators and in the next section we will turn our attention to the bilingual nature of CAS and its jurisprudence.

The idea that law, like other social phenomena, is rooted in and surrounded by tradition is well established. The common understanding of what characterizes a legal tradition and what constitutes distinct legal traditions have been refined and reconsidered over time,[73] but lawyers nevertheless largely agree with the basic propositions that legal tradition affects how they think about and practice law, that legal traditions at least to some extent and in some regards differ between legal systems, and that such differences affect the interaction between legal systems and between lawyers based in different legal systems.[74]

Researchers have paid attention to how differences in legal traditions affect the interaction between actors in international adjudicatory institutions, including international courts and international arbitration tribunals.[75] For example, one can reasonably suspect that a CAS arbitrator that lives in Sweden, that has been trained in the Swedish legal system, and that practices Swedish law might approach a case that comes before CAS in a slightly different way than, for example, a Canadian

---

69 Giordetti 2013; Greenwood and Baker 2015.

70 Van Harten 2012.

71 See Sect. 8.3.

72 Giordetti 2013, p. 485.

73 One much discussed issue is the distinction between legal systems, legal families, and legal traditions and which is the best basis for a useful taxonomy. Compare e.g. David and Brierly 1985 and Glenn 2014.

74 See e.g. Mattei 1997, p. 7. One of the most debated issues in comparative law in the last two decades is whether legal traditions represent "irreducibly distinctive modes of legal perception and thinking" that prevent legal convergence. Legrand 1996, p. 81.

75 See e.g. Elsing and Townsend 2002; Swigart and Terris 2015, p. 623; Zhang et al. 2018.

colleague. In line with this, some view international adjudication as an arena where old traditions converge into new practices, others as one where cultures clash.[76]

Scholars have previously suggested that the relative involvement of arbitrators from different legal traditions – a frequent example being legal traditions belonging to the common law and civil law traditions – may have bearing on how disputes are settled.[77] Opinions on the role of legal traditions in CAS does however differ. Some have suggested that the legal traditions that CAS arbitrators have their backgrounds in may affect their work as arbitrators and distinguish them from one another. For example, Soek has argued that CAS used a different approach in *Aanes*[78] than in previous, similar cases and that this was in part attributable to the *Aanes* panel consisting of arbitrators that had their background in the so-called civil law tradition.[79] By comparison, Beloff argues "that concepts of justice are, at any rate to ethical lawyers, shared across the globe" and that this serves as a solid basis for appropriately mixing concepts from different legal traditions.[80]

A well-established approach for studying these types of differences is to categorize national legal orders into legal traditions. The core idea behind the theory of legal traditions is that although legal systems are unique, different, and diverse it is both possible and valuable to group them together based on similar characteristics. In order to belong to the same legal tradition, legal systems should use sufficiently similar legal methods and sources and be based on similar principles and these similarities should distinguish them from legal systems that belong to another legal tradition.[81] Lawyers have traditionally grouped the majority of all national legal systems into two major groups: those belonging to the civil law tradition and those belonging to the common law tradition. This historically-based distinction focuses on whether the main features of a legal system can be traced back to the law of Rome in the 4th century B.C. (the civil law tradition) or to the law of England as it developed after 1066 A.D. (the common law tradition).[82] The civil law tradition is sometimes further divided into sub-traditions, such as the Germanic civil law tradition, the Romantic civil law tradition, and the Nordic civil law tradition.

[76] See Ginsburg 2003, pp. 1335–1336.

[77] See Latty 2007, p. 261 ("Le nombre élevé d'arbitres et leur extrême diversité culturelle ne sont pas de nature à favoriser l'émergence d'un courant jurisprudentiel homogène."); Oschütz 2002, p. 702 ("one should clearly consider that the different legal cultures of the arbitrators may also cause certain differences as to the understanding of the legal concepts.").

[78] CAS 2000/A/317.

[79] Soek 2003, p. 167. ICAS has to some extent accepted the view that there are relevant differences between legal traditions in its attempt to provide a diverse list of arbitrators. Even if the members of ICAS do not themselves subscribe to the theory that the arbitrators' legal traditions matter, this behavior suggests that they at least believe that parties and other actors, whose view of the legitimacy of CAS matters, subscribe to this theory.

[80] Beloff 2005, p. 52. See also e.g. Bersagel 2012, pp. 203–204.

[81] See e.g. David and Brierly 1985, pp. 17–21; De Cruz 2007, pp. 32–43; Merryman 1985, pp. 1–2.

[82] See e.g. De Cruz 2007, pp. 32; Merryman 1985, pp. 2–4. A third previously often-mentioned tradition is the socialist legal tradition. This category has however lost much of its relevance over the last decades.

Although well established and frequently used, this approach for classifying national legal systems into traditions is contested. The hegemony of the civil law/common law-distinction has been heavily criticized, including for being too simplistic and Western-centric.[83] In response, legal comparatists have increasingly sought to expand the classification process to consider, for example, religious legal traditions and customary law.[84] As discussed above, there is a lack of geographic diversity when it comes to CAS arbitrator appointments and this is in some regards problematic.[85] The fact that most CAS arbitrators are based in nations with legal systems that fit the traditional civil law/common law-dichotomy relatively well does however make it less problematic to use it as the basis for studying the role of legal traditions in CAS.[86]

A first question regarding the role of legal tradition in CAS is to what extent arbitrators belonging to different traditions are represented and to what extent they interact. 59 percent of all CAS arbitrators featured in the dataset are based in a nation whose legal system is considered to belong to the civil law tradition (civil law arbitrators) compared to 28 percent for arbitrators based in a nation with a legal system that belongs to the common law tradition (common law arbitrators). Remaining 12 percent are based in a nation that has what can be described as a mixed legal tradition.[87] Civil law arbitrators are also on average more frequently appointed than common law arbitrators, receiving 70 percent of all appointments.[88] If we believe that arbitrators' background in a particular legal tradition may influence how they act as arbitrators, the civil law tradition's influence on CAS and its jurisprudence is in this regard potentially significantly stronger than the common law tradition.[89]

An important factor in this regard is how arbitrators with backgrounds in different legal traditions work together within CAS. This is an important and complex question that ought to be studied using different methods, including qualitative methods such as for example interviews. One approach for furthering our knowledge that is possible using the current data is to analyze to what extent CAS arbitrators with backgrounds in different legal traditions appear together on CAS panels (co-appearances),[90] creating a social map where we can compare connections within and between civil law and common law CAS arbitrators.[91]

---

[83] De Cruz 2007, pp. 33–34.

[84] See e.g. Glenn 2014.

[85] See above Sect. 9.2.4.

[86] This examination relies on the JuriGlobe project's classifications. Fathally and Mariani 2008.

[87] The data contains codes for combinations of civil law, common law, the Muslim (Islamic) legal tradition, and customary law.

[88] See below Table 9.2 *Arbitrator Legal Traditions and Decision Mean Centrality*.

[89] CAS can in this regard be compared to ICSID with a stronger mix of civil and common law arbitrators. See Puig 2014.

[90] See also Sect. 8.4.

[91] See below Fig. 9.8 *Arbitrator Co-Appearances and Legal Tradition*. This approach is inspired by Puig 2014, pp. 409–410 (studying ICSID arbitrators).

This approach produces some interesting findings. First, as a group, civil law arbitrators occupy a more central role in the CAS arbitrator co-appearance network than common law arbitrators.[92] The "inner core" of the network is heavily dominated by civil law arbitrators. While there are three or four prominent common law arbitrators that can be considered part of this "inner core",[93] common law arbitrators are generally more peripheral in the network.

Second, CAS arbitrators have a tendency to cluster based on whether they have a civil law or common law background, that is that common law arbitrators tend to co-appear on panels together with other common law arbitrators and the same goes for civil law arbitrators. That does not mean that CAS panels are generally mono-traditional;[94] there are many examples of pairs of civil law and common law arbitrators that have appeared together on a number of CAS panels, particularly involving the aforementioned three or four prominent common law arbitrators.[95] The social map does however reveal that legal tradition on a general level appears to be an important factor with regard to with whom CAS arbitrators appear.

A different and in some ways more fundamental questions is whether there is a correlation between, on the one hand, the legal tradition in which CAS arbitrators have their background and, on the other, the CAS decisions that they have delivered. To test this empirically, we must select factors that relate to CAS decisions that are both reliably measurable and that we reasonably would expect could differ depending on the legal tradition of the author.

As previously discussed, one difference between legal systems belonging to the civil law and common law traditions is the role of precedent. While precedent is used as a source of law in both common law and civil law jurisdictions, the latter generally do not adhere to a formal rule of *stare decisis* and lawyers from civil law legal orders may therefore be more inclined to depart from or overrule previous decisions than lawyers from common law legal orders.[96] There is also, supposedly, a clear difference in style between how judgments are written in common law and civil law courts. For example, German courts tend to cite many previous decisions

---

[92] The vertices' positions in the graph were decided using the Fruchterman-Reingold algorithm according to which vertices repel each other but where edges act as an attractive force. This type of force-directed placement algorithm pushes weakly-connected nodes to the periphery and keeps strongly-connected nodes in the center. Fruchterman and Reingold 1991.

[93] E.g. Michael Beloff (UK) and Richard McLaren (Canada).

[94] Of the 694 CAS decisions decided by three arbitrator panels included in the dataset, 321 (46.2%) were decided by three arbitrators with a background in the same legal tradition. See below Table 9.2 *Arbitrator Legal Traditions and Decision Mean Centrality*.

[95] See below Fig. 9.8 *Arbitrator Co-Appearances and Legal Tradition*.

[96] See e.g. Merryman 1985, p. 22 ("the familiar common law doctrine of *stare decisis* [is] rejected by the civil law tradition. Judicial decisions are not law."); Siems 2014, pp. 57–58; Vogenaur 2006, p. 894 ("the fact that the common law systems acknowledge precedent as a binding source of law was long taken to be the essential difference between the common law and the civil law."). See also Chap. 4.

Table 9.2 Arbitrator Legal Traditions and Decision Mean Centrality. [*Source* The author]

Category	Individuals	Appointments	Persuasive power		Precedential power	
			Outdegree	Hub score	Indegree	PageRank
All arbitrators	229	2,195	2.65	0.055	2.65	0.00089
Civil law tradition[a]	136	1,509	3.51	0.071	2.60	0.00090
Germanic tradition	60	871	3.17	0.074	2.31	0.00086
Romantic tradition	71	534	3.71	0.062	2.82	0.00098
Nordic tradition	11	86	3.07	0.050	3.48	0.00096
Common law tradition	65	571	2.86	0.064	2.17	0.00084
Mixed legal tradition	28	115	3.58	0.0395**	2.01	0.00092
Single-tradition panels						
All common law		47	3.47	0.105**	2.77	0.00084
All civil law		274	3.62**	0.074	3.39	0.00096

$*p \leq 0.05$, $**p \leq 0.01$, $***p \leq 0.001$
[a]Subtypes include relevant mixed tradition systems

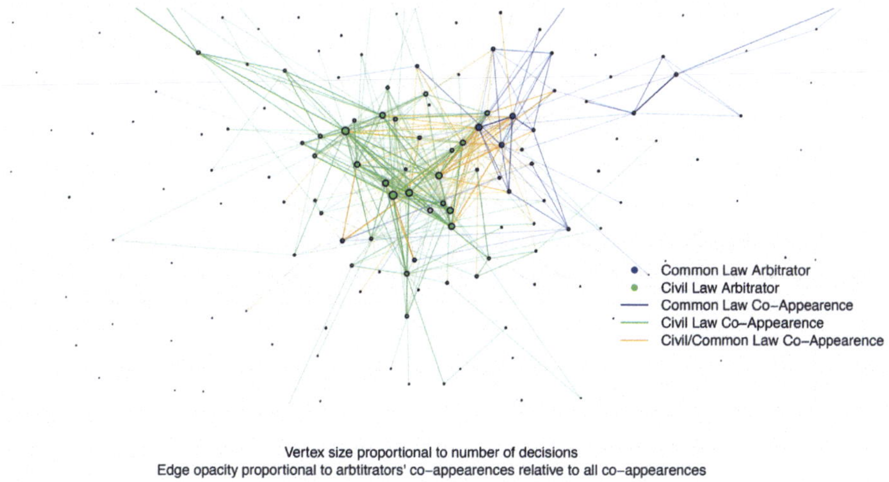

Fig. 9.8 Arbitrator Co-Appearances and Legal Tradition. [*Source* The author]

but without the more extensive discussion commonly associated with common law courts and French courts traditionally did not cite precedent at all.[97]

Over time it has been questioned how significant the differences between legal traditions are in practice,[98] and research suggests that these differences may be less clear in international courts and tribunals.[99] In practice there may be few tangible, relevant differences between how common law and civil law lawyers use precedent as a source of law (or generally act as arbitrators). However, if there are significant differences between how civil and common law lawyers think about and approach the law, one of the most obvious areas where one would expect to find such differences is how they use previous decisions as precedent.

One approach for studying this is to focus on to what extent a decision contains references to previous decisions and which previous decisions (persuasive power).[100] If there are differences between how common law and civil law arbitrators use previous decisions as a source of law, we would expect to see a difference in terms of how many previous decisions they cite and/or to what extent the decisions that they cite are particularly important in CAS jurisprudence. How many previous decisions arbitrators tend to cite can be measured as the mean outdegree of all decisions that they participated in delivering.[101] This can be used to compare if in this regard there are significant differences between arbitrators with backgrounds in different legal traditions. Outdegree treats all references to previous decisions equally regardless of those decisions' other characteristics. It is however reasonable to consider not only the quantity of references but also their quality, something that we can approximate using Hub Score. Hub Score takes into account not the only the number of decisions cited but also their relative importance in terms of how many other decisions have also cited the cited decisions and their relative importance.[102]

When we look at all arbitrators included in the dataset, there are few statistically significant differences between arbitrators with regard to legal tradition. The only statically significant result is that CAS arbitrators with a mixed legal tradition background tend to cite previous decisions that do not otherwise have a strong, precedential position.[103]

The fact that a majority of all CAS panels are composed of arbitrators with a background in different legal traditions may however hide some tradition-based tendencies of individual arbitrators. One way to test this possibility is to focus on cases decided by single-tradition CAS panels, that is CAS panels consisting of three

---

[97] Siems 2014, pp. 55–56.

[98] Vogenaur 2006, pp. 894–895.

[99] Several researchers that have studied the role of precedent in international arbitration courts point to the complexity of the issue. See e.g. Bersagel 2012; Guillaume 2011; Kaufmann-Kohler 2007.

[100] See Sect. 6.3.2.

[101] I.e. the average number of references to previous decisions.

[102] See Sect. 1.6.

[103] I.e. low hub score. See above Table 9.2 *Arbitrator Legal Traditions and Decision Mean Centrality*.

arbitrators with a background in the same legal tradition. When we do this, we find that there are indeed some statistically significant differences in persuasive power between CAS decisions delivered by all-civil-law and all-common-law CAS panels: whereas all-civil-law panels tend to cite a greater than average number of previous decisions,[104] all-common-law panels tend to cite previous decisions that are structurally more important for CAS's overall jurisprudence.[105] It thus appears that, contrary to what one might have expected, common law CAS arbitrators tend to cite fewer previous decisions than civil law CAS arbitrators. However, many of the decisions that civil law arbitrators cite are relatively unimportant in the sense that they are not cited in many or important previous decisions. Even though common law arbitrators cite fewer decisions than civil law arbitrators, they cite decisions that are structurally more important. One possible explanation for this could be that common law arbitrators are more experienced than civil law arbitrators when it comes to identifying and relating to well-established previous decisions as a source of law.

9.4 The Role of Language

CAS's "working languages are French and English,"[106] the traditional languages of the Olympic movement.[107] Subject to permission of the panel and CAS, parties may select a different language as the working language, but this is rare and almost all of the studied CAS decisions were written in French or English.[108] CAS can be described as a bilingual institution, both in the sense that its proceedings are conducted in either French or English and in the sense that CAS jurisprudence can be divided into two language groups: a French group and an English group.

The role of language in CAS is partially connected to the issue of CAS arbitrators' geographical origin as lawyers that have a proficiency in a particular language are more likely to have their backgrounds in certain legal system or legal tradition, and when it comes to CAS's working languages this is more likely to be the case with French than with English as "fluency in English is more likely to be disconnected from acculturation in a particular legal system."[109] According to Mavromati, the choice of language also "often reflects the legal tradition of the

[104] High mean outdegree.

[105] High hub score.

[106] Article R29 CAS Code.

[107] Mavromati and Reeb 2015, p. 76.

[108] The data includes 3 decisions written in German and 3 written in Italian. See however Mavromati 2012, Fig. 3 (showing that 5% of all proceedings before CAS are conducted in Spanish).

[109] Cohen 2016, p. 510.

country concerned, and from this scope, it might have an impact on the outcome of the dispute."[110]

Between the two main working languages, English is far more commonly used in CAS and its dominance has increased over time. Based on the collected decisions, the absolute number of CAS decisions published in French has remained relatively stable over time. However, as a result of a steadily increasing number of CAS decisions written in English over time, the French CAS decisions' portion of CAS's jurisprudence has decreased, both on a yearly basis and overall. 79 percent of all decisions decided by CAS in or before 1994 were written in French,[111] but by 2014 this had dropped to 17 percent, and there are no indications that the portion of CAS decisions published in French will not continue to decline.[112] Despite this decline, the role of French in CAS remains so substantial that the bilingual nature of the institution should be examined further.

On a structural level, the bilingual nature of CAS raises the question to what extent CAS jurisprudence constitutes one single body of jurisprudence or, alternatively, whether CAS decisions are separated based on language. One can suspect that all CAS arbitrators are not equally strong in French and in English and that this is reflected in the language of the proceedings of the cases that arbitrators adjudicate. For example, it is highly likely that CAS arbitrators that appear on cases where the language of the proceedings is French are more proficient in French than CAS arbitrators that only appear in proceedings where English is the working language. Moreover, one would expect that arbitrators who are less proficient in one of CAS's working languages will be less able to access, and will consequently be less familiar with, CAS jurisprudence written in that language. Depending on the extent of the language barrier that this creates it may have a tangible effect on CAS jurisprudence. In an extreme case, a multilingual adjudication body may end up with several, distinct, language-based bodies of jurisprudence where decisions written in one language predominantly consider and follow decisions written in the same language and where the lack of communication between such language-based bodies of jurisprudence result in diverging strands of case law.

To test whether CAS is at risk of such development we will consider to what extent CAS panels working in English and in French differ when it comes to citing previous CAS decisions written in their working language and the other language respectively. In evaluating this, one must take into account that the two working languages are not equally represented in CAS jurisprudence. Thus, one should not expect CAS panels to cite French and English decisions to an equal extent in the absence of a language barrier. Rather, one should expect CAS panels to cite French

---

[110] Mavromati 2012, p. 40.

[111] The representativeness of the data in this regard is supported by Mavromati 2012, Fig. 3, who reports that in 21% of cases registered with CAS before 20 April 2011, the language of the proceedings was French. This is comparable to the 19.8% of the studied CAS decisions delivered before or in 2011 being written in French.

[112] During the last three years of the period studied, 10.1% of all collected CAS decisions were in French.

and English decisions to an extent equal to their proportion of CAS's total body of jurisprudence. For example, as discussed above, CAS decisions in French constituted 17 percent of CAS jurisprudence at the end of 2014. In the absence of a language barrier it is therefore reasonable to expect that approximately 17 percent of the decisions cited in CAS decisions delivered in 2015, regardless of language, were written in French. Conversely, if that portion varies significantly between CAS decisions written in French and in English, that would suggest the existence of a language barrier and the size of that barrier can be inferred from the size of the deviation. However, because the two languages' respective representation in CAS jurisprudence has shifted significantly over time, the language of the decisions referred to must be evaluated with regard to the language composition of CAS jurisprudence at the time when the reference was made.[113]

When we test this, we find a quite substantial difference between French and English CAS decisions. CAS decisions written in French over-cite French CAS decisions by an average of 67 percent relative to the French decisions' portion of CAS jurisprudence at the time when the citation was made. CAS decisions written in English, by comparison, cite only half as many French CAS decisions as they would if they would follow the proportions of CAS jurisprudence. This indicates that there is a quite significant language barrier in CAS and there are no indications in the data that the size of this barrier is shifting over time.

Moreover, the data shows a very strong correlation between, on the one hand, the number of deciding arbitrators from a nation where French is an official language[114] and, on the other, how well-represented French decisions are among the previous CAS decisions cited in the decision. Given the expectations outlined above it is not so surprising that CAS panels on which there are no arbitrators from a French-speaking nation tend to cite 60 percent fewer French CAS decisions than warranted by their portion of CAS jurisprudence, much less than all-French-speaking CAS panels.[115] What is more notable is that this measurement increases linearly with the panelists' language skills. CAS panels with one French-speaking arbitrator cite a more proportional number of French decisions than panels with no French-speaking arbitrator and panels with two French-speaking arbitrators even more so but they still do not do as well as an all-French-speaking CAS panel. This is somewhat surprising as one could perhaps expect that a single French-speaking arbitrator would be able to close or at least

---

[113] For example, CAS's decision in CAS 96/156, *Foschi*, which is written in English, cites six previous CAS decisions, 50% of which are written in French: CAS 92/63, *Gundel* (French); CAS 94/128, *UCI & CONI* (French); CAS 94/129, *Quigley* (English); CAS 95/141, *Chagnaud* (French); CAS 95/142, *Lehtinen* (English); CAS 96/149, *Cullwick* (English). On the day when *Foschi* was decided, 22 October 1997, there were 35 CAS decisions included in the studied dataset. 19 or 54% of those decisions were written in French. The decisions cited in *Foschi* were thus highly representative of CAS jurisprudence at the time.

[114] Which we here use as a proxy for the arbitrators' language skills.

[115] All-French-speaking CAS panels, by comparison, tend to only very slightly over-cite French decisions.

significantly reduce the language barrier by introducing relevant French decisions to his or her non-French-speaking fellow panelists. The linear correlation suggests that the language barrier is not merely a question of the panel as a collective having the necessary language skills but a more deep-rooted, language-based difference between arbitrators with regard to relying on or at least citing previous decisions.

References

Alvarez J E (2007) The Democratization of the Invisible College. The American Society of International Law, IL Post, 8 November 2007. http://www.law.nyu.edu/sites/default/files/ECM_PRO_065334.pdf. Accessed 25 May 2017

Beloff M (2005) Is there a lex sportiva? International Sports Law Review 3:49–60

Bersagel A (2012) Is There a Stare Decisis Doctrine in the Court of Arbitration for Sport? An Analysis of Published Awards for Anti-Doping Disputes in Track and Field. Pepperdine Dispute Resolution Law Journal 12:189–207

Boigeol A (2013) Feminisation of the French 'Magistrature': Gender and Judging in a Feminised Context. In: Schultz U, Shaw G (eds) Gender and Judging. Hart Publishing, Oxford, pp. 125–144

Cohen M (2016) On the linguistic design of multinational courts: The French capture. ICON 14 (2):498–517

David R, Brierley J (1985) Major Legal Systems in the World Today. Stevens and Sons, London

De Cruz P (2007) Comparative Law in a Changing World, 3rd edn. Routledge-Cavendish, Oxon

Dezalay Y, Garth B (1996) Dealing in Virtue: International Commercial Arbitration and the Construction of a Transnational Legal Order. The University of Chicago Press, Chicago

Elsing S, Townsend J (2002) Bridging the Common Law-Civil Law Divide in Arbitration. International Arbitration 18(1):59–65

Fathally J, Mariani N (2008) World Legal Systems, 2nd edn. http://www.juriglobe.ca. Accessed 19 May 2017

Franck S (2007) Empirically Evaluating Claims About Investment Treaty Arbitration. North Carolina Law Review 86:1–88

Franck S, Freda J, Lavin K, Lehmann T, van Aaken A (2015) Diversity Challenge: Exploring the 'Invisible College' of International Arbitration. Columbia Journal of Transnational Law 53:429–506

Fruchterman T, Reingold E (1991) Graph drawing by force-directed placement. Software: Practice and Experience 21(11):1129–1164

Ginsburg T (2003) The Culture of Arbitration. Vanderbilt Journal of Transnational Law 36:1335–1345

Giordetti C (2013) Who Decides Who Decides in International Investment Arbitration? University of Pennsylvania Journal of International Law 35:431–486

Glenn H P (2014) Legal Traditions of the World, 5th edn. Oxford University Press, Oxford

Greenwood L, Baker C M (2015) Is the balance getting better? An update on the issue of gender diversity in international arbitration. Arbitration International 31:413–423

Guillaume G (2011) The Use of Precedent by International Judges and Arbitrators. Journal of International Dispute Settlement 2(1):5–23

Kaufmann-Kohler G (2007) Arbitral Precedent: Dream, Necessity or Excuse? Arbitration International 23(3):357–378

Kenney S J (2013) Which Judicial Selection Systems Generate the Most Women Judges? Lessons from the United States. In: Schultz U, Shaw G (eds) Gender and Judging. Hart Publishing, Oxford, pp. 461–480

Latty F (2007) La lex sportiva: Recherche sur le droit transnational. Martinus Nijhoff, Leiden

Legrand P (1996) European Legal Systems are Not Converging. International and Comparative Law Quarterly 45(1):52–81
Ludewig R, LaLlave J (2013) Professional Stress, Discrimination and Coping Strategies: Similarities and Differences between Female and Male Judges in Switzerland. In: Schultz U, Shaw G (eds) Gender and Judging. Hart Publishing, Oxford, pp. 233–254
Mack K, Roach Anleu S (2013) Skills for Judicial Work: Comparing Women Judges and Women Magistrates. In: Schultz U, Shaw G (eds) Gender and Judging. Hart Publishing, Oxford, pp. 211–232
Mattei U (1997) Three Patterns of Law: Taxonomy and Change in the World's Legal Systems. The American Journal of Comparative Law 45(1):5–44
Mavromati D (2012) Language of procedure before CAS: Practice, criteria and impact of the language on the outcome of the case. CAS Bulletin 2012(1):39–48
Mavromati D, Reeb M (2015) The Code of the Court of Arbitration for Sport: Commentary, Cases and Materials. Wolters Kluwer, Alphen aan den Rijn
Merryman J (1985) The Civil Law Tradition, 2nd edn. Stanford University Press, Stanford
Oschütz F (2002) Harmonization of Anti-Doping Code Through Arbitration: The Case Law of the Court of Arbitration for Sport. Marquette Sports Law Review 12:675–702
Puig S (2014) Social Capital in the Arbitration Market. The European Journal of International Law 25(2):387–424
Puig S (2016) Blinding International Justice. Virginia Journal of International Law 56(3):647–700
Reeb M (1998) The Court of Arbitration for Sport (CAS). In: Reeb M (ed) Digest of CAS Awards I. Kluwer Law International, The Hague, pp. xxiii–xxxi
Schachter O (1977) The Invisible College of International Lawyers. Northwestern University Law Review 72(2):217–226
Siems M (2014) Comparative Law. Cambridge University Press, Cambridge
Soek J (2003) The Strict Liability Principle and the Human Rights of Athletes in Doping Cases. T.M.C. Asser Press, The Hague
Swigart L (2010) The 'National Judge': Some Reflections on Diversity in International Courts and Tribunals. McGeorge Law Review 42:223–242
Swigart L, Terris D (2015) Who are International Judges? In: Romano C, Alter K, Shany Y (eds) The Oxford Handbook of International Adjudication. Oxford University Press, Oxford, pp. 619–638
Terris D, Romano C, Swigart L (2007) The International Judge: An Introduction to the Men and Women Who Decide the World's Cases. Brandeis University Press, Waltham
Van Harten G (2012) The (lack of) women arbitrators in investment treaty arbitration. Columbia FDI Perspectives 59, Vale Columbia Center on Sustainable International Investment, New York
Vogenaur S (2006) Sources of Law and Legal Method in Comparative Law. In: Reimann M, Zimmermann R (eds) The Oxford Handbook of Comparative Law. Oxford University Press, Oxford, pp. 869–898
Zhang A H, Liu J, Garoupa N (2018) Judging in Europe: Do Legal Traditions Matter? Journal of Competition Law and Economics 14(1):144–178

Chapter 10
CAS from the Litigants' Perspective

Abstract The Court of Arbitration for Sport (CAS) exists to resolve sports-related disputes, but what is a sports-related dispute? This chapter explores CAS from the perspective of athletes, clubs, sports governing bodies (SGBs), and other actors that appear as litigants before CAS. This examination reveals that CAS plays different roles to different classes of litigants, many of which are not generally associated with international arbitration tribunals. The chapter also examines and compares the success rate of different classes of litigants, as well as the geographical origin of CAS litigants.

10.1 Forms of Arbitration

All forms of arbitration have certain things in common but the role and nature of arbitration varies quite significantly and it has evolved over time.[1] It should also be acknowledged that the actors that choose to resolve disputes through arbitration constitute a rather diverse group.[2] Parties to arbitration can broadly be divided into three categories: (i) natural persons, (ii) corporations, associations, and other, similar legal persons, and (iii) states and state entities. Although there is no firm and clear distinction between the two it is also common to distinguish between domestic arbitration and international arbitration, the latter being one that relates to multiple countries, either due to the international character of the subject of the dispute or to the parties being based in different countries.[3] Using these categories we can identify some typical forms of arbitration.

---

[1] See Rigozzi 2005, pp. 172–175.

[2] Arbitration always, at least on some level, rests on a consensual arbitration agreement. However, as highlighted by the German courts' decisions in the *Pechstein* case, it is debatable whether athletes' consent to CAS arbitration can always be characterized as genuine. See LG München I's decision of 26 February 2014 in 37 O 28331/12; OLG München's decision of 15 January 2015 in 1110/14 Kart; BGH's decision of 7 June 2016 in KZR 6/15.

[3] Blackaby et al. 2015, pp. 7–10; Tweeddale and Tweeddale 2005, pp. 46–50. Cf. Article 1(3) Model Law on International Commercial Arbitration (amended 2006) (defining what constitutes international arbitration for the purpose of the model law).

J. Lindholm, *The Court of Arbitration for Sport and Its Jurisprudence*,
ASSER International Sports Law Series,
https://doi.org/10.1007/978-94-6265-285-9_10

A first and most obvious form of arbitration is arbitration resolving disputes involving natural and legal persons, particularly for the purpose of resolving commercial disputes (commercial arbitration).[4] Businesses have resolved commercial disputes through arbitration since antiquity,[5] but more recently it has also become increasingly common to resolve disputes between consumers and businesses through arbitration (consumer arbitration).[6] Domestic arbitration of commercial disputes tend more commonly to involve natural persons, whereas international arbitration largely revolves around disputes between and among legal persons and states.[7]

Despite its importance for determining whether a dispute is arbitrable, the distinction between commercial and non-commercial disputes for the purpose of arbitration is not clear and firm.[8] The UNCITRAL Model Law advocates for a broad interpretation of the term "commercial":[9]

> The term "commercial" should be given a wide interpretation so as to cover matters arising from all relationships of a commercial nature, whether contractual or not. Relationships of a commercial nature include, but are not limited to, the following transactions: any trade transaction for the supply or exchange of goods or services; distribution agreement; commercial representation or agency; factoring; leasing; construction of works; consulting; engineering; licensing; investment; financing; banking; insurance; exploitation agreement or concession; joint venture and other forms of industrial or business cooperation; carriage of goods or passengers by air, sea, rail or road.

Under this definition, many disputes decided by the Court of Arbitration for Sport (CAS) can be said to be of a commercial character.[10] One of the earliest examples of CAS resolving a dispute that can be clearly characterized as commercial in nature is *X v. HC Y* where CAS in 1989 was asked to determine the duration of an employment contract involving X, a hockey coach, and HC Y, a hockey club and the damages that HC Y was to pay X as a result of his wrongful termination.[11]

A second, major form of international arbitration is arbitration between states (inter-state arbitration).[12] Like commercial arbitration, inter-state arbitration has a history that goes back to antiquity,[13] but the disputes that are resolved through inter-state arbitration are fundamentally different from those resolved through

[4] Tweeddale and Tweeddale 2005, pp. 40–41.

[5] Born 2014, pp. 24–53.

[6] See e.g. Drahozal and Friel 2002, p. 357; Ware 2001, p. 89.

[7] Blackaby et al. 2015, p. 7.

[8] See Blackaby et al. 2015, pp. 11–12; Tweeddale and Tweeddale 2005, pp. 51–57.

[9] Explanatory footnote to Article 1(1) Model Law on International Commercial Arbitration (amended 2006).

[10] Blackshaw 2013, pp. 19–21.

[11] CAS 87/10 (relying, *inter alia*, on the principle of good faith, CAS concluded that the parties had entered into an agreement covering a two-year period).

[12] Sometimes also referred to as "state-to-state arbitration" or "state-state arbitration".

[13] Born 2014, pp. 7–15.

commercial arbitration. They may for example concern the drawing of national borders[14] or the payment of war reparations,[15] issues that might otherwise be resolved by international courts or through armed conflict.

The third and final major form of international arbitration is arbitration between investors and states (investor-state arbitration).[16] By entering into a bilateral or multilateral investment treaty, the contracting states agree on the terms governing individuals based in one contracting state investing in another contracting state.[17] Under these treaties, which became increasingly common towards the end of the twentieth century, individuals that invest in a foreign state covered by an investment treaty may enforce their rights under the treaty,[18] for example protecting against legislation that drastically reduces the value of the investment,[19] directly against that state through arbitration. This is a venue for natural and legal persons to end up as applicant with a state as respondent.

CAS engages in neither of the latter two forms of international arbitration as states do not appear before CAS. Instead CAS engages in forms of adjudication that are distinguishable from the above-described three major forms of international arbitration, as would be expected from an international arbitration institution that invites a broad range of sports-related disputes.[20]

The majority of all cases that come before CAS are disciplinary in nature, for example against an individual on the grounds of doping violations or corruption, and where CAS is asked to review the decision of a sports governing body (SGB). The legal basis of such disciplinary actions is contractual[21] and the outcome of such disciplinary actions may carry significant economic consequences, although this is not necessarily the case. It is nevertheless difficult to characterize these types of disputes as disputes that arise from "relationships of a commercial nature", at least in some cases. Take for example the case of *Raducan* where CAS was asked to determine whether a sixteen-year-old Romanian gymnast who had taken a cold medicine that, unbeknownst to her, contained a banned substance, should be allowed to keep her Olympic medal.[22] Only under a very broad definition that would place it with many fundamentally distinguishable types of disputes could

---

[14] See e.g. PCA's award in Case 1996–04, *Eritrea v. Yemen*.

[15] See e.g. PCA's award in Case 2001–02, *Ethiopia v. Eritrea*.

[16] Tweeddale and Tweeddale 2005, pp. 41–44.

[17] E.g. including the right to fair and equitable treatment and protection from expropriation.

[18] Hobér 2004, pp. 139–141.

[19] See e.g. NAFTA Chap. 11 Arbitration Tribunal's award of 7 August 2005, *Methanex Corp. v. the United States of America*.

[20] See Sect. 2.2. Cf. Blackshaw 2013, p. 18 (referring to disputes that concern "purely sporting issues"); Valero 2014, p. 4 (drawing a distinction between regulatory issues, such as doping, and "more commercial" issues).

[21] See e.g. CAS 2011/O/2422, *USOC v. IOC*, para 45 ("The WADA Code is neither a law nor an international treaty. It is rather a contractual instrument binding its signatories in accordance with private international law.").

[22] OG 00/011.

Raducan be characterized as an example of a commercial dispute. CAS describing disciplinary actions as "quasi-penal" in nature is a clear acknowledgement of the distinctive character of these disputes.[23]

CAS also adjudicates many cases that can broadly be described as involving regulatory disputes. An example of this are cases where SGBs are uncertain or in disagreement about the interpretation and validity of sports rules. This includes cases brought under the consultation procedure,[24] but also many cases brought under other procedures. An illustrative example of these types of cases are the so-called Osaka Rule cases. During its meeting in Osaka in 2008, the Executive Board of the International Olympic Committee (IOC) enacted a rule according to which an athlete that was suspended for more than six months for a doping violation would be ineligible from participating in the next Olympic Games taking place following the expiration of the suspension period.[25] The British Olympic Committee (BOA) had fifteen years earlier implemented a similar rule that made all British athletes who had been found guilty of a doping offence forever ineligible from representing Great Britain.[26] CAS found that the IOC regulation and the BOA Bye-Law were functionally equivalent to a suspension under the World Anti-Doping Code (WADC). CAS determined that the IOC and BOA rules were in conflict with the WADC that contains a complete and mandatory set of sanctions and takes precedent over the rules in question.[27] These types of disputes sometime resemble inter-state arbitration, even though the underlying relationship rests on private rather than public international law grounds.

CAS thus to some extent engages in forms of international arbitration that are distinguishable from the major forms of international arbitration outside the field of sports. In this regard, CAS is a unique example of what international arbitration is and can be and contributes to the evolution of the understanding of the phenomenon.

This chapter will explore CAS and its activities from the perspective of the litigants that come before CAS. They can be divided into three main classes:

---

[23] CAS 98/222, *Bernhard*, paras 26, 41, 43; CAS 2000/A/289, *Chiotti*, para 7; CAS 2009/A/1782, *Volandri*, para 6. It should be noted, however, that a distinction must in this regard be made between the ability to invoke certain penal principles and the status of a dispute as penal for the purpose of determining arbitrability. See further Rigozzi 2005, pp. 374–379.

[24] See e.g. CAS 93/109, *FFTri & ITU* (regarding a conflict between anti-doping rules and general legal principles); CAS 98/215, *IBA* (regarding the proper interpretation of IBA's rules on changes of nationality); CAS 2000/C/267, *AOC* (regarding whether use of full body swimsuits contravened FINA's rules). See also CAS 95/145, *Federation Y* (jurisdiction denied), where the applicant asked CAS "to confirm that the Federation Y. was the relevant governing body of the sport X." Ibid., para 2.

[25] See CAS 2011/O/2422, *USOC v. IOC*.

[26] CAS 2011/A/2658, *BOA v. WADA*.

[27] By signing the WADC the IOC and BOA surrendered their autonomy to impose conflicting rules.

(i) individuals, primarily athletes; (ii) clubs; and (iii) SGBs.[28] All three classes are extensively engaged in litigation before CAS. However, as developed below, there are some clear differences between the three regarding what types of cases they engage in, whether they appear on the applicant[29] or respondent side of the litigation, who appears on the other side, and whether other classes of litigants appear on the same side of the litigation. Exploring these questions will give insight into how different classes of litigants interact with CAS and a deepened understanding of the different roles that CAS plays.

As previously discussed in this book, CAS decisions have normative implications as CAS panels tend to adhere to previous decisions. To most litigants that come before CAS, and particularly to those who are neither SGBs nor repeat litigants, the most important thing is not the precedent that CAS's decision might set for the future but the outcome in the individual case. It can be difficult to assess to what extent the outcome in an individual case is beneficial to a particular litigant. For example, an athlete that receives a one-year suspension for a doping violation may view this outcome either as a win or a loss depending on the circumstances of the individual case and his or her expectations.[30] It is even more difficult to objectively determine whether CAS reached a substantially correct outcome in an individual case and to do so on a large scale is unfeasible.

However, for the about 77 percent of the studied decisions that are brought under the Appeals Arbitration Procedure CAS provides a simple but reliable outcome measurement.[31] If CAS finds that an appeal is admissible and that it has jurisdiction over the case it will either (i) dismiss the appeal (upholding the appealed decision), (ii) uphold the appeal (annulling the appealed decision), or (iii) uphold the appeal in part (amending the appealed decision).

In order to compare outcomes between groups of cases grouped on the basis of the litigants, all studied appeals cases that meet these criteria are assigned an *outcome score* that ranges between a respondent win/appellant loss (−1) and an appellant win/respondent loss (1). It is quite clear that a CAS decision constitutes a win for the respondent if the appeal is dismissed (−1) and a win for the appellant if the appeal is upheld (1). It is less obvious how one for these purposes should treat an outcome where CAS partially upholds the appeal. It is obviously not the ideal

---

[28] This data was manually coded for all studied CAS decisions on the basis of party names or, in the rare instances where this was ambiguous, on the basis of CAS's description of the parties.

[29] The term applicant as used in this context covers both applicants in cases brought under the Ad Hoc Procedure, claimants in cases brought under the Ordinary Arbitration Procedure, and appellants in cases brought under the Appeals Arbitration Procedure.

[30] Compare e.g. CAS 99/A/223, *Korda*, where CAS against the athlete's request set aside a decision that carried no suspension and imposed a one-year suspension, and CAS 2000/A/312, *Leipold II*, where CAS replaced a two-year suspension with a one-year suspension. *Leipold II* is a good illustration of the complexity involved in quantifying outcome as the appellant had asked CAS to revoke the appealed decision in its entirety.

[31] See below Table 10.2 *Litigant Combinations and Mean Outcome*. This obviously includes decisions under the Appeals Arbitration Procedure, but also many decisions under the Ad Hoc Procedure.

outcome for neither the appellant nor the respondent and the distance from those ideals depends on what lies in the term "partially".[32] In the absence of an objective basis for a finer classification, partially upheld appeals are treated as CAS splitting the outcome between what would be the ideal outcomes according to the appellant and respondent respectively (0).

The mean outcome score for all studied decisions that meet the criteria described above is −0.26. This means that respondents overall have been slightly more successful than appellants in cases brought under the Appeals Arbitration Procedure.[33] This is not particularly surprising. As discussed in greater detail below, one would expect respondents to have a considerable edge in Appeals Arbitration cases. In fact, if anything it is surprising that respondents are not more successful.[34] However, as explored below, this varies considerably depending on who the litigants are and the type of case.[35]

10.2 Individuals as CAS Litigants

The three classes of litigants described above are represented to fairly the same extent when it comes to bringing cases to CAS, each appearing as applicant to roughly the same extent as the others, but who they bring these cases against varies quite significantly. It is fairly uncommon that individuals bring cases against other individuals or clubs. Individuals instead overwhelmingly bring claims against SGBs, making what can be referred to as individual-SGB disputes a type of dispute that is quite common in CAS. In most cases individuals bring such cases alone or together with other individuals.[36] More than four out of five CAS decisions that include an individual applicant features at least one SGB on the respondent side.[37] These individual-SGB disputes make up a significant portion of CAS's caseload as

---

32 In line with the discussion above, an appellant that received a reduced suspension, but a suspension nonetheless, might consider that deeply disappointing or grossly unjust.

33 It is worth clarifying that success in this context does not relate to what in some general sense ought to have been the outcome or, in that sense, how well a party argued their case. A party might refer to what is here characterized as a win as a bad win and what is here characterized as a loss as a good loss. Success in this context only refers to whether the applicant after CAS's review ended up in a better situation compared to under the reviewed decision. A certain class of litigant is successful in that regard if it does significantly better than other classes of litigants.

34 See below Sect. 10.6.

35 See below Table 10.2 *Litigant Combinations and Mean Outcome*.

36 83.4% of all decisions involving an individual applicant only involved individual applicants. See below Table 10.2 *Litigant Combinations and Mean Outcome*.

37 83.5% of all respondents facing individual applicants were SGBs. See below Table 10.1 *Litigant Appearances by Class and Side*.

Table 10.1 Litigant Appearances by Class and Side. [*Source* The author]

			Applicant side includes			
			Individual	Club	SGB	Total
Respondent side includes	Individual	Count	24	54	174	252
		% within respondent	9.5%	21.4%	69.0%	21.9%
		% within applicant	5.7%	18.5%	39.5%	
	Club	Count	45	111	11	167
		% within respondent	26.9%	66.5%	6.6%	14.5%
		% within applicant	10.8%	38.0%	2.5%	
	SGB	Count	349	127	255	731
		% within respondent	47.7%	17.4%	34.9%	63.6%
		% within applicant	83.5%	43.4%	58.0%	
	Total	Count	418	292	440	
		% within applicant	36.3%	25.4%	38.3%	

one-third of all CAS decisions studied involved an applicant side consisting of only individual applicants against a respondent side that consisted only of SGBs.[38] Almost three-quarters of all individual-SGB disputes involved international and regional SGBs, predominantly the IOC, certain major international sport federations,[39] and regional football federations,[40] and one-third involved national SGBs,[41] particularly from Australia, the United States, and Italy.[42]

This is not entirely unexpected considering that most cases that come before CAS fall under the Appeals Arbitration Procedure and many of those involve appeals of SGBs decisions against individuals in disciplinary actions, in particular relating to anti-doping violations, and decisions concerning athletes' eligibility to compete.[43] It is also unsurprising that almost two-thirds of all individual-SGB disputes concern doping-related matters,[44] including many landmark CAS

[38] 278 decisions.

[39] E.g. FEI, FINA, FIFA, ITF, and FIS.

[40] 201 decisions.

[41] 91 cases. Some cases involved both international/regional and national SGBs as respondents.

[42] Most of those were brought against the Australian and Italian Olympic committees (AOC and CONI) and the United States Anti-Doping Agency (USADA).

[43] As discussed in Sect. 2.2, most CAS decisions fall under Appeals Arbitration Procedure.

[44] 179 decisions. This is based on CAS's subject matter classification.

Table 10.2 Litigant Combinations and Mean Outcome. [*Source* The author]

			Applicants							
			Individual	Individual and club	Individual, club, and SGB	Individual and SGB	Club	Club and SGB	SGB	Total
Respondents	Individual	All cases	5				24		31	60
		Appeals w/ outcome	5				23		17	45
		mean outcome	−0.60				−0.22		0.35**	−0.04
	Individual and club	All cases		4			9		1	14
		Appeals w/ outcome		1			9		1	11
		Mean outcome		0.00			−0.67		−1.00	−0.64
	Individual, club, and SGB	All cases		4			7			11
		Appeals w/ outcome		3			6			9
		Mean outcome		−0.67			−0.50			−0.56
	Individual and SGB	All cases	1			10	5		131	147
		Appeals w/ outcome	1			6	5		92	104
		Mean outcome	1.00			−0.17	−0.60		0.35***	0.27***
	Club	All cases	18				65	1	3	87
		Appeals w/ outcome	13				59	1	3	76
		Mean outcome	−0.38				−0.42	−1.00	−0.33	−0.42

(continued)

Table 10.2 (continued)

			Applicants							
			Individual	Individual and club	Individual, club, and SGB	Individual and SGB	Club	Club and SGB	SGB	Total
	Club and SGB	All cases	11	8			11	1	4	35
		Appeals w/ outcome	8	5			8	1	3	25
		Mean outcome	−0.50	−0.4			−0.88*	−1.00	0.67	−0.48
	SGB	All cases	278	10	1	25	78	2	81	475
		Appeals w/ outcome	222	8	1	18	64	1	55	369
		Mean outcome	-0.34	0.00	0.00	−0.44	−0.42	−1.00	−0.45	−0.37***
	Total	All cases	313	26	1	35	199	4	251	829
		Appeals w/ outcome	249	17	1	24	174	3	171	639
		Mean outcome	−0.35*	−0.22	0.00	−0.38	−0.44***	−1.00	0.07***	−0.26

−1 represents outcome entirely in favor of respondent(s), 1 represents outcome entirely in favor of appellant(s)
$^{*}p < 0.05$, $^{**}p < 0.01$, $^{***}p < 0.001$

decisions,[45] such as *Squizzato*,[46] *Susin*,[47] *Hipperdinger*,[48] and *Knaus*.[49] However, there are also many individual-SGB disputes where athletes challenge SGBs' decisions to sanction, disqualify, or otherwise eliminate them from competing for actions unrelated to doping,[50] or even directly to sports activities.[51]

Judging by the outcome of CAS decisions heard under the Appeals Arbitration Procedure, individuals are rather unsuccessful as CAS applicants,[52] including in individual-SGB disputes where CAS upholds one appeal for each two that it dismisses.[53] This number drops to one appeal upheld for each seven dismissed under the Ad Hoc Procedure.[54] The decrease in appellant success rate is likely attributable to the expedited procedure in ad hoc cases, at least in part. The prospective applicant must decide quickly whether to appeal a decision within the competition in question and this can possibly sometimes lead to applicants appealing decisions they would not have appealed had they had more time to consult and consider the merits. Also, because CAS in these cases is under pressure to quickly render a decision, during the Olympic Games within twenty-four hours of the lodging of the application,[55] applicants have less time to prepare arguments and a reduced ability to present evidence.[56] Finally, it is unrealistic to expect that decisions that are made in a single day will be as well-considered as those that are made over a period of seven-and-a-half months.[57] While the issues decided by the CAS Ad Hoc Division are arguably on average less complicated than those decided by the Appellate Division, a reduction in quality is expected, even inevitable given the urgency, and this may have some effect on the outcome.

It should finally be noted that the significantly low success rate of individual appellants should not be taken to mean that individuals should generally refrain from appealing SGB decisions. If one also considers partially upheld appeals,

---

[45] Regarding why these constitute landmark cases, see Chap. 5.

[46] CAS 2005/A/830.

[47] CAS 2000/A/274.

[48] CAS 2004/A/690.

[49] CAS 2005/A/847.

[50] See e.g. CAS 99/A/246, *Ward* (disqualification, suspension, and fine for horse abuse); CAS 2008/A/1594, *Sheykhov* (disqualification for rigged wrestling match); OG 00/013, *Segura* (disqualification for infraction in walking competition).

[51] See e.g. CAS 92/80, *B. v. FIBA* (double nationality and eligibility to compete for national team); CAS 2008/A/1574, *D'Arcy* (elimination from Olympic team due to off-field misconduct).

[52] See above Table 10.2 *Litigant Combinations and Mean Outcome*. There are no significant differences in this regard based on subject matter. Individuals perform more average if they appear together with a club. Ibid. See further below Sect. 10.3.

[53] 38 compared to 114.

[54] 3 compared to 26.

[55] Article 18 Arbitration Rules applicable to the CAS Ad Hoc Division for the Olympic Games.

[56] See Mavromati 2016, p. 10.

[57] On average 223.7 days passed between the moment when the studied CAS decisions brought under the Appeal Arbitration Procedure were lodged with CAS and its decision was rendered.

individual appellants end up in a better position than they would have had they not appealed in almost half of all cases.[58]

Individuals are not generally less successful than other classes of CAS litigants when appearing as respondents. One important exception to this is however cases brought by an SGB appellant. Unlike appeals cases generally, which overall tend to go the respondents' way, these cases tend to go the appellants' way and quite clearly so.[59] However, this has likely more to do with the appellant and the nature of these cases than that there is an individual respondent.[60]

10.3 Clubs as CAS Litigants

Much like individuals, clubs predominantly appear alone as applicants when they bring cases to CAS.[61] Cases where only clubs appear on the applicant side can be divided into three major groups: those brought against individuals (club-individual disputes), against other clubs (inter-club disputes), and against SGBs (club-SGB disputes).[62]

The club-individual and inter-club disputes found in the dataset are in many ways similar to each other. All of the decisions studied that belong to these two categories were football-related and quite commercial in nature. Most club-individual disputes concerned an employment relationship between a football player and a football club where the nature of the dispute was either that the club argued that the player had violated the terms of the employment agreement,[63] or that the club according to the player had terminated the employment relationship without just cause.[64] In both of these cases, the dispute mainly concerned the applicants' claim for monetary damages. Most inter-club disputes are characterized by one football club appealing a decision by the FIFA Dispute Resolution Chamber (FIFA DRC) that was favorable to another football club and that in some way concerns the transfer of football players. Those cases primarily concern the

58 108 out of 222.

59 See above Table 10.2 *Litigant Combinations and Mean Outcome*.

60 See further below Sect. 10.4.

61 85.8% of all decisions that involved a club applicant only involved club applicants. See above Table 10.2 *Litigant Combinations and Mean Outcome*.

62 See above Table 10.2 *Litigant Combinations and Mean Outcome*.

63 See e.g. CAS 2006/A/1192, *Mutu II*; CAS 2009/A/1856 & 1857, *Club X v. A*; CAS 2010/O/2132, *Pereira Dias*.

64 See e.g. CAS 2006/A/1062, *Etoga*; CAS 2007/A/1233 & 1234, *Da Silva & Magri*; CAS 2008/A/1517, *Pajuelo Chávez*; CAS 2009/A/1956, *Club Tofta Itróottarfelag, B68 v. R*. In these cases the appellant club asked CAS to overturn or modify a previous decision in favor of the player.

calculation and payment of transfer compensation,[65] training compensation,[66] or solidarity payments.[67]

Club-SGB disputes are also dominated by football-related cases, but not quite to the same extent as club-individual and inter-club disputes. In this category we also find cases relating to, for example, athletics, basketball, and cycling. Cases belonging to this category are also quite heterogeneous in terms of subject matter. Like club-individual and inter-club disputes, some club-SGB disputes concern player transfers and employment relationships.[68] However, in this category we also find cases concerning, for example, the enforcement of CAS decisions[69] and SGBs' liability for damages they have caused clubs.[70]

The most interesting cases belonging to this category are however, in my opinion, those where the limits of SGBs' powers to govern sport are challenged and CAS clarifies those limits. This includes cases concerning SGBs' power to regulate the conditions for participation,[71] and to apply and enforce such regulation, thereby deciding who can compete, who is promoted, who is relegated, and who is a champion.[72] While such actions can frequently carry significant financial consequences, they are also heavily connected both to the very core of the competitive aspect of sports and to aspects of sports law that in a functional sense can be likened to administrative or constitutional law.[73]

There are no obvious patterns with regard to which football clubs appear as litigants in such cases. Although there are some clubs that appear multiple times in the dataset,[74] the overwhelming majority of all clubs appear only once and when a

[65] See e.g. CAS 2003/O/486, *Fulham FC v. Olympique Lyonnais*; CAS 2005/O/985, *Feyenoord Rotterdam NV v. Cruzeiro Esporte Club*; CAS 2011/A/2557, *FC Dynamo Kyiv v. AS Nancy-Lorraine*.

[66] See e.g. CAS 2006/A/1181, *FC Metz v. FC Ferencvarosi*; CAS 2010/A/2069, *Galatasaray AS v. Aachener TSV*; CAS 2012/A/2919, *FC Seoul v. Newcastle Jets FC*.

[67] See e.g. CAS 2005/A/896, *Fulham FC v. FC Metz*; CAS 2010/A/2098, *Sevilla FC v. RC Lens*; CAS 2012/A/2875, *Helsingborgs IF v. Parma FC*.

[68] See e.g. CAS 98/201, *Celtic v. UEFA*; CAS 2007/A/1251, *Aris II*; CAS 2008/A/1485, *FC Midtjylland v. FIFA*; CAS 2009/A/1928 & 1929, *Bompastor & Abily*.

[69] CAS 2005/A/957, *Clube Atlético Mineiro v. FIFA*; CAS 2008/A/1658, *SC Fotbal Club Timisoara v. FIFA & RFF*; CAS 2012/A/2689, *SC Sporting Club SA Vaslui v. FIFA*.

[70] CAS 93/103, *SC Langnau v. LSHG* (damages for erroneous decision by a referee); CAS 2013/A/3273, *Cruz Azul v. FFC & FIFA* (damages for player injured while playing for national team).

[71] See e.g. CAS 98/200, *AEK Athens* (ban on multi-club ownership); CAS 2009/A/1869, *FC La Chaux-de-Fonds v. SFL* (restrictions of the legal form of member clubs).

[72] See e.g. CAS 98/185, *RSC Anderlecht v. UEFA* (refusal to admit club to compete on grounds of corruption); CAS 2010/A/2170 & 2171, CAS 2010/A/2170 & 2171, *Iraklis & OFI v. HFF* (promotion and relegation); CAS 2011/A/2529, *FC Nouadhibou v. FFRIM* (selection of national champion); CAS 2013/A/3199, *Rayo Vallecano de Madrid SAD v. RFEF* (refusal to grant license after bankruptcy).

[73] See also Sect. 7.2.

[74] For example, the French football club FC Metz appears in four unrelated disputes and in different positions: CAS 2005/A/896, *Fulham FC v. FC Metz* (requesting solidarity payment for

club appears in several cases they frequently relate to the same underlying factual circumstances.[75]

Clubs are generally unsuccessful as appellants, at least when appearing without the support of individuals or SGBs. They are also unsuccessful in cases where they face a combination of clubs and SGBs as respondents. Looking at this same combination of litigants but from the opposite side, it is the only one where clubs are significantly successful as respondents.[76]

10.4 Sports Governing Bodies as CAS Litigants

Federations and other SGBs are by far the most common class of litigants that come before CAS. Of all CAS decisions studied, 85 percent contained an SGB on at least one side of the dispute. SGBs appear before CAS particularly often as respondents, having almost two-thirds of their appearances as a respondent compared to little more than one-third as an applicant.[77] The reason for this is, as discussed above, that a large portion of CAS's caseload consists of appeals of SGB decisions.

It is perhaps more unexpected, at least at first glance, that 58 percent of all cases brought by SGBs and 31 percent of all cases in the dataset have an SGB on both sides of the disputes.[78] Thus, almost one-third of all decisions studied involved CAS resolving a dispute between SGBs, what will here be referred to as an inter-SGB dispute.

These inter-SGB disputes can be split into two groups. Roughly half of all inter-SGB disputes involve SGBs bringing a case against a combination of individual and SGB respondents,[79] in all but a few instances concerning a doping violation. Almost two-thirds of those decisions involved the World Anti-Doping Agency (WADA) as an appellant, by itself or together with an international SGB, appealing a national or international SGBs decision in a doping matter that it

---

player L.); CAS 2006/A/1181, *FC Metz v. FC Ferencvarosi* (being requested to pay training compensation); CAS 2009/A/1756, *FC Metz v. Galatasaray SK* (requesting solidarity payment for player F.); CAS 2013/A/3417, *FC Metz v. NK Nafta Lendava* (being requested to pay training compensation).

[75] See e.g. CAS 2005/A/927, *Parma FC v. Manchester United FC*; CAS 2009/A/1908, *Parma FC v. Manchester United FC* (both regarding Manchester United paying Parma training compensation for the same player).

[76] See above Table 10.2 *Litigant Combinations and Mean Outcome*. It can be noted that while clubs have a better than average outcome score as respondents in certain litigant combinations, those differences are not statistically significant.

[77] See above Table 10.1 *Litigant Appearances by Class and Side*.

[78] Ibid. It is much less common that individuals and SGBs team up as applicants. Ibid.

[79] See above Table 10.2 *Litigant Combinations and Mean Outcome*.

considered to be too lenient, naming both the deciding SGB and the athlete accused of a doping violation as respondents.[80]

While some of the decisions belonging to the other half of the inter-SGB disputes relate to doping,[81] this is not particularly common. Those cases more commonly concern a broad range of other issues, including recognition of federations,[82] recognition of officials,[83] the nationality of athletes related to their eligibility to compete,[84] other issues relating to team selection,[85] disciplinary sanctions,[86] observance of proper norm-making procedures,[87] and the outcome of sport competitions.[88] These examples illustrate the breadth and importance of issues that are settled by CAS in inter-SGB disputes. When this is considered in conjunction with the noticeable volume of such disputes that passes through CAS, it is clear that one of the important roles that CAS plays is to serve as a forum for resolving inter-SGB disputes.

Inter-SGB disputes are also interesting from a structural perspective. CAS decisions in inter-SGB disputes are slightly better grounded in existing CAS jurisprudence than the average CAS decision, both in a quantitative and qualitative sense.[89] However, the long-term impact of these decisions on CAS jurisprudence as precedent is lower than the average CAS decision.[90] Inter-SGB disputes stand out in this regard as these two aspects of the structural importance of jurisprudence otherwise generally tend to point in the same direction, or at least not in different directions.[91]

One possible explanation for decisions in inter-SGB disputes being more well-grounded in CAS jurisprudence is the high level of experience, expertise, and resources that may come with having SGBs on both sides of a dispute. All else

---

[80] See e.g. CAS 2007/A/1434 & 1435, *Pinter*; CAS 2008/A/1551, *Cherubin*; CAS 2008/A/1738, *Busch*; CAS 2013/A/3112, *Chernova*.

[81] See e.g. CAS 95/122, *NWBA v. IPC*; CAS 2003/A/442, *FFE v. FIE*.

[82] See e.g. CAS 2004/A/776, *FCP v. FIRS*; CAS 2001/A/329, *GBA v. IBF;* CAS 2002/O/410, *GFA v. UEFA*; CAS 2006/A/1088, *RBF v. IBF*; CAS 2007/A/1424, *FEB v. FIQ & FCBB*.

[83] See e.g. CAS 2007/A/1392, *FPJ & FVJ v. IJF*; CAS 2008/O/1808, *KFF v. FIFA*.

[84] See e.g. CAS 94/132, *PRABF v. USAB*; CAS 98/209, *FEB v. FIBA*.

[85] See e.g. 2004/A/544, *CBH v. FEI*; CAS 2008/A/1502, *AOC & AWU v. FILA*.

[86] See e.g. CAS 96/157, *FIN v. FINA*; CAS 2004/A/725, *USOC v. IOC & IAAF*.

[87] See e.g. CAS 99/O/229, *FFESSM et al. v. CMAS*; CAS 2003/O/450, *FSSE v. FEI*; CAS 2008/O/1455, *Boxing Australia v. AIBA*.

[88] See e.g. CAS 2000/A/305, *CPC v. IPC*; CAS 2008/A/1641, *NAOC v. IAAF & USOC*.

[89] CAS decisions in intra-SGB disputes have a mean outdegree of 3.8, compared to a general mean of 3.6, and a mean hub score of 0.086, compared to a general mean of 0.075. Thus, to use the same terminology as above, decisions in intra-SGB disputes generally have greater persuasive power than other CAS decisions.

[90] CAS decisions in intra-SGB disputes have a mean indegree of 2.2, compared to a general mean of 2.9, and a mean PageRank of 0.00081, compared to a general mean of 0.00091. To use the terminology used above, decisions in intra-SGB disputes generally have less precedential power than other CAS decisions.

[91] Compare Tables 6.3, 6.4, 6.5, 6.6, 6.7 and 6.8.

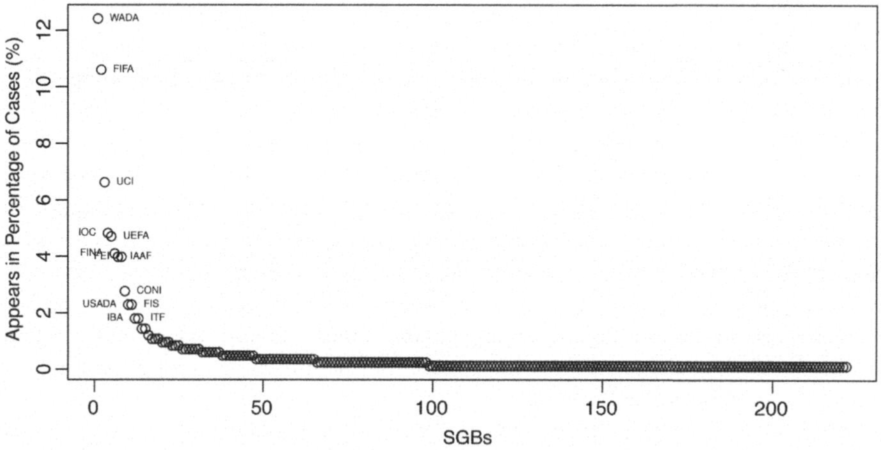

Fig. 10.1 Appearances by SGBs as Litigants. [*Source* The author]

being equal, we would reasonably expect experienced and well-resourced litigants to be able to present more well-developed arguments, including arguments supported by more and/or more well-selected previous decisions. The overall comparatively low precedential power of CAS decisions in inter-SGB disputes does however indicate that these decisions are primarily important to the parties to the individual dispute and that their contribution as precedents that is relevant to rely upon in subsequent decisions is relatively low compared to other CAS decisions.

While SGBs as a class frequently appear as litigants in CAS, not all SGBs are repeat litigants. Much like arbitrator appointments,[92] party appearances in CAS follow a power law distribution with considerable differences between SGBs with regard to how frequently they appear before CAS. As one might have expected, most of the repeat litigants before CAS are major international federations, like those governing football (FIFA), cycling (UCI), swimming (FINA), and athletics (IAAF), and other international SGBs, like WADA and IOC.

WADA is by far the one single actor that most frequently appears as a litigant before CAS, appearing in more than 12 percent of all studied decisions.[93] Although this is a fairly large portion, it is actually misleadingly low considering that WADA appeared before CAS for the first time in 2005 and that it has consistently appeared more frequently over time. The disputes that WADA is involved in follow a clear profile. In four out of five decisions, WADA appears as the appellant with a combination of an individual athlete and an SGB[94] as co-respondents. In these

---

[92] See Sect. 8.3.

[93] See above Fig. 10.1 *Appearances by SGBs as Litigants.*

[94] An international federation, NADO, or NOC.

cases, WADA typically acts as the enforcer of the WADC, appealing a decision by the respondent SGB where the respondent athlete was suspected of doping and, according to WADA, was wrongfully acquitted or received a too lenient sanction.[95] That WADA would need to police that federations and other SGBs applied the WADC in an efficient and consistent manner in the years following its implementation was to be expected. It is also natural that there will always be some need for such actions. It is however somewhat puzzling that there is no clear indication in the data that such actions have become less common over time and towards the later parts of the studied period.[96] This could indicate that SGBs as a group are not sufficiently improving how they apply and enforce the WADC. However, another possible explanation that fits the findings is that SGBs are improving in this regard but that WADA at the same time have increased its efforts to monitor and appeal decisions in doping-related matters.

SGBs are successful as litigants in CAS. SGBs is the only class of appellants that win more cases than they lose and if we exclude disputes that only involve SGBs their success over respondents is quite extensive.[97] WADA is particularly successful as an appellant, being at least partially successful in 86 percent of the appeals that it brings to CAS.[98] SGBs are also overall more successful than average as respondents. This is particularly true if one disregards disputes where SGBs appear as respondents together with an individual against an SGB, many of which are, as discussed above, doping-related cases brought by WADA.

While most CAS repeat litigants are SGBs, not all SGBs are CAS repeat litigants. Many international federations, like for example the International Rowing Federation (FISA) and the International Canoe Federation (ICF), only appear in a few of the studied decisions and there are several national Olympic committees (NOCs) and anti-doping organizations (NADOs) who have appeared in more CAS disputes than some international sport federations. There are even some non-SGB actors, particularly football clubs, that appear more often as litigants before CAS than some international federations.[99]

[95] See e.g. CAS 2007/A/1370 & 1376, *Lucas Dodô*; CAS 2007/A/1396 & 1402, *Valverde III*; CAS 2009/A/1870, *Hardy*.

[96] These types of actions' portion of all doping-related decisions vary markedly, between 10 and 60% on a year-by-year basis but there is no clear trend.

[97] See above Table 10.2 *Litigant Combinations and Mean Outcome*.

[98] Decisions that involve WADA on the applicant side has an average outcome score of 0.46.

[99] One of the more frequently appearing non-SGB parties is the Turkish football club Galatasaray, which was a party in six studied decisions: CAS 2004/A/659, *Felipe II*; CAS 2004/A/701, *Sport Club Internacional v. Galatasaray SK*; CAS 2005/A/811, *Galatasaray SK v. MSV Duisburg*; CAS 2006/A/1180, *Ribery*; CAS 2009/A/1756, *FC Metz v. Galatasaray SK*; CAS 2010/A/2069, *Galatasaray SK v. Aachener TSV*.

10.5 Geographic Origin of CAS Litigants

CAS was originally conceived and is frequently described as a global or international arbitration institution.[100] For example, Kane describes CAS as "the superior arbitral body competent to hear international sporting disputes."[101] Some have however questioned CAS's international character. In 1992, Nafziger commented on CAS's distinctly European character, claiming that "[a]lthough the CAS was intended to have a global scope, it is essentially a European institution."[102] Nafziger points to the heavy European influence on CAS's institutional composition,[103] and that its influence is limited by its "European orientation".[104] Much time has passed since Nafziger made those comments and it is appropriate to examine to what extent CAS has been able to expand beyond its "European orientation" such that it can be described as a "true" international or global institution.

We have previously examined the international character of CAS in terms of the geographical origin of its arbitrators. In doing so, we found that the diversity found on ICAS's list of CAS arbitrators is not reflected in arbitrator appointments as arbitrators based in Oceania and North America but above all Europe receive an overwhelming majority of all appointments. Arbitrators from these continents have received more than nine out of ten appointments and CAS may in that regard come across as more of a Western than global dispute resolution institution.[105]

In this section we will continue the examination of the international character of CAS by in a similar manner considering the geographical origin of the litigants that come before CAS. To have geographically well-distributed litigants is not the final or ultimate measurement of the international nature of a dispute resolution institution. However, if an institution that is intended to be international in nature suffers from a distinct lack of geographical diversity among its litigants, further investigations are prudent.

In order to examine where CAS litigants come from, we compile and compare the nationality of all litigants involved in the studied CAS disputes, regardless of which side of the dispute they appeared, whether they are private individuals, clubs, or federations, or whether they appeared together with other litigants on the same side of the dispute. International federations and other international SGBs are however excluded from consideration since they have no strong connection to any particular nation. For example, one could arguably characterize the IOC and FIFA as being Swiss considering that they have their seats and principle centers of activity in Switzerland. However, to do so would dramatically skew the results towards Switzerland in a way that has no bearing on the type of litigant

[100] See e.g. Reeb 1998, pp. xxiii–xxxiv and Sect. 1.1.

[101] Kane 2003, p. 636.

[102] Nafziger 1992, p. 507.

[103] Ibid., p. 507.

[104] Ibid., p. 508.

[105] See Sect. 9.2.4.

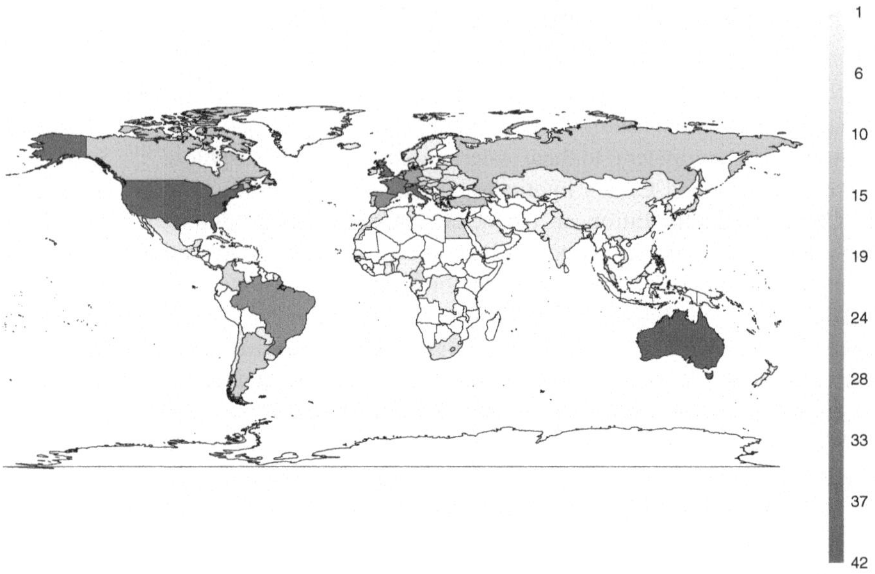

Fig. 10.2 Geographic Origin of CAS Litigants - First Half (Color figure online). [*Source* The author]

geographical diversity that we are interested in here. Finally, to detect possible developments in the geographical origin of CAS parties over time, the studied decisions will be divided into two halves, an earlier and a later half, based on when the decisions were delivered.[106]

This approach produces several, interesting findings. First, although a large portion of the parties that come before CAS are based in European nations, they are not so dominant that CAS, solely on that ground, can be described as "European oriented". However, on a general level, CAS litigants, much like CAS arbitrators, are heavily concentrated in Western Europe, North America, and Australia. This is particularly clear in the first half of the collected CAS decisions.[107] For example, there are only a few examples of African, Middle-Eastern, and South-East Asian litigants appearing before CAS in the first half. Although Brazil is one notable exception, it would not be entirely unfair to claim that CAS during this period was to some extent "Western oriented" in terms of who in practice made use of its services.

Second, most of the nations that produced a large number of CAS litigants in the first half remain in the top in the second half where there is still a noticeable

[106] The median decision date of the studied decisions, which is used to split the decisions, is 16 July 2008.

[107] See above Fig. 10.2 *Geographic Origin of CAS Litigants - First Half.*

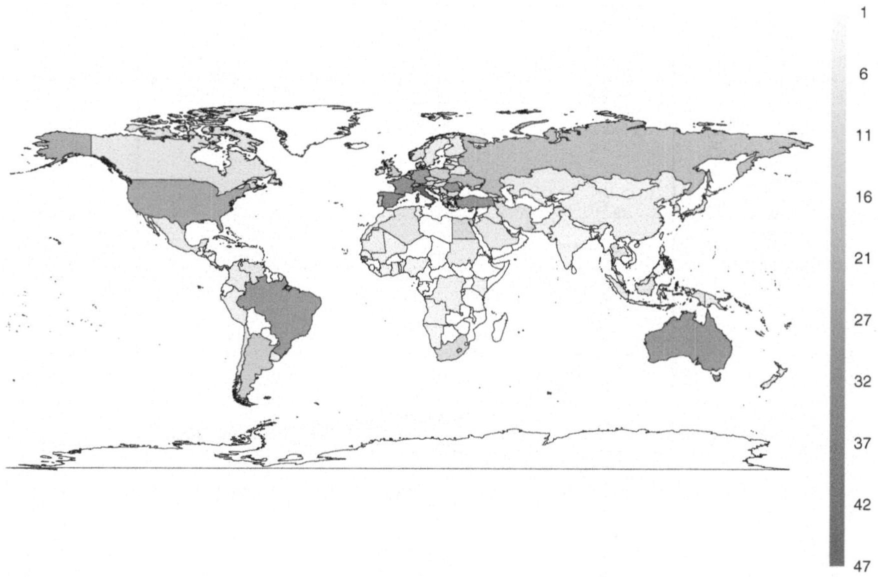

Fig. 10.3 Geographic Origin of CAS Litigants – Second Half (Color figure online). [*Source* The author]

Western-orientation.[108] However, while there is still room for increased geographical diversity with regard to the litigants that appear before CAS, it is quite clear that it has improved over time. In CAS decisions from the second half we find litigants from many nations that were not represented in the first half, particularly nations located in Africa, South America, the Middle East, and South-East Asia. There is also a noticeable increase of litigants from the Eastern parts of Europe. Litigants from Turkey, Romania, Ukraine, and Russia are common in the second half of the decisions. In order to allow for increased diversity in terms of the geographical origin of CAS litigants, litigants from some nations must become less dominant.[109] While many Western nations have been affected by this, the United Kingdom, Canada, the United States, and Australia have been particularly affected. Thus, while English has become more dominant as CAS's main working language over time,[110] litigants from the world's main English-speaking nations have interestingly become less dominant as CAS litigants.

[108] See above Fig. 10.3 *Geographic Origin of CAS Litigants – Second* Half. For example, Italy, the United States, Spain, France, and Germany.

[109] It should be noted that this is type of dominance is relative and does not, of course, affect the absolute number of litigants from a particular nation. The total number of litigants in CAS, as the total number of cases, has increased over time.

[110] See Sect. 9.4.

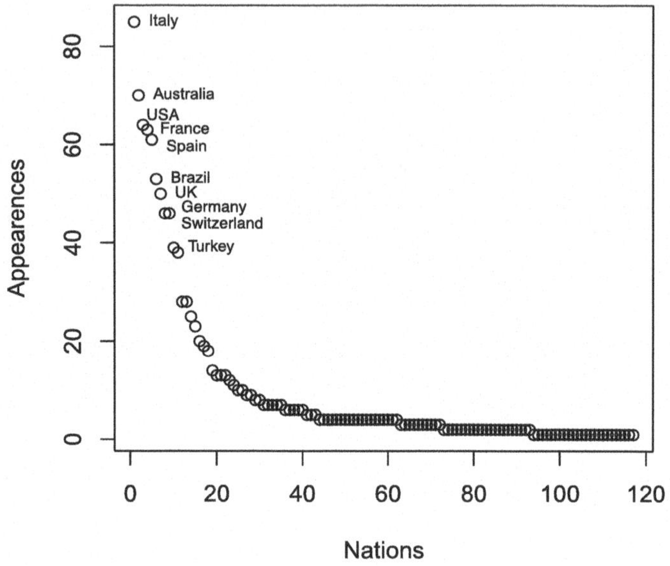

Fig. 10.4 Geographical Origin of CAS Litigants by Nation. [*Source* The author]

Third and finally, although a trend towards a more equal geographic distribution is detectable over time, it is still far from equal and most litigants that come before CAS are based in a relatively limited number of nations.[111]

There is no immediately obvious reason why litigants that come before CAS tend to be based in particular nations. A first factor that obviously could affect how frequently actors from individual nations appear as CAS litigants is population size. One could imagine that the more people there are in a nation, the greater the number of actors involved in sports and the greater the risk that a sports-related dispute involving these actors will arise. The economic situation in a nation could also help explain the relative number of litigants it sends to CAS. A substantial portion of the disputes that come before CAS involve commercial dealings and monetary damages. Actors also have greater incentives to bring an action – which takes energy, money, and other resources – the greater the amounts at stake. Along similar lines, applicants have greater incentives to bring monetary claims against respondents of financial means.[112] It is therefore plausible that disputes connected to nations where there is more money involved in sports are more likely to end up before CAS. One problem with this approach is that there is not any reliable global data on the size of the sports economy of different nations.[113] A rough but reliable, straightforward,

[111] See above Fig. 10.4 *Geographical Origin of CAS Litigants by Nation.*

[112] Cf. Franck 2007, p. 29 (finding that applicants in investor-state disputes tend to be based in high-income nations).

[113] At least as far as I have been able to determine.

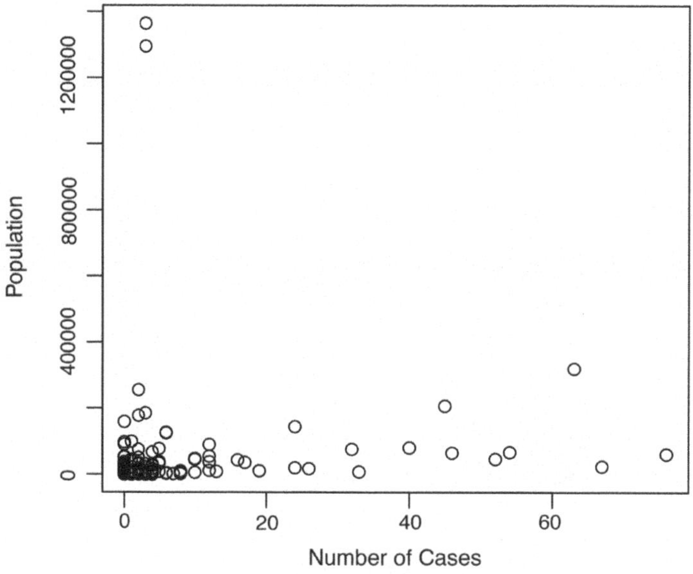

Fig. 10.5 CAS Litigants and Population by Nation. [*Source* The author]

commonly used, and fairly objective measurement for comparing different nations' economic situations is however gross national income (GNI) per capita.[114]

There does not appear to be any relevant correlation between the size of a nation's population and the number of litigants it sends to CAS. While many CAS litigants come from more populous nations, like the United States and Brazil, nations with relatively small populations, like Australia and Italy, dwarfs the most populous nations in the world, like China and India.[115]

GNI per capita is a somewhat better predictor for how frequently litigants from certain nations appear before CAS: nations with very low GNI per capita have very few CAS litigants and nations that send a high number of litigants also have a relatively high GNI per capita.[116] The correlation between GNI per capita and CAS litigants is however far from absolute. For example, the United States, Canada, and Australia have comparable GNI per capita, but there are many more CAS decisions involving Australian and American parties than Canadian parties. Consistent with the reasoning above, one might expect CAS to settle more disputes involving American parties than Canadian parties simply because there are more Americans

[114] The analysis in this part uses the World Bank's dataset for GNI per capita (Alpha method) as per 8 January 2015.

[115] See above Fig. 10.5 *CAS Litigants and Population by Nation*. For example, when measuring the number of CAS decisions involving a litigant from particular nations per 1 million inhabitants, there are around 2.9 decisions for Australia and around 0.002 decisions for both China and India.

[116] See below Fig. 10.6 *CAS Litigants and GNI by Nation*.

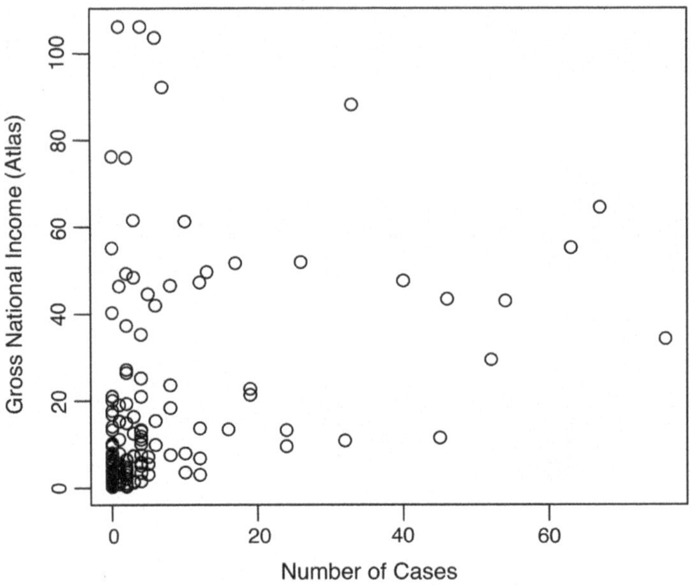

Fig. 10.6 CAS Litigants and GNI by Nation. [*Source* The author]

than Canadians but that would not explain why there are so many Australian CAS litigants.

A third possible factor is what sports are popular in particular nations. A significant portion of CAS jurisprudence concerns football and we could therefore expect litigants from nations where football is a relatively large sport to appear more frequently in CAS decisions. However, while the distribution of nationalities of CAS litigants in non-football-related decisions is somewhat different from the overall distribution, the difference is not particularly strong. Moreover, it is not necessarily the nations that one would expect to be affected by removing football cases that are affected. European nations, where many of the most commercially successful football clubs are located, become slightly less dominant but are still very strong. For example, Italy is still among the three most well-represented nations in CAS even if we disregard football-related disputes. Despite Italy's strong reputation as a football nation, a closer examination of CAS decisions that include at least one Italian litigant reveals that only approximately one-third of those cases concern football.[117] The generally strong position of American and Australian litigants becomes even more accentuated if we remove football-related cases while African nations, along with some South American and Latin American nations, almost entirely disappear. Thus, it appears that the above-observed increase in

[117] Among Italy-related CAS disputes, the single largest sport concerned is cycling.

litigant nationality diversity in the latter half is to some extent connected to football-related disputes.

The examination has thus far focused on the geographical distribution of CAS litigants generally, that is across all CAS decisions. This reveals the international character of CAS's "clientele" which is one important factor when considering the international or global character of a dispute resolution institution. A related but distinctly different factor is the international character of the disputes, that is if the resolved disputes are in some way connected to multiple nations. An overall geographically diverse set of litigants could mean that the underlying disputes have an international character, but this is not necessarily the case. It would be consistent with the findings above, albeit unlikely, that CAS primarily resolves disputes with litigants from the same nation but that those such essentially national disputes come from multiple different nations. While this would confirm CAS's status as an international dispute resolution institution, it would make it so in a rather particular sense.

There is no established or uncontestable way of determining whether a particular dispute is national or international in nature. For example, a dispute may have arisen between two football clubs located in the same nation concerning training compensation for a player that was transferred to a third club located in a second nation. Reasonable minds could differ as to whether this is a national dispute, an international dispute, or something in between. However, the geographic diversity of the litigants involved in a particular dispute should overall function as a fairly good proxy for the international character of the underlying dispute, at least on a general level. Geographic diversity here refers to whether a case involves non-international litigants[118] based in different nations. This can obviously only be measured for cases that involves at least two non-international litigants.[119] Since international SGBs make up a large portion of all CAS litigants,[120] this unfortunately drastically reduces the number of observations.[121] Studying these decisions reveals that little more than half of them involved litigants of different nationalities.[122] Differently phrased, little less than half of these decisions could be described as international disputes in the sense that the non-international litigants involved were based in different nation.

While CAS's portion of international disputes in this sense is perhaps lower than one might expect from an international dispute resolution institution, two things should be born in mind. First, it is important to point out that one in five of those cases involved an international SGB as litigant. While it measures yet another

[118] I.e. litigants that are not international SGBs.

[119] Whether these litigants appeared on the same side of the litigation is not taken into consideration. It would be relevant and interesting to consider differences within and between the sides but to do so would require a larger data sample.

[120] See above Sect. 10.4 and immediately below.

[121] 329 of the 830 collected decisions (39.6%) meet this criterion.

[122] 54.7%. The mean number of unique nationalities in this set was 1.6, but the data includes cases involving litigants of as many as six different nationalities.

aspect of the international character of CAS's activities, it is important to keep in mind the internationalization that takes place by involving an international SGB as a litigant. If viewed from this perspective, CAS is quite clearly an international dispute resolution institution as two out of three studied decisions involved at least one international SGB, most commonly on the respondent side.[123] This can be viewed to reflect, as one might have expected, the international character of sports and the extensive involvement of international SGBs.

Second, a non-negligible number of these disputes can be referred to as examples of domestic arbitration in the sense that the dispute involved two Swiss-based parties that came before a Swiss-based arbitration court.[124] The fact that many international federations and other international SGBs are based in Switzerland significantly contribute to this, but there is also a number of domestic Swiss disputes settled by CAS in the dataset that does not include an international SGB on either side of the dispute. Most of these cases are actions brought by Swiss clubs against a Swiss SGB, such as the Swiss ice hockey federation (Ligue Suisse de Hockey sur Glace, LSHG)[125] and the Swiss Football League.[126]

10.6 The Roles of CAS

This review has revealed that CAS plays many different roles and that these different roles to some extent overlap with different classes of litigants. To individual litigants, and particularly athletes, CAS is predominantly an institution where they challenge decisions by SGBs preventing them from competing. Thus, one could say that from the athletes' perspective CAS is the one that watches, or at least is capable of watching, the warders.[127] CAS's role in adjudicating those disputes can be compared to that of an administrative court, seeking to ensure that SGBs and their disciplinary bodies follow proper procedure, respect fundamental rights, and interpret and apply the applicable rules in a correct and consistent manner.

CAS also quite frequently plays this type role in relation to clubs and SGBs. However, in relation to those classes of litigants, CAS also plays other significant roles. In many inter-SGB disputes CAS serves a function that is somewhat similar to that of arbitration tribunals in inter-state disputes in that it acts as a neutral arbiter that settles disputes between policy- and norm-making bodies that to some extent

---

[123] 67.1%. However, only 3.6% of the decisions involved an international SGB on both the applicant and respondent side.

[124] There are different rules under Swiss law governing CAS when it engages in domestic arbitration compared to international arbitration. See Sect. 2.1.

[125] CAS 86/1, *Niederhasli HC v. LSHG*; CAS 93/103, *SC Langnau v. LSHG*; CAS 98/190, *HC Prilly v. LSHG*.

[126] CAS 2006/A/1095, *FC Zurich v. SFL & FC Sion*; CAS 2006/A/1154, *FC Locarno v. SFL*; CAS 2009/A/1869, *FC La Chaux-de-Fonds v. SFL*.

[127] Cf. Juvenal 1918, Satire VI, lines 347–348.

consider themselves autonomous and independent of each other, disputes for which there are no obvious alternative formal dispute resolution mechanisms.[128] A comparison can also be made with courts that resolve constitutional conflicts regarding the division of power between different political entities within a shared system. Finally, many of the cases that come before CAS and that involve disputes between clubs have a quite strong commercial dimension. In those cases and to those litigants, CAS plays a role that is similar to commercial arbitration tribunals, with the major differences being the nature of the issues involved in the dispute and the rules governing those issues. CAS makes an important contribution with regard to all its three main roles and it is difficult to identify another institution that could easily fill its shoes in any of them.

At first glance, the data seems to support that the three classes of litigants can be ranked in terms of outcome. Most obviously, SGBs tend to do significantly better than average both as appellants and respondents against individuals and as respondents against clubs.[129] Observing this pattern might cause one to speculate that these entities have a competitive edge in proceedings before CAS. One could speculate that such a competitive edge could come from them having more resources or greater litigation experience or, more sinisterly, because they, in the words of the European Court of Human Rights, have exercised "a real influence over the arbitration appointment mechanism" in CAS.[130]

However, I would caution against drawing such a conclusion. First, as discussed in this chapter, the most common disputes between combinations of litigants are frequently quite different from each other and it is far from given that litigants with comparable resources and influence can be expected to win to the same extent regardless of the nature of the disputes. Second, there is no observable correlation between litigation experience and mean outcome among SGBs,[131] and there is not, as far as I can see, an obvious explanation why these factors would be correlated between classes of litigants but not within classes of litigants.

Finally, it is worth pointing out that CAS, based on the collected decisions, overturn, in whole or in part, almost 55 percent of all appealed decisions. This spontaneously seems like a rather high overturn rate, although it is difficult to find another arbitration tribunal that exercise a similar appellate function as CAS and to which CAS can be fairly compared. Also, the nature of the disputes that come before CAS and the rules governing them have no perfect corollary in national and international legal orders. One can however note that the overturn rate in national

[128] See above Sect. 10.1.

[129] See above Table 10.2 *Litigant Combinations and Mean Outcome*.

[130] ECtHR's decision 2 October 2018 in *Mutu & Pechstein v. Switzerland*, appl. no. 40575/10 & 67474/10, para 157 ("Si la Cour est prête à reconnaitre que les organisations susceptibles de s'opposer aux athlètes dans le cadre de litiges portés devant le TAS exerçaient une réelle influence dans le mécanisme de nomination des arbitres en vigueur à l'époque des faits") (my translation).

[131] For example, FINA and FEI appear as litigants in the data roughly the same number of times and in similar types of disputes, but whereas FINA as a respondent is more successful than average (-0.45) FEI is less successful than average (-0.17).

appellate courts generally appears to be significantly lower. For example, the United States Courts of Appeal reverse between 3 and 14 percent of the lower courts' decisions, depending on the type of dispute and year-to-year variations,[132] and one study shows that the overturn rate of Canadian appellate courts is even lower.[133] One way to interpret this observation is that SGBs and their decision-making bodies quite frequently get their decisions wrong, at least in part, if we believe that CAS gets it right. If so, one should reasonably also conclude that CAS serves an important function in setting those decisions right.

References

Blackaby N, Partasides C, Redfern A and Hunter M (2015), Redfern and Hunter on International Arbitration, 6th edn. Oxford University Press, Oxford

Blackshaw I (2013) ADR and Sport: Settling Disputes Through the Court of Arbitration for Sport, the FIFA Dispute Resolution Chamber, and the WIPO Arbitration & Mediation Center. Marquette Sports Law Review 24(1):1–57

Born G (2014) International Commercial Arbitration, 2nd edn. Wolters Kluwer, Alphen aan den Rijn

Drahozal C, Friel R (2002) Consumer Arbitration in the European Union and the United States. North Carolina Journal of International Law and Commercial Regulation 28(2):357–394

Franck S (2007) Empirically Evaluating Claims About Investment Treaty Arbitration. North Carolina Law Review 86:1–88

Hobér K (2004) Arbitration Involving States. In: Newman L, Hill R (eds) The Leading Arbitrators' Guide to International Arbitration. Juris, pp. 139–162

Kane D (2003) Twenty Years On: An Evaluation of the Court of Arbitration for Sport. Melbourne Journal of International Law 4:611–635

Lubetsky M H, Krane J A (2009) Appealing Outcomes: A Study for the Overturn Rate of Canada's Appellate Courts. Osgoode Hall Law Journal 47(1):131–149

Mavromati D (2016) The Rules Governing the CAS Anti-Doping and Ad Hoc Divisions at the Olympic Games, 29 August 2016. https://ssrn.com/abstract=2816482. Accessed 6 July 2018

Nafziger J (1992) International Sports Law: A Replay of Characteristics and Trends. American Journal of International Law: 86:489–518

Reeb M (1998) The Court of Arbitration for Sport (CAS). In: Reeb M (ed) Digest of CAS Awards I. Kluwer Law International, The Hague, pp. xxiii–xxxi

Rigozzi A (2005) L'arbitrage international en matière de sport. Helbing & Lichtenhahn, Basel

Tweeddale A, Tweeddale K (2005) Arbitration of Commercial Disputes: International and English Law and Practice. Oxford University Press, Oxford

Valero A (2014) In search of a working notion of lex sportiva. The International Sports Law Journal 14:3–11

Ware S (2001) Paying the Price of Process: Judicial Regulation of Consumer Arbitration Agreements. Journal of Dispute Resolution 2001(1):89–101

---

[132] United States Courts, "Just the Facts: U.S. Courts of Appeals", Chart 3. http://www.uscourts.gov/news/2016/12/20/just-facts-us-courts-appeals#chart3. Accessed 16 June 2018 (bankruptcy cases ignored because of the special nature of such disputes and the lack of similarity with CAS's cases).

[133] Lubetsky and Krane 2009.

Table of Cases

Decisions by the Court of Arbitration for Sport

CAS 86/1, Niederhasli HC v. Ligue Suisse de Hockey sur Glace (LSHG)
CAS 86/02, International Olympic Committee (IOC) & NOC
CAS 91/53, G. v. Fédération Equestre Internationale (FEI)
CAS 91/56, S v. Fédération Equestre Internationale (FEI)
CAS 92/63, Gundel v. Fédération Equestre Internationale (FEI)
CAS 92/71, SJ v. Fédération Equestre Internationale (FEI)
CAS 92/73, N v. Fédération Equestre Internationale (FEI)
CAS 92/80, B. v. Fédération Internationale de Basketball (FIBA)
CAS 92/81, L v. Y. SA
CAS 92/86, W. v. Fédération Equestre Internationale (FEI)
CAS 93/103, SC Langnau v. Ligue Suisse de Hockey sur Glace (LSHG)
CAS 93/109, Fédération Française de Triathlon (FFTri) & International Triathlon Union (ITU)
CAS 95/122, National Wheelchair Basketball Association (NWBA) v. International Paralympic Committee (IPC)
CAS 94/123, Fédération Internationale de Basketball (FIBA) v. W. & Brandt Hagen e. V. (Brandt Hagen)
CAS 94/128, Union Cycliste Internationale (UCI) & Comitato Olimpico Nazionale Italiano (CONI)
CAS 94/129, USA Shooting & Quigley v. Union Internationale de Tir (UIT)
CAS 94/132, Puerto Rico Amateur Baseball Federation (PRABF) v. USA Baseball (USAB)
CAS 95/141, Chagnaud v. Fédération Internationale de Natation Amateur (FINA)
CAS 95/142, Lehtinen v. Fédération Internationale de Natation Amateur (FINA)
CAS 95/144, Comités Olympiques Européens (COE)
CAS 95/145, Federation Y
CAS 96/149, Cullwick v. Fédération Internationale de Natation Amateur (FINA)

J. Lindholm, *The Court of Arbitration for Sport and Its Jurisprudence*,
ASSER International Sports Law Series,
https://doi.org/10.1007/978-94-6265-285-9

CAS 95/150, Volkers v. Fédération Internationale de Natation Amateur (FINA)
CAS 96/153, Watt v. Australian Cycling Federation (ACF) & Tyler-Sharman
CAS 96/156, Foschi v. Fédération Internationale de Natation Amateur (FINA)
CAS 96/157, Federazione Italiana Nuoto (FIN) v. Fédération Internationale de Natation Amateur (FINA)
CAS 97/168, Fédération Française des Sociétés d'Aviron (FFSA), Federazione Italiana Canottaggio (FIC), Fédération Royale Néerlandaise des Sociétés d'Aviron (FNSA) v. Fédération Internationale des Sociétés d'Aviron (FISA)
CAS 97/169, Menegotto v. Federazione Ciclistica Italiana
CAS 97/176, Union Cycliste Internationale (UCI) v. Jogert & NCF
CAS 98/185, RSC Anderlecht v. Union of European Football Associations (UEFA)
CAS 98/190, HC Prilly v. Ligue Suisse de Hockey sur Glace (LSHG)
CAS 98/192, Union Cycliste Internationale (UCI) v. S, Danmarks Cykle Union (DCU) & Danmarks Idraets-Forbund (DIF)
CAS 98/200, AEK Athens & SK Slavia Prague v. Union of European Football Associations (UEFA)
CAS 98/201, Celtic v. Union of European Football Associations (UEFA)
CAS 98/208, Wang et al. v. Fédération Internationale de Natation Amateur (FINA)
CAS 98/209, Spanish Basketball Federation (FEB) v. Fédération Internationale de Basketball (FIBA)
CAS 98/211, de Bruin v. Fédération Internationale de Natation Amateur (FINA)
CAS 98/214, Bouras v. Fédération Internationale de Judo (FIJ)
CAS 98/215, International Baseball Association (IBA)
CAS 98/218, Hall v. Fédération Internationale de Natation Amateur (FINA)
CAS 98/222, Bernhard v. International Triathlon Union (ITU)
CAS 99/A/223, International Tennis Federation (ITF) v. Korda
CAS 99/O/229, Fédération Française d'Etudes et de Sports sous-marins (FFESSM) et al. v. Confédération Mondiale des Activités Subaquatiques (CMAS)
CAS 99/A/234 & 235, Meca Medina & Majcen v. Fédération Internationale de Natation Amateur (FINA) (Meca-Medina & Majcen I)
CAS 1999/A/246, Ward v. Fédération Équestre Internationale (FEI)
CAS 2000/A/260, Beashel & Czislowski v. Australian Yachting Federation (AYF)
CAS 2000/C/267, Australian Olympic Committee (AOC)
CAS 2000/A/270, Meca Medina & Majcen v. Fédération Internationale de Natation Amateur (FINA) (Meca-Medina & Majcen II)
CAS 2000/A/274, Susin v. Fédération Internationale de Natation Amateur (FINA)
CAS 2000/A/281, Haga v. Fédération Internationale de Motocyclisme (FIM)
CAS 2000/A/289, Union Cycliste Internationale (UCI) v. Chiotti & Fédération Française de Cyclisme (FFC)
CAS 2000/A/305, Canadian Paralympic Committee (CPC) v. International Paralympic Committee (IPC)
CAS 2000/A/310, Leipold v. International Olympic Committee (IOC) (Leipold I)
CAS 2000/A/312, Leipold v. International Olympic Committee (IOC) (Leipold II)
CAS 2001/A/317, Aanes v. Fédération Internationale de Luttes Associeés (FILA)
CAS 2001/A/318, Virenque v. Fédération Cycliste Suisse (Swiss Cycling)

CAS 2001/A/329, Gibraltar Badminton Association (GBA) v. International Badminton Federation (IBF)
CAS 2001/A/330, Reinhold v. Fédération Internationale des Sociétés d'Aviron (FISA)
CAS 2001/A/337, Bray v. Fédération Internationale de Natation Amateur (FINA)
CAS 2001/A/343, Union Cycliste Internationale (UCI) v. H.
CAS 2001/A/345, Meier v. Fédération Cycliste Suisse (Swiss Cycling)
CAS 2001/A/354-355, Irish Hockey Association (IHA) v. Lithuanian Hockey Federation (LHF) & International Hockey Federation (FIH) & Lithuanian Hockey Federation (LHF) v. International Hockey Federation (FIH)
CAS 2001/A/357, Nabokov, Russian Olympic Committee (ROC) & Russian Ice Hockey Federation (RIHF) v. International Ice Hockey Federation (IIHF)
CAS 2002/A/361, Berchtold v. Skiing Australia Limited (SAL)
CAS 2002/A/363, Pastorello v. United States Anti-Doping Agency (USADA)
CAS 2002/A/370, Lazutina v. International Olympic Committee (IOC) (Lazutina I)
CAS 2002/A/371, Danilova v. International Olympic Committee (IOC)
CAS 2002/O/372, Norwegian Olympic Committee & Confederation of Sports (NOCCS) et al. v. International Olympic Committee (IOC)
CAS 2002/O/373, Canadian Olympic Committee (COC) & Scott v. International Olympic Committee (IOC)
CAS 2002/A/378, Simeoni v. Union Cycliste Internationale (UCI) & Federazione Ciclista Italiana (FCI)
CAS 2002/A/383, International Association of Athletics Federations (IAAF) v. Confederação Brasileira de Atletisimo (CBAT) & Dos Santos
CAS 2002/A/385, Tchachina v. Fédération Internationale de Gymnastique (FIG)
CAS 2002/A/397, Lazutina v. Fédération Internationale de Ski (FIS) (Lazutina II)
CAS 2002/O/410, Gibraltar Football Association (GFA) v. Union of European Football Associations (UEFA)
CAS 2002/A/417, International Association of Athletics Federations (IAAF) v. Confederación Argentina de Atletismo & Witteveen
CAS 2002/A/431, Union Cycliste Internationale (UCI) v. Roux & Fédération Française de Cyclisme (FFC)
CAS 2003/A/442, Fédération Française d'Escrime (FFE) v. Fédération Internationale d'Escrime (FIE)
CAS 2003/O/450, Fédération Suisse de Sports Equestres (FSSE) v. Fédération Equestre Internationale (FEI)
CAS 2003/O/453, Felipe I
CAS 2003/A/461, 471 & 473, WCM-GP Ltd. v. Fédération Internationale de Motocyclisme (FIM)
CAS 2003/O/486, Fulham FC v. Olympique Lyonnais
CAS 2003/A/506, Unknown
CAS 2003/O/527, Hamburger Sport-Verein v. Odense Boldklub
CAS 2004/A/544, Confédération Brésilienne de Hippisme (CBH) v. Fédération Equestre Internationale (FEI)

CAS 2004/A/549, Deferr & Real Federacion Española de Gimnasia (RFEG) v. Fédération Internationale de Gymnastique (FIG)
CAS 2004/A/574, Associação Portuguesa de Desportos v. Club Valencia
CAS 2004/A/594, Hapoel Beer-Sheva v. Real Racing Club de Santander
CAS 2004/A/607, Boevski v. International Weightlifting Federation (IWF)
CAS 2004/A/628, International Association of Athletics Federations (IAAF) v. USA Track & Field (USATF) & Young
CAS 2004/A/635, Barcelona v. Velez Sarsfield
CAS 2004/A/651, French v. Australian Sports Commission & Cycling Australia
CAS 2004/A/659, Galatasaray SK v. Fédération Internationale de Football Association (FIFA) & Club Regatas Vasco da Gama & Felipe (Felipe II)
CAS 2004/A/676, Ismailia SC v. Confédération Africaine de Football (CAF)
CAS 2004/A/690, Hipperdinger v. Association of Tennis Professionals (ATP)
CAS 2004/A/701, Sport Club Internacional v. Galatasaray SK
CAS 2004/A/707, Millar v. British Cycling Federation
CAS 2004/A/714, Fazekas v. International Olympic Committee (IOC)
CAS 2004/A/725, United States Olympic Committee (USOC) v. International Olympic Committee (IOC) & International Association of Athletics Federations (IAAF)
CAS 2004/A/727, De Lima & Brazilian Olympic Committee (BOC) v. International Association of Athletics Federations (IAAF)
CAS 2004/A/748, Russian Olympic Committee (ROC) & Ekimov v. International Olympic Committee (IOC), United States Olympic Committee (USOC) & Hamilton
CAS 2004/A/776, Federacio Catalana de Patinatge (FCP) v. International Roller Sports Federation (FIRS)
CAS 2004/A/777, ARcycling AG v. Union Cycliste Internationale (UCI)
CAS 2004/A/780, Henning v. Prudentópolis SC & Prudentópolis SC v. Henning & Eintracht Frankfurt Fußball AG
CAS 2004/A/794, Unknown
CAS 2005/A/811, Galatasaray SK v. MSV Duisburg
CAS 2005/A/830, Squizzato v. Fédération Internationale de Natation Amateur (FINA)
CAS 2005/A/835 & 942, PSV Eindhoven v. Fédération Internationale de Football Association (FIFA) & Federação Portuguesa de Futebol (FPF) & PSV Eindhoven v. Bomfim & Fédération Internationale de Football Association (FIFA)
CAS 2005/C/841, Comitato Olimpico Nazionale Italiano (CONI)
CAS 2005/A/847, Knauss v. Fédération Internationale de Ski (FIS)
CAS 2005/A/884, Hamilton v. United States Anti-Doping Agency (USADA) & Union Cycliste Internationale (UCI)
CAS 2005/A/889, Mathare United FC v. Al-Arabi SC
CAS 2005/A/893, Metsu v. Al-Ain Sports Club
CAS 2005/A/896, Fulham FC v. FC Metz

CAS 2005/A/899, FC Aris Thessaloniki v. Fédération Internationale de Football Association (FIFA) & New Panionios NFC (Aris I)
CAS 2005/A/902–903, Mexès & AS Roma v. AJ Auxerre (Mexès II)
CAS 2005/A/908, World Anti-Doping Agency (WADA) v. Wium
CAS 2005/A/916, AS Roma v. Fédération Internationale de Football Association (FIFA)
CAS 2005/A/927, Parma FC v. Manchester United FC
CAS 2005/A/951, Cañas v. ATP Tour
CAS 2005/A/952, Cole v. Football Association Premier League (FAPL)
CAS 2005/A/957, Clube Atlético Mineiro v. Fédération Internationale de Football Association (FIFA)
CAS 2005/C/976 & 986, Fédération Internationale de Football Association (FIFA) & World Anti-Doping Agency (WADA)
CAS 2005/A/983 & 984, Club Atlético Peñarol v. Suarez et al.
CAS 2005/O/985, Feyenoord Rotterdam NV v. Cruzeiro Esporte Club
CAS 2006/A/1008, Rayo Vallecano de Madrid v. Fédération Internationale de Football Association (FIFA)
CAS 2006/A/1018, CA River Plate v. Hamburger SV
CAS 2006/A/1025, Puerta v. International Tennis Federation (ITF)
CAS 2006/A/1029, Maccabi Haifa FC v. Real Racing Club Santander
CAS 2006/A/1062, Da Nghe FC v. Etoga
CAS 2006/A/1082 & 1104, Real Valladolid CF SAD v. Barreto Caceres & Club Cerro Porteno
CAS 2006/A/1088, Russian Badminton Federation (RBF) v. International Badminton Federation (IBF)
CAS 2006/A/1095, FC Zurich v. Swiss Football League (SFL) & FC Sion
CAS 2006/A/1102 & 1142, Eder v. Ski Austria & World Anti-Doping Agency (WADA) v. Eder & Ski Austria
CAS 2006/A/1125, Hertha BSC Berlin v. Stade Lavallois Mayenne FC
CAS 2006/A/1153, World Anti-Doping Agency (WADA) v. Portuguese Football Federation & Lopes de Almeida
CAS 2006/A/1154, FC Locarno v. Swiss Football League (SFL)
CAS 2006/A/1165, Ohuruogu v. UK Athletics & International Association of Athletics Federations (IAAF)
CAS 2006/A/1175, Daniute v. International DanceSport Federation
CAS 2006/A/1177, Aston Villa FC v. B.93 Copenhagen
CAS 2006/A/1180, Galatasaray SK v. Ribéry & Olympique de Marseille
CAS 2006/A/1181, FC Metz v. FC Ferencvarosi
CAS 2006/A/1189, IFK Norrköping v. Trinité Sports FC & Fédération Française de Football (FFF)
CAS 2006/A/1192, Chelsea FC v. Mutu (Mutu II)
CAS 2007/A/1201, Baggaley v. Australian Canoeing, International Canoe Federation & Surf Life Saving Australia (Baggaley II)
CAS 2007/A/1217, Feyenoord Rotterdam v. Union of European Football Associations (UEFA)

CAS 2007/A/1233 & 1234, Universitatea Craiova v. Da Silva & Magri
CAS 2007/A/1251, Aris FC v. Fédération Internationale de Football Association (FIFA) (Aris II)
CAS 2007/A/1252, Fédération Internationale de Natation Amateur (FINA) v. Mellouli & Federation Tunisienne de Natation (FTN)
CAS 2007/A/1286, 1288 & 1289, Eder et al. v. International Olympic Committee (IOC)
CAS 2007/A/1298–1300, Wigan Athletic FC v. Heart of Midlothian & Heart of Midlothian v. Webster & Wigan Athletic FC & Webster v. Heart of Midlothian
CAS 2007/A/1320 & 1321, Feyenoord Rotterdam v. Clube de Regatas do Flamengo
CAS 2007/A/1329 & 1330, Chiapas FC v. Cricuma Esporte Clube
CAS 2007/A/1362, Comitato Olimpico Nazionale Italiano (CONI) & World Anti-Doping Agency (WADA) v. Petacchi
CAS 2007/A/1358, FC Pyunik Yerevan v. Lombe, AFC Rapid Bucaresti & Fédération Internationale de Football Association (FIFA)
CAS 2007/A/1359, FC Pyunik Yerevan v. Bete, AFC Rapid Bucaresti & Fédération Internationale de Football Association (FIFA)
CAS 2007/A/1363, TTF Liebherr Ochsenhausen v. European Table Tennis Union (ETTU)
CAS 2007/A/1370 & 1376, Fédération Internationale de Football Association (FIFA) & World Anti-Doping Agency (WADA) v. Superior Tribunal de Justica Desportiva do Futebol (STJD), Confederacao Brasileira de Futebol (CBF) & Lucas Dodô
CAS 2007/O/1381, Real Federacion Espanola de Ciclismo (RFEC) & Valverde v. Union Cycliste Internationale (UCI) (Valverde I)
CAS 2007/A/1392, Federacion Panamena de Judo (FPJ) & Federacion Venezolana de Judo (FVJ) v. International Judo Federation (IJF)
CAS 2007/A/1394, Landis v. United States Anti-Doping Agency (USADA)
CAS 2007/A/1396 & 1402, World Anti-Doping Agency (WADA) & Union Cycliste Internationale (UCI) & World Anti-Doping Agency (WADA) v. Real Federacion Espanola de Ciclismo (RFEC) & Valverde (Valverde III)
CAS 2007/A/1415, Benjamin v. Fédération Equestre Internationale (FEI)
CAS 2007/A/1424, Federacion Espanola de Bolos (FEB) v. Federation Internationale des Quilleurs (FIQ) & Federacion Catalana de Bitlles i Bowling (FCBB)
CAS 2007/A/1429 & 1442, Sall v. Fédération Internationale de Football Association (FIFA) & IK Start
CAS 2007/A/1434 & 1435, International Olympic Committee (IOC) & World Anti-Doping Agency (WADA) v. Fédération Internationale de Ski (FIS) & Pinter
CAS 2008/A/1448, Razek & Zamalek SC v. PAOK FC & Fédération Internationale de Football Association (FIFA)
CAS 2008/O/1455, Boxing Australia v. International Boxing Association (AIBA)

CAS 2008/A/1458, Union Cycliste Internationale (UCI) v. Vinokourov & Kazahkstan Cycling Federation (KCF)
CAS 2008/A/1471 & 1486, Fédération Internationale de Natation Amateur (FINA) & World Anti-Doping Agency (WADA) v. Tagliaferri, Federazione Italiana Nuoto & Comitato Olimpico Nazionale Italiano (CONI)
CAS 2008/A/1480, Pistorius v. International Association of Athletics Federations (IAAF)
CAS 2008/A/1485, FC Midtjylland A/S v. Fédération Internationale de Football Association (FIFA)
CAS 2008/A/1489 & 2008/A/1510, Despres & Canadian Centre for Ethics and Sport (CCES) & World Anti-Doping Agency (WADA) v. Despres, Canadian Centre for Ethics and Sport (CCES) & Bobsleigh Canada Skeletion (BCS)
CAS 2008/A/1502, Australian Olympic Committee (AOC) & Australian Wrestling Union (AWU) v. FILA
CAS 2008/A/1511, O'Hara v. World Anti-Doping Agency (WADA) & Union of European Football Associations (UEFA)
CAS 2008/A/1513, Hoch v. Fédération Internationale de Ski (FIS) & International Olympic Committee (IOC)
CAS 2008/A/1517, Ionikos FC v. Pajuelo Chávez
CAS 2008/A/1518, Ionikos FC v. Rebelo Lopes
CAS 2008/A/1519-1520, FC Shakhtar Donetsk v. Matuzalem, Real Zaragoza SAD & Fédération Internationale de Football Association (FIFA) & Matuzalem & Real Zaragoza SAD v. FC Shakhtar Donetsk & Fédération Internationale de Football Association (FIFA)
CAS 2008/A/1545, Anderson et al. v. International Olympic Committee (IOC)
CAS 2008/A/1549, Michael v. Australian Canoeing
CAS 2008/A/1551, World Anti-Doping Agency (WADA) v. Comitato Olimpico Nazionale Italiano (CONI), Federazione Italiana Giuoco Calcio (FIGC) & Cherubin
CAS 2008/A/1557, Federazione Italiana Giuoco Calcio (FIGC), Comitato Olimpico Nazionale Italiano (CONI), Mannini & Possanzini v. World Anti-Doping Agency (WADA)
CAS 2008/A/1564, World Anti-Doping Agency (WADA) v. IIHF & Busch
CAS 2008/A/1568, Mica & FC Wil 1900 v. Fédération Internationale de Football Association (FIFA) & Club PFC Naftex AC Bourgas
CAS 2008/A/1574, D'Arcy v. Australian Olympic Committee (AOC)
CAS 2008/A/1576 & 1628, Fédération Internationale de Football Association (FIFA) & World Anti-Doping Agency (WADA) v. Malta Football Association & Grech
CAS 2008/A/1583 & 1584, Sport Lisboa, Benfica Futebol SAD & Vitoria Sport Clube de Guimaraes v. Union of European Football Associations (UEFA) & FC Porto Futebol SAD
CAS 2008/A/1594, Sheykhov v. FILA
CAS 2008/A/1600, Unknown
CAS 2008/A/1605, Jongewaard v. AOC

CAS 2008/A/1615, Hellenic Modern Pentathlon Federation (HMPF) v. Union Internationale de Pentathlon Moderne (UIPM), Australia Olympic Committee (AOC), Modern Pentathlon (MPA) & Darby
CAS 2008/A/1633, FC Schalke 04 v. Confederaçã Brasileira de Futebol (CBF)
CAS 2008/A/1634, Hertha BSC v. Football Association of Serbia (FAS)
CAS 2008/A/1636, Hoy v. Fédération Equestre Internationale (FEI)
CAS 2008/A/1641, NAOC v. International Association of Athletics Federations (IAAF) & USOC
CAS 2008/A/1652 & 1664, World Anti-Doping Agency (WADA) v. Troy & Australian Rugby Union (ARU) & International Rugby Board (IRB) v. Troy
CAS 2008/A/1658, SC Fotbal Club Timisoara v. Fédération Internationale de Football Association (FIFA) & RFF
CAS 2008/A/1665, J. v. Udinese Calcio SpA
CAS 2008/A/1705, Neue Grasshopper Fussball AG v. Club Alianza de Lima
CAS 2008/A/1708, Football Federation Islamic Republic of Iran (IRIFF) v. Fédération Internationale de Football Association (FIFA)
CAS 2008/A/1718–1724, International Association of Athletics Federations (IAAF) v. All Russian Athletic Federation (ARAF) & Yegorova et al.
CAS 2008/A/1738, World Anti-Doping Agency (WADA) v. Deutscher Eishockey Bund e.V. (DEB) & Busch
CAS 2009/A/1752 & 1753, Devyatovskiy & Tsikhan v. International Olympic Committee (IOC)
CAS 2009/A/1756, FC Metz v. Galatasaray SK
CAS 2009/A/1757, MTK Budapest v. FC Internazionale Milano S.p.A.
CAS 2009/A/1768, Hansen v. Fédération Equestre Internationale (FEI)
CAS 2009/A/1782, Volandri v. International Tennis Federation (ITF)
CAS 2008/O/1808, Kenya Football Federation (KFF) v. Fédération Internationale de Football Association (FIFA)
CAS 2009/A/1810 & 1811, SV Wilhelmshaven v. Club A. Excursionistas & Club A. River Plate
CAS 2009/A/1823, Panamerican Judo Union (PJU) v. International Judo Federation (IJF)
CAS 2009/A/1856 & 1857, Club X v. A
CAS 2009/A/1869, La Chaux-de-Fonds v. Swiss Football League (SFL)
CAS 2009/A/1870, World Anti-Doping Agency (WADA) v. Hardy & USADA
CAS 2009/A/1879, Valverde v. Comitato Olimpico Nazionale Italiano (CONI), World Anti-Doping Agency (WADA) & Union Cycliste Internationale (UCI) (Valverde II)
CAS 2009/A/1880 & 1881, FC Sion & El-Hadary v. Fédération Internationale de Football Association (FIFA) & Al-Ahly Sporting Club
CAS 2009/A/1889, Unknown
CAS 2009/A/1892, World Anti-Doping Agency (WADA) v. Comitato Olimpico Nazionale Italiano (CONI), Slay & Diaz Gonzalez
CAS 2009/A/1908, Parma FC SpA v. Manchester United FC
CAS 2009/A/1910, Telecom Egypt Club v. Egyptian Football Association (EFA)

CAS 2009/A/1912 & 1913, Pechstein & Deutsche Eisschnelllauf Gemeinschaft e. V. (DESG) v. International Skating Union (ISU)
CAS 2009/A/1919, Club Salernitana Calcio 1919 SpA v. CA River Plate & Costa
CAS 2009/A/1920, FK Pobeda, Zabrcanec & Zdraveski v. Union of European Football Associations (UEFA)
CAS 2009/A/1926 & 1930, International Tennis Federation (ITF) & World Anti-Doping Agency (WADA) v. Gasquet
CAS 2009/A/1928 & 1929, Olympique Lyonnais v. US Soccer Federation (Bompastor & Abily)
CAS 2009/A/1935, Fédération Royale Marocaine de Football v. Fédération Internationale de Football Association (FIFA)
CAS 2009/A/1956, Club Tofta Itróottarfelag, B68 v. R
CAS 2009/A/1960 & 1961, Trabzonspor v. LOSC Lille Métropole & LOSC Lille Métropole v. Trabzonspor & Sylva
CAS 2009/A/1988, Belize Basketball Federation v. Fédération Internationale de Basketball (FIBA)
CAS 2009/A/2011, Schumacher v. International Olympic Committee (IOC)
CAS 2010/A/2041, Chepalova v. Fédération Internationale de Ski (FIS)
CAS 2010/A/2069, Galatasaray AS v. Aachener TSV
CAS 2010/A/2090, Finnish Ski Association & Saarinen v. Fédération Internationale de Ski (FIS)
CAS 2010/A/2091, Lachter v. Boateng Owusu
CAS 2010/A/2098, Sevilla FC v. RC Lens
CAS 2010/O/2132, FC Shakhtar Donetsk v. Pereira Dias
CAS 2010/A/2145–2147, Sevilla FC SAD v. Udinese Calcio SpA & De Sanctis v. Udinese Calcio SpA & Udinese Calcio SpA v. De Sanctis & Sevilla FC SAD
CAS 2010/A/2170 & 2171, Iraklis Thessaloniki FC & OFI v. Hellenic Football Federation (HFF)
CAS 2010/A/2172, Oryekhov v. Union of European Football Associations (UEFA)
CAS 2010/A/2178, Caucchioli v. Comitato Olimpico Nazionale Italiano (CONI) & Union Cycliste Internationale (UCI)
CAS 2010/A/2203 & 2214, Larpe & Fédération Française de Cyclisme (FFC) v. Union Cycliste Internationale (UCI)
CAS 2010/A/2226, Leal Queiroz v. Autoridade Antidopagem de Portugal (ADoP)
CAS 2010/A/2268, I v. Fédération Internationale de l'Automobile (FIA)
CAS 2010/A/2275, Croatian Golf Federation (CGF) v. European Golf Association (EGA)
CAS 2010/A/2288, Union Cycliste Internationale (UCI) v. Giunti, Federazione Ciclistica Italiana (FCI) & Comitato Olimpico Nationale Italiano (CONI)
CAS 2010/A/2311 & 2312, Stichting Anti-Doping Autoriteit Nederland & KNSB v. W
CAS 2010/A/2315, Netball New Zealand v. International Netball Federation Limited (IFNA)

CAS 2011/A/2325, Union Cycliste Internationale (UCI) v. Paulissen & Royale Ligue Vélocipédique Belge (RLVB)
CAS 2011/A/2539, Monchengladbach v. Boca Juniors
CAS 2011/A/2364, Butt v. International Cricket Council
CAS 2011/A/2384 & 2386, Union Cycliste Internationale (UCI) v. World Anti-Doping Agency (WADA), Contador & Real Federacion Espanola de Ciclismo (RFEC)
CAS 2011/O/2422, United States Olympic Committee (USOC) v. International Olympic Committee (IOC)
CAS 2011/A/2425, Fusimalohi v. Fédération Internationale de Football Association (FIFA)
CAS 2011/A/2426, Adamu v. Fédération Internationale de Football Association (FIFA)
CAS 2011/A/2433, Diakite v. Fédération Internationale de Football Association (FIFA)
CAS 2011/A/2435, World Anti-Doping Agency (WADA) v. Thys, Athletics South Africa (ASA) & South African Institute for Drug-Free Sport (SAIDS)
CAS 2011/A/2472, Al-Wehda Club v. Saudi Arabian Football Federation (SAFF)
CAS 2011/A/2479, Sinkewitz v. Union Cycliste Internationale (UCI)
CAS 2011/A/2499, Subirats v. Fédération Internationale de Natation Amateur (FINA)
CAS 2011/A/2529, FC Nouadhibou v. Fédération de Football de la République Islamique de Mauritanie (FFRIM)
CAS 2011/A/2557, FC Dynamo Kyiv v. AS Nancy-Lorraine
CAS 2011/A/2563, CD Nacional v. FK Sutjeska
CAS 2011/A/2612, Hui v. International Weightlifting Federation (IWF)
CAS 2011/A/2616, Union Cycliste Internationale (UCI) v. Rivera & Real Federación Española de Ciclismo (RFEC)
CAS 2011/A/2625, Bin Hammad v. Fédération Internationale de Football Association (FIFA)
CAS 2011/A/2646, Club Rangers de Talca v. Fédération Internationale de Football Association (FIFA)
CAS 2011/A/2658, BOA v. World Anti-Doping Agency (WADA)
CAS 2011/A/2671, Union Cycliste Internationale (UCI) v. Rasmussen & National Olympic Committee and Sports Confederation of Denmark (Dansk Idraetsforbund)
CAS 2011/A/2678, International Association of Athletics Federations (IAAF) v. Real Federación Española de Atletismo (RFEA) & Fernández Peláez
CAS 2011/A/2681, KSV Cercle Brugge v. FC Radnicki
CAS 2012/A/2689, SC Sporting Club SA Vaslui v. Fédération Internationale de Football Association (FIFA)
CAS 2012/A/2699, Al-Birair v. Confédération Africaine de Football (CAF)
CAS 2012/A/2707, AS Nancy-Lorraine v. FC Dynamo Kyiv

CAS 2012/A/2731, Brazilian Olympic Committee, Brazilian Taekwondo Confederation & Ferreira v. World Taekwondo Confederation, Comite Olympico Mexicano & Valadez
CAS 2012/A/2750, FC Shakhtar Donetsk v. Real Zaragoza SAD
CAS 2012/A/2791, World Anti-Doping Agency (WADA) v. Jamaludin et al.
CAS 2012/A/2837, Beresford v. Equestrian Australia
CAS 2012/A/2875, Helsingborgs IF v. Parma FC
CAS 2012/A/2900, FC Otelul Galati SA v. FC Banik Ostrava
CAS 2012/A/2912, Murofushi & Japanese Olympic Committee v. International Olympic Committee (IOC)
CAS 2012/A/2917, British Paralympic Association (BPA) v. International Association for Disabled Sailing (IFDS) & Norwegian Olympic and Paralympic Committee and Confederation of Sports (NIF)
CAS 2012/A/2919, FC Seoul v. Newcastle Jets FC
CAS 2012/A/2922, World Anti-Doping Agency (WADA) v. Federaçao Pernambucana de Futebol & Fernandes
CAS 2012/A/2981, Desportivo Nacional v. FK Sutjeska
CAS 2012/A/3031, Katusha Management SA v. Union Cycliste Internationale (UCI)
CAS 2012/A/3033, Pešić v. FC OFI Crete
CAS 2012/A/3035, Parma FC v. VFL Wolfsburg
CAS 2013/A/3062, Sammut v. Union of European Football Associations (UEFA)
CAS 2013/A/3077, World Anti-Doping Agency (WADA) v. Casas Biutrago & General Disciplinary Commission of the Colombian Olympic Committee (GCD)
CAS 2013/A/3112, World Anti-Doping Agency (WADA) v. Chernova & Russian Anti-Doping Agency (RUSADA)
CAS 2013/A/3139, Fenerbahçe SK v. Union of European Football Associations (UEFA) (I)
CAS 2013/A/3151, Millar v. Fédération Equestre Internationale (FEI)
CAS 2013/A/3199, Rayo Vallecano de Madrid SAD v. RFEF
CAS 2013/A/3256, Fenerbahçe SK v. Union of European Football Associations (UEFA) (II)
CAS 2013/A/3258, Besiktas Jimnastik Kulübü v. Union of European Football Associations (UEFA)
CAS 2013/A/3264, Achhakir v. Fédération Internationale de Football Association (FIFA)
CAS 2013/A/3273, Club Deportivo Social y Cultural Cruz Azul v. Federación de Fútbol de Chile (FFC) & Fédération Internationale de Football Association (FIFA)
CAS 2013/A/3297, FC Metalist v. Union of European Football Associations (UEFA) & PAOK FC
CAS 2013/A/3323, Deportivo Petare FC v. Fédération Internationale de Football Association (FIFA)

CAS 2013/A/3380, Club Atlético Independiente v. Fédération Internationale de Football Association (FIFA)
CAS 2013/A/3411, Al Gharafa SC & Bresciano v. Al Nasr Sports Club & Fédération Internationale de Football Association (FIFA)
CAS 2013/A/3417, FC Metz v. NK Nafta Lendava
CAS 2014/A/3488, World Anti-Doping Agency (WADA) v. Lallukka
CAS 2014/A/3536, Racing Club Asociación Civil v. Fédération Internationale de Football Association (FIFA)
CAS 2014/A/3546, Manisaspor Club v. Dixon
CAS 2014/A/3625, Sivasspor Kulübü v. Union of European Football Associations (UEFA)
CAS 2014/A/3628, Eskişehirspor Kulübü v. Union of European Football Associations (UEFA)
CAS 2014/A/3861, Izaguirre v. Club Tigres de la UANL & Federación Mexicana de Fútbol Asociación
CAS 2015/A/4153, Al-Gharafa SC v. Fedor & Fédération Internationale de Football Association (FIFA)
OG 96/001, US Swimming v. Fédération Internationale de Natation Amateur (FINA)
OG/96/003 & 004, Korneev & Gouliev v. International Olympic Committee (IOC)
OG 96/005, Andrade et al. v. NOC Cape Verde (NOC CV) (II)
OG 96/006, Mendy v. Association Internationale de Boxe (AIBA)
OG 98/002, Rebagliati v. International Olympic Committee (IOC)
OG 00/004, Comité Olympique Congolais (COC) & Kibunde v. Association Internationale de Boxe (AIBA)
OG 00/005, Perez v. International Olympic Committee (IOC) (Perez II)
OG 00/009, Perez (Perez III)
OG 00/011, Raducan v. International Olympic Committee (IOC)
OG 00/013, Segura v. International Association of Athletics Federations (IAAF)
OG 00/014, Fédération Française de Gymnastique (FFG) v. Sydney Organizing Committee for the Olympic Games (SOCOG)
OG 02/001, Prusis & Latvian Olympic Committee (LOC) v. International Olympic Committee (IOC)
OG 02/005, Billington v. Fédération Internationale de Bobsleigh et de Tobogganing (FIBT)
OG 02/006, New Zealand Olympic Committee (NZOC) v. Salt Lake Organizing Committee for the Olympic Winter Games of 2002 (SLOC)
OG 02/007, Korean Olympic Committee (KOC) v. International Skating Union (ISU)
OG 04/001, Russian Olympic Committee (RNOC) v. Fédération Equestre Internationale (FEI)
OG 04/003, Edwards v. International Association of Athletics Federations (IAAF) & USA Track and Field (USATF)
OG 04/009, Hellenic NOC & Kaklamanakis v. International Sailing Federation (ISAF)

OG 06/002, Deutscher Skiverband & Evi Sachenbacher-Stehle v. International Ski Federation (FIS)
OG 06/003, Azzimani v. Comité National Olympique Marocain
OG 08/002, Simms v. Fédération Internationale de Natation Amateur (FINA)
OG 08/006, Moldova National Olympic Committee (MNOC) v. International Olympic Committee (IOC)
OG 12/005, Sterba v. World Anti-Doping Agency (WADA)
OG 12/011, Russian Olympic Committee (ROC) v. International Sailing Federation (ISAF)

Decisions by National Courts

Germany

OLG Frankfurt's decision 18 April 2001 in case 13 U 66/01 (Baumann v. DLV)
LG München I's decision of 26 February 2014 in 37 O 28331/12 (Pechstein v. ISU)
OLG München's decision 15 January 2015 in case 1110/14 Kart (Pechstein v. ISU)
BGH's decision 7 June 2016 in case KZR 6/15 (Pechstein v. ISU)

Belgium

Cour d'appel Bruxelles's decision 29 August 2018 in case 2016/AR/2048 (Doyen Sports et al. v. URBSFA et al.)

United Kingdom

London Street Tramways Co Ltd v. London County Council [1898] AC 375

United States

Anastasoff v. United States, 223 F.3d 898 (8th Cir. 2000)

Switzerland

SFT's decision 15 March 1993 in case 4P.217/1992, ATF 119 II 271 (Gundel v. FEI)
SFT's decision 31 March 1999 in case 5P.83/1999 (Wang et al. v. FINA)
SFT's decision 27 May 2003 in case 4P.267–270/2002, 129 ATF 445 (Lazutina & Danilova v. IOC)
SFT's decision 20 December 2005 in case 4C.1/2005, BGE 132 III 285 (X. AG v. Y)
SFT's decision 27 March 2012 in case 4A_558/2011 (Matuzalem v. FIFA)
SFT's decision 9 October 2012 in case 4A_110/2012 (Paulissen)
SFT's decision 22 March 2007 in case 4P.172/2006, ATF 133 III 235 (Cañas v. ATP Tour)

Decisions by international courts and tribunals

European Court of Human Rights

ECtHR's decision 17 September 2009 in Scoppola v. Italy (no. 2), appl. no 10249/03

ECtHR's decision 2 October 2018 in Mutu & Pechstein v. Switzerland, appl. no. 40575/10 & 67474/10

Court of Justice of the European Union

Case 11/70, Internationale Handelsgesellschaft mbH v. Einfuhr- und Vorratsstelle fur Getreide und Futtermittel, EU:C:1970:114

Case 120/78, Rewe-Zentral AG v Bundesmonopolverwaltung für Branntwein (Cassis de Dijon), EU:C:1979:42

Case C-415/93, Union Royale Belge des Sociétés de Football Association (ASBL) v Bosman, Royal club liégeois SA v Bosman et al. & Union des associations européennes de football (UEFA) v Bosman, EU:C:1995:463

Case C-126/97, Eco Swiss China Time Ltd v. Benetton International NV, EU: C:1999:269

Case T-313/02, Meca-Medina & Majcen v. Commission, EU:T:2004:282

Case C-519/04 P, Meca-Medina & Majcen v. Commission, EU:C:2006:492

Joined Cases C-295-298/04, Manfredi et al. v. Assitalia SpA., EU:C:2006:461

Case C-8/08, T-Mobile Netherlands BV et al. v. Raad van bestuur van de Nederlandse Mededingingsautoriteit, EU:C:2009:343

NAFTA Ch. 11 Arbitration Tribunal

NAFTA Ch. 11 Arbitration Tribunal's award of 7 August 2005, Methanex Corp. v. the United States of America

Decisions by Other Sports Adjudicatory Bodies

FIFA Dispute Resolution Chamber

FIFA DRC decision of 28 March 2008, Club AAA v. Club BBB

FIFA DRC decision of 3 July 2008, Club J v. Club A

FIFA DRC decision of 3 October 2008, Club A v. Club O

FIFA DRC decision of 19 February 2009, Club B FF v. Club S

FIFA DRC decisions of 16 July 2009, Club H v. Club M

FIFA DRC decision of 10 December 2009, Club C v. Player M & Club S

FIFA DRC decision of 5 February 2010, Player X v. Club FC-S

FIFA DRC decision of 6 May 2010, Player M v. Club K.

FIFA DRC decisions of 23 January 2013, Club N v. Club R

FIFA DRC decisions of 23 January 2013, Club F v. Club B
FIFA DRC decision of 30 August 2013, Player L v. Club Y
FIFA DRC decisions of 17 January 2014, Club R v. Club G
FIFA DRC decision of 27 February 2014, Club J v. Club P
FIFA DRC decision of 3 September 2015, Player A v. Club C
FIFA DRC decisions of 17 June 2016, Club A v. Player C
FIFA DRC decision of 18 August 2016, Club A v. Club C

Basketball Arbitration Tribunal

BAT 436/11

Table of Sources

Agnoloni T (2014) Network Analysis of Italian Constitutional Case Law. Semantic Processing of Legal Texts (SPLeT) 2014:24–28

Alexander L (1989) Constrained by Precedent. Southern California Law Review 63:1–64

Alexy R (2002) A Theory of Constitutional Rights. Oxford University Press, Oxford

Alexy R (2011) A Theory of Legal Argumentation: The Theory of Rational Discourse as Theory of Legal Justification. Oxford University Press, Oxford

Alter K J (1988) Who are the 'Masters of the Treaty'?: European Governments and the European Court of Justice. International Organizations 52:121–147

Alvarez J E (2007) The Democratization of the Invisible College. The American Society of International Law, IL Post, 8 November 2007. http://www.law.nyu.edu/sites/default/files/ECM_PRO_065334.pdf. Accessed 25 May 2017

Anderson J (2010) Modern Sports Law. Hart, Oxford

Anderson J (ed) (2013) Leading Cases in Sports Law. T.M.C. Asser Press, The Hague

Anter A (2014) Max Weber's Theory of the Modern State: Origins, Structure and Significance. Palgrave Macmillan, Basingstoke

Arroyo M (2013) Arbitration in Switzerland: The Practitioner's Guide. Kluwer Law International, Alphen aan den Rijn

Barabási A-L and Albert R (1999) Emergence of Scaling in Random Networks. Science 286:509–512

Barak A (2012) Proportionality: Constitutional Rights and Their Limitations. Cambridge University Press, Cambridge

Barents R (2004) The Autonomy of Community Law. Kluwer Law International, The Hague

Barrett A C (2003) Stare Decisis and Due Process. University of Colorado Law Review 74:1011–1075

Beloff M (2001) Drugs, Laws and Versapaks. In: O'Leary J (ed) Drugs and Doping in Sport: Socio-Legal Perspectives, Cavendish, London, pp. 39–56

J. Lindholm, *The Court of Arbitration for Sport and Its Jurisprudence*,
ASSER International Sports Law Series,
https://doi.org/10.1007/978-94-6265-285-9

Beloff M (2005) Is there a lex sportiva? International Sports Law Review 3:49–60

Beloff M (2011) Is There Such a Thing as Sports Law? The Circuiteer 33:13–15

Beloff M, Kerr T, Demetriou M and Beloff R (2012) Sports Law. 2nd ed. Hart Publishing, Oxford

Benz, J and Sternheimer W (2015) Expedited Procedures before the Court of Arbitration for Sport. CAS Bulletin 2015(1):6–11

Berger B (2013) The Legal Framework: Rights and Obligations of Arbitrators in the Deliberations. In: Berger B and Schneider M (eds) Inside the Black Box: How Arbitral Tribunals Operate and Reach Their Decisions, Juris Publishing, New York, pp. 7–12

Bersagel A (2012) Is There a Stare Decisis Doctrine in the Court of Arbitration for Sport? An Analysis of Published Awards for Anti-Doping Disputes in Track and Field. Pepperdine Dispute Resolution Law Journal 12:189–207

Bhala R (1999) The Myth About Stare Decisis and International Trade Law. American University International Law Review 14:845–956

Bjorklund A (2009) The Emerging Civilization of Investment Arbitration. Penn State Law Review 113:1269–1300

Blackaby N, Partasides C, Redfern A and Hunter M (2015), Redfern and Hunter on International Arbitration. 6th ed. Oxford University Press, Oxford

Blackshaw I (2006) Introductory Remarks. In: Blackshaw I, Siekman R and Soek J (eds) The Court of Arbitration for Sport 1984–2004, T.M.C. Asser Press, The Hague, pp. 1–5

Blackshaw I (2011) Towards a "Lex Sportiva". The International Sports Law Journal 2011(3/4):140–144

Blackshaw I (2012) Introductory Remarks. In: Wild A (ed) CAS and Football: Landmark Cases, T.M.C. Asser Press, The Hague, pp. 5–10

Blackshaw I (2013a) ADR and Sport: Settling Disputes Through the Court of Arbitration for Sport, the FIFA Dispute Resolution Chamber, and the WIPO Arbitration & Mediation Center. Marquette Sports Law Review 24(1):1–57

Blackshaw I (2013b) CAS 92/A/63, Gundel v. FEI. In Anderson J (ed) Leading Cases in Sports Law, T.M.C. Asser Press, The Hague pp. 65–74

Blei D (2012) Probabilistic Topic Models. Communications of the ACM 55 (4):77–84

Blei D and Lafferty J (2009) Topic Models. In Srivastava A and Sahami M (eds) Text Mining: Classification, Clustering, and Applications, Chapman and Hall, Boca Raton, pp. 71–93

Blei D, Ng A and Jordan I (2003) Latent Dirichlet Allocation. Journal of Machine Learning Research 3:993–1022

Blondel, V, Guillaume J-L, Lambiotte R, and Lefebvre E (2008) Fast unfolding of communities in large networks. Journal of Statistical Mechanics 2008(10): P10008

Boigeol A (2013) Feminisation of the French 'Magistrature': Gender and Judging in a Feminised Context. In: Schultz U and Shaw G (eds) Gender and Judging, Hart Publishing, Oxford, pp. 125–144

Bond S (1991) The International Arbitrator: From the Perspective of the ICC International Court of Arbitration. Northwestern Journal of International Law and Business 12(1):1–22

Born G (2014) International Commercial Arbitration. 2nd ed. Wolters Kluwer, Alphen ann den Rijn

Bowers L (2010) Science and the Rules Governing Anti-Doping Violations. In: Thieme D and Hemmersbach P (eds) Doping in Sports, Springer, Berlin, pp. 513–531

Brin S and Page L (1998) The anatomy of a large-scale hypertextual Web search engine. Computer Networks and ISDN Systems 30:107–117

Brower C and Schill S (2009) Is Arbitration a Threat or a Boon to the Legitimacy of International Investment Law? Chicago Journal of International Law 9 (2):471–498

Buy F, Maramyou J-M, Poracchi D and Rizzo F (2015) Droit du Sport. 4nd ed. LGDJ, Paris

Cahoy D (2010) Considerations in the Rise of Empirical Legal Scholarship. American Business Law Review 47:v–ix

Cane P and Kritzer H (2010) The Oxford Handbook of Empirical Legal Research. Oxford University Press, Oxford

Cardozo B (1921) The Nature of the Judicial Process. Yale University Press, New Haven

CAS (1991) Guide to Arbitration. http://sportrecht.org/cms/upload/10verbands/CASguideArbitration.pdf. Accessed 7 September 2018

CAS (2016), Statistics 2016. http://www.tas-cas.org/fileadmin/user_upload/CAS_statistics_2016_.pdf. Accessed 7 September 2018

Casini L (2011) The Making of Lex Sportiva by the Court of Arbitration for Sport. German Law Journal 12(5):1317–1340

Cavalieros P and Kim J (2015), Can the Arbitral Community Learn from Sports Arbitration? Journal of International Arbitration 32(2):237–260

Chiassoni P (2012) The Philosophy of Preced: Conceptual Analysis and Rational Reconstruction. In: Bustamante T and Bernal Pulido C (eds) On the Philosophy of Precedent, Proceedings of the 24th World Congress of the International Association for Philosophy of Law and Social Philosophy III, Franz Steiner Verlag, Stuttgart, pp. 13–33

Coccia M (2013a) International Sports Justice: The Court of Arbitration for Sport. European Sports Law Bulletin 2013(1):23–76

Coccia M (2013b) The jurisprudence of the Swiss Federal Tribunal on challenges against CAS awards. CAS Bulletin 2013(2):2–17

Cohen M (2016) On the linguistic design of multinational courts: The French capture. I•CON 14(2):498–517

Commission J (2007) Precedent in Investment Treaty Arbitration: A Citation Analysis of a Developing Jurisprudence. Journal of International Arbitration 24 (2):129–158

Cornelius S (2013) CAS 2008/A/1480 Pistorius v. IAAF. In: Anderson J (ed) Leading Cases in Sports Law, T.M.C. Asser Press, The Hague pp. 229–238

Craig P (2001) The Jurisdiction of the Community Courts Reconsidered. In: de Búrca G and Weiler J (eds) The European Court of Justice, Oxford University Press, Oxford, pp. 177–214

Craig P (2006) EU Administrative Law. Oxford University Press, Oxford

Cross R and Harris J W (1991) Precedent in English Law. 4th ed. Clarendon Press, Oxford

Dasser F and Wójtowicz P (2016) Challenges of Swiss Arbitral Awards: Updated and Extended Statistical Data as of 2015. ASA Bulletin 34(2):280–300

David R and Brierley J (1985) Major Legal Systems in the World Today. Stevens and Sons, London

Davies T, Vernon M, and Schofield J (2014) Is sport doing enough to catch drug cheats? In: Clive Palmer (ed) The Sports Monograph: Critical Perspectives on Socio-Cultural Sport, Coaching and Physical Education, SSTO Publications, Preston, pp. 65–78

De Cruz P (2007) Comparative Law in a Changing World. 3rd ed. Routledge-Cavendish, Oxon

Derlén M and Lindholm J (2014) Goodbye *van Gend en Loos*, Hello *Bosman*? Using Network Analysis to Measure the Importance of Individual CJEU Judgments. European Law Journal 20(5):667–687

Derlén M and Lindholm J (2015) Characteristics of Precedent: The Case Law of the European Court of Justice in Three Dimensions. German Law Journal 16 (5):1073–1098

Derlén M and Lindholm J (2016a) Bosman: A Legacy Beyond Sports. In: Duval A and Van Rompuy B (eds) The Legacy of Bosman, T.M.C. Asser Press, The Hague, pp. 31–49

Derlén M and Lindholm J (2016b) Judiciell aktivism eller prejudikatbildning? En empirisk granskning av Högsta domstolen. Svensk Juristtidning 2016:143–158

Derlén M and Lindholm J (2017a) Peek-a-boo, It's a Case Law System. German Law Journal 18(3):647–686

Derlén M and Lindholm J (2017b), Is It Good Law? Network Analysis and the CJEU's Internal Market Jurisprudence. Journal of International Economic Law 20(2):257–277

Derlén M, Lindholm J, Mirshahvalad A, and Rosvall M (2013) Coherence Out of Chaos: Mapping European Union Law by Running Randomly Through the Maze of CJEU Case Law. Europarättslig Tidskrift 16(3):517–535

Dezalay Y and Garth B (1996) Dealing in Virtue: International Commercial Arbitration and the Construction of a Transnational Legal Order. The University of Chicago Press, Chicago

Douglas Z (2010) Can a Doctrine of Precedent Be Justified in Investment Treaty Arbitration? ICSID Review 25(1):104–110

Drahozal C (2003) Of Rabbits and Rhinoceri: A Survey of Empirical Research on International Commercial Arbitration. Journal of International Arbitration 20 (1):23–34

Drahozal C (2005) Behavorial Analysis of Arbitral Decision Making. In: Drahozal C and Naimark R (eds) Towards a Science of International Arbitration: Collected Empirical Research, Kluwer Law International, The Hague, pp. 319–337

Drahozal C and Friel R (2002) Consumer Arbitration in the European Union and the United States. North Carolina Journal of International Law and Commercial Regulation 28(2):357–394

Drahozal C and Naimark R (2002) Towards a Science of International Arbitration: Collected Empirical Research. Kluwer Law International, The Hague

Duffy J (2013) Proportionality of sanctions under the WADA Code: CAS jurisprudence and the need for a strict approach. Australasian Dispute Resolution Journal 24(1):26–40

Duval A (2013) *Lex Sportiva*: A Playground for Transnational Law. European Law Journal 19(6):822–842

Duval A (2015) La Lex Sportiva Face au Droit de Européenne: Guerre et Paix dans l'Espace Juridique Transnational. Academic thesis, European University Institute, Florence

Duval A (2017) Not in My Name! Claudia Pechstein and the Post-Consensual Foundations of the Court of Arbitration for Sport. Max Planck Institute for Comparative Public Law & International Law (MPIL) Research Paper No. 2017-01. https://papers.ssrn.com/sol3/papers.cfm?abstract_id=2920555. 7 September 2018

Duxbury N (2008), The Nature and Authority of Precedent. Cambridge University Press, Cambridge

Dworkin R (2016) Law's Empire. Bloomsbury, London

Dworkin R (2013) Taking Rights Seriously. Bloomsbury, London

Elsing S and Townsend J (2002) Bridging the Common Law-Civil Law Divide in Arbitration. International Arbitration 18(1):59–65

Emerson F (1970) History of Arbitration Practice and Law. Cleveland State Law Review 19(1):155–164

Epstein L and King G (2002) The Rules of Inference. University of Chicago Law Review 69:1–133

Erbsen A (2006) The Substance and Illusion of Lex Sportiva. In: Blackshaw I, Siekman R, and Soek J (eds) The Court of Arbitration for Sport 1984–2004, T.M.C. Asser Press, The Hague, pp. 441–454

Euler L (1741) Solutio problematis ad geometriam situs pertinentis. Commentarii academiae scientiarum Petropolitanae 8:128–140

Fathally J and Mariani N (2008) World Legal Systems. 2nd ed. http://www.juriglobe.ca. Accessed 19 May 2017

Fortunato S (2010) Community Detection in Graphs. Physics Reports 486:75–174

Foster K (2003) Is There a Global Sports Law? Entertainment Law 2(1):1–18

Foster K (2006) Lex Sportiva and Lex Ludica: The Court of Arbitration for Sport's Jurisprudence. Entertainment and Sports Law Journal 3(2)

Fowler J and Jeon S (2008) Authority of Precedent. Social Network 30:16–30

Fowler J, Johnson T, Spriggs II J, Jeon S, and Wahlbeck P (2007) Network Analysis and the Law: Measuring the Legal Importance of Precedents at the U.S. Supreme Court. Political Analysis 15:324–346

Franck S (2007) Empirically Evaluating Claims About Investment Treaty Arbitration. North Carolina Law Review 86:1–88

Franck S, Freda J, Lavin K, Lehmann T and van Aaken A (2015) Diversity Challenge: Exploring the 'Invisible College' of International Arbitration. Columbia Journal of Transnational Law 53:429–506

Franck S, van Aaken A, Freda J, Guthrie C, and Rachlinski J (2017) Inside the Arbitrator's Mind. Emory Law Journal 66(5):1115–1173

Freeman L (1979) Centrality in Social Networks: Conceptual Clarification. Social Networks 1:215–239

Fruchterman T and Reingold E (1991) Graph drawing by force-directed placement. Software: Practice and Experience 21(11):1129–1164

Fuller L (1969) The Morality of Law. 2nd ed. Yale University Press, New Haven

Gardiner S, O'Leary J, Welch R, Boyes S, and Naidoo U (2012) Sports Law. 4th ed. Routledge, Oxon

Gascón M (2012) Rationality and (Self) Precedent: Brief Considerations Concerning the Grounding and Implications of the Rule of Self Precedent. In: Bustamante T and Bernal Pulido C (eds) On the Philosophy of Precedent, Proceedings of the 24th World Congress of the International Association for Philosophy of Law and Social Philosophy III, Franz Steiner Verlag, Stuttgart, pp. 35–50

Geeraert A, Alm J, and Groll M (2014) Good governance in international sport organizations: An analysis of the 35 Olympic sport governing bodies. International Journal of Sport Policy and Politics 6(3):281–306

Geist A (2010) The Open Revolution: Using Citation Analysis to Improve Legal Text Retrieval. European Journal of Legal Studies 2(3):137–145

George T (2006) An Empirical Study of Empirical Legal Scholarship: The Top Law Schools. Indiana Law Journal 81:141–160

Ginsburg T (2003) The Culture of Arbitration. Vanderbilt Journal of Transnational Law 36:1335–1345

Giordetti C (2013) Who Decides Who Decides in International Investment Arbitration? University of Pennsylvania Journal of International Law 35:431–486

Girvan M and Newman M (2002) Community Structure in Social and Biological Networks. PNAS 99(12):7821–7826

Glenn H P (2014) Legal Traditions of the World. 5th ed. Oxford University Press, Oxford

Gorbylev S (2013) A short story of an athlete: Does he question independence and impartiality of the Court of Arbitration for Sport? The International Sports Law Journal 13:294–298

Greenwood L and Baker C M (2015) Is the balance getting better? An update on the issue of gender diversity in international arbitration. Arbitration International 31:413–423

Guillaume G (2011) The Use of Precedent by International Judges and Arbitrators. Journal of International Dispute Settlement 2(1):5–23

Hansford T and Spriggs II J (2008) The Politics of Precedent on the U.S. Supreme Court. Princeton University Press, Princeton

Hart H L A (2012) The Concept of Law. 3rd ed. Oxford University Press, Oxford

Hayek F A (2007) The Road to Serfdom. Chicago University Press, Chicago

Heise M (1999) The Importance of Being Empirical. Pepperdine Law Review 26:807–834

Hess B (2015) The Development of Lex Sportiva by the Court of Arbitration for Sport. In: Vieweg K (ed) Lex Sportiva, Duncker and Humblot, Berlin, pp. 59–76

Hobér K (2004) Arbitration Involving States. In: Newman L and Hill R (eds) The Leading Arbitrators' Guide to International Arbitration, Juris, pp. 139–162

IBA, Report on the Public Policy Exception in the New York Convention. Report by the Subcommittee on Recognition and Enforcement of Foreign Arbitral Awards, October 2015. https://www.ibanet.org/LPD/Dispute_Resolution_Section/Arbitration/Recogntn_Enfrcemnt_Arbitl_Awrd/publicpolicy15.aspx. Accessed 7 September 2018

Ioannidis G (2016) The Influence of Common Law Traditions on the Practice and Procedure Before the Court of Arbitration for Sport (CAS). In: Duval A and Rigozzi A (eds) Yearbook of International Sports Arbitration 2015, T.M.C. Asser Press, The Hague pp. 17–38

Marc J (2014) Precedent and Case-Based Reasoning in the European Court of Justice. Cambridge University Press, Cambridge

James M (2013) Sports Law. 2nd ed. Palgrave Macmillan, Basingstoke

Jansen N and Michaels R (2008) Beyond the State? Rethinking Private Law: Introduction to the Issue. American Journal of Comparative Law 56(3):527–539

Juvenal (1918) Satires. Ramsay G (trans), Heinemann, London

Kane D (2003a) Twenty Years On: An Evaluation of the Court of Arbitration for Sport. Melbourne Journal of International Law 4:611–635

Kane O (2003b) The CAS Mediation Rules. The International Sports Law Journal 2003(1):33–35

Kaufmann-Kohler G (2007) Arbitral Precedent: Dream, Necessity or Excuse? Arbitration International 23(3):357–378

Kaufmann-Kohler G and Bärtsch P (2006) The Ordinary Arbitration Procedure of the CAS. In: Blackshaw I, Siekman R, and Soek J (eds) The Court of Arbitration for Sport 1984–2004, T.M.C. Asser Press, The Hague, pp. 69–98

Kaufmann-Kohler G and Rigozzi A (2015) International Arbitration: Law and Practice in Switzerland. Oxford University Press, Oxford

Kelsen H (1970) The Pure Theory of Law. Knight M trans., University of California Press, Berkeley

Kenney S J (2013) Which Judicial Selection Systems Generate the Most Women Judges? Lessons from the United States. In: Schultz U and Shaw G (eds) Gender and Judging, Hart Publishing, Oxford, pp. 461–480

Kerchove M van de and Ost F (1994) Legal Systems Between Order and Disorder. Stewart I trans., Oxford University Press, Oxford

Kinsella S and Duke A (2014) Who are the Real Winners and Losers in the General Court? Competition Policy International Europe Column. http://www.competitionpolicyinternational.com/who-are-the-real-winners-and-losers-in-the-general-court. Accessed 6 June 2018

Kleinberg J M (1999) Authoritative Sources in a Hyperlinked Environment. Journal of the ACM 46:604–632

Kleinberg J M (2000) The Small-World Phenomenon: An Algorithmic Perspective. In: Proceedings of the Thirty-Second Annual ACM pp. 163–170

Komárek J (2011) Judicial Lawmaking and Precedent in Supreme Courts. LSE Law, Society and Economy Working Papers 4/2011. http://ssrn.com/abstract=1793219. Accessed 6 July 2018

Krähe C (2006) The Appeals Procedure before the CAS. In: Blackshaw I, Siekman R, and Soek J (eds) The Court of Arbitration for Sport 1984–2004, T.M.C. Asser Press, The Hague, pp. 99–104

Kramer M H (1999) In Defense of Legal Positivism: Law Without Trimmings. Oxford University Press, Oxford

Kramer M H (2007) Objectivity and the Rule of Law. Cambridge University Press, Cambridge

Kwak H, Lee C, Park H and Moon S (2010) What is Twitter, a social network or a news media? In: Proceedings of the 19th international conference on World wide web, ACM, pp. 591–600

Kye C (2015) A Quagmire of Delays at the European General Court: Any Escape? Maastricht Journal of European and Comparative Law 22(3):453–471

Lagarde P (1982) Approche critique de la 'lex mercatoria'. In: Le Droit des Relations Economiques Internationales: Etudes Offertes a Berthold Goldman, Litec, Paris pp. 125–150

LaLive P (1984) On the Neutrality of the Arbitrator and of the Place of Arbitration. In: Reymond C and Bucher E (eds) Swiss Essays on International Arbitration, Schulthess, Zürich, pp. 23–33

Lancichinetti A and Fortunato S (2009) Community detection algorithms: A comparative analysis. Physical Review E 80(5):56117

Landes W M and Posner R A (1976) Legal Precedent: A Theoretical and Empirical Analysis. The Journal of Law and Economics 19:249–307

Landes W M and Posner R A (1979) Adjudication as a Private Good. The Journal of Legal Studies 8(2):235–284

Latour B (2010) The Making of Law: An Ethnography of the Conseil d'Etat. Brilman M and Pottage A trans., Polity, Cambridge

Latty F (2007) La lex sportiva: Recherche sur le droit transnational. Martinus Nijhoff, Leiden

Latty F (2011) Transnational Sports Law. The International Sports Law Journal 2011(1-2):34–38

Lee I (2008) Practice and Predicament: The Nationality of the International Arbitrator (with Survey Results). Fordham International Law Journal 31:603–633

Legrand P (1996) European Legal Systems are Not Converging. International and Comparative Law Quarterly 45(1):52–81
Legum B (2008) The Definitions of 'Precedent' in International Arbitration. In: Gaillard E and Banifatemi Y (eds) Precedent in International Arbitration, Juris Publishing, New York, pp. 5–14
Leskovec J and Horvitz E (2008) Planetary-scale views on a large instant-messaging network. Proceedings of the 17th international conference on World Wide Web, ACM, pp. 915–924
Llewellyn K N (1960) The Common Law Tradition: Deciding Appeals. Little, Brown and Co., Boston
Louw A M (2012) Ambush Marketing and the Mega-Event Monopoly: How Laws are Abused to Protect Commercial Rights to Major Sporting Events. T.M.C. Asser Press, The Hague
Lubetsky M H and Krane J A (2009) Appealing Outcomes: A Study for the Overturn Rate of Canada's Appellate Courts. Osgoode Hall Law Journal 47 (1):131–149
Ludewig R and LaLlave J (2013) Professional Stress, Discrimination and Coping Strategies: Similarities and Differences between Female and Male Judges in Switzerland. In: Schultz U and Shaw G (eds) Gender and Judging, Hart Publishing, Oxford, pp. 233–254
Lupu Y and Voeten E (2011) Precedent in International Courts: A Network Analysis of Case Citations by the European Court of Human Rights. British Journal of Political Science 42:413–439
MacCormick N (1999) Questioning Sovereignty. Oxford University Press, Oxford
MacCormick N (2003) Legal Reasoning and Legal Theory. Oxford University Press, Oxford
MacCormick N and Summers R (1997) Appendix: Final Version of the Common Questions, Comparative Legal Precedent Study, September 1994. In: MacCormick N, Summers R, and Goodhart A (eds) Interpreting Precedent, Ashgate, Farnham, pp. 551–562
Mack K and Roach Anleu S (2013) Skills for Judicial Work: Comparing Women Judges and Women Magistrates. In: Schultz U and Shaw G (eds) Gender and Judging, Hart Publishing, Oxford, pp. 211–232
Maduro M P and Azoulai L (2010) Introduction. In: Maduro M P and Azoulai L (eds) The Past and Future of EU Law: The Classics of EU Law Revisited on the 50th Anniversary of the Rome Treaty, Hart, Oxford, pp. xiii–xx
Malatesta A and Sali R (eds) (2013) The Rise of Transparency in International Arbitration. JurisNet, Huntington
Mangan M (2009) The Court of Arbitration for Sport: Current Practice, Emerging Trends and Future Hurdles. Arbitration International 25(4):591–602
Martens D-R (2006) CAS Landmark Decisions. In: Blackshaw I, Siekman R and Soek J (eds) The Court of Arbitration for Sport 1984–2004, T.M.C. Asser Press, The Hague, pp. 235–245
Mattei U (1997) Three Patterns of Law: Taxonomy and Change in the World's Legal Systems. The American Journal of Comparative Law 45(1):5-44

Mavromati D (2012) Language of procedure before CAS: Practice, criteria and impact of the language on the outcome of the case. CAS Bulletin 2012(1):39–48

Mavromati D (2016) The Rules governing the CAS Anti-Doping and Ad Hoc Divisions at the Olympic Games, 29 August 2016. https://ssrn.com/abstract=2816482. Accessed 6 July 2018

Mavromati D and Reeb M (2015) The Code of the Court of Arbitration for Sport: Commentary, Cases and Materials. Wolters Kluwer, Alphen aan den Rijn

Mbaye K (2002) Foreword. In: Reeb M (ed) Digest of CAS Awards 1998–2000, Kluwer Law International, The Hague, pp. xi–xii

Mbaye K (2006) Une nouvelle institution d'arbitrage: le tribunal arbitral du sport (TAS). Annuaire français de droit International XXX:409 (1984). Reprinted in: Blackshaw I, Siekman R, and Soek J (eds), The Court of Arbitration for Sport 1984–2004, T.M.C. Asser Press, The Hague, pp. 6–20

McArdle D (2015) Dispute Resolution in Sport: Athletes, Law and Arbitration. Routledge, Oxon

McAuliffe W and Rigozzi A (2013) Sports Arbitration. The European, Middle Eastern and African Arbitration Review 2013:15–22

McCain K W (1986) Co-cited author mapping as a valid representation of intellectual structure. Journal of the American Association for Information Science 37:111–122

McLaren R (1998) A New Order: Athletes' Rights and the Court of Arbitration at the Olympic Games. Olympika: The International Journal of Olympic Studies 7:1–24

McLaren R (2001) The Court of Arbitration for Sport: An Independent Arena for the World's Sports Disputes. Valparaiso University Law Review 35:379–405

McLaren R (2006) CAS Advisory Opinions. In: Blackshaw I, Siekman R, and Soek J (eds) The Court of Arbitration for Sport 1984–2004, T.M.C. Asser Press, The Hague, pp. 180–193

McLaren R (2011) The Court of Arbitration for Sport. In: Nafziger J and Ross S (eds) Handbook on International Sports Law, Edward Elgar Publishing, Cheltenham, pp. 32–64

Merryman J (1985) The Civil Law Tradition. 2nd ed. Stanford University Press, Stanford

Michaels R (2007) The True Lex Mercatoria: Law Beyond the State. Indiana Journal of Global Legal Studies 14(2):447–468

Milgram S (1967) The Small World Problem. Psychology Today 1:61–67

Mitten M (2014) The Court of Arbitration for Sport and its Global Jurisprudence: International Legal Pluralism in a World Without National Boundaries. CAS Bulletin 2014(2):48–79

Mitten M J and Davis T (2008) Athlete Eligibility Requirements and Legal Protection of Sports Participation Opportunities. Virginia Sports and Entertainment Law Journal 8:71–146

Mitten M J and Opie H (2010) 'Sports Law': Implications for the Development of International, Comparative, and National Law and Global Dispute Resolution. Tulane Law Review 85:269–322

Nafziger J (1992) International Sports Law: A Replay of Characteristics and Trends. American Journal of International Law: 86:489–518

Nafziger J (1999) Globalizing Sports Law. Marquette Sports Law Journal 9:225–238

Nafziger J (2004) Lex Sportiva. The International Sports Law Journal 2004 (1-2):3–8

Nafziger J (2006) Lex Sportiva and CAS. In: Blackshaw I, Siekman R, and Soek J (eds) The Court of Arbitration for Sport 1984–2004, T.M.C. Asser Press, The Hague, pp. 409–419

Nafziger J (2011) International Sports Law. In: Nafziger J and Ross S (eds) Handbook on International Sports Law, Edward Elgar Publishing, Cheltenham, pp. 3–31

Nafziger J (2015) Defining the Scope and Structure of International Sports Law: Four Conceptual Issues. In: Vieweg K (ed) Lex Sportiva, Duncker and Humblot, Berlin, pp. 161–178

Neale T (2013) Citation Analysis of Canadian Case Law. Journal of Open Access to Law 1(1):1–60

Nelson C (2001) Stare Decisis and Demonstrably Erroneous Precedents. Virginia Law Review 87(1):1–84

Newman M (2004) Fast algorithm for detecting community structure in networks. Physical Review E 69:066133

Newman M (2006) Modularity and community structure in networks. Proceedings of the National Academy of Sciences 103(23):8577–8582

Newman M (2011) Networks: An Introduction. Oxford University Press, Oxford

Newman M (2012) Communities, modules and large-scale structure in networks. Nature Physics 8:25–31

Newman M and Girvan M (2004) Finding and evaluating community structure in networks. Physical Review E 69(2):026113

Noussia K (2010) Confidentiality in International Commercial Arbitration: A Comparative Analysis of the Position under English, US, German and French Law. Springer Verlag, Berlin

Oschütz F (2002) Harmonization of Anti-Doping Code Through Arbitration: The Case Law of the Court of Arbitration for Sport. Marquette Sports Law Review 12:675–702

Page L, Brin S, Motwani R, and Winograd T (1998) The PageRank Citation Ranking: Bringing Order to the Web, 29 January 1998. http://ilpubs.stanford.edu:8090/422/1/1999-66.pdf. Accessed 6 July 2018

Panagiotopoulos D (2011) Lex Sportiva and International Legitimacy Governing: Protection of Professional Players. US-China Law Review 8:121–136

Panagiotopoulos D (2013) Sporting Jurisdictional Order and Arbitration. US-China Law Review 10:130–140

Panagis Y, Christensen M L, and Sadl U (2016) On top of topics: leveraging topic modeling to study the dynamic case-law of international courts. In: Bex F and Villata S (eds) Legal Knowledge and Information Systems, Frontiers in Artificial Intelligence and Applications 294, pp. 161–166

Parrish R (2012) Lex sportiva and EU sports law. European Law Review 37 (6):716–733
Paulsson J (1993) Arbitration of International Sports Disputes. Arbitration International 9(4):359–369
Paulsson J (2010) Moral Hazard in International Dispute Resolution. ICSID Review 25(2):339–335
Paulsson J (2011) Arbitration in Three Dimensions. International and Comparative Law Quarterly 60(2):291–323
Pauwelyn J (2015) The Rule of Law Without the Rule of Lawyers? Why Investment Arbitrators Are From Mars, Trade Adjudicators Are From Venus. The American Journal of International Law 109(4):761–805
Peel L, Larremore D, and Clauset A (2017) The ground truth about metadata and community detection in networks. Science Advances 3:e1602548
Pinna A (2006) The Trials and Tribulations of the Court of Arbitration for Sport: Contribution to the Study of the Arbitration of Disputes Concerning Disciplinary Sanctions. In: Blackshaw I, Siekman R, and Soek J (eds) The Court of Arbitration for Sport 1984–2004, T.M.C. Asser Press, The Hague, pp. 386–408
Plato (1921) Cratylus. In: Fowler H (trans), Twelve Volumes 12, Harvard University Press, Cambridge
Posner R (1995) Overcoming Law. Harvard University Press, Cambridge
Prechal S (2016) The Many Formations of the Court of Justice: 15 Years After Nice. Fordham International Law Journal 39(5):1273–1288
Puig S (2014) Social Capital in the Arbitration Market. The European Journal of International Law 25(2):387–424
Puig S (2016) Blinding International Justice. Virginia Journal of International Law 56(3):647–700
Radicchi F, Castellano C, Cecconi F, Loreto V, and Parisi D (2004) Defining and identifying communities in networks. PNAS 101(9):2658–2663
Ramberg C (2017) Prejudikat som rättskälla i förmögenhetsrätten. Wolters Kluwer, Stockholm
Ravjani A (2009) The Court of Arbitration for Sport: A Subtle Form of International Delegation. Journal of International Media and Entertainment 2:241–284
Raz J (2009) The Authority of Law. 2nd ed. Oxford University Press, Oxford
Redner S (1998) How Popular is Your Paper? An Empirical Study of the Citation Distribution. European Physical Journal B4:131–134
Reeb M (1998) The Court of Arbitration for Sport (CAS). In: Reeb M (ed) Digest of CAS Awards I, Kluwer Law International, The Hague, pp. xxiii–xxxi
Reeb M (2002) The Court of Arbitration for Sport: History and Operation. In: Reeb M (ed) Digest of CAS Awards II, Kluwer Law International, The Hague, pp. xxiii–xxx
Reeb M (2004) The Court of Arbitration for Sport: History and Operation. In: Reeb M (ed) Digest of CAS Awards III, Kluwer Law International, The Hague, pp. xxvii–xxxv

Reilly L (2012) An Introduction to the Court of Arbitration for Sport (CAS) and the Role of National Courts in International Sports Disputes. Journal of Dispute Resolution 2012(1):63–81
Reynolds W and Richards W (1978) The Non-Precedential Precedent: Limited Publications and No-Citation Rules in the United States Courts of Appeal. Columbia Law Review 78:1167–1206
Rigozzi A (2005) L'arbitrage international en matière de sport, Helbing & Lichtenhahn, Basel
Rigozzi A (2010a) Challenging Awards of the Court of Arbitration for Sport. Journal of International Dispute Settlement 1(1):217–265
Rigozzi A (2010b) The recent revision of the Code of sports-related arbitration (CAS Code). Jusletter 13 September 2010
Rigozzi A and Hasler E (2013) Sports Arbitration under the CAS Rules. In: Arroyo M (ed) Arbitration in Switzerland: The Practitioner's Guide, Wolters Kluwer, Alphen aan den Rijn, pp. 936–1206
Rigozzi A, Hasler E, and Quinn B (2013) The 2011, 2012 and 2013 revisions to the Code of Sports-related Arbitration. Jusletter 3 June 2013
Rincón A (2007) EC Competition and Internal Market Law: On the Existence of a Sporting Exemption and its Withdrawal. Journal of Contemporary European Research 3(3):224–237
Rogers C (2006) Transparency in International Commercial Arbitration. Kansas University Law Review 54:1301–1345
Rosvall M, Axelsson D, and Bergstrom C T (2009) The Map Equation. European Physics Journal Special Topics 178:13–23
Schachter O (1977) The Invisible College of International Lawyers. Northwestern University Law Review 72(2):217–226
Schauer F (1987) Precedent. Stanford Law Review 39(3):571–605
Schauer F (2007) Has Precedent Ever Really Mattered in the Supreme Court? Georgia State University Law Review 24:381–401
Schauer F (2008a) Authority and Authorities. Virginia Law Review 94 (8):1931–1961
Schauer F (2008b) Why Precedent in Law (and Elsewhere) is Not Totally (or Even Substantially) About Analogy. Perspectives on Psychological Science 3 (6):454–460
Schepel H and Blankenburg E (2001) Mobilizing the European Court of Justice. In: de Búrca G and Weiler J (eds) The European Court of Justice, Oxford University Press, Oxford, pp. 9–42
Schill S (2012) International Arbitrators as System-Builders. American Society of International Law 106:295–297
Schreuer C and Weiniger M (2008) A Doctrine of Precedent? In: Muchlinksi P, Ortino F, and Shreuer C (eds) The Oxford Handbook of International Investment Law, Oxford University Press, Oxford, pp. 1188–1206
Schultz T (2014) Transnational Legality: Stateless Law and International Arbitration. Oxford University Press, Oxford
Scott J (2017) Social Network Analysis. 4th ed. Sage, London

Segal J, Spaeth H, and Benesh S (2005) The Supreme Court in the American Legal System. Cambridge University Press, Cambridge

Segan J (2013) Does the Court of Arbitration for Sport need a 'Grand Chamber'? Sports Law Bulletin, 19 April 2013. https://www.sportslawbulletin.org/does-the-court-of-arbitration-for-sport-need-a-grand-chamber/. Accessed 9 January 2018

Siekmann R (2011) What is Sports Law? Lex Sportiva and Lex Ludica: A Reassessment of Content and Terminology. The International Sports Law Journal 2011(3-4):3–13

Siems M (2014) Comparative Law. Cambridge University Press, Cambridge

Simma B (2006) The Court of Arbitration for Sport. In: Blackshaw I, Siekman R, and Soek J (eds) The Court of Arbitration for Sport 1984–2004, T.M.C. Asser Press, The Hague, pp. 21–30

Slaoui F-Z (2009) The Rising Issue of 'Repeat Arbitrators': A Call for Clarification. Arbitration International 25(1):103–119

Small H (1973) Co-citation in the scientific literature: A new measure of the relationship between two documents. Journal of the American Association for Information Science 24:265–269

Smeureanu I (2011) Confidentiality in International Commercial Arbitration. Wolters Kluwer, Alphen aan den Rijn

Soek J (2003) The Strict Liability Principle and the Human Rights of Athletes in Doping Cases. T.M.C. Asser Press, The Hague

SOU 2003:102 En öppen domarrekrytering

Stone Sweet A (2006) The New Lex Mercatoria and Transnational Governance. Journal of European Public Policy 13(5):627–646

Stone Sweet A and Brunell T (1998) Constructing a Supranational Constitution: Dispute Resolution and Governance in the European Community. American Political Science Review 92:63–81

Stone Sweet A, Chung M Y, and Saltzman A (2017) Arbitral Lawmaking and State Power: An Empirical Analysis of Investor–State Arbitration. Journal of International Dispute Settlement 8(4):579–609

Strömholm S (2000) General Features of Swedish Law. In: Bogdan M (ed) Swedish Law in the New Millenium, Norstedts Juridik, Stockholm, pp. 31–47

Swigart L (2010) The 'National Judge': Some Reflections on Diversity in International Courts and Tribunals. McGeorge Law Review 42:223–242

Swigart L and Terris D (2015) Who are International Judges? In: Romano C, Alter K, and Shany Y (eds) The Oxford Handbook of International Adjudication, Oxford University Press, Oxford, pp. 619–638

Tarissan F and Nollez-Goldbach R (2014) The Network of the International Criminal Court Decisions as a Complex System. In: Sanayei A, Zelinka I, and Rössler O (eds) ISCS 2013: Interdisciplinary Symposium on Complex Systems, Springer, Berlin pp. 255–264

Ten Cate I (2013) The Costs of Consistency: Precedent in Investment Treaty Arbitration. Columbia Journal of Transnational Law 51:418–478

Terris D, Romano C, and Swigart L (2007) The International Judge: An Introduction to the Men and Women Who Decide the World's Cases. Brandeis University Press, Waltham

Teubner G (ed) (1997) Global Law Without a State. Dartmouth, Andover

Teubner G (2002) Breaking Frames: Economic Globalization and the Emergence of Lex Mercatoria. European Journal of Social Theory 5(2):199–217

Teubner G (2008) State Policies in Private Law. American Journal of Comparative Law 56:835–843

Tridimas T (2006) The General Principles of EU Law. 2nd ed. Oxford University Press, Oxford

Tucker T (2016) Inside the Black Box: Collegial Patterns on Investment Tribunals. Journal of International Dispute Settlement 7:183–204

Tuori K (2011) Ratio and Voluntas: The Tension Between Reason and Will in Law. Ashgate, Farnham

Tweeddale A and Tweeddale K (2005) Arbitration of Commercial Disputes: International and English Law and Practice. Oxford University Press, Oxford

Vaitiekunas A (2014) The Court of Arbitration for Sport: Law-making and the question of independence. Stämpfli Verlag, Bern

Valero A (2014) In search of a working notion of *lex sportiva*. The International Sports Law Journal 14:3–11

van Gerven W (2000) Of Rights, Remedies and Procedures. Common Market Law Review 37:501–536

Van Harten G (2012) The (lack of) women arbitrators in investment treaty arbitration. Columbia FDI Perspectives 59, Vale Columbia Center on Sustainable International Investment, New York

van Opijnen M (2012) Citation Analysis and Beyond: in Search of Indicators Measuring Case Law Importance. Frontiers in Artificial Intelligence and Applications 250:95–104

Vauchez A (2016) What is a Classic in Law? Methodological Notes on Grandes arrêts at the European Court of Justice. In: Davies B and Nicola F (eds) EU Law Stories: Contextual and Critical Histories of EU Jurisprudence, Cambridge University Press, Cambridge, pp. 21–34

Vieweg K and Staschik P (2015) The Lex Sportiva: The Phenomenon and its Meaning in the International Sporting Arena. In: Vieweg K (ed) Lex Sportiva, Duncker & Humblot, Berlin, pp. 17–58

Viswanath B, Mislove A, Cha M, and Krishna G (2009) On the evolution of user interaction in Facebook. Proceedings of the 2nd ACM workshop on Online social networks, ACM, pp. 37–42

Vogenaur S (2006) Sources of Law and Legal Method in Comparative Law. In: Reimann M and Zimmermann R (eds) The Oxford Handbook of Comparative Law, Oxford University Press, Oxford, pp. 869–898

von Bogdandy A and Venzke I (2012) Beyond Disputes: International Judicial Institutions as Lawmakers. In: von Bogdandy A and Venzke I (eds) International Judicial Lawmaking, Springer, Berlin, pp. 3–33

Wallace M, Gingras Y, and Duhon R (2009) A new approach for detecting scientific specialties from raw co-citation networks. Journal of the American Society for Information Science and Technology 60(2):240–246

Ware S (2001) Paying the Price of Process: Judicial Regulation of Consumer Arbitration Agreements. Journal of Dispute Resolution 2001(1):89–101

Watts D and Strogatz S (1998) Collective Dynamics of 'Small-World' Networks. Nature 393:440–442

Wax A (2015) Public International Sports Law and the Lex Sportiva. In: Vieweg K (ed) Lex Sportiva, Duncker & Humblot, Berlin, pp. 145–160

de Weger F (2016) The Jurisprudence of the FIFA Dispute Resolution Chamber. T. M.C. Asser Press, The Hague

Weidemaier, W C M (2010) Toward a Theory of Precedent in Arbitration. William and Mary Law Review 51:1895–1958

Weidemaier, W C M (2012) Judging-Lite: How Arbitrators Use and Create Precedent. North Carolina Law Review 90:1091–1146

Weston M (2009) Simply a Dress Rehearsal? U.S. Olympic Sports Arbitration and De Novo Review at the Court of Arbitration for Sport. Georgia Journal of International and Comparative Law 38:97–129

Wild A (ed) (2012) CAS and Football: Landmark Cases. T.M.C. Asser Press, The Hague

Wise A and Meyer B (1997) International Sports Law and Business. Kluwer Law International, Boston

Wolaver E (1934) The Historical Background of Commercial Arbitration. University of Pennsylvania Law Review 83(2):132–146

Wolbring G (2008) Oscar Pistorius and the future nature of Olympic, Paralympic and other sports. Scripted 5(1):139–160

Yi D (2006) Turning Medals into Metal: Evaluating the Court of Arbitration for Sport as an International Tribunal. Asper Review of International Business and Trade Law 6:289–341

Zetie K (2003) Getting a buzz from flight. Physics Education November 2003:476

Zhang A H, Liu J, and Garoupa N (2018) Judging in Europe: Do Legal Traditions Matter. Journal of Competition Law and Economics 14(1):144–178

Zuberbühler T, Müller C, and Habegger P (2013) Swiss Rules of International Arbitration. 2nd ed. Schulthess, Zürich

Index

J. Lindholm, *The Court of Arbitration for Sport and Its Jurisprudence*,
ASSER International Sports Law Series,
https://doi.org/10.1007/978-94-6265-285-9

The manufacturer's authorised representative in the EU is Springer
Nature Customer Service Centre GmbH, Europaplatz 3, 69115 Heidelberg,
Germany. If you have any concerns regarding our products, please
contact ProductSafety@springernature.com

Printed and bound by CPI Group (UK) Ltd, Croydon, CR0 4YY
30/09/2026
02225446-0013